Lutosławski on Music

Edited and Translated by
Zbigniew Skowron

THE SCARECROW PRESS, INC.
Lanham, Maryland • *Toronto* • *Plymouth, UK*
2007

SCARECROW PRESS, INC.

Published in the United States of America
by Scarecrow Press, Inc.
A wholly owned subsidiary of
The Rowman & Littlefield Publishing Group, Inc.
4501 Forbes Boulevard, Suite 200, Lanham, Maryland 20706
www.scarecrowpress.com

Estover Road
Plymouth PL6 7PY
United Kingdom

British Library Cataloguing in Publication Information Available

Library of Congress Cataloging-in-Publication Data

Lutoslawski, Witold, 1913–1994.
  Lutoslawski on music / edited and translated by Zbigniew Skowron.
    p. cm.
  Includes bibliographical references and index.
  ISBN-13: 978-0-8108-4804-7 (hardcover : alk. paper)
  ISBN-13: 978-0-8108-6013-1 (pbk. : alk. paper)
  ISBN-10: 0-8108-4804-X (hardcover : alk. paper)
  ISBN-10: 0-8108-6013-9 (pbk. : alk. paper)
  1. Music—History and criticism. 2. Lutoslawski, Witold, 1913—1994.
3. Composers—Poland—Biography. I. Skowron, Zbigniew. II. Title.
ML60.L96 2007
780—dc22   2007020482

∞^TM The paper used in this publication meets the minimum requirements of
American National Standard for Information Sciences—Permanence of Paper for
Printed Library Materials, ANSI/NISO Z39.48-1992.
Manufactured in the United States of America.

At a time when a bewildering multitude of styles, techniques, and mutually exclusive aesthetic credos characterizes the musical scene of the world, Witold Lutosławski's art steadfastly proclaims the continuity of the Western musical heritage. His towering creations, deeply rooted in the traditions of the past, point toward new horizons yet to be reached in a distant future. In a new language, they speak to contemporary audiences of permanent and essential values which have their being in the art of light and shade, of motion and stillness, of sound and silence, of the human drama of life itself. In a unique way, his music stands before us as a powerful affirmation of the relevance, strength, and vitality of new art forms of our time . . .

—Victor Babin (fragment of a speech delivered by Victor Babin during the ceremony of granting Witold Lutosławski an honorary degree of the Cleveland Institute of Music on June 2, 1971. CIM Notes, Vol. 9, No. 2, Summer 1971, p. 1. Used with permission of the Cleveland Institute of Music)

Contents

viii   *Contents*

Preface

$\mathcal{A}$lthough writings about music are a substantial part of Witold Lutosławski's creative output, they have not so far been the subject of a thorough study. The fact that they are dispersed in various sources makes this task even more difficult. Moreover, many of his writings remain unpublished to this day, so that only a complete edition of them would allow a deep insight into their various topics and aspects. To provide a fuller accounting of Lutosławski's writings on music is the main goal of the present collection, which, for the first time, includes his most important texts arranged in six parts, as follows: (1) writings on beauty, musical form, compositional technique, and perception; (2) essays on his own works; (3) essays on composers and musicians; (4) various opinions on contemporary music in Poland and abroad; (5) occasional speeches; and (6) his artistic diary from the years 1959–1984.

From the very beginning of Lutosławski's activity as a writer (that is, from the late 1930s), his texts revealed their idiosyncratic profile, which made them quite different from such prolific writers on music as Cage, Boulez, or Stockhausen. Whereas all three leading avant-gardists openly proclaimed their aesthetic (or, as it is sometimes called, antiaesthetic) manifestos and their radical attitudes, Lutosławski chose a pragmatic approach, addressing first and foremost *practical* problems in his own compositional technique. Thus, his writings attempted to explain the concrete solutions in particular works in order to help listeners to understand them, rather than build a theory of aesthetics in their own right. Another difference between Lutosławski and the postwar avant-gardists is his attitude toward the idea of contemporary music. Being an enthusiast of it, he always kept a critical distance from the radical innovations, especially those that in the process of musical communication totally neglected the feedback of the audience. This is why many of his texts often display a *critical* reappraisal of the basic tenets of both the pre- and postwar avant-garde.

Most of Lutosławski's writings consist of the lectures he delivered at various courses for young composers, both abroad and in Poland, showing them the details of his compositional workshop. His activity as a lecturer dates only from the early 1960s when the political change in Poland in October of 1956, which marked the end of the doctrine of socialist realism in art, allowed his new ideas to materialize, starting with *Five Iłłakowicz Songs* (1956–1957), *Musique funèbre* (1958), Three Postludes (1958–1960), and *Jeux vénitiens* (1961).

Among the many Lutosławski texts that are now kept in the Paul Sacher Foundation in Basel are some unpublished lectures that he wrote with the intention of delivering at courses for composers at Tanglewood in 1962. There are both Polish and English versions of these texts, but—as in case of many Lutosławski's writings in English—no translator is credited. Steven Stucky gave the following details about them:

> As the result of a telephone invitation from Aaron Copland, in the summer of 1962 Lutosławski made his first visit to the United States, where he spent a busy and fruitful three months. For eight weeks he conducted the composition course at the Berkshire Music Center (Tanglewood) in western Massachusetts. For the course Lutosławski prepared a cycle of four formal lectures: an introduction summarizing historical developments since the nineteenth century, a discussion of rhythmic problems in new music, an address on the problem of constructing large-scale form in the twentieth century, and an explanation of his own approach to pitch organisation and harmony in the context of limited aleatorism.[1]

The texts of all four lectures are included in this present collection. It seems possible that this group of lectures was even bigger, since among the typescripts for these four lectures is another text marked with number V and entitled *Aleatorism*. When asked in interviews about the details of his compositional technique, Lutosławski often answered that if he had enough time he would write a kind of treatise on it, maybe similar to that of Olivier Messiaen. It seems that those unpublished lectures, along with some published texts that complement them, give us an idea of the main chapters of this unwritten treatise.

Apart from explaining his concepts of basic musical categories, Lutosławski often discussed historical and aesthetic issues. The main purpose of these kinds of texts, which were mostly published both in Poland and abroad, was to express his attitude toward tradition and, on the other hand, toward the newest avant-garde phenomena surrounding him. Hence, many of these texts reveal his creative choices on his own path toward modernity, and his attempts at placing himself in the context of twentieth-century music, more precisely—in the movement that included Debussy, Stravinsky, Bartók, and, in new Polish music, Karol Szymanowski.

Still another group of texts shows him as an active participant in musical life who attempted not only to register the plethora of events he witnessed as a man and an artist, but also to discover his own criteria for evaluating them. Among these texts may also be found many occasional articles dedicated to Polish and foreign composers and musicians. What is telling in this context is that this group of texts starts with a commemorative article written in 1937 after the death of Karol Szymanowski.

A separate, final part of the present collection consists of the "Notebook of Ideas," which is in fact a kind of artistic diary that Lutosławski kept, more or less systematically, from 1959 to 1984. For this purpose he used a typical, green square-ruled school notebook (150 × 218 mm) of eighty-eight pages from the early 1950s, which had a stiff, dark blue cover with a grainy surface. All the entries are made in pencil, and the frequent crossings-out of single words and larger parts of the text prove that he was writing down his notes spontaneously and correcting them immediately.

A characteristic feature of Lutosławski's artistic diary is its clear division in two parts. The first part (unnumbered pages 1–9) seems to be at first glance a typical compositional sketchbook. This is shown by the composer's detailed remarks on the elements of some works that he was then considering, such as the Nonet, Piano Concerto, *Lamentations, Elegy,* or a work for choir and two (or one) soloists with orchestra and electro-acoustic means, based on Franz Kafka's short story *Before the Law.* None of these was completed as an immediate result of the sketches—he composed the Piano Concerto in the late 1980s, and never apparently returned to the other projects.

In the initial part of the "Notebook," two dates appear that allow us to establish, at least approximately, the chronology of his entries. The first of them, 18 X 58 (signifying October 18, 1958), which the composer put for some reason in a frame, appears on page 8, and the second one, 24 X 58, on page 9, which is on the last page of the initial, "sketchy" part of the "Notebook." Its second part differs from the first in having a textual character (musical elements appear there only sporadically). Beginning with the date 22 I 59 (also put in a frame), Lutosławski apparently decided to notate his thoughts systematically, expressing them both in a concise way and in longer sections of prose. In the final, unnumbered part of the "Notebook," the entries appear more rarely. On two occasions they are separated by periods of almost five years: November 25, 1974 to August 26, 1979, and November 24, 1979 to January 10, 1984. The latter date ends the entire "Notebook of Ideas."

Bearing in mind the variety of Lutosławski's writings, it was impossible to apply uniform criteria in organizing them in particular chapters of the present collection. So, some of the texts, as in part 1, are arranged according to the hierarchy of their content, some, as in parts 2, 4, and 5, are put in a chronological order, whereas the others, as in part 3, are arranged alphabetically. Apart from the obvious dates of Lutosławski's printed works and texts, the chronology of his unpublished writings presents problems, because he rarely dated his manuscripts. In some cases, when the texts remained unpublished, it is impossible to date them. Each of the edited Lutosławski texts is provided with the information on its source and with the notes. As I already mentioned, this collection includes writings that were originally published (or presented as lectures) in English, and also the texts translated by myself from Polish.

In a collection such as this, which aims to give a more or less complete image of Lutosławski as a writer on music, the reader might expect some biographical information. Yet instead of the usual, encyclopedic data, which is often given in such instances, I decided to start with a vivid autobiographical text (most probably written in English by Lutosławski himself) titled "Life and Music."[2]

In conclusion, I would like to thank first of all Bruce Phillips, who encouraged me to start this collection and who has patiently guided me through all its stages. My special thanks go to Mary Whittall, and to Elizabeth and Martin Rumbelow, who helped me generously and incessantly with translating and editing many of Lutosławski's texts. I am also particularly grateful to Jonathan W. Bernard of the University of Washington for his highly efficient assistance in identifying English versions of various quotations used by Lutosławski, and for valuable editorial advice. Among the people who helped me to obtain some of Lutosławski's texts, both in Europe and in the United States, and to clarify their details, are Katarzyna Naliwajek, Robert Piencikowski, and Nick Reyland, whom I thank warmly for their kindness. To Piotr Maculewicz of the University of Warsaw I owe my thanks for his meticulous work on diagrams and musical examples. I am also grateful to Renée Camus and Kellie Hagan of Scarecrow Press, for their assistance in preparing this book for publication. Last but not least, I would like to express my gratitude to all the institutions and people who allowed me use of their copyrighted materials, especially to Marcin Bogusławski, Witold Lutosławski's stepson, and to Dr. Felix Meyer, the Director of the Paul Sacher Foundation in Basle, for his kind agreement for me to use the Lutosławski sources which are housed there in the Witold Lutosławski Collection.

NOTES

1. Steven Stucky, *Lutosławski and His Music* (Cambridge, UK: Cambridge University Press, 1981), 85.
2. He wrote this text, which apparently sums up both events from his life and his artistic achievement, for the ceremony of receiving the Kyoto Prize in October 1993.

Introduction

Witold Lutosławski's Life and Music

This text, originally written for the Inamori Foundation and never published, was preceded by the following paragraph: "From the correspondence I received from the Secretariat of the Inamori Foundation, I understand that the wish of the Organizers of this meeting is that I speak about my life from childhood up to now. I don't mind, although I am not sure whether such a topic of my lecture would be interesting enough to engage your attention for three quarters of an hour. So I will try to add to it here and there some thoughts that, as I hope, are not quite commonplace."

⁂

I was born on 25 January 1913, to a family of landowners, whose estate was about 150 kilometers north of Warsaw.[1] The place was beautiful, with a splendid view from the garden on the valley of the river Narew. It was not without influence on my character that I spent my early years in contact with nature. Beautiful forests, fields, rivers, meadows, and gardens are still in my memory, although the estate has not belonged to my family for many years.

One year after my birth, the First World War began. Poland was then largely under the domination of the Russian empire. The German offensive against Russia began in 1915 and it took place on the territory of Poland. So masses of Poles looked for shelter in Russia. My family joined them, which is why I spent three years in Moscow. This stay had a tragic end. My father was involved in some underground activity among emigrants organizing Polish military troops to be used at a suitable time to free Poland. After the 1917 revolution in Russia, the Bolsheviks arrested my father, and in September 1918 they executed him. Soon after, Poland became free and we could come back to our country. Our estate was ruined by the war and never returned to its former state. I stayed there until I had to go to school in 1924 in Warsaw. A few years earlier, I began to learn to play the piano. In fact, I don't remember being indifferent to music. It has always fascinated me and I could not imagine myself having another profession than that of a musician, or even a composer. Already by the age of six I had improvised on the piano, and the first preludes for piano I wrote down correctly at the age of nine. At that time I frequently attended the concerts of the Warsaw Philharmonic. This was the most important source of my musical experience. I owe the development of my musical taste and knowledge to that institution. Of course, what I was then listening to was mainly the standard repertoire of concerts for the audiences of subscribers: Beethoven, Tchaikovsky, Grieg, and the like.

The true revelation came a little earlier, when I was eleven years old. At a concert of the Warsaw Philharmonic, I heard for the first time the Third Symphony ("Song of the Night") by Karol Szymanowski, certainly a great composer of his time.[2] The music is fascinating in its harmony, sound-colors, and emotional force of great originality. At that moment to hear the Third Symphony of Szymanowski was as if the door of a miraculous garden opened in front of me. I was in a state of excitement for weeks. I tried to recreate Szymanowski's harmonies on the keyboard. At that time I discovered the whole-note scale, up to then unknown to me. The entire experience was a true initiation into the music of the twentieth century. Strangely enough, however, the music of Szymanowski had practically no influence on what I composed later. As a teenager I deciphered Ravel's and Debussy's music and whatever twentieth-century music was available in our country. At twelve I had interrupted piano lessons and begun to study violin, which I then abandoned six years later to come back to piano. I then continued to study the piano and graduated from the Warsaw Conservatory. But earlier, at the age of fourteen, I began a private study of composition with Professor Witold Maliszewski, who was a composer and pupil of Rimsky-Korsakov and Glazunoff. Later I entered his class of composition at the Warsaw Conservatory. I graduated in 1936 for piano and in 1937 for composition. My last year of composition studies was somewhat peculiar. My professor was very conservative in his musical opinions and tastes. I thought that the piece for orchestra that I began to compose then would probably be unacceptable for him. So, being afraid of discouragement, I stopped coming to his class and planned to come only when I had finished work on my Symphonic Variations. But in the middle of it, the professor called me and demanded that I come to the class. I brought half of the score. But his decision was a model of his honesty as a teacher. He said that if I was to continue writing such music he could not teach me any more, as he did not understand it. But to finish my studies, I must write something that he could approve. I did it and received my diploma.

Symphonic Variations had to wait to be completed until I finished my one year of military service in 1938.[3]

During the years of my studies (two years of mathematics, five years of composition and four years of piano, all of it between 1931 and 1937) I had the opportunity to attend concerts of some of the greatest musicians of our century. The pianists: Józef Hofman, Robert Casadesus, Walter Gieseking, Alfred Cortot, Wilhelm Backhaus; the violinists: Joseph Szigeti, Georg Kulenkampf, Bronisław Huberman, Paweł Kochański, Jacques Thibaud; cellist Emmanuel Feuerman; and conductors: Bruno Walter, Ernest Ansermet, Georg Georgescu, Klemens Kraus. I heard great composers playing their works: Hindemith playing viola; and Prokofiev playing his Piano Concertos I, II, III, and V, and also a solo recital. I heard Ravel conducting his Piano Concerto with Marguerite Long as soloist,[4] Szymanowski playing his *Symphonie Concertante* in the Warsaw Philharmonic.[5] It is a list of historical names now. They enriched my whole life. Certain performers remain still in my memory, such as the last sonatas of Beethoven by Józef Hofman and Symphonic Variations of Franck by Casadesus. They were all the inspiration for my conducting of my works now. It was a great lesson in understanding the art of performance of music.

In the autumn of 1939 I planned to go to Paris to go on studying composition. But the Second World War broke out on September 1st and instead of going to Paris I went to Kraków as commander of a military radio station by the Headquarter of the First Army. The war in Poland without any other country's help, when our country was attacked from the west by Germany and the east by the Soviet Union, lasted no more than six weeks. After eight days as a prisoner of war I escaped from the moving camp and went to Warsaw on foot (about 400 kilometers).

The period of German occupation in Poland from 1939 to 1945 was very peculiar. Besides the more or less known atrocities like concentration camps, executions on the streets, arrests etc., there was also a situation that affected especially the culture of Poland. The Germans treated the Polish nation as one destined to be annihilated entirely. That is why any cultural activity was forbidden. There were no universities, libraries, theatres, concerts etc. The whole musical life, as modest as it was, concentrated in cafés, where even the most important Polish musicians performed sometimes quite serious music. Fellow composer and colleague Andrzej Panufnik and I performed a duet of two pianos and played every day in cafés.[6] We made over two hundred transcriptions for two pianos of quite a serious repertoire: from Bach's organ toccatas to Ravel's *Bolero*. We made also some free paraphrases, such as waltzes of Strauss harmonized *à la* Ravel and the like. One of the paraphrases I created was—so to say—a "private" version of Paganini's Twenty-fourth Capriccio. It was the only piece from among our transcriptions that remained, as the rest (over two hundred pieces) were destroyed during the uprising of the Polish underground army in Warsaw in 1944. The piece won some popularity after the war, as the number of the gramophone recordings of new duets was over 20. During the period of the German occupation I tried to keep composing. I managed to complete the first movement of my First Symphony, some sketches of the other movements, two piano studies, a trio, and quite a number of small pieces.

It was by chance that I did not remain in Warsaw during the uprising. If I did, I would probably not be able to speak to you now.

In January 1945 came the so-called liberation. In fact it was a great disappointment. It was not a true liberation, but rather a taking over. Although the state of Poland was formally re-created, it was not a free country as it is now, but almost a Russian colony. Nevertheless, everybody in Poland felt the strong will to reconstruct the ruined country, along with the totally destroyed capital—Warsaw. My modest contribution to this work was connected with my profession. There was strong need for so-called functional music: the repertoire for music schools, for small ensembles, for children (songs and easy pieces), etc. I composed quite a number of these, very often using folk tunes as the raw material.

But at the same time, I was working on my more important compositional work. I completed my First Symphony, whose first performance took place in 1948 in Katowice. (Warsaw was then still in ruins, having no concert hall and a rather modest orchestra.) The performers of my First Symphony were the Radio Orchestra conducted by Grzegorz Fitelberg. He was a very important conductor in Poland, a friend and a promoter of the new music and particularly of the music of the young Polish composers.

In 1949 began the so-called Stalinism in Poland, the terribly gloomy period, during which the cultural policymakers wanted to follow the Soviets and tried to impose upon the artists the principles of *socialist realism* and to eradicate what they called *formalism*. Nobody knew what the word *formalism* could mean and how *realism* could be realized in music. The authorities organized a congress of composers and musicologists at a provincial castle in Łagów Lubuski[7] to inaugurate a new period of music, along the lines mentioned above. The result was a state of depression shared by many of us. I thought then that only my so-called functional music would be publicly performed, but the more important music of mine would remain in a drawer up to the end of my life. I tried to understand the purpose of this kind of policy, why artists should be deprived of their own style, their aesthetics, their artistic personality. The answer to these questions came later, when we began to understand the principles of a totalitarian regime. The authorities had to absolutely dominate the whole nation. Nobody beyond the leading group could have any kind of influence on the society. That is why the great artistic personalities, such as Shostakovich and Prokofiev in music, were criticized most severely in the Soviet Union, even persecuted. In this respect, the situation in Poland was not so serious as in the Soviet Union. I was one of the first victims. My First Symphony, performed at the inaugural concert of the Chopin Competition in 1949,[8] produced a true scandal and was declared "formalist." For ten years it was not performed. Up to that point, I didn't understand what the new policies could mean. After the concert—as I was told—the vice-minister of culture, the man who enforced the cultural policy in communist Poland, declared that a composer like Lutosławski should be thrown under a street-car. Of course, I was very proud of this declaration. Later, the same man tried to convince me to compose something like Shostakovich's *Song of the Forests*, a terrible piece of kitsch, which this great composer was probably compelled to write. I simply refused, saying that that didn't interest me. There was no reaction. That proves that the authorities didn't really persecute the composers in Poland as seriously as they did in the Soviet Union.

That period lasted for a much shorter time in Poland than in the Soviet Union and in the other countries of middle-eastern Europe. By 1955 the authorities were no longer interested in what the composers did and what kind of music was performed. I guess they came to understand that music was not efficient enough for the purposes of political propaganda, and that they gave up trying to influence the composers.

In 1956, the international festival of contemporary music Warsaw Autumn was inaugurated. In the program, beside the classic works of the twentieth century and those of the living composers, there were also the most experimental works. The authorities interfered very little with the program made up by the composers and musicologists. The authorities assumed a considerable budget for the festival, which, besides the leading Polish orchestras and soloists, included some foreign ensemble performances: Orchestre National de la Radiodiffusion et Télévision of Paris, Wiener Philharmoniker, State Orchestra of the USSR from Moscow, State Philharmonic from Bucharest, State Philharmonic from Brno, Tatrai Quartet from Budapest, and the Quartet Parrenin from Paris. The festival was a true sensation not only for Polish, but also for Eastern European audiences. The music of our century had not been performed in those countries for nearly thirty years. Some important twentieth-century works were performed in Poland for the first time. They were received with enthusiasm by the audiences. Webern's Five Pieces op. 10, for example, had to be encored in its entirety. The festival had an enormous influence on the young generation of Polish composers. It was a true breakthrough for the young Polish musicians. For my generation, Warsaw Autumn had no such a great importance, since before losing contact with the rest of the world we had heard much of what was played at the festival.

For many years after the end of the war I earned my living composing functional music: incidental music for theatres and radio plays, children's songs for radio broadcasts etc. Our State Music Publications (PWM) couldn't do anything to help our music to be performed in other countries, especially in the West. So until I was over fifty, I remained almost entirely unknown as a composer outside Poland. To publish in a Western country was strictly forbidden for years. My contract with my present publisher in England (Chester Music, London) was concluded in 1966 when I was 53. Only since then has my music been available for performances wherever people wished. The author rights (royalties) enabled me to stop composing functional music, as my works began "to work" for me.

In 1962 I went for the first time to the United States. For eight weeks in that summer I taught composition in Tanglewood, Massachusetts. In that period I had the opportunity to regularly attend the concerts of the Boston Symphony Orchestra and some great conductors: Charles Münch, Pierre Monteux, William Steinberg, and Erich Leinsdorf. After the stay in Tanglewood, the International Institute of Education offered us a one-month trip across the country. During a short stay in New York I had the opportunity to pay a visit to Mr. and Mrs. Edgar Varèse.

In 1963 for the first time I publicly conducted my music. It was at the occasion of the first performance of my *Trois poèmes d'Henri Michaux* at the Musical Biennale in Zagreb.[9] The work is written for a twenty-part chorus and an instrumental ensemble. Two conductors are necessary and I was asked to conduct the instruments. As conductor I was not quite a beginner, as since my school years I had always conducted my functional music, that is, the incidental music for theatres and radio plays, children's music for the radio broadcasts, etc. The reason I decided to begin conducting my concert music was, above all, some entirely new problems connected with the introduction of the element of chance into my music. The so-called controlled aleatorism, about which I shall be talking another time, requires an entirely new kind of conducting. At the occasion of the first performance of my Second Symphony that I conducted[10] I wanted to test myself: is this kind of music at all possible to play, is the result obtained precisely such as foreseen? The result of this experiment turned out quite positively and since then I have been using this technique of composition very often. It offers quite new, earlier unknown possibilities, particularly in the domain of rhythm. Some conductors of the older generation treat such music rather mistrustfully, since it is without meter and without bar lines. On the other hand, for the younger conductors, the technique of controlled aleatorism is something quite obvious.

After the first performances of my Second Symphony, which I conducted in Poland, I began to be engaged to conduct concerts of my music in other

European countries, and later also in the United States and Australia. I have had the chance to conduct concerts of my music with the best orchestras of the world, such as the Berliner Philharmoniker, Wiener Philharmoniker, Orchestre de Paris, Orchestre Philharmonique de Paris de la Radio France, BBC Symphony, the Philharmonia Orchestra of London, Hallé Orchestra, and the Scottish National Orchestra (at present the Royal Scottish Orchestra), as well as the leading American orchestras, those of New York, Philadelphia, Boston, Cleveland, Los Angeles, San Francisco, Pittsburgh, Houston, Saint Louis, Louisville, and some others. The contact with such elite orchestras has been a priceless experience for me not only as conductor, but also as composer. To form the sound one wants to hear, to discover all the possible secrets of one's own works, to get in direct contact with various kinds of audience, all this is of supreme importance for a composer. Nowadays I give about fifteen concerts of my music a year. I prefer to give concerts exclusively of my music rather than to share a concert with someone else conducting a traditional program. I know, then, that a big part of the audience has come to hear their beloved symphony of Schubert and only wait for it during my part of the program. On the other hand, when the program is exclusively made up of my works, I can be sure that those who came, did it to hear my music. The atmosphere in the hall is then particularly favorable for a better performance. I have been very lucky to have the opportunity of collaborating with some of the best soloists of our time: the pianist Krystian Zimerman, the violinist Anne-Sophie Mutter, the cellist Mstislav Rostropovich, the singers Peter Pears, Dietrich Fischer-Dieskau, Solveig Kringelborn, the oboist Heinz Holliger and his wife, the harpist Ursula Holliger, and many others. I owe them all the moments of true inspiration in my compositional work. My programs sometimes contain some old pieces of mine, such as Symphonic Variations (1938). Reporters and listeners ask me often what I feel when conducting my old music, which, after all, is so different from what I compose now. My answer is this: I try not to think of myself being a composer presenting his works to the audience, but rather a conductor, an interpreter performing works of his younger colleague, about whom he knows more than any other conductor. Of course, I have to accept the works I decide to perform myself. There are some that I never conduct. It is not that I discard them entirely, I just don't like performing them. Some require too much time to prepare, and they are time consuming, even if quite performable. I think orchestral music must be playable. It is very easy to compose music that is difficult to play. The true art is to be able to compose not very difficult music without artistic compromises.

Another question I am often asked concerns teaching. I am not a teacher and there are some young composers who would like to study composition with me and probably reproach me for my refusal. But to tell the truth, there are several reasons for my attitude. Firstly, I don't believe that teaching composition is really advisable for an active composer. The best thing a composition teacher can do is to analyze as many kinds of music as possible. To do so, the teacher must himself study a lot of works, which for an active composer might be damaging to his own creative work. So I think I would be a rather bad teacher.

Still another question I am asked is why I have not composed an opera. It is true that I had been looking for a subject for an opera that would be acceptable to me. It was rather difficult, bearing in mind that I am a bad opera viewer. Some fragments of even the greatest master works, when seen in the theatre, make me laugh: an embracing couple singing instead of whispering, looking at the conductor instead of into the eyes of each other etc., etc. Of course, this kind of thing concerns purely realistic theatre. That is why the subject I was looking for would have to be nonrealistic, for instance, a fairy tale, dream, surrealistic or fantastic play, etc. In such a play, singing instead of speaking would be a small detail of an accepted convention. One of model solutions could be Ravel's *L'enfant et les sortilèges*. A singing armchair is not stranger than a speaking one.

The largest part of my work is composed for a symphony orchestra, which is a rather traditional means of expression. The instruments are constructed with the harmonic scale as the base. The majority of them are, above all, diatonic instruments and they were not meant to serve the sound ideas of the composers of our century. But we have nothing to replace them. No instrument could compete with violin, oboe, horn, and the others. The electronic or electro-acoustic music is a different kind of art and it is an error to see in it the successors of traditional instruments. Although I am not an enthusiastic listener of electronic music, I must admit there is some reason to consider it more in spirit of our time than the traditional instrumentarium. However, it is significant that, in spite of quite fantastic possibilities offered by some studios such as IRCAM in Paris or Stanford in the United States, there is still no one true masterpiece produced by them. It may be due to the fact that a great number of composers are preoccupied with the means of expression rather than the expression itself; the technique of composing rather than the purpose it is meant to serve. Music is, after all, not only a composition of sounds, but also is, maybe above all, the composition of human reactions to them. The perception of the arts occurs in our psyche, the senses are but an intermediary factor.

Now I come to a fundamental question (also often asked): for whom do I compose music? My answer is apparently a highly controversial one and may even provoke indignation. But I will try to explain that this attitude is the only one that can be considered honest from a creative artist. This answer is: I compose music for myself. I shouldn't be astonished if the first reaction to such a statement were: what a disgusting egoism. I can understand such a reaction, but it is a terribly superficial one, and I can easily retort to it: yes, I compose for myself, but I am sure that there are a number of people I resemble, who have similar tastes and even possibly similar wishes, so they can find in my music something for themselves. As I said before, it is the only honest attitude of a creative artist. Why do I say so? Suppose I should like to satisfy the tastes and wishes of other people, to please them, to be appreciated. First of all, I don't believe one can really know what the musical wishes of another man are like. Everybody hears music in a different way, so it is beyond my imagination to know how other people really hear my music. But there is a more important justification of my apparent egoism: if I composed music to satisfy someone else, I should have to deceive myself, to resign from following my own taste and wishes, my aesthetics, to resign from saying what I believe in, in other words—to resign from saying the truth. It would be as if I offered others false money.

Some artists, writers, and philosophers maintain that the duty of a creative artist is to express the world in which we live. The great writer Joseph Conrad says even that the duty of the artist is to do justice to the visible world.[11] I am definitely against such a view. I think the visible world, the world in which we live, has no difficulty in expressing itself without our help. We are not predestined to express the real world in the art. The ideal world, the world of our dreams, of our wishes, of our vision of perfection is the domain of the arts. Access to this ideal world is given to creative artists. Their duty is to enable access to this world to other people through their works. This is one of the most important tasks of artists. They must not forget about another very important fact: talents are not the exclusive property of the artist. They are entrusted to him. He must not use them freely, for example, to get money or fame. The talents are not to be used, they are to be served. They require a lot of work, of thought, of consideration. In other words, the talents are not just a gift, they lay a heavy responsibility on the artist. Perhaps all this makes his life difficult, requires patience, persistence, and endurance, but—on the other hand—the life offers the artist experiences and satisfactions that cannot be compared with anything else.

Music fills almost my whole day, but not entirely. I find time to read literature, although less and less fiction; to visit collections of paintings; to go to theatres, etc. For several years I have been sailing on the lakes and rivers of Poland.

As I said at the beginning of this lecture, the topic of it, according to the wishes of its organizers, is the history of my life. From time to time I had to make reference to the political events that inevitably interfered in my life and work. Major changes in my country began in 1980 at the moment when Solidarity, a workers' national movement, came into being. The possibility of a little more freedom had already had an enormous influence on my state of mind. The first free Congress of Culture,[12] organized exclusively by scientists and artists, took place in December 1981. In my speech I denounced the purposes of the authorities' cultural policy. My allusion to what happened in the Soviet Union resulted in my music being forbidden for public performance there for seven years, and my name could not appear in their press.

The martial law[13] weakened for some years the activity of the opposition, but soon a Citizen Committee was brought to being by Lech Wałęsa[14] and I had the privilege to join it. To demonstrate the protests against martial law, the internment of the activists of the opposition, and other annoyances, many of us who were artists boycotted the media. We refused to appear on television, to give interviews to the press etc. I refused to be decorated by the minister of culture and resigned from appearing publicly as conductor, and did not appear on television. The situation was gradually changing in a favorable direction, the Soviet Union gradually withdrew its domination, and the freedom of Poland was becoming a fact. This fundamental change has a tremendous significance for me, as it does for every honest Pole. There are certainly many problems, which make the situation of our country difficult and disquieting, but there is no price that the majority of us would not pay for one thing: the resumption, after several decades, of the independence of our country.

Source

Typescript in English. Copyright Witold Lutosławski Collection, Paul Sacher Foundation. All rights reserved. Printed by permission.

Notes

1. Witold Lutosławski was born on January 25, 1913 on his family estate in Drozdowo near Łomża, in the Kurpie region northeast of Warsaw.

2. Lutosławski witnessed the Polish premiere of Szymanowski's Third Symphony, *Pieśń o nocy* ("Song of the Night") by the Warsaw Philharmonic, under the direction of Grzegorz Fitelberg. This concert, which was one of the most important events of that season and was reviewed in many Warsaw newspapers, took place on April 11, 1924.

3. The first performance of Lutosławski's Symphonic Variations took place in Kraków under the direction of Fitelberg, on June 17, 1939, three months before the outbreak of the Second World War.

4. Concert by the Warsaw Philharmonic, on March 11, 1933.

5. Concert by the Warsaw Philharmonic, on February 15, 1935.

6. See Andrzej Panufnik, *Composing Myself* (London: Methuen, 1987).

7. This congress was organized in the autumn of 1949. Among its main speakers was Włodzimierz Sokorski—representative of the Polish Ministry of Culture—who in his speech titled "Formalism and Realism in the Arts" proclaimed officially the idea of *socialist realism* in Polish music. The report from that congress was published in *Ruch Muzyczny*, no. 14 (1949): 12–31.

8. Lutosławski means the Fourth International Chopin Piano Competition, that is, the first one that took place in Warsaw after the Second World War from September 18 until October 17, 1949.

9. The world premiere of *Trois poèmes d'Henri Michaux* took place on May 9, 1963 in Zagreb, during Musički Biennale. This work was performed by the Zagreb Radio Orchestra and Choir, conducted by Lutosławski (orchestra) and Slavko Zlatić (chorus).

10. Lutosławski means the Polish premiere of his Symphony no. 2, which took place on June 9, 1967 in Katowice, with the Polish Radio National Symphony Orchestra conducted by the composer.

11. See: Joseph Conrad, *Typhoon, The Nigger of the "Narcissus," and Other Stories* (London: The Folio Society, 2000), 229. The full passage from this novel Lutosławski referred to says: "A work that aspires, however humbly, to the condition of art should carry its justification in every line. And art itself may be defined as a single-minded attempt to render the highest kind of justice to the visible universe, by bringing to light the truth, manifold and one, underlying its every aspect."

12. This congress was organized in Warsaw in December 1981 and was broken with the introduction of the martial law in the whole country.

13. The martial law was introduced in Poland on December 13, 1981 and was cancelled on July 22, 1983.

14. Lech Wałęsa (b. 1943), the first leader of the Polish independent trade union Solidarity, created in 1980. He was the president of Poland in 1990–1995.

• *1* •

On Beauty, Musical Form,
Compositional Technique, and Perception

ON BEAUTY

$\mathcal{I}$ can't formulate a definition of beauty; after all it has countless and very varied faces.

There is beauty in the eyes of a smiling child, and in Vermeer's *The Art of Painting*,[1] and in the cry of a bird flying over a lake at dawn, and in Chopin's Prelude in E-flat major;[2] in the poplar growing in my garden, and in the cathedral at Chartres.

But also, and—perhaps—first of all there is beauty in the impulse of the soul of a man who is sacrificing his life for others.

Beauty is able to evoke joy and to bring relief in suffering; to fire the imagination and to restore calm to quivering nerves.

In the end beauty allows a man to sense what could have been happiness.

Source

Manuscript in Polish. Copyright Witold Lutosławski Collection, Paul Sacher Foundation. All rights reserved. Printed by permission.

Notes

1. This painting (original title *De Schilderkonst*, 1666–1667) is now kept in the Kunsthistorisches Museum in Vienna.
2. Prelude op. 28, no. 19.

1

NOTES ON THE CONSTRUCTION OF LARGE-SCALE FORMS

When composing large-scale closed forms, I always remember that what I am principally engaged in doing is organizing the process of the perception of my work. To my mind a piece of music is not only an arrangement of sounds, but also a set of impulses transmitted by these sounds to the listener and the reactions those impulses then awaken in him. To command these impulses and reactions, the composer can only follow his own experience in listening to the music and assume that his potential audience will include a certain number of people with responses similar to his own.

Two kinds of music perception might be distinguished: the active and the passive. The latter is how I would describe the kind of perception in which the listener's attention is totally absorbed by what he is hearing at a given moment. Active perception, on the other hand, occurs when a part of the listener's attention is, at certain moments, occupied in assimilating what he has heard earlier or in anticipating, foreseeing, or waiting for what he is about to hear. The bulk of the following remarks will be devoted to those elements of a composition that are designed to direct the audience backward, that is, into the immediate past, or forward, that is, into the immediate future of the course of the music. In other words, I propose to talk about the means available to the composer for stimulating both the listener's memory and his powers of anticipation.

Music forms can be divided into a number of categories, according to the degree to which a composition depends on the involvement of the audience's memory or anticipation. At one end of the scale, we have forms whose perception does not require the exercise of either the listener's memory or his anticipation; at the other, ones where the maximum participation of both is essential. Among the latter belong what are called "large-scale closed forms," such as sonatas, fugues, and the like. The former include some of the forms of primitive music. In our own day, music that brings neither memory nor anticipation into play is going through an extremely interesting evolution and is reaching a high level of sophistication. A composer working in this vein strings together a series of sound-occurrences that follow in no consequential order and without revealing any other ulterior pattern that might guide the process of perception. All that matters is the "now" of hearing; no other effort is needed for the perception of the music except that required by listening at a given moment. It is revealing that forms of this sort should just now be attracting the most distinguished composers of the day (witness Stockhausen's important achievements in this field). The spate of interest in this direction is quite understandable.

What makes me think so? Well, I have said that this form involves a succession of sound-occurrences without any consequential relationship to each
other. Now in the case of music, the idea of a consequential relationship is very
mistily defined. In contrast to logic, mathematics, and so on, music does not
deal in unambiguous elements, or indeed in any elements at all that have some
meaning other than a conventional one. Accordingly, the notion of a consequential relationship can be applied to music only metaphorically: the elements
hang together solely on the strength of an accepted, familiar convention, and
their concatenation bears only a passing resemblance to the relationship between cause and effect. It works only if there exists a convention to which the
listener is sufficiently well attuned for the composer to be able to create the
illusion of something self-evident with all the persuasiveness of a logical chain
of reasoning.

The ages of Baroque and Classicism were periods of grand conventions
founded primarily on the tonal system, and so it is not surprising that they
should have given birth to large-scale closed forms of supreme accomplishment. Nowadays, however, we lack conventions that have taken firm enough
root in the listener's mind. Those that have been developed are either in a
constant process of flux, or else tend to give way to new ones before audiences
have had time to grasp them.

To illustrate what I have just said, let me give you a simple example (J.
S. Bach, Brandenburg Concerto no. 4, measures 79–82). After that we would
expect something along these lines: (J. S. Bach, Brandenburg Concerto no. 4,
measures 83–85).

After this: (Beethoven, *Egmont*, measures 86–91) we might be surprised if,
instead of again hearing this: (Beethoven, *Egmont*, measures 88–89) we heard
this: (Beethoven, *Egmont*, measures 92–95).

In both cases we were anticipating something; but, while in the first
example what we expected did in fact follow, in the second the sequel took
us aback. In both instances, however, we were listening actively, switching on
our powers of anticipation and being able to do so because of the existence of
conventions with which we are conversant.

Now, in contrast, listen to this: (H. M. Górecki, *Scontri*, first *ffff* on page 5
up to the end of the first measure on page 6).[1] Here, there is no saying what
may come next. We have nothing specific to look for, so if what follows is this:
(the following part on page 6, from the two measures rest) it strikes us neither
as inevitable nor totally unexpected.

The same goes for this: (A. Dobrowolski, *Music for Magnetic Tape and Oboe
Solo*, from 1'25" on page 6 up to 2'15" on page 7).[2] After that we would not
be anticipating this: (the following part on page 7) or anything else either. Anticipation is quite impossible here, since the organization of the sounds is not

governed by any generally known rules. There is no established musical syntax to give us a lead to what might follow.

Given such a state of affairs, there is nothing remarkable about the interest in forms where the relationships between the sound-occurrences are immaterial, each coming across to the listener in isolation from the others without calling on either his memory, his ability to integrate single sound-occurrences into a larger whole, or his powers of anticipation.

Nevertheless, it would be wrong to assume that large-scale closed forms are a hopeless proposition for the modern composer. His only problem is to find ways of activating the listener's memory and anticipation despite the absence of recognized conventions, which could serve as a cue, or of a congenial basis of listening habits. It is such devices that I have been hunting for over the past years, and they form the chief subject of today's seminar.

My explorations in this field can be divided roughly into two groups.

The first is a matter of providing a basis for the listener's powers of recall and anticipation through the creation of *once-only conventions*, which is how I would describe the simple rules behind the construction of each section of a composition. These rules must be lucid enough to be communicated in the actual course of the music so that they can be used in the same way as the more solidly planted and longer-lived conventions of the past. What happens is that the process of acclimatization to the convention proposed by the composer is condensed into a few seconds. To understand what I am getting at, remember that if you are to respond to each phase in the development of a Beethoven sonata as he intended, you must first have listened to a number of works by him and by other composers as well, and so digested the whole complex system of conventions within which Beethoven was working. Naturally, this takes time. In the case of once-only conventions, the composer assumes that the listener lacks the grounding that would enable him to respond properly to each stage of the form's development, let alone anticipate anything whatsoever. Hence, he can bank only on what he is capable of intimating during the actual unfolding of his work.

In the later part of this lecture I shall give some examples of how this idea can be put into practical effect.

The second, much less important area, into which the search for ways of organizing the perception of a large-scale form has taken me, lies in the direction of borrowings from the other arts, principally the theatre. This can be fruitful when the aim is to create more intricate formal situations in which the simple, elementary once-only conventions I have mentioned are no longer enough. Of course, looking beyond the boundaries of pure music for ideas from other spheres is something of a makeshift. But you have to remember that in the realm of pure music there cannot be found at present any durable, universally known, conventions to which reference could be meaningfully made. For instance, we have no universal system of organizing pitch that would promise the composer that his audience will, at any given moment, be waiting to hear a particular sound, harmony, or even more complex musical occurrence, as was the case during the reign of the tonal system. In these circumstances, to venture outside music as such in search of some familiar phenomenon on whose sequences might be modeled the construction of a musical form seems to be a natural reflex. The drawback with this procedure, of course, is not only that it detracts from the homogeneity of music, but also that it is bound to be arbitrary in its methods of converting the grammar of nonmusical idioms into the language of music. This weakness is offset to some extent by the freshness that music gains through such transplants from outside.

The modes I have termed once-only conventions serve chiefly to stimulate the listener's powers of anticipating what is about to take place in a work. In other words, their purpose is to direct his attention forward, that is, into the immediate future. In order to switch his mind back into the immediate past, to make him recall what he has just heard and also instinctively piece together a section of music, we can fall back on certain typical mental reactions that have been partly shaped by the old musical conventions.

Let us now briefly consider the impulses that are intended to generate the responses sought by the composer in the listener's mind, that is to say, to direct the attention backward.

In the perception of a tonal work, the integration of a short section of music and its recollection usually occur after the cadence which ends the section. As far as we are concerned, cadences have vanished together with the tonal system, but this does not mean that we are forced to forfeit integration of each musical section by the listener and its memorization during perception of the work. The role of the cadence may be assumed by other phenomena that do not belong wholly to the tonal system. One possibility is the introduction of various kinds of changes in the course of the music, especially ones that are abrupt and radical. The most obvious device is simply to insert a hiatus. This gives the listener a chance to take brief stock of the preceding passage and to prime himself for the next one (Symphony no. 2, figures 4–5).

Other possibilities are changes in tempo, dynamics, tone-color, disposition of sounds, and so on. The sudden introduction of such a change at the beginning of a new section acts as a prompt, in the process of perception, to the recapitulation of what has gone immediately before. Its novel variations form a kind of background against which the preceding section takes on a different shape from that immediately registered by our senses, and is revealed in a new light. For its part the ensuing section may do exactly the same for its successor.

The switches may be extremely radical. Take this for instance: (*Jeux véni-tiens*, part I, from the beginning up to figure 7). Here there has been a change in tempo from fast to slow; in the orchestration from winds to strings; in the texture from a tissue of seven animated parts, each of which has its own wayward rhythm owing nothing to the others, to a combination of sustained notes forming an eight-note chord that provides the setting for the brief entries of the solo instrument; in the dynamics from *f* to *pp*; in the register from higher to lower; in the nature of the harmony from a twelve-note chord with a fourth-major second structure to an eight-note chord with a minor second structure.

But less sweeping changes can also work. A minor innovation—in the following example, the introduction of sustained notes—can equally well trigger an instinctive "summing up" of a preceding passage into a single whole (String Quartet, from the beginning of page 4 up to figure 4).[3]

These were examples of sound phenomena generating an impulse to "sum up," or integrate, a short passage just heard. The same thing may also occur with longer sections or even whole stages in the development of the form of a work. In this case the switch that induces the integration reflex must consist of the introduction of an element that is a complete novelty in relation to all the preceding sections of the work. A simple example of such a contrivance is the appearance of solo voices and chorus in the last movement of Beethoven's Ninth Symphony. The moment we hear the first entrance of the voice and then the chorus we automatically fuse in our memory everything that has gone before from the very beginning of the symphony. The introduction of the vocal element instantly defines the previous movements as a separate whole, that is, as the instrumental part of the symphony.

There is a similar device in Boulez's *Le marteau sans maître*. Here the change in regard to the preceding music consists of the appearance for the first time of the low notes of the tam-tam. It is only on hearing those that we become fully aware that everything beforehand had taken place in a medium and high register without descending below the small octave.

So much for the means of stimulating the listener's memory in the course of the perception of a work, in other words, of ways of causing a retrospective action of his consciousness.

As I have said, the listener's mind can be directed not only backward, but also forward, toward things that at a given moment have yet to take place in the work. Of course this is possible only to a very limited degree and much more vaguely than is the case with recollection, integration, and "summing up" of music already heard.

One way of jogging the listener into anticipation of what may be about to occur is the introduction of changes that are of a continuing nature and point in a single, specific direction. To grasp the mechanism of such changes, let us first consider some sections of music in which there are no changes whatsoever, that is, passages which might be called static (E. Varèse, *Intégrales*,[4] from page 12, measure 4, up to page 14, measure 2; *Trois poèmes d'Henri Michaux*, figures 29–30).

In these examples nothing changes as time passes. The melodic themes are repeated. Register, dynamics, tone-color, tempo, etc., remain the same without undergoing development. These passages do not prompt us in the course of listening to direct our attention either backward or forward. We do not know and we cannot imagine what may happen next and only common sense prevents us from supposing that such music may go on *ad infinitum*.

The same cannot be said of our next batch of examples. In each case we can detect certain changes leading in a recognizable direction and taking place in a continuous manner (*Trois poèmes d'Henri Michaux*, figures 89–90).

Here there is no question of wondering whether the work will last indefinitely, since loudness has its limits, and we realize that it will not be long before these are reached. In this way we can anticipate the moment at which the passage we are hearing must come to an end. But what is more important is that from the beginning of this passage we are aware not only of its variability, but also of the direction and speed of these changes. In our example there is a shift in loudness, moving from *p* to *f*.

In the next examples it is the arrangement of the sounds that changes continuously, running from higher to lower notes with diminishing speed: (*Trois poèmes d'Henri Michaux*, from the beginning up to figure 12, without *sfz*).

From a broad and sparse arrangement to one that is narrow and condensed in the middle of the scale: (String Quartet, figure 14).

From a broad and sparse arrangement to two that are narrow and condensed at the top and bottom of the scale: (*Jeux vénitiens*, part III, from section S up to the end of this part).

In the next example, the density of the accents increases continuously (*Trois poèmes d'Henri Michaux*, figures 12–27); in the next one there is a change in orchestration: the strings gradually give way to woodwinds, brass and percussion: (*Jeux vénitiens*, part II, from the beginning up to figure 32); in the next one the number of sounds used rises from three to twelve: (Symphony no. 2, figure 1).

In these examples of changes in the arrangement of sounds I have confined myself to illustrating the simplest situations, that is, ones where the changes follow a certain steady direction. But these continuing changes may also take a more intricate course—for instance, a transition from one sound to a set of several sounds lower down the scale followed by reversion to a single sound, the lower one in our aggregation: (*Trois poèmes d'Henri Michaux*, figures 74–84).

A more complex situation arises when the run of the music is divided into horizontal layers and the beginning of the continuous changes in each of them takes place at a different moment. In the next example the changes involve the arrangement of the sounds in one stratum and the time density of the sounds in the other. In the orchestral stratum we can distinguish several short sections, each of which displays a differently orientated, continuously changing arrangement of sounds, namely—to take them in order—from condensed at the top of the scale to broad, from higher to lower, from lower to higher, and so on. In the vocal parts, on the other hand, the time density of the sounds changes identically in each section: from greater to lesser. The beginnings of each section in the chorus part do not take place at the same moments as the beginnings of the sections in the orchestra (*Trois poèmes d'Henri Michaux*, words *qui glissez en nous*, figures 98–142).

Changes pointing in a specific direction and occurring in a continuous manner may, like the abrupt changes discussed earlier, take place not only within the span of short sections, but also in the course of whole stages in the development of a large-scale form containing a large number of sections. Such changes also have the effect of spurring the listener's powers of anticipation. This is an extremely crucial point in the construction of large-scale forms and in the process of their perception. Since a practical example would take up too much time, I shall confine myself to a verbal description. In the second part of my Symphony no. 2, the rhythm, tempo, and, to some extent, the scoring undergo a parallel, gradual transformation over a period of fifteen or so minutes. This transformation acts as a kind of scaffolding supporting the whole form. It consists of several sections with a great deal of variety, all of them, however, subordinated to a common principle that enables them to come over as a single whole.

"Metamorphoses," the main part of my *Musique funèbre,* is organized along similar lines. In it there is a gradual transformation of rhythm, dynamics, harmony, and melody that knits all the stages in the development of the form into a single fabric (one single whole).

The form of the principal, central part of the last movement of *Jeux vénitiens* consists of an increasingly rapid succession of several sections of music played by separate groups of instruments. This takes place in three stages, with the sections crowding more closely upon one another each time, until at the climax they form a thick mass of sound: (*Jeux vénitiens*, part IV, sections a_1–G).

In all three cases, the direction in which the changes are tending can be quite easily identified by the listener in the initial sections of the form. As the latter unfolds, the listener gains a firmer grasp of the direction he has identified and this strengthens the main formal construction of the work. As a result, the composer can allow himself certain deviations from the basic formal plan without damage to the construction and occasionally he can swing away from the specified direction of the ongoing changes. For example, in the second part of my Second Symphony there is a general intensification of rhythmical activity, but there are brief moments in which the activity slackens. This does not impair the overall impression we receive while listening and it may perhaps even have the opposite effect, serving as a reminder of the direction in which the changes are taking place when it is restored after a short digression.

The principle of continuity of change can also be waived without detriment to the general formal plan. These changes can be made in jerks and, as long as the general direction is consistent, the listener will already be glimpsing it in his mind after the second such switch. Here is an example. In it the dynamics change from *f* to *p*, the arrangement of sounds from a broad one embracing several octaves to one condensed in the middle of the scale, and the time density of the sounds from greater to smaller. But all this takes place not in a continuous process, but in a series of jumps (*Jeux vénitiens*, part IV, batt., *pf*, etc., figures 101–140).

In all the previous examples of continuous changes with a single specific direction, the purpose of the composer has been to convey as early and as clearly as possible both the nature of these changes and the direction they are following. As I have said, this awakens the listener's powers of anticipation. But changes may also be introduced in a deliberately surreptitious fashion so that the listener notices them only after they are to a large extent accomplished. In this case the composer is bent not on arousing, but on lulling the listener's anticipation. Here is an example (Symphony no. 2, figures 42–44).

The beginning of the section is static, that is, we cannot observe any changes in the course of the music. It is some time before we realize that the regularly recurring elements have been reinforced by a percussion group that carries on to the end, whereas the other instruments are gently faded out. The change here has taken place in a way almost imperceptible to the listener.

I have already mentioned that another area of my formal experimentation has revolved around borrowing from the other arts, especially the theatre. This is a matter that needs to be approached with the greatest caution and with many reservations. Everything that I am going to say on this point is imprecise, slippery, arguable, and defies purely musical analysis. As a result, to make certain things clearer I shall have to resort occasionally to purely literary terms. Of course, I quite appreciate the shortcomings of talking about music in this fashion. But I would rather not pass over these matters, since they can form an element in the process of composition and in my own case they have played a certain part in the construction of large-scale forms.

Here is the beginning from my String Quartet. In its patterning there can be detected an analogy with a scene from a stage play. It opens with a soliloquy by the first violin. It is composed of a number of very brief phrases that are punctuated from time to time by a four-note refrain (four sounds, section α).

Each of the phrases represents a separate musical idea, none of which are developed, but instead are discarded after a brief while. The structure of the phrases is characteristic: each of them starts with a fair amount of energy that is quickly exhausted. In one case, for example, this involves a rapid climb to the top of the scale and then a gradual descent (section β).

In another, there is a large piling-up of sounds in time that are then slowly thinned out (section γ). In a third, there is a certain intensification of the dynamics followed by a rapid weakening (section δ).

The rhythm is to a certain extent modeled on human speech, with its typical inflections to match meaning and accent phrases, words, and even syllables. It should not be supposed from this that the music is here intended actually to say something literally. All that it has borrowed from speech is its outward habit, its purely vocal features, and the manner in which it flows in time. The same goes for the end of the soliloquy and the passage that follows. Only the actual laws governing a certain stage situation have been adapted to music. It is no part of its purpose to reproduce the situation itself. What is the point of this situation? Well, at the end of the soliloquy, the four-note refrain, slightly altered, will be repeated three times: *mp*, *p*, and *p*. But in the third repetition, the first note is followed by a two-second rest, after which the three remaining instruments enter in succession. The model for this passage is a stage situation in which a character breaks off in midspeech with a short sentence repeated more and more softly, having perhaps noticed the presence of other persons who are not supposed to hear what he has been saying. These other people then begin to speak (section ε).

The brief motif is repeated by the second violin, viola, and cello, at first on three neighboring steps of a quarter-tone scale, but it then proceeds to develop more and more broadly, and the listener might be led to imagine that this passage will run for a long time. The musical discourse is, however, abruptly cut short by the entry of the first violin (figure 2). At the moment that the energy reaches its peak, with C having been repeated for the fifth time, there follows a three-second break, after which C is once more repeated *piano* (the third note before figure 3).

Once again there is a distinct analogy with a line spoken excitedly and suddenly broken off as a result of some outside factor or some inner psychological impulse. The final repetition *piano* of C brings the incursion of the first violin to an end and, at the same time, opens a new episode in which the first violin is joined by the viola and second violin. Here is the passage in full: (String Quartet, from the beginning up to page 5).

The fact that certain conventions have been taken from outside the sphere of music to govern the method of developing the musical discourse does not mean that the piece should be described as illustrative or program music. In program music the composer is trying to make the listener associate certain nonmusical ideas with the music he hears. In the case described here, nothing was further from my purpose. I do not care whether the analogies between music and speech or music and stage situation are detected by the listener or not. In fact I might even say that I would rather they were not. However, I have drawn attention to them here because they form part of the set of devices that I have used in the construction of large-scale closed forms. Without a doubt, this method falls far short of what I would ideally like, but that, at a time when there are no accomplished, durable conventions, is quite unattainable. Despite its obvious crudities, however, this method stands me in good stead, especially when I am trying to organize more complex formal situations.

∽

I have discussed some of the elements of constructing large-scale closed forms. I was particularly concerned to demonstrate the ways of nudging the listener's mind in the course of perception in either direction—backward and forward—in other words, ways of evoking an instinctive integration and memorization of the music just heard by the listener, and of stimulating his ability to anticipate, expect, and await music which at that given moment he has yet to hear.

In addition, I have drawn attention to the possibility of borrowing simple exemplars from outside the province of music (from the theatre in this specific case) that, after adaptation to music, can act as a substitute for musical conventions.

I have dealt with these problems piecemeal. On another occasion I shall talk about the construction of the form of the whole of a longer work.[5]

Source

Unpublished typescript in English, written with the intention to be presented in Darmstadt in 1967. Copyright Witold Lutosławski Collection, Paul Sacher Foundation. All rights reserved. Printed by permission.

Notes

1. See Henryk M. Górecki, *Scontri* per orchestra, 2nd ed. (Kraków: Polish Musical Edition, 1976).

2. See Andrzej Dobrowolski, *Music for Magnetic Tape and Oboe Solo* (Simplified Score + Record). (Kraków: Polish Musical Edition, 1973).

3. See Witold Lutosławski, String Quartet. Study Score (Kraków: Polish Musical Edition, 1968).

4. See Edgar Varèse, *Intégrales* for Small Orchestra and Percussion. Full Score (New York: G. Ricordi, 1956).

5. The two last paragraphs are crossed out.

PROBLEMS OF MUSICAL FORM

This lecture is concerned with certain problems relating to musical form. I should like it to be regarded as a collection of suggestions, which may prove of practical value to the composer, rather than a theoretical study.

I shall treat the conception of musical form in its narrow sense here, that is, as an arrangement of specific kinds of musical material within the period of time that the composer has designed for his composition—in other words—in the sense in which we use the word *form* when speaking, for example, of sonata form or variation form.

We are all aware of the fact that our epoch has produced very little in the way of musical form as thus understood. Really, no characteristic form has arisen of which we can say that its name at least is common to many contemporary works. And it is so in spite of the undeniable fact that in the sphere of form in the wider meaning of the term, that is, the shaping of the musical material itself, no earlier epoch has actually produced such variety and richness as have the last few decades.

If—as I have said—there does not really exist any fixed form characteristic of our epoch, then the simple consequence of this is the necessity of creating this form every time we compose a musical work. At any rate, this is true in those cases where we do not wish to base ourselves on the old forms, which no longer belong to our epoch, and surely only those cases should truly interest us nowadays. My main purpose in this lecture is to present you with a few personal suggestions concerning the creation of new forms.

There are probably many different ways of approaching this problem. It depends on the particular goal we are aiming at—in our case—on the kind of form we are seeking. There exist today various tendencies in this field, and one of the more characteristic, especially in the case of composers using the serial technique, is the elaboration of a so-called open form. This should be thought of not as a whole with a beginning and an end, but rather as a segment of some imagined longer span of time. A further stage in explorations of this type is represented by the so-called instantaneous form, in which the composer does not establish any connection between each particular moment of his music and all the rest and, consequently, between each of these moments and the whole work. In other words, in such a form, importance is attached only to what we hear at a given moment. In this way there arises something which could be called *anti-form*; an aggregate of events following one upon the other, which demand no continuity of concentration, not only during listening but even in the hearing itself. And thus, according to Stockhausen, his work *Carré* for four instrumental-vocal ensembles may be listened to in its entirety, or in parts, and with a varying degree of concentration—all depending on the inclination of the listener.[1]

I do not in the least dispute the compelling psychological motives that may induce the composer to seek this kind of solution, but—nevertheless—I personally regard it as a kind of formal atrophy, which in its application does not call for any especially arduous or intensive training. In other words, it is not difficult to master this kind of form. And so I confine myself to merely mentioning it.

A much harder task these days is the construction of a closed form, and it is with *this* problem that I now propose to deal. But before doing so, I must return once more to the classical period, in order to elucidate and trace one of the most important factors in the structure of musical form, the factor certain old theorists call "the character of the music." What this "character" of the music signifies will become apparent as I develop my theme further. But I must warn you straight away that this term does not have so much in common with the conventional meaning of the word *character*. However, so long as you bear this in mind, I see no necessity to substitute it for another word.

Now by the character of the music in a given section of a musical form, we understand the relation of this particular section to the form as a whole. Or we can express it differently by saying that the character of the music in a given section of the form determines the function of this section in the creation of the overall form. From this point of view we differentiate four musical characters in classical music: narrative, transitional, introductory, and terminative.

In a section that has a narrative character, the musical content itself is the most important thing and it dominates the listener's attention. The perception of this section proceeds as follows: "I hear this and nothing else occupies my attention." As a rule, the narrative character is manifested in expositions and in recapitulations of entire themes.

The course of a section of form of a transitional character is different. Here the musical content is not the most important element and does not dominate the listener's attention. This section is composed chiefly of fragments of the material already heard in the exposition. The listener feels that he is about to pass over to another moment of the overall form. He finds himself, as it were, en route, going somewhere. His perception of this section is along the following lines: "I hear this, but, above all, I feel that what I now hear is leading me on to something different I shall hear in a moment." In classical music, bridge-passages from a main theme to a subsidiary one, development sections, and also certain moments in extended codas all have this character.

Both introductory and terminative characters are features of a section of the form in which, as in the previous one, the musical content is not the most important element. The perception of the introductory section is as follows: "I hear this, but I realize that actually, I am anticipating hearing something else." The perception of a terminative section, on the other hand, may be indicated thus: "I hear this, but I realize that in a moment the whole form or some stage of it is about to end."

It is clear that these various kinds of perception do not depend on the inclination of the listener himself, but they are suggested to him or even forced upon him by the "character" of the music.

It is not difficult in classical music to examine the way in which the composer achieves the specific musical character of a given section of form. In the classics, the narrative character is to be found predominantly in themes built in the form of periods. It is marked by harmonic inactivity, is more or less restricted to the tonic key, and is strongly imbued with melodic-rhythmic content. Sections of a character are most often based on melodic-rhythmic material that has been heard before and is now undergoing fragmentation into smaller motifs repeated many times. In such a section, attention is diverted from the melodic-rhythmic content and focused on other factors, especially on the harmony, which now becomes markedly more active.

The changing nature of the harmony, dependent on the cycle of modulations, gives the listener a feeling of approaching some unknown point far distant in time. Toward the end of a section of a character, the harmonic situation usually becomes clear, tending to dominant tonality, in which the narrative section in turn makes its appearance. During this period, the melodic-rhythmic content depends mainly on further repetitions of already familiar material, or on a new material of no great significance, and *this* reinforces the feeling of waiting for something new, and even induces a sort of impatience or boredom, a feeling of emptiness demanding to be filled. That the listener should feel thus is precisely the composer's aim, and this is one of the formal masterstrokes to be found in the Viennese classics.

This specific impatience or boredom is a necessary preparation for the narrative section that is just about to be heard. This section may contain a new theme, or perhaps recapitulation of a theme that has already been heard. Without preparation, without the creation of a suitable atmosphere, without that characteristic expectancy allied to impatience or boredom, the entry of a new narrative would not have the intended effect and would not play its intended role. The entry of a new narrative section after preparation by a lengthy section is like the entry of a new character in a drama, preceded and *prepared for* by a suitable situation. Sections of an introductory character are distinguished by a sparing use of melodic material, which may often be purposely insignificant and of somewhat secondary importance, so as to ensure that the musical content in this case will not absorb the whole of the listener's attention. This is a way of creating a state of expectancy for what is to follow. Harmonically, sections of an introductory character are mainly static, inclining for the most part to the dominant tonality in which the next narrative section is to appear. Coming finally to sections of a terminative character, we find that they may even be rich in melodic interest, as in the case, if you remember, of so-called closing themes. In regard to harmony, sections of a terminative character depend mostly on the strong perfect cadence, often repeated several times over.

I have recalled here in very simplified terms phenomena well known to *every one* of us, but I am doing this so as to be able later to draw conclusions from them, which may be usefully applied to present-day composition.

The elements that the classical composers made use of in the construction of their forms consisted primarily of themes, motives, and a harmonic scheme. These elements served to produce the desired musical character in the sections of each form, and they frequently afforded possibilities of subtle interplay, sudden changes, and unexpected transitions from one character to another.

Of course the means we employ today are quite different. All the same, it is worthwhile reflecting upon the manner in which the old means were employed so that we in turn, in the construction of our large forms, may take advantage of possibilities analogous to those that gave the classics their particular musical characters. And at any rate, it is worth reflecting upon the relationship of each section of our new form to the whole. In other words—upon the function of each section in the construction of the overall form.

It seems to me that when embarking upon a construction of a large form, our first consideration should be the moments of intense musical significance, that is, those that have a certain measure of independent interest, and which, even if taken out of the context of the overall form, would still have an intrinsic meaning. With these moments we place others, less arresting, which would *lose* their meaning if taken out of their context, because the significance of such moments depends above all on their relationship to other moments of the form and also to the whole. In other words: their significance depends *first and foremost* on their formal function. This function consists of indicating to us the exact places in which we find ourselves at different stages of the form, in rousing our expectancy with regard to what is about to happen, or in warning us that either the whole form itself or some stage of it is to finish.

These two types of music constitute the foundation upon which to build a large form, and the architectural worth of our large form depends upon our ability to manipulate them. To illustrate what I mean by this ability, I shall give an elementary example: it concerns merely the quantity of music of each of the two above-mentioned types in a large form. If we fill the whole form with music of the first type, that is, with music of intense musical significance, of which the individual moments attract attention to themselves quite independently of the context, then our form becomes a sort of "potpourri," and the most attractive moments do not compensate for its structural weakness. If, on the other hand, we deprive our form entirely of moments of independent musical interest and base everything on contrast, preparation, transition, anticipation, that is to say, on the manifold formal functions, then we get a form that is labored, empty, and unsatisfactory. The fault in both cases is a lack of balance between forces acting in opposite directions; namely the two opposite directions to which our attention is drawn in the course of our perception of the work. One of these directions is represented by the music which we are actually hearing at the moment, and the other by the relationships of the music heard at a given moment to other moments, as well as to the overall form.

In order, then, to tackle the construction of a large form, we must possess a certain number of ideas of intrinsic value. The French call such an idea *idée clef*—a key idea. In the case of the classics, the key ideas were themes, that is to say, concepts of a melodic-rhythmic nature. The theme, too, was clothed in its own characteristic harmony, and summarized within itself the main idea of the whole work and determined its general physiognomy.

Nowadays, the key idea of a composition cannot be a theme for the simple reason that, in the texture of contemporary music, the theme, in the sense in which it is defined here, just does not exist. It will be represented instead by a single structure or "sound object" or, to put it differently, an independent complex of sounds bounded in time. It can fulfill its function on the condition that it has intrinsic value for us and makes sense even when removed from its context. These key ideas determine the cast of the whole work just as themes do in classical music.

However, key ideas alone are not the whole answer to the problem. It would not be true to say that everything else was now just a matter of technique, knowledge, craftsmanship, or logical reasoning. I am deeply convinced that in an authentic work of art everything, without exception, is an act of invention. Technique is, at bottom, only a species of invention, for actually it is a collection of ideas that lend themselves to repeated application. And so I regard all kinds of ideas of a formal nature, which go into the making of a large scale composition, as being of equal importance to key ideas themselves.

At this point we come up against a basic problem: what possibilities do we have at our disposal in the construction of a large form, when our key ideas consist of individual structures or of sound-objects? In which direction must we search for formal ideas, which will enable us to construct a large work? In classical music, the creative elements needed for building a formal structure were, firstly, thematic material of a melodic-rhythmic nature and, secondly, tonal harmony with its established system of tonalities, modes, modulations, and cadences. Let us consider what kind of devices serve this purpose nowadays. Let us enumerate the special types of musical material available to us in the event of our constructing a modern form:

1. Disposition of sounds in the musical gamut. What is under consideration here is the *compass* of the sounds of the structure in a given period of time, the position of this compass in relation to our middle register, the compactness or looseness of the sound-texture vertically, or the distribution of this compactness and looseness, if at a given moment it is not uniform. With regard to the fact that these are features which are variable in time, we must think here of their average proportions in a given section of the form, that is, the average compactness, the average extent of the compass, etc. And thus we can speak, for example, of placing a given section of the music within a certain compass bounded by two sounds, provided that these latter are not overstepped in this particular section of the form.

2. Timbre. Here we are considering not only the timbre of individual instruments and groups of similar instruments, but also—at the same time—the degree of differentiation among the timbres used when we operate simultaneously with different timbres. Timbre here should be understood as meaning one of the possible tone-colors, of which each instrument possesses a large number, depending on register, tone-production, dynamics, the kind of attack, and, above all, depending on the musical text performed and its harmonic physiognomy.

3. Types of rhythm and frequency of impulses. Here I see the possibility of operating with all kinds of modular rhythm and, above all, with nonmodular ones, whereas frequency of impulses I understand as a concept of tempo extended into the realm of nonmodular rhythm.

4. Intensity. Here dynamics comes into play and another influencing factor in the case of ensemble music is the number of instruments employed in a given section of the form.

5. Harmony. This requires special discussion. As you know, in serial music we cannot speak of harmony as being an independent, form-creating factor. Now, I personally do not use the serial technique in my compositions and so my approach to harmony is somewhat different. (I shall be discussing some other time how I make use of vertical sound ag-

gregations and their variants—in short—harmony.[2] In my own work, as a composer, I must say I find this harmonic aspect of sound material one of the most important in constructing large forms.)

I have enumerated here some of the basic features of the musical texture that may be utilized in the construction of our form. Thus: in order to make a large form clear and to give it a definitive shape, capable of being comprehended and remembered, we must indicate clearly its several stages or divisions. These stages or divisions must be sufficiently differentiated from one another, so that together they will form a construction that may be grasped in the course of performance. They may differ as regards the features already mentioned, that is, as regards the disposition of sounds within the musical gamut, the timbre, the type of rhythm, frequency of impulses, intensity, harmony, etc. To each section of our form we can apportion certain features that are maintained throughout its duration and differentiate it in this way from the section which follows.

The distribution of the features, mentioned here, over the whole form is, however, only one aspect of the problem. Probably more important from the point of view of the whole composition itself, is what happens inside each section.

As I have already said, in classical music we distinguish four so-called characters of the music: narrative, transitional, introductory, and terminative. Now let us say that of these four characters, the narrative may be regarded as a kind of *static* musical character. For what is most important in it is what is happening at a given moment. We remain, as it were, in a state of balance, directing our mind neither forward nor backward. Let us call the remaining three characters *dynamic*, because they are distinguished by a lack of balance, they exert some sort of force, and direct our attention to what is just about to follow. It was possible in classical music to achieve this dynamic effect by a suitable play of harmonic functions and by certain manipulations of the thematic material. Nowadays, in order to be able to construct a large form, we must seek elsewhere for this dynamic character; and I now intend to indicate the new possibilities in this direction.

If all the features of a musical composition are maintained for some time without change, if—in other words—the music remains in the same register, with the same timbre and intensity, then its character may be described as static. A sudden change of one, several, or even all the features of the musical texture does not basically alter this static character. It will only bring about a juxtaposition of two contrasting but static sections of the music. We can find many examples to illustrate this in Stravinsky's works.

We only obtain the dynamic character when one, several, or all the features of the musical texture undergo change in a *continuous* way. The observation by the listener of this change, and especially his awareness of the direction in which it is taking the music, incline him to divert his attention from what he is hearing at the moment, that is to say, from the actual musical content of the given section. At such a moment part of the listener's attention is taken up by matters of a formal nature, such as—for example—anticipation of a new stage of the form, or conclusion of the present stage or of the whole work.

The changes in particular features of the musical texture may, of course, pursue a very varied course, both as regards their direction and also the speed at which these changes are effected. This offers the composer a whole wealth of possibilities for the shaping of the particular stages of a large musical form. Indeed, the wealth of possibilities seems here to be no less than in the classical period, when the dynamic force of a given section of the music was determined by the course of the harmony and the use made of thematic material.

Now, I think, would be a fitting moment to let you hear several examples, which illustrate the way I have just mentioned of shaping particular parts of our large form.

For reasons I mentioned at the beginning of my lectures, I am using excerpts from my own works.

Here is an example of a section of musical form possessing a distinctly static character. All the features of the musical texture remain unchanged for a while. A sudden alteration of the majority of these features introduces a new section of a no less static character. This is the equivalent of what in classical music we define as narrative character (*Jeux vénitiens*, part I, sections A–B).

Here is a second example of an analogous static character. Certain pitch changes of the sound groups do not violate this character. We listen to this music without any thought of what comes next. The music being listened to says nothing to us about this; for the given moment it is self-sufficient (*Jeux vénitiens*, part II, measures 1–25).

Now I am going to give you examples of sections of form in which the character is not static but dynamic. Let me just remind you that this means that in this section, progressive changes take place in one or more features of the musical texture. In the example you are now going to hear, the musical content is purposely, so to speak, diluted. Nothing essential is happening in this music. The listener has the feeling that the music here is not intended to absorb his full attention. It suggests that something more important is on the way. This impression is intensified when the accents, which at first are introduced sparingly, gradually begin to accumulate. At this point we feel certain that at any moment now we are going to hear something significant, something for which this whole section has been preparing us. And this feeling of anticipation is duly confirmed when we hear the first intervention of the piano. In this case, the particular feature undergoing progressive change is the frequency of impulses (*Jeux vénitiens*, part IV, from the beginning to b_1 [exclusively]).

And here is the next example, also of music of a dynamic character. Here several features undergo change, but it should be noted that these changes take place in a series of steps and not in a smooth continuous way, so that it is only after some considerable time that we realize *where* they are leading. These changes are as follows: the volume of tone decreases in the percussion section, so that each entry of this group of instruments becomes weaker and weaker. In this same group, there is a decrease in the frequency of impulses. As for the other instruments, their volume of sound remains constant, but the placement of sounds previously spread over a wide band of the scale is now confined within a narrow range of the middle register. The frequency of impulses is gradually reduced, and the harmonic aspect also undergoes change: from a widely-spaced twelve-note chord we pass gradually to one built up of minor seconds superimposed one upon another in close formation.

As you can see, this is a section in which various changes take place simultaneously, creating a kind of counterpoint. The reduction to a minimum of the musical content of this section, and the fact that the whole emphasis is laid on the process of change of several features of the musical texture, compels us to perceive this music as a typical transition from one stage of the form to the next, which we are now conditioned to expect as a matter of course (*Jeux vénitiens*, part IV, figures 101–145).

At this point I am purposely cutting short these reflections on the subject of constructing a large form, although really it would seem that I am only now coming to the most important part. Perhaps I ought to show you the ways to combine sections with different formal functions; examine everything concerning the temporal proportions of particular parts of the form; and reflect upon the degree of concentration of the musical content at particular moments of the form, in order to obtain what might be called the "psychological balance of the form." In other words, perhaps I ought to consider everything that would enable us to construct a large form in such a way as to ensure that the listener's perception of it would be a complete, independent experience.

If, however, I were to do *that*, we should have to listen to a number of works in their entirety and repeat their long parts, for which, of course, we have no time. Besides, I am not sure whether this would really be of any great advantage. For to push theoretical considerations too far in this direction could be of no practical benefit to you as composers. Moreover, it might give rise to the false idea that one could indeed learn to create large forms in this way. I am convinced that, in spite of the undoubted necessity for intensive thought on this subject, the creation of a large form is always—in the final analysis—an act of inspiration.

I have spoken here about many things that I am sure are already familiar to you, and no doubt at times I have stated the obvious, but it was not my purpose to present some new theory about musical form, or even new recipes for composing. Sometimes the attaching of names to phenomena that are familiar to us, and the marshaling of them into some kind of order, acts as a stimulus to our own processes of thought on a given subject. This stimulation of your minds to undertake independent research into the problem of building a large form was in truth the purpose of my lecture.

Source

Unpublished typescript in English (third lecture at Tanglewood, 1962). Copyright Witold Lutosławski Collection, Paul Sacher Foundation. All rights reserved. Printed by permission.

Notes

1. See Karlheinz Stockhausen: *Carré* für vier Orchester und vier Chöre, in id. *Texte zu eigenen werken, zur Kunst Anderer, aktuelles. Aufsätze zur musikalischen praxis* (Cologne, Germany: Verlag M. DuMont Schauberg, 1964), 102–103.
2. See Lutosławski's text "Pitch, the Interval and Harmonic Aggregate" in this chapter.

PITCH, THE INTERVAL, AND HARMONIC AGGREGATE

In considering the history of music of the first half of the twentieth century, I have arrived at the conclusion that a singular duality prevails among composers of this period as regards the use of pitch. I have developed the term *use of pitch* to connote everything that relates to the interval in composition, the sequence of sound of various pitch, and also to simultaneous sound or the vertical aggregate or—if we wish to resort to an older form—the chord. I feel that the duality of the tendencies lies, on the one hand, in the basically different treatment of the above factors by the Schoenberg school and, on the other, by the spiritual heirs of Debussy, like Stravinsky in his first period, Bartók, Messiaen, or Varèse.

I have counterposed Schoenberg to Debussy with deliberate intent. As a matter of fact, it is significantly characteristic of their period that two great artist reformers, whose objectives and aims of reform were so diametrically opposed, should emerge almost simultaneously. It may seem that this contradiction is a paradox. But as I stop to reflect about it longer, my observation is that extreme difference between the two opposing tendencies was instrumental in compelling them to appear at the same time. One tendency complements the other; they constitute a mutual counterbalance and I feel that the logic of the historical development of music in the first half of the twentieth century lies in this mutual counterposition. This singular counterpoise has continued for several decades. But there is something that unites the two opposing movements. And, despite the diametrical opposition, they also fulfill a certain common historical role. Both tendencies liquidate the tonal system, the major-minor key system, the system of functional harmony.

I shall now try to tell you briefly just where I feel the contradiction between the Debussy and Schoenberg schools lies. The simplest way to explain this problem is to consider the attitude of each of these movements to the question of the harmonic aggregate or, to put it very simply, to the treatment of the chord.

Debussy, as we all know, started a new period regarding the knowledge of harmonic aggregate. The knowledge was not the result of theoretical research, but was gained by the empirical method. It is a gift of nature, a consequence of a deep spiritual need, and, at the same time, of a specific sensual temperament. Debussy discovered an extraordinary wealth of possibilities, developed by the large number of his followers, by directing the maximum intensity of his attention to harmonic aggregate in its thousands of variations as a phenomenon that has its own independent value of expression and is independent of functional purpose. One of the things that astonishes me in Debussy's genius is that in a comparatively short time, the composer demonstrated such a scope of impenetrable and unexplored possibilities that were concealed in the twelve-tone scale of equal temperament, a creation we know was derived from the overtone series. I wish to draw particular attention to the last fact, because I shall return to it frequently in my lecture.

To Schoenberg, however, the astonishing discovery made by Debussy seems to be reduced to naught. This fact was not entirely obvious in the first stages of Schoenberg's creativity. But upon studying the subsequent periods in his work as well as that of his followers, we realize that Schoenbergianism stands in plain opposition to the future vision of the world of sound we may sense in Debussy. To Schoenberg, the chord is not an independent creation. It is the result of experience only in a small degree. The role of meaning of the chord is not of primary importance in the course of the composition. Above all, simultaneous sound is not the result of a choice made according to its qualities of expression or sound color (I cannot find words that would give a more precise description), but is simply the function of the use of the row that is the foundation of the dodecaphonic technique. In this manner, the simultaneous combination of tones is subordinated to new functional laws, laws that establish the sequence of horizontal and vertical sounds. It is clear that this state of affairs signifies a complete relinquishing of the great wealth of possibilities inherent in the development of the chord system, the prospects of which were demonstrated in the works of Debussy. In place of this, Schoenberg introduces other elements of sound material or rather a completely separate concept of the world of sound, a concept that is completely alien to Debussy's sensualism. In the ultimate aim, this concept is to lead to the disappearance of qualitative differences between the intervals or, in other words, to a maximum departure from those properties of the twelve-tone scale of equal temperament that are derived directly from the fact that there are intervals in this scale belonging to the overtone series. In Schoenberg's system, I sense an instinctive desire to go beyond the twelve-tone scale. Unlike the one preceding it, the world of sound of Debussy and of his followers is indissolubly bound with the phenomenon of the overtone series and the twelve-tone scale of equal temperament. Debussy discloses prospects for the maximum exploitation of this scale with its characteristic qualitative differences between the separate intervals. I cannot undertake here a study of all the reasons that led to the virtually simultaneous emergence of two such contradictory musical ideas, which divided the body of music artists into two opposing camps, and gave rise to two separate traditions that have began to permeate each other only in the course of the last few years.

The source of this singular division should be sought in the deep layers of the human psyche. This is why I can scarcely hope to divine the cause of this phenomenon.

One of the reasons may be the two different types of human reactions to sound. I shall not go into a detailed analysis and I will only give a rather primitive illustration. To the representatives of one of the two types, the perfect fifth represents a completely different quality than tritone, while to the representative of the second type (I am referring to the serialists) this difference is rather quantitative, that is, they are concerned with the difference in the number of semitones contained in each of the respective intervals. I have deliberately used this elementary example. But I constantly bear in mind the numerous and diversified consequences deriving from this juxtaposition I have chosen in illustration. Thus we have here the different role performed by the intervals, that is, by simultaneous combination of sounds and sound sequences, which may be treated as arrangements of different psychological impulses that differ in quality or as an expression of numerical relations. Developing the generalization from this observation, one may speak of the prevalence of the sensual element in one and of the intellectual element in the second of the two types of reaction to sound phenomena. I am by no means convinced either by those who accord priority to one of the two types or by those who allege that the second is on the wane.

I have already risked the assertion that, beginning with Schoenberg, dodecaphony and serial music are, among other things, an expression of the doctrine's logical development toward its ultimate stage, that is, to go beyond the twelve-tone scale of equal temperament. Many convincing arguments may be quoted in support of this assertion. I have spoken of the fact that one of the principal traits of the traditional chromatic scale is its dependence on the overtone series and, consequently, the use of qualitative differences between the intervals. I have given a brief definition of qualitative difference. May I add, however, that qualitative difference also includes everything that differentiates the intervals from each other, apart from the difference in their range and the distance between separate pairs of tones (the difference in the number of semitones that separate every two tones of a pair or everything that differentiates intervals with the exception of the pure differences in quantity). It is true that the quality of the interval does correspond in a certain sense to the degree of complexity of the relations between the arithmetical number of vibrations of its tones. But above all, the qualitative differences between the intervals correspond to the different reactions of our ear to these intervals, in that we consciously register certain individual traits of each separate interval irrespective of its range.

The serial technique in its various phases aims to abolish all qualitative differences between the intervals, principally by using the largest possible number of various intervals in the smallest possible space. The ear then registers impulses that vary so quickly that it can react in the given time only to the distances between the tones and not to the separate qualities. Another example of this same tendency is to employ the most complex relations between the number of vibrations, which also may in a certain moment obliterate qualitative differences. This may be achieved by giving a preference to the intervals whose tones remain in the most complicated relation to each other, thus, for instance, the minor second and tritone, and by avoiding the simplest intervals like the octave, the perfect fifth, and others. The constant use of intervals in which the tones are far apart (a manner deeply rooted in the compositions of later day serialism) is also one of the methods used in obliterating qualitative differences. All these methods achieve their aim only to a certain degree and I feel convinced that the complete elimination of qualitative differences between intervals in the conventional scale is impossible.

That is why I feel that Schoenberg's ultimate aim in choosing this direction of development of the musical language—an aim that was probably subconscious—was to go beyond the present scale. Or at least to establish in the previous scale a state of affairs that would strip the scale of its basic and characteristic features and would reduce the relations between the tones of the intervals to numerical relations.

Today, by using electronic generators it is possible to create any arbitrary scale, hence a scale that would ideally fulfill that aim of the serialism. That is why its continuation in the area of the old scale—it seems to me—would be totally groundless. It is an anachronism and always remains in an overt and deliberate contradiction to the very concept of qualitative differences between intervals—a concept that lies at the foundation of the twelve-tone scale.

The conclusions I arrived at after these deliberations were not only the reason why I was never interested for long in the use of serial techniques in my own work. Lack of faith in the development of this technique at the present moment is not the only thing. A more important reason, perhaps, is that I feel more strongly attracted by the twelve-tone scale, with the qualitative differences between the intervals as a point of departure. This accords far more closely with my natural predispositions than the serial technique. Another sphere of my search lies in the world of sound that goes beyond the twelve-tone scale of equal temperament. One of the problems I am working on at present is a new type of musical scale that it will be possible to use in compositions only by creating sound with electronic devices. I am also interested in all other methods of producing sound, known as concrete music, not to mention the whole range of sound that may be drawn from conventional instruments in the area of the production of sound of an undefined pitch.

I have spoken of my search in the sphere of the twelve-tone scale of equal temperament. I shall not endeavor to describe the whole evolution that led me to the basic element of my musical material, namely the twelve-note chord. This chord contains all the notes of the scale, a chord that, as we know, has a vast number of variations. By way of experiment, I classified the twelve-note chord in a system of classes, grouping them according to similarity of the reaction they provoke and, consequently, to similarity of structure. The choice of a suitable class of the twelve-note chord depends in the composition on the purpose it is to serve at a given moment from the point of view of expression, formal function, and the like.

Here are a few examples of the twelve-note chords and the manner in which they are used in my compositions.

I shall begin with the simplest illustration so that you may easily grasp the most essential properties of this technique, that is, the properties that make it possible to employ a factor that I call the qualitative difference between two intervals and their groupings and, in this instance, the qualitative differences that separate the different varieties of the twelve-note chord.

Here we have the songs called *Children Rhymes*, set to the lyrics taken from a collection by Kazimiera Iłłakowicz, a Polish woman poet.[1] The childlike quality of these texts inspired me to reduce the means of expression to an absolute minimum. Depending on the expression desired, I used the suitable twelve-note chord, and in certain cases, two or even one type of the chord provided sufficient material for one song. We shall now hear the song "Zima" (Winter), throughout which we hear the twelve-note chord constructed of four chords of major third (*Five Songs,* "Zima" [Winter]).

Other types of twelve-note chords predominate in the song called "Wiatr" (The Wind). These are twelve-note chords of a cluster construction that oscillate between the aggregates of minor seconds, minor seconds with major seconds, and major seconds (*Five Songs,* "Wiatr" [The Wind]).

Now we come to an example of a more complex construction, in which a series of various twelve-note chords are used side by side. Despite the differences, they all belong to three quite closely related types. Consequently, the fragment has a certain intended fairly uniform and harmonic colour (*Jeux vénitiens,* part I, figures 55–83).

And in a conclusion, an example of sharp contrasts achieved by placing side by side two twelve-note chords of a diametrically different effect and a diametrically different structure. This example is taken from one of my older compositions for strings called *Musique funèbre* (part III, *Apogeum,* figures 235–245).

Source

Unpublished typescript in English (fourth lecture at Tanglewood, 1962). Copyright Witold Lutosławski Collection, Paul Sacher Foundation. All rights reserved. Printed by permission.

Note

1. *Five Songs,* to poems of Kazimiera Iłłakowicz (1956–1957), include: "Morze" (The Sea), "Wiatr" (The Wind), "Zima" (Winter), "Rycerze" (Knights), and "Dzwony cerkiewne" (Orthodox Church Bells).

SOME PROBLEMS IN THE AREA OF RHYTHM

In this lecture I intend to make a few remarks about the methods undertaken by certain composers to organize time in a musical work. Some phenomena in this field observable in various moments in the history of music will attract our attention, but we shall concentrate particularly upon the period concerning us most, that is, upon the recent years. We shall choose one of the classical periods of European music as our starting point, and then we shall move in two directions, namely forward, toward the present era, and backward, toward the remote past. According to this plan we shall analyze some musical examples in the following sequence: we shall begin with some fragments of Haydn's and Beethoven's sonatas, then we shall take a closer look at the "Danse sacrale" from Stravinsky's *Rite of Spring*; further at a fragment taken from a St. Martial organum; at fragments of works by Messiaen, Boulez, Nono, and Stockhausen; and at a fragment of Syrian psalmody from the fifth century; references will also be made to the works of Bussotti and Penderecki.

We shall begin with the finale from Haydn's Sonata no. 20 in D major, *Tempo di minuetto*. We can distinguish several parts in the musical form as a whole owing to the allocation of musical content in the work and to the placing of cadences in it. Having thus divided this form we come to the conclusion that it falls into five segments, each of equal length, that is, having thirty-two measures. Let us borrow a term from the language of architecture and call such a segment a *module*. We could go on dividing further and thus obtain a larger number of equal segments, though smaller in size. Let us agree to reserve the term *module* only for the longest segments of musical form, which arise from the natural division of this form and are of equal length. The module is therefore a relative unit of duration, similar to such rhythmic values as a whole note, a half note, etc. The form we have chosen as an example consists of five modules, each module of thirty-two measures long.

The second example is almost as simple. It is the "Andante con moto" from Beethoven's Piano Sonata no. 23 in F minor, op. 57 (the "Appassionata"). Here we have to deal with a theme with variations, which are performed *attaca*, so that the form is a continued whole. The first division, according to the allocation of musical content and the placing of the cadences, allows us to distinguish five segments in the form as a whole, namely, the theme, three variations, and the recapitulation of the theme in a form shortened to half of its original length. These segments are not equal; four of them have thirty-two measures, and one has sixteen measures. The next division allows us to halve each of the first four segments because—as a matter of fact—each of them always consists of sixteen measures twice repeated. In such a perfectly natural way, we obtain eight segments and, after adding the last segment left over from the previous division, nine segments. This time they are all of equal length, namely they have sixteen measures each. Thus, we can say that our form consists of nine modules of sixteen measures each, arranged so that the first eight modules are always braced together in pairs.

The next example is the "Menuetto" from Beethoven's Piano Sonata no. 18 in E-flat major, op. 31. It is a ternary form ABA. The lengths of individual segments are: A—thirty-two measures, B—forty-four measures, A—thirty-two measures, and a coda of eight measures. In order to obtain segments of equal

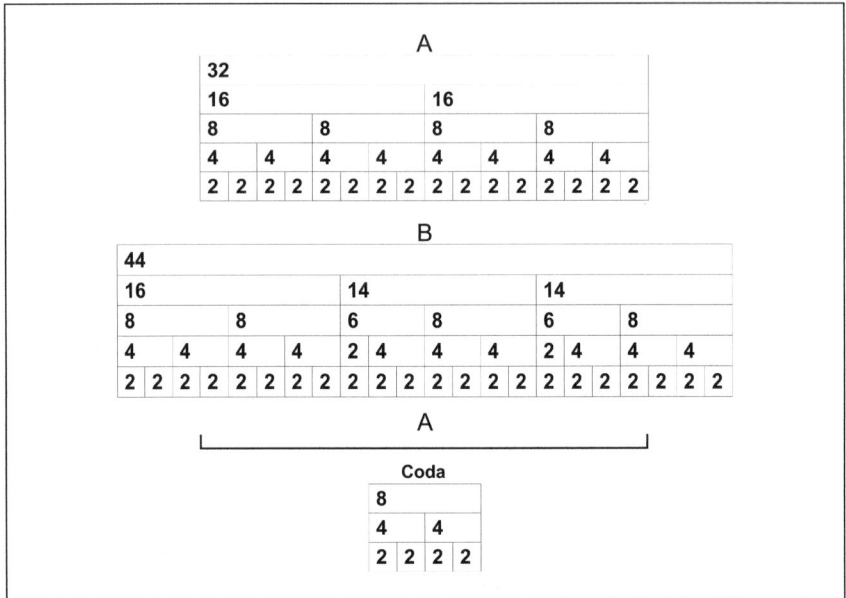

A

32															
16								16							
8				8				8				8			
4		4		4		4		4		4		4		4	
2	2	2	2	2	2	2	2	2	2	2	2	2	2	2	2

B

44																					
16								14						14							
8				8				6			8			6			8				
4		4		4		4		2	4		4		4	2	4		4		4		
2	2	2	2	2	2	2	2	2	2	2	2	2	2	2	2	2	2	2	2	2	2

A

Coda

8			
4		4	
2	2	2	2

Example 1-1.

length by our previous method, we must take four more divisions, according to the allocation of musical content and to the placing of the cadences. It is only after the fourth division that we have segments of two measures that can be looked upon as modules. These modules are grouped as shown in example 1-1.

We have hitherto followed the allocation of musical content and the placing of the cadences when dividing our form into segments. But while applying the same principles of division we may not obtain any segments of equal length at all. This will be shown in our next example. In order, however, to find there the basic constructive element of the music of this period, that is, the module, we shall assume yet another principle of division. We shall use it where the previous principles cannot already be used. I shall now explain what this new principle of division should consist of. In the works of classical composers, the measure is not only a conventional unit, but also a real unit of duration. In the perception of classical music, a measure is distinctly divided into parts corresponding to the accepted meter, though the musical thread remains unbroken while the measure lasts. The same can be said about a period of several measures, which are homogenous as regards musical content and unbroken by any cadence. In such a period we can discern smaller groups of several measures or, at any rate, single measures. Let us apply all the principles of dividing in analyzing the next example, which is the "Adagio cantabile" from Beethoven's

16						12				
8			8			7			5	
2	2	4	2	2	4	2	3	2	2	3
1	1	1	1	1	1	1	1	1	1	1	1	1	1	1	1	1	1	1	1	1	1	1	1	1	1

Example 1-2.

Piano Sonata no. 8 in C minor, op. 13. The form consists of six segments. It is only when we divide the form for the fifth time that we obtain a module of one measure's length. The fifth division involves the following grouping of the modules in the first two segments, as shown in example 1-2.

It can be said that the size of the module in the examples previously analyzed is equal to at least one measure, while the number of measures in larger modules is one of the multiples of the number two, namely two, four, eight, sixteen, and thirty-two, and the duration of the module in our first example exceeds forty seconds. The way in which the modules form groups testifies to the preference for the number two and its multiples, that is, two, four, eight, etc. The grouping of modules by three, which results in such groupings as 2 + 3 = 5, 2 + 2 + 3 = 7, etc., is less common.

These general remarks refer to a very characteristic feature of musical works created mainly in the eighteenth and nineteenth centuries, though this feature can also be discovered in music created in very remote times. This is best corroborated by the first example in the anthology by Davison and Apel[1]: the Chinese hymn from 1000 BC that, as we would describe it today, has a clearly recognizable module of four measures. It took a very long time before such a structure of musical form gained predominance and it did not disappear and die all of a sudden. Let us pass at once to an example that has introduced a radical change in the phenomena under discussion without dwelling upon the intermediate stages or the exceedingly numerous "leftovers" of the classical structure of form in the music of later times.

The "Danse sacrale" from Stravinsky's *Rite of Spring* can be divided into seven sections. As no cadences come into question here, the allocation of musical content is the sole principle of division.

The first section only (shown in example 1-3), as the most characteristic for the problem we are discussing, is the one I shall deal with. This section (from figure 142 to figure 149) consists of thirty-three measures of unequal length. The first striking feature that distinguishes this example from all the preceding ones is the variable character of the meter. As a result of this feature, the module cannot be equal here to one measure. We can state, however, even at a superficial glance at the text, that the module exists here, and that it is smaller than one measure, that is, it is equal to one

Example 1-3.

semiquaver. Needless to say, the modules are forming groups here, too. The first grouping we see is the combining of two modules in one rhythmical value, that is, a quaver. The only rhythmic values in this text are semiquavers and quavers. Further, the modules group in variable numbers into measures of variable length, equal to two, three, four, or, at most, five modules. The interesting feature of the fragment is that this length changes irregularly (in spite of some repetitions). The essential feature of Stravinsky's innovation is, firstly, diminishing the module to the length of a part of a measure, lasting for only a fraction of a second (in our example less than one-quarter of a second) and, secondly, discarding the multiples of the number two in forming the modules into groups.

A similar rhythmic structure can be found in medieval music, though we are not quite sure that it was then performed in such a way as the present-day transcriptions show. Let us have a look at a fragment of the Organum from St. Martial's Abbey (Limoges) dating from the twelfth century.

Example 1-4 is a two-part piece; the upper part is written continuously in short, equal rhythmic values, whereas the values in the lower part are longer and unequal. In this case one single rhythmic value of the upper part is the module, whereas the lower part denotes the groups of the modules. Thus, we can distinguish in this fragment the groups of unequal length, containing successively 2, 4, 5, 4, 2, 2, etc., modules.

In the one-part Polish thirteenth-century spiritual song *Bogurodzica* (The Mother of God, see example 1-5) only two rhythmic values appear (if we consider its present, probably simplified, notation). The shorter rhythmic value is here the module and the way of setting the text allows us to divide this frag-

Example 1-4.   Organum from the school of St. Martial.

ment into sections (corresponding to present-day measures). These sections are of unequal length and they contain successively 8, 6, 8, 8, 10, 7, 12, 8, etc., modules. The number eight recurring four times in this fragment in no way impairs the basic irregularity, because the groups of modules within the sections containing eight of them assume the shape 3 + 3 + 2 twice.

Stravinsky's innovations, which—as we saw—have their counterparts in the past, not only found many imitators, but also a number of creative followers. Messiaen's *valeurs ajoutées* (added values) are in fact a variant of the rhythmic structure of the first fragment of Stravinsky's "Danse sacrale," although the source of Messiaen's invention was Indian rhythm.

In the next example of a rhythmic structure with the added values,[2] the module is equal to one semiquaver, and the groups make in sum one measure that contains twenty-five modules, as shown in example 1-6.

These groupings contain successively 5, 4, 4, 5, and 7 modules. The module is here even smaller than in the "Danse sacrale"; its length is probably no bigger than one-fifth of a second.

In examples 1-7 and 1-8, taken from Boulez's *Structures* for two pianos

Example 1-5.   *Bogurodzica*.

Example 1-6.

(measures 48–56), we find a still smaller module. It is equal to one demisemi-quaver, which takes no longer than one-eighth of a second. The modules are grouped successively, according to the following numbers: 5, 4, 1, 1, 1, 4, 1, 3, 1, 1, 4, 1, 3, 1, 1, 2, 3, 1, 1, 3, 1, 5, 1, 4, 1, 1, 1, 1, 7, 1, etc.

Yet when we aggregate the single demisemiquavers into groups (this is most likely how this rhythm is perceived), we obtain: 5, 4, 3, 4, 1, 3, 2, 4, 1, 3, 2, 2, 3, 2, 3, 1, 5, 1, 4, 4, 7, 1, etc.

When listening to this kind of rhythm in a fast tempo (the composer

Example 1-7.

Example 1-8. Pierre Boulez, Structures for two pianos, measures 48–55. Copyright Universal Edition AG Vienna. Reprinted by permission.

marked this section *très rapide*) we are not likely to grasp its modular structure. However, it is very probable that if we introduced some changes in an absolutely precise performance of this fragment (obtained, for instance, through the medium of tape) by lengthening or shortening some rhythmic values so they would not comprise the whole number of our modules, this change would be immediately noticeable. This means that even when the module is very small and occurs in the irregularly variable groups, the perception of such a rhythmic structure differs from the perception of the nonmodular structure. We have to admit, however, that in this case we approach the moment in which the module, becoming still smaller, approximates zero or disappears completely. This will occur initially in the perception of a given rhythmic structure and, later on, also in its notation. A step in this direction is to superimpose incommensurable rhythmic values. Examples 1-9 and 1-10 are such a structure, taken from Luigi Nono's *Cori di Didone*, measures 22 and 23.

By taking a crotchet as a unit, the composer simultaneously uses values equal to the whole numbers of the third, fourth, fifth, sixth, and seventh parts of a crotchet. Needless to say, there is no module in such a structure. In other words, the structure is devoid of any, even very small, rhythmic value, the grouping of which would allow us to obtain all the rhythmic values occurring in this fragment, as was suggested in the preceding example. If we wanted to find the rhythmic value, the complete multiples of which would

Example 1-9.

Example 1-10.   Luigi Nono, *Cori di Didone*, measures 22 and 23. Copyright Ars Viva Verlag GmBH Mainz. Reprinted by permission.

$$\frac{1}{3} \cdot \frac{1}{4} \cdot \frac{1}{5} \cdot \frac{1}{7} = \frac{1}{420}$$

Example 1-11.

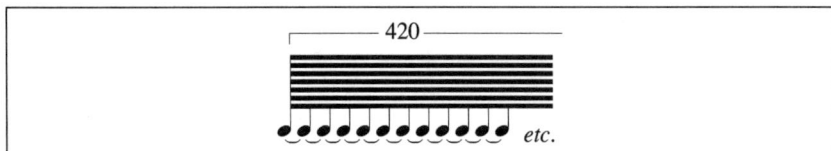

Example 1-12.

give us all the rhythmic values of our fragment, we should have done the multiplication in example 1-11.

In transferring this into musical notation we would have to express each of the rhythmic values in our fragment by means of a grouping of modules equal to 1/420 of a crochet. This would create remarkable difficulty if one keeps in mind that, for instance, one-seventh of a crochet would be represented graphically as sixty notes linked together with slurs, and marked with the number 420, which would mean that one crotchet would consist of 420 notes instead of 512 (i.e., two to the power of nine). (See example 1-12.)

It is evident that this kind of notation would be at variance with the intentions of the composer, who purposely used the overlapping, incommensurable rhythmic values, in order to obtain nonmodular rhythmic structure. This is why, when attempting to represent this nonmodular structure by means of a modular notation, we reach the point of absurdity. I have demonstrated this purposely, however, in order to examine an interesting process of the reduction of the module toward its total disappearance. At the same time we see quite clearly that the musical notation we have used so far is adapted first and foremost to a modular rhythmic structure and that it gives priority to such groups of modules as 2, 3, 4, 6, 8, 12, etc., which we can represent with the help of single signs (see example 1-13).

Other groupings, such as 5, 7, 9, 11, 13, etc., can be represented graphically only by means of composite signs, and this obscures the real picture of the rhythmic structure (see example 1-14).

Yet this notation suggests the division of each of these rhythmic values into fragments, which is in most cases at variance with the composer's intention.

Our notation is even less adapted to express graphically the wholly nonmodular structures. For instance, a contemporary transcription of a fragment of

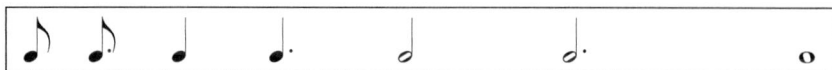

Example 1-13.

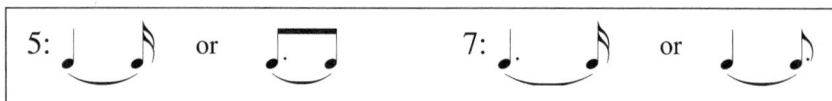

Example 1-14.

Example 1-15.   Syrian psalmody.

the Syrian psalmody of the fifth century seems to be an unconvincing notation of the nonmodular rhythmic structure, as shown in example 1-15.

The nonmodular rhythmic structures occur more and more frequently in the repertoire of today's compositional means of expression (see, for instance, Sylvano Bussotti's *Pour clavier* and Krzysztof Penderecki's *Quartetto per archi*). Also more frequently, the composer gives up the attempt of making a precise rhythmic notation, while leaving to the performer the care of rendering the nonmodular structure during the execution of the work. Some examples of such structures and their notations are given below. In certain instances it is the only possible way of notation. However, the composer always risks a false understanding of his or her text by the performer. The most common error in performing these kinds of structures is for the performer to fall into some regularity, which resembles the performance of modular structures. We must assume that, as happened in the past, some tradition of execution will evolve in our times, and this will help to re-create music from notation that is far from precise.

This brief overview of the issues concerning rhythm is, of course, incomplete. I had no intention to submit a hypothesis concerning a possible regularity of the historical developments of the matters under discussion. I am not interested in the question of which of the two kinds of rhythmics, modular or nonmodular, could be said to be superior, or which of them should be considered as more or less useful in our time. My intention was to demonstrate the widest imaginable spectrum of modes of the rhythmic shaping of music; a spectrum that is today available to a composer. At the extremes of this spectrum, I included in my lecture two examples: a fragment of Haydn's sonata, consisting of five thirty-two-measure modules, and a couple of contemporary compositions, not only without any modules, but also with an approximate time structure. Between these extremes there exists an infinite number of possibilities for rhythmic shaping, and I have presented here only some of them.

One could probably adopt another method of classification of the phenomena under discussion. However, what is most important for us as composers is not the way in which we arrange and classify these phenomena, but the awareness of their variety and extent. This is what could be useful in our work.

As a supplement to what has been presented here I would like to add some remarks of a rather practical nature concerning the problem of composition and execution of certain kinds of rhythm.

As the module diminishes and the easily perceptible regularity in the grouping of modules in larger wholes disappears, the degree of difficulty in performing a musical work increases. The difficulties are considerable when the work is written for a large group of performers. A precise performance then often becomes quite impossible, not only because of the difficulty, for the performers, of familiarizing themselves with their parts, but also the distance of the performers from each other. Thus, the time for propagation of sound from one member of the group to the other, who might be, for instance, twenty meters away, can be longer than the duration of the module itself. Composers overcome these difficulties in various ways.

Stravinsky's "Danse sacrale" does not raise serious problems for the performers. But certain of Messiaen's rhythms, particularly in his orchestral works, do demand a new method for their performance. In order to perform such rhythms as shown in example 1-16, Messiaen suggests conducting successively in three, four, and two time, yet these times are of unequal length, and are marked with special signs. He marks the pattern composed of two, three, and four modules as follows:

$$2 = \sqcap \qquad 3 = \triangle \qquad 4 = |\sqcap|$$

These signs are supposed to help the conductor's reading of the musical text. And example 1-17 is how the notation of the rhythm mentioned above appears.

Example 1-16.

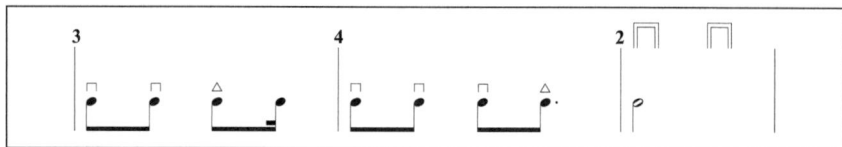

Example 1-17.

It is certainly a practical method, but it can be applied to a relatively limited number of rhythmic combinations, that is, to those that can be expressed as a succession of groups of two or three modules. We divide these kinds of rhythms into measures, if possible, so as to place the group containing three modules at the end of each measure. This latter example is, of course, a particular one. It can only point to one of the trends in searching for the most practical notation of rhythmic structures with a very small module in works for conducted groups.

The old way of notating complex rhythmic structures, which was still used—among others—by Bartók, is to treat the meter purely conventionally. The composer chooses the most suitable meter to express a given fragment of his work, for instance 2/4 or 3/4, and he expresses all the rhythmic structures in this meter, without bothering that the measure-line becomes a purely conventional sign with no other meaning. This notation is also applied where incommensurable rhythmic values appear simultaneously. We have noticed this already in the quoted example from Luigi Nono's *Cori di Didone*. The composer placed at the beginning of the first part of this work the sign 3/4, and he used this meter only as a frame for rhythmic values. In this particular instance, one should admit that this way of notating the text, although probably the best possible, is very difficult for performers, and it gives the conductor little possibility of controlling the performance. The composer depends here on the ability of each performer to sing the rhythmic values containing the whole number of the modules, the length of which changes nearly every measure, moving—for instance—from one-fifth to one-seventh of a crotchet. This requires an enormous effort of concentration, and one can hardly count upon high precision in performance, still less on the ease and lack of constraint on the part of the performers.

Example 1-18. Karlheinz Stockhausen, Klavierstück I. Copyright Universal Edition AG Vienna. Reprinted by permission.

Similar difficulties emerge in the performance of chamber works, such as Boulez's *Structures I* for two pianos, and even in certain fragments of soloist works, such as Stockhausen's *Klavierstück I.* In this work, the variability of the length of a module in a small space of time requires from the performer a great precision in feeling the flow of time, to a degree that is difficult to imagine. Example 1-18 is the beginning of Stockhausen's *Klavierstück I.*

The basic time-unit here is a crotchet. However, it appears only in the third measure, whereas in the first measure the time, which equals five applied units (5/4), has been divided straight away into eleven equal parts, of which the first six constitute a basis for building a simple, modular rhythmic structure. The time allotted to the remaining 5/11 parts of the measure is once more divided by the composer, this time into seven equal parts, in order to create out of them a new, relatively simple rhythmic structure based upon a new module. Thus, within the space of one measure, the duration of which is equal to five applied units, the composer creates two rhythmic structures based upon modules of various length. It is easy to calculate the lengths of these two modules in their relation to the applied time-unit, that is, a crotchet. The length of the first module is simply 5/11, whereas the length of the second one is a result of the following operation (see example 1-19).

One can admire the precision of the composer's rhythmic vision, which differentiates so subtly the durations of a module within such a short segment. My only objection would be that the composer has not chosen the proper medium to carry his vision into effect. The musical text poses difficulties that are almost impossible to surmount in a live performance, whereas the realization of the same rhythmic structure by means of a montage of tape would be quite simple. One can assume, however, that the composer cared not so much for an absolutely precise realization of complex rhythmic structures as for the causing an impression of irregularity and of nonmodular character of these

$$\frac{5}{11} \cdot \frac{5}{7} = \frac{25}{77}$$

Example 1-19.

structures, that is, about a result that was possible to obtain in spite of a not entirely precise performance.

These last examples bring us to the conviction that the problem of notation of more complex rhythmic structures can be solved in two ways:

1. Through an absolutely precise notation and through giving up its faithful reading in the performance of a work, as we saw in the examples of the works of Nono, Boulez, and Stockhausen, or
2. Through a notation that is not precise and that appeals to the performer's assumed understanding of the composer's intention. The performer, in turn, may find some assistance in the composer's commentaries written in the score. We saw examples of such a notation in Bussotti's and Penderecki's compositions.

Each of these systems of notation has its advantages and disadvantages. The advantage of the first system is a precision of the rhythmic image that is to serve as a model for the performers. This system excludes any essential misunderstanding of the composer's intentions on the part of the performer. Such a notation, however, discourages and alarms the performers and awakes in them a distrust of the use of this notation by the composer. Above all, it unsettles and hampers the performers, since it imposes requirements that can be much better fulfilled by a machine. The second, imprecise system of notation aims at inciting and mobilizing the initiative of performers, giving them greater freedom and releasing their natural tendency to display creativity in playing or singing. The use of this system, however, risks deviating too far from the composer's intentions and may lead to a complete misunderstanding of them. Another difficulty arises from the use of the approximate notation in a routine orchestral environment when the musicians may not employ their initiative in the interpretation of a musical text, but will expect precise instructions from the notation.

I have pointed here to some problems of a practical nature that confront a composer with the development of rhythm in recent years. What I have said here belongs already in great part to history, but I think that looking backward and contemplating what has happened in the past might help us to solve new problems that confront us in today's world.

Source

Unpublished typescript in English (second lecture at Tanglewood, 1962). Copyright Witold Lutosławski Collection, Paul Sacher Foundation. All rights reserved. Printed by permission. The Polish version of this text, titled "Kilka problemów z dziedziny rytmiki," was printed in *Res Facta*, no. 9 (1982): 114–28.

Notes

1. See: Archibald T. Davison and Willi Apel, eds., *Historical Anthology of Music*, vol. I (Oriental, Medieval, and Renaissance Music) (Cambridge, Mass.: Harvard University Press, 1949).
2. Lutosławski did not indicate the source of this example.

ALEATORISM

The last lecture of mine I am devoting to a subject that is, nowadays, more and more often engaging the attention of music writers, not only in professional publications, but also in articles intended for a wider public. The subject I am referring to is aleatorism.

I would advise those who desire to acquaint themselves with the theoretical aspect of this problem to read some of the very thorough dissertations that are available on this theme, such as, for example, the lecture delivered by John Cage in 1958 in Darmstadt, which is published under the title "Indeterminacy" in a collection of Cage's writings titled *Silence*[1]; an article titled "Aléa" by Boulez, which appeared in 1957 in *Darmstädter Beiträge*[2]; and parts of an article by Werner Meyer-Eppler in the first volume of the journal *Die Reihe*.[3]

As we are unable on the basis of these articles to give a consistent definition of the word *aleatorism*, I prefer to treat the subject from a practical angle rather than a theoretical one. What may appear in my lecture to be a theoretical discourse will actually be a report of my own reflections on the subject of aleatorism, reflections arising directly out of my work as a composer, and of an exclusively practical nature.

Broadly speaking, I distinguish two kinds of aleatorism, which we might call "large-scale" aleatorism and "small-scale" aleatorism, or aleatorism of form and of texture, or aleatorism of "the whole" and of "details," or something of the kind. In the first case, the whole form of the work is decided by chance, whereas in the second its details are subject to chance, while the main formal contours remain stable.

Let us consider for a moment this first kind of aleatorism, that is, the kind I styled "larger scale." Let us imagine that the whole work consists of several sections, for example, A, B, and C, and that the composer leaves the performer full freedom to determine the order of these sections, that is he makes the ultimate form of the whole form dependent on chance. Let us pause for a moment to consider what the composer has created in this way. It is not difficult to see that he has become the author of six very similar works, and moreover, he never knows which of them will be performed. It may even turn out that one of them, or even more than one, will never be performed, because the choice of work depends on the performer and it is impossible to know beforehand whether blind fate will select all the possibilities offered by the composer. It may well be that this element of surprise or unexpectedness contributes a certain value to the work and adds to its charm. But don't forget that this charm, contributed by the element of surprise, is not fully operative at a first performance, because the listener, hearing the work for the first time, and hearing it only once, is not in a position to realize that the title in the program embraces no less than six works, all similar to one another, and that the particular piece he is listening to at the moment is just one of them, nor does he realize that the composer was not aware beforehand which of these six works would actually be performed. To the listener hearing the work for the first time all these facts are of no significance whatsoever. He hears a certain piece of music and that's all.

Only a second, or third, or even more performances can acquaint him with the fact that this same title applies to six separate works, all very similar to each other, and that we can never know which of them will be performed.

But the very fact that these six works are very similar to each other deprives the surprise element the composer is aiming for of much of its charm. So that, in my opinion, the element of surprise, of unexpectedness, is not a sufficient raison d'être for this form of aleatorism. I have often wondered what it is that attracts present-day composers to this kind of aleatorism, which, for my own practical purposes, does not interest me personally. I found a certain answer to this question in an interesting article by György Ligeti, entitled *Wandlungen der musikalischen Form.*[4] Ligeti writes there that a characteristic feature of many present-day composers is a dislike of repetition. In its extreme form, this dislike, which Ligeti terms *alergy*, means that not only within the work itself nothing is repeated, but also that no single performance of the work is ever an exact repetition of a previous performance. In this alergy, Ligeti sees the origin of aleatorism, the kind that I have named large scale or aleatorism of form. Ligeti's explanation seems to me correct, and I can easily imagine how the mechanism of large-scale aleatorism came into being, although I personally do not feel this particular alergy. In fact, the presence of certain repetitions in the work itself does not disturb me in any way, and I even do not hesitate to introduce them quite frequently into my own works. And that is why the kind of aleatorism I have just described has, till now, never had more than a passing interest for me, and I have never applied it in my own compositions.

The second kind of aleatorism, the kind I termed "small scale," or aleatorism of texture or of details, is quite a different matter. Here I see great possibilities of enriching the language of music, and I have a certain amount of experience in this direction, which I intend to tell you about in the rest of my lecture.

At this point it would be appropriate to cite a comparatively accurate definition of this kind of aleatorism, which is to be found in the article I have already mentioned by Meyer-Eppler: "Aleatorisch (von Alea = Würfel) nennt man Vorgänge deren Verlauf im Groben festliegt, im einzelnen aber vom Zufall abhängt" (We call events aleatory [from alea—meaning "dice"] when their course is fixed, as regards their general outlines, but depends on chance, as far as their details are concerned).[5]

There are two fields in which this kind of aleatorism offers the composer possibilities such as he cannot obtain with the help of any other technique. First of all, it offers him new rhythmic possibilities and, secondly, new ways of taking advantage of the expressive and technical resources of individual performers in ensemble playing. I shall try to analyze both these features of aleatory technique by means of examples taken from my composition, *Jeux vénitiens*.

Before I do so, though, I should like to draw your attention to the importance of the second of the two features just mentioned, that is, to taking advantage of the expressive and technical resources of individual performers in ensemble playing.

We are all aware that the development of the art of ensemble playing has, till now, been in the direction of an ever greater precision in the simultaneity of performance of the individual parts. The development of style in music-making has advanced to such an extent that big ensembles of one hundred players perform in such a way that the effect is of one instrument combining many different tone-colors. There is, of course, a special kind of beauty in this, which the listener can find quite fascinating. But in this perfection of ensemble playing there is not much room for the personal artistic expression of individual performers, who are but elements of a wonderfully functioning, collective mechanism, rather than independent cointerpreters of the music. This is painfully evident in certain recent works, which make particularly stringent demands upon the players in regard to rhythm and ensemble playing. Many scores in the prealeatory period reduced the role of the performer to that of a counting-machine, thus making it impossible for him to play freely and naturally, and depriving him, therefore, of all the pleasure one usually associates with the performing

Example 1-20.

Example 1-21.

Example 1-22.

Example 1-23.

Example 1-24.

of ensemble music. In this situation the advent of aleatorism can be regarded as a true liberation, as it restores to the performer the possibility of exploiting his own artistic resources, in contradiction to former techniques, which led to a complete mechanization and automatism.

The elementary example that I am going to give you now will make clear to you the nature of my first explorations into the realm of aleatory technique.

Imagine the triad C–E–G lasting for ten seconds. In the period of Monteverdi we would probably confine ourselves to the version shown in example 1-20. In the Mozartian period, we would find something like example 1-21 or example 1-22. An imitator of Stravinsky's middle period would probably prefer something like example 1-23, which already presents certain difficulties to the performer. A young composer of our own times, modeling himself on the early work of Stockhausen or Nono, would write something like example 1-24.

In this example we have a very subtle kind of rhythm, introduced usually in such cases with the help of serial operations. This version of our triad C–E–G will make very great demands on the skill of the performers. Each one of them will be intent, above all, on seeing that each note is performed at the right time and is of the required duration, a task that in itself presents a lot of difficulties. If we add to this the fact of the changing, and very precisely indicated, dynamic, then free and unhampered music-making is here just out of the question. The function of the performer can be compared to that of a mechanism, which, in most cases unfortunately, functions with insufficient precision.

And now for the final version of our chord C–E–G, lasting ten seconds. This time the example (1-25) is my own personal proposition.

What can be observed in this text? All the parts are played *ad libitum*, and the performers do not have to worry how each separate part will sound in relation to the other parts. The conductor gives one signal for them to commence playing and a second for them to stop. The repetition marks indicate a return to the beginning, if the situation demands it, that is to say, if a performer has finished playing his part before the conductor has given the signal to stop. The rhythm, being the sum of all the parts, cannot be foreseen in detail, yet its general aspect depends to a large extent on the rhythm of the individual parts and so on the will of the composer. Caesurae allow the performers a breathing space and let them concentrate their attention on the entry to follow. Playing *ad libitum* permits a great variety and richness of expression in the playing of each individual performer, and the fact of playing in an ensemble in no way diminishes this. We mustn't forget that all this involves a quite elementary concept, such as the chord C–E–G lasting ten seconds.

I have given this elementary example to show you the starting point in the application of aleatorism in my own music writing.

Example 1-25.

I come now to some concrete examples taken from my work *Jeux vénitiens*.

Here is the first page of the score. In essence this does not greatly differ from my example with the chord C–E–G. Only here we have another chord—one consisting of twelve notes:

G–A–C4–D4–E4–F sharp–B4–C5 sharp–E5 flat–F5–A5 flat–B5 flat (see *Jeux vénitiens*, part I, sections A–B).

The next fragment is an example of free, capricious, predominantly solo playing, in which all the instruments are subordinated to the soloist. Here all the rhythmic values are rendered approximately, and the only time limitation is the boundary between the separate sections, indicated by vertical lines. However, the player is at liberty to perform the music within these boundaries with complete freedom. The conductor gives a sign only at the beginning of a new section, accommodating himself to the playing of the soloist.

Perhaps it would be an exaggeration to speak here of aleatorism. It is rather a loosening of the time bonds between sounds, enabling the whole ensemble to play in a free, rhapsodic manner, such as is not possible with the traditional technique (*Jeux vénitiens*, part III, sections A–J).

Before proceeding to my next example, I should like to say a few words about the concept of *objet sonore* (sound object) introduced by Pierre Schaeffer, the originator of concrete music.

The term *objet sonore* can be applied aptly both to instrumental and vocal music, and in certain cases the use of this term makes it easier to understand the construction of a work. What is *objet sonore* in instrumental and vocal music? It is an aggregate of sounds, bounded in time and pitch range, and the separate sounds of this aggregate are more closely related to each other than to sounds of other *objets sonore* appearing before, afterward, or even simultaneously. What is it that causes the relationship of sounds to be closer within the framework of one subject? Actually, many factors are conducive to this: the close proximity of the sounds in time, similarity of rhythm, tone-color, attack, dynamic, expressiveness, etc. In my example, the harmonic aspect of the various sound objects plays a big role, because each of them is characterized by a different kind of twelve-note sound—the aggregate of all the sounds of the respective "object."

The fragment to which we are listening is a typical construction by means of sound object. Each of these is played *ad libitum*, the conductor indicates only its beginning. The tempo and rhythm of each particular object is markedly different from the tempo and rhythm of the others. Thus, each object has its own tempo and its own rhythmic physiognomy, so to speak. Notice that, in addition to this microrhythm appearing in the different objects, there is still a macro-rhythm, a rhythm resulting from the collocation in time of the individual objects, regarded as a whole. This macrorhythm appears in our fragment as a cycle of ever shorter time sections, apportioned by the beginnings of the separate objects. Represented in seconds, this macrorhythm would appear as follows: (*Jeux vénitiens*, part IV, sections a_1–G).

By the end of the fragment we already cease to distinguish clearly the beginnings of separate objects, and proceed gradually to a thickly scored, polyrhythmic orchestral *tutti*, almost verging on chaos. This effect, I may add, is what the composer intended.

And now I come to the last illustration—the conclusion of the whole work. This is also a typical construction with sound objects. Each of these objects—there are four of them altogether—has its characteristic physiognomy, differentiating it from the others. I should like to draw your attention to one feature that all four objects possess in common, namely a thinning-out of the density of their impulses. The greatest density is found near the beginning, after which there follows a gradual thinning out. Owing to this, each of the objects has its own special and distinctive terminative course. I would remind you here of the concept of a *terminative character* of music that I used in my lecture on forms.[6] These individual terminative characters of the various objects combine in our perception to form the conclusion of the work.

The separate parts are played *ad libitum*, the conductor indicates only the beginnings of each of the four separate objects (*Jeux vénitiens*, part IV, page 44 up to the end).

From what I have said and from the examples given, it can be seen that with the introduction of aleatorism of texture, or detail, or—in other words—of what I called "small-scale" aleatorism, we composers are confronted with a whole host of entirely new problems calling for solutions. The two most important of these are, firstly, the necessity of creating a whole system of rules to ensure that the operation of chance shall not overstep the limits set by the composer and, secondly, the need to overcome the manifold difficulties in the way of performing this new music and bound up with the problem of notation.

The purpose of this lecture was only to acquaint you with the existence of these problems. To understand their full implications would require a greater number of lectures and also some work of a practical nature.

Source

Unpublished typescript in English (possibly fifth lecture at Tanglewood, 1962). Copyright Witold Lutosławski Collection, Paul Sacher Foundation. All rights reserved. Printed by permission.

Notes

1. John Cage's "Indeterminacy" was the second of the three lectures he delivered in Darmstadt in September 1958 under the common title *Composition as Process*. See J. Cage, *Silence* (Middletown, Conn.: Wesleyan University Press, 1961), 35–40.
2. Pierre Boulez, "Aléa," trans. by Heinz-Klaus Metzger, *Darmstädter Beiträge zur neuen Musik* 1 (1957): 44–56. The first English translation of this essay was published by *Perspectives of New Music* 3, no. 1 (Fall–Winter 1964): 42–53. Another English version was included in Boulez's *Stocktakings from an Apprenticeship*, collected and presented by Paule Thévenin, translated from the French by Stephen Walsh (Oxford: Clarendon Press, 1991), 26–38). "Aléa" was originally published in *La nouvelle revue Française* 59 (November 1957): 839–57.
3. Werner Meyer-Eppler, "Statistische und Psychologische Klangprobleme," *Die Reihe* Vol. 1, *Elektronische Musik* (Vienna: Universal Edition, 1955), 22–28.
4. György Ligeti, "Wandlungen der musikalischen Form," *Die Reihe* Vol. 7, *Form-Raum* (Vienna: Universal Edition, 1960), 5–17.
5. Werner Meyer-Eppler, "Statistische," p. 22. Another English version of that quotation is: "A process is said to be aleatoric (from Lat. *Alea* = dice) if its course is determined in general but depends on chance in detail." See *Die Reihe*, Vol. 1, *Electronic Music* (New Jersey: Universal Edition, 1958), 55.
6. See Lutosławski's text "Problems of Musical Form" in this chapter.

ABOUT THE ELEMENT OF CHANCE IN MUSIC

Between 1958 and 1961 I wrote Three Postludes for symphony orchestra. These works were not named at random. The word *postludium* is connected by meaning with the conclusion of something. In the case of my works, this still holds. The postludiums for orchestra are the final works in which I did not apply the element of chance. This element has played an important role in everything I have written since the time of the Postludes. The performance of the third work of this kind, my String Quartet, is a suitable occasion for considering this important change in my method of composing, and for making some general observations on the subject of chance in music.

The phenomenon about which I am speaking is not simple and not so devoid of ambiguity that it could be either accepted or dismissed completely. It is possible to define a composer's aesthetic and even, to a certain extent, his philosophic attitude to his task according to the role he designates to chance in his work. I consider the standpoint of those who make chance the actual author of the work, and who limit their own role to organizing the circumstances in which chance can appear in the form of the actual sound result, to be the most radical. Here the composer is merely the initiator of play that, after it has been initiated by a series of chance operations, continues to play itself out by itself. Consequently the sound result can, naturally, be foreseen only to a very limited extent. It is, however, not entirely unforeseeable: we can say with complete certainty, for instance, that Brahms's Fourth Symphony could not be due to chance operations. If we are still going to maintain the negative aspect of our former statement, we can go on further and say that the majority of Neoclassical works cannot be the result of chance operations. If we were to be even bolder, we might dare to say that chance operations have led to sound productions that together have a certain style of their own.

Although a composer, in composing in this way, does not entirely eliminate himself from the work, and although the result of his activity is not entirely unforeseeable, I would define this standpoint as being the most radical. It was just this standpoint that John Cage most probably had in mind when he wrote: "A performance of a composition which is indeterminate cannot be grasped as an object in time," and when he defined the activity of performing such a composition as "non-knowledge of something that has not yet happened."[1] It was about just this standpoint that Luigi Nono sarcastically wrote: "treating chance as a source of cognition can be the method only of people who are afraid of making their own decisions and of the freedom involved in this."[2] Pierre Boulez attributes this standpoint to a predilection for orientalism "that masks a basic weakness in compositional technique; it would be a protection against the asphyxia of invention, the resort to a more subtle poison that destroys every last embryo of craftsmanship."[3] A certain American musician, having read a few words on aleatorism, which I had said in an interview for the *New York Times*,[4] was probably thinking about the same standpoint when he wrote to me saying "aleatoric music is the antithesis of form, its amorphousness is the negation of artistic creation."

I have no intentions to condemn a method of composing merely to support a principle that I myself have accepted in advance. Any principle, any method of composing, or any artistic standpoint toward a given problem can only be defended or attacked in one way—on the basis of the work itself. Unfortunately this means it has no objective value, just as no judgment on a work of art has any objective value.

Consequently, if I myself am an opponent of the standpoint described above, which depends on elevating the role of chance to that of a factor playing a decisive role in a work of art, it is for completely different reasons than those given by Nono, Boulez, and my American correspondent. The standpoint described here does not interest me simply because in it I do not find anything that could, even to the slightest extent, help me to find what I am looking for. I am not even partially interested in avoiding responsibility for my work. I am not interested in music entirely determined by chance. I want my piece to be something that I myself have created, and I would like it to be the expression of what I have to communicate to others.

The "absolute" aleatorism, which I am thinking about here, is not therefore a usable method in my work as a composer.

The case is the same with the other form of aleatorism, which I would like to call the aleatorism of form. Its essential feature is that the performers are given the freedom of establishing the order in which the formal elements, as composed by the author, are finally presented to the listeners. This procedure can be compared to the designing of architectural segments from which the customer can freely establish the whole, depending on his needs or fantasy. This method is an expression of the composer's reluctance to permit repetition rather than a predilection for chance. Does it, however, fulfill its function? Does it in fact ensure individuality to every possible version of a work composed in this way? It would be difficult for me to give an answer to this question because I have not had any experience, as a composer, in this field. There is nothing strange in this since I do not in the least feel any special disinclination to repetition, even within the limits of one and the same work. This method does not seem to me to be new, and I do not feel anything especially exciting in it, just as I am not particularly interested in each of the successive twenty-four (!) possible performances of Chopin's twenty-four preludes. A composer's desire for each performance of his work to be different would ultimately be understandable if he were composing on a deserted island and if he were the only person to listen to his work. In most cases this, however, is not so, and it seems to me to be far more natural to leave what I have written to the listeners, and to satisfy that continual desire for something new, which every composer feels, by continually creating new compositions. Is it not on this, among other things, that the creative mechanism depends?

It is high time that I define the essential feature of the kind of aleatorism that for several years has been the object of my work as a composer. This aleatorism could be called limited or an aleatorism of texture. In order to give a brief definition of this phenomenon I can here cite the well-known Meyer-Eppler definition: "Aleatorisch nennt man Vorgänge deren Verlauf im Groben festliegt aber im einzelnen vom Zufall abhängt" (We call events aleatory when their course is fixed, as regards their general outlines, but depends on chance, as far as their details are concerned).[5] Music as defined in this way clearly belongs to the conventions and traditions typical of Europe.

Moreover, a musical work is above all an occurrence. It is not a state. John Cage's definition of this fact is very much to the point: "The form aspects essentially conventional to European music are for instance, the presentation of a whole as an object in time having a beginning, a middle, and an ending, progressive rather than static in character."[6]

The introduction of elements of chance into music, understood in this way, need not essentially change its character. This is the case when the range within which chance operates is sufficiently limited by the author, when chance does not play a controlling part in the work and is subordinated to the aim indicated by the composer, and finally, when it enriches the means of expression consciously used by the composer and is not used to organize sound occurrences to be a surprise not only for the listeners but also for the composer himself.

Aleatorism, understood in this way, is perhaps no great innovation; it radically changes, however, the character of the music.

The most typical form of limited aleatorism is collective *ad libitum* playing within an instrumental or vocal ensemble. The most characteristic feature of music performed in this way is the absence of a common division of time to which all performers must comply in the same way. In my works this concerns only those phenomena that appear within the limits of the particular sections of the given musical form. On the whole, the dividing lines between the larger particular parts of the form are common for all performers, that is, they fall at the same moments. Consequently, it follows that the form of the work, as a set of the particular larger parts, is fixed completely by the composer. The breaking down of the common division of time into several particular divisions of time takes place only in shorter parts of the form. This is sufficient, however, for the rhythmical physiognomy of such music to differ essentially from that of any other music. The difference about which we are speaking could be compared to that between poetry and prose, although this is of course a far-reaching simplification. In reality, the structure of rhythmical collective *ad libitum*, is the overall sum of the rhythmical structures appearing in the particular parts. This overall sum is a phenomenon far more complex than any polyrhythmic structure appearing in traditional music. It is influenced, for example, by the possibility of the nonsimultaneous occurrence of acceleration and slowing down, in the different parts, in the performance of a section of the music. There are many similar possibilities. The result is based on the principle, accepted by the composer in advance, that each musician performs within a preestablished section of time, as if he were playing alone—rather than basing his performance on those of the other members of the ensemble. In this way, the rhythmical texture assumes a flexibility that is a characteristic feature of this music and cannot be achieved in any other way.

Here the question arises: to what degree can the composer control the ultimate result of the entire procedure? One of the most characteristic features of this music is, moreover, that decisions are not centralized with the composer, but are split up among several performers. The extent to which the composer controls the situation can only be defined in relation to what his original intention was. In my works this intention was always a particular sound picture, the essential features of which remain undisturbed despite the accepted method of collective *ad libitum* playing. Moreover, this picture must be such that its nature cannot be changed by certain notes, and even groups of notes, not ultimately falling always in the same order. In composing such a sound picture I have to foresee all possible versions that could result from my text, and to compose this text in such a way that all these versions would correspond to my intention. This can be done in a relatively easy way. Namely, it depends on composing only one version of a given section of the music that, with respect to the original intention, could be called the least advantageous. In other words, of all the possible situations that might arise from the combined elements of my sound picture as the outcome of *ad libitum* playing, I choose the one that produces the result most divergent from my intention. By imagining the least advantageous situation that can arise from these elements, I can, if necessary, easily make the necessary corrections so that even this least advantageous situation will fulfill the required conditions. In doing this, I can be completely sure that all other possible versions will be even more certain to fulfill the required conditions. It is clear that the conditions, which a sound picture composed in this way must fulfill, cannot be defined too precisely. Moreover, in composing in this way, clear-cut rhythmical contours, in which the slightest shift in time would introduce an essential change into the picture, are not brought into play. These clear-cut contours can, indeed, appear in the particular parts; they are, however, subject to a process in which they are partially leveled out as a result of the lack of a common rhythmical pulsation for all performers. Thus a sound texture arises, the essential feature of which is its instability. This feature does not in any way exclude the possibility of bringing sharp rhythmical contrasts into play. One of the main aims of collective *ad libitum* is to enrich rhythm by elements that a traditional technique does not possess.

Here I have described some of the features of the composing technique called limited aleatorism. I have tried to point out certain possibilities that this technique can give rise to in the field of rhythm. The way of performing music thus composed constitutes a completely different aspect of the same subject. It is easy to foresee that the performing of such music requires something entirely different from the performers than any other form of music does. As a result of following the common pulsation of the entire group for many years, performers may have difficulties in overcoming this obstacle when they must play with complete ease, without any restraint, and independently of what is happening at the same moment in the other parts. Performers must accept the fact that each performance will bring something new in its small details, and that what they once heard in the parts of the colayers may never be repeated in an identical way. This is exclusively the result of the lack of a common pulsation; it involves a shift in time and also a shortening and lengthening of the particular compositional elements. Collective *ad libitum*, moreover, gives the performers the possibility of benefiting from all the advantages that in traditional music are kept exclusively for solo pieces. For example, *tempo rubato* is possible, in the performance of ensemble music with a common pulsation, only within a limited field. Here in collective *ad libitum* all the variations of *rubato* playing are possible. The superimposing of several parts played *rubato*, in a way quite independent of each other, is the most characteristic feature of the texture described above. The difficulties that might possibly arise in the performance of this kind of music merely consist of overcoming the performing habits of a long tradition. I am convinced (and many of my personal experiences support this conviction) that these difficulties are far less than those that sometimes arise in the performance of music that has a division of time common to the entire ensemble. The very concept of collective *ad libitum* can be considered as a reaction of a composer-performer to the often absurd demands that some composers have made of performers in the last few years. Such demands are the result of a completely abstract approach to music considered exclusively as a series of acoustic phenomena occurring in time. I consider such an approach to music as being flagrantly one-sided. I understand music not only as a series of sound phenomena but also as an activity carried out by a group of human beings—the performers of the piece. Each of these persons is endowed with many far greater possibilities than those that a purely abstract score demands. I want to include in the repertoire of compositional means the wealth that is presented by the individual psyche of a human being—the performer. I believe it is an element of musical subject matter that has, up to now, been little used, and, until a short time ago was almost completely ignored. I also believe that it has new and still completely unknown possibilities. I am not, on the other hand, counting at all on the possible creative ability of the performers. I do not presuppose any improvised

parts, even the shortest, in my works. I am an adherent of a clear-cut division between the role of the composer and that of the performer, and I do not wish even
partially to relinquish the authorship of the music I have written. In this paper I
have concentrated exclusively on problems directly connected with time and the
means of its division in a piece of music in which chance plays a certain role. It is
obvious that the influence of chance on the disposition of sound, considered with
respect to pitch, is an equally important aspect of the problem. This question has of
course also been the object of my efforts. It could be called aleatoric counterpoint.
This subject is however too wide for me to have included it in this text.

∞

This paper is in no way a collection of dogmas or even of principles of procedure
that I have accepted. It is also no program for the future—according to which I
might proceed in my future works. It has merely been a fragmentary chronicle
of my activity as a composer, describing the thoughts that have accompanied my
work during the last few years. Will these thoughts retain their current significance very long for me? Will they be subject to revision or to changes, or shall I
one day dismiss them completely? This does not concern me. I take good heed
only to ensure that none of these ideas comes to dominate me, even to the slightest extent, and that none of them restricts my freedom in attempting to attain
everything that my imagination might give rise to in the future.

Source

Györgi Ligeti, Witold Lutosławski, Ingvar Lidholm, *Three Aspects of Music. From
the Composition Seminar in Stockholm.* Publications issued by The Royal Academy of Music and The Royal Swedish College of Music Publications, No. 4.
(Stockholm: Nordiska Musikförlaget, 1968), 47–53. Printed by permission of
Ehrlingförlagen AB, Stockholm, Sweden.

Notes

1. This quotation, which consists in fact of two short quotations, was based on
the following passage from the second part (subtitled "Indeterminacy") of Cage's
text *Composition as Process* (the fragments Lutosławski referred to are italicized): "An
experimental action is one the outcome of which is not foreseen. Being unforeseen,
this action is not concerned with its excuse. Like the land, like the air, it needs none. *A
performance of a composition which is indeterminate* of its performance is necessarily unique.
It cannot be repeated. When performed for a second time, the outcome is other than it
was. Nothing therefore is accomplished by such a performance, since that performance

cannot be grasped as an object in time. A recording of such a work has no more value than a postcard; it provides *a knowledge of something that happened,* whereas the action was non-knowledge of something that had not yet happened." See John Cage, *Silence* (Middletown, Conn.: Wesleyan University Press, 1961), 39.

2. This quotation seems to be close to the following passage from Nono's essay "The Historical Reality of Music Today," *The Score* (July 1960): 41–45 (see the italicized fragments): "Composers can always talk about the 'chance element' as long as it does not become a panacea. It will be valid as long as it is used as a means of widening our empirical experience, as a means of exploring new possibilities. But *to replace artistic determinism by chance is possible and attractive only to the composer who is unable to make decisions.* (We need not wait for history to judge because fraud is immediately obvious.) Such freedom is a form of intoxication which prevents those who believe in it from seeing the bars which obstruct their view of the heavens." This passage appears near the end (p. 45) of Nono's essay. (No translator is credited.)

3. See Pierre Boulez, "Aléa," *Perspectives of New Music* 3, no. 1 (Fall–Winter 1964): 42. Here is another version of this quotation from *Stocktakings from an Apprenticeship,* collected and presented by Paule Thévenin, translated from the French by Stephen Walsh (Oxford: Clarendon Press, 1991): "The most basic embodiment of chance is to be found in the adoption of a quasi-oriental philosophy in order to conceal a fundamental weakness in compositional technique: a cure for creative suffocation with a more subtle disease, which destroys the smallest embryo of craftsmanship." In this volume, "Aléa" appears on pp. 26–38; the quotation itself on p. 26.

4. See Howard Klein, "Notes from Underground," *New York Times,* August 7, 1966, D13.

5. See note 5 to the text "Aleatorism" in this chapter.

6. J. Cage, *Silence,* 36.

RHYTHM AND ORGANIZATION OF PITCH IN COMPOSING TECHNIQUES EMPLOYING A LIMITED ELEMENT OF CHANCE

Werner Meyer-Eppler has written: "Aleatorisch nennt man Vorgänge deren Verlauf im Groben festliegt, im Einzelnen aber von Zufall abhängt" (We call events aleatory when their course is fixed, as regards their general outlines, but depends on chance, as far as their details are concerned).[1] Compositions written within the terms of this definition do not really go beyond the basic conventions and traditions of European music, where a piece of music is, typically, an occurrence rather than a state. John Cage has made this point most lucidly: "The form aspects essentially conventional to European music are, for instance, the presentation of a whole as an object in time having a beginning, a middle and an ending, progressive rather than static in character, which is to say possessed of a climax or climaxes and in contrast a point or points of rest."[2]

The introduction of an element of chance into music of this kind need not involve a violation of its intrinsic features, as specified by Cage. The work will continue to be "an object in time" so long as the play of chance is sufficiently held in check by the composer and does not become the controlling impulse of the work but is kept subservient to the composer's design, being used to amplify the range of intentionally employed means of expression rather than in the organization of sounds that are to come as a surprise to the audience of even the composer himself.

Conceived in this way, aleatorism does not appear to be much of an innovation. But although it is true that it makes no fundamental change in the treatment of a musical work as an object in time, it has an utterly radical effect on its rhythmic and expressive physiognomy, and this is enough to give music composed in this vein a totally different sound from that in which chance makes no appearance whatsoever.

One of the typical devices of controlled aleatorism is the introduction of collective *ad libitum* passages for a number of instruments or voices. The quintessential feature of this type of music—that one that distinguishes it from the traditional kind—is the absence of a common time division to be followed by all the performers. In my works, this is the case only with what is played within the particular sections of the composition. The breakdown into sections (whose length may be anywhere from several seconds to several minutes) is a fixed one and the same for all performers. Thus the form of the work, in the sense of the weaving together of particular sections, is entirely determined by the composer. Although the division of the common time scheme into a number of independent ones is confined to the sections within themselves, this is enough—as I have said—to transform the rhythmic physiognomy of such music out of all recognition. This is because the rhythmic structure developed in a collective *ad libitum*, in itself the sum of all the rhythmic structures of the individual parts, is far more complex than any polyrhythmic structure to be found in traditional music. One for the reasons for this is that there may be nonsimultaneous *accelerandos* and *rallentandos* within particular parts. There are many other similar possibilities. All of them spring from the composer's assumption that each of the performers will, within a specified time-unit, play as though he were on his own, without worrying whether he is in time with the others. In this way the rhythmic structure acquires a distinctive "suppleness" not attainable otherwise (see String Quartet, figures 37–38; Symphony no. 2, figures 7–13).

Now, it may be asked: to what extent does the composer control the end product of this procedure? After all, one of the specific features of such music is the composer's inability to anticipate precisely the sequence of the notes played in each section or even their final duration. The degree to which he is master of the situation he creates can only be measured in terms of his original intention. If, to take the extreme instance, he is out to compose any sort of music whatsoever, he can be said, a little paradoxically, to be in control of the situation even if the shaping of his work is left wholly to chance. Cases in point are compositions where the score is marked with such directions as "play anything," "switch on the radio," and so on. By its very nature, such an intention is bound to be meticulously fulfilled as long as the performers follow the specified instructions, however little difference they make to the ultimate pattern of the sound.

In my works the primary intention is always a certain specific sound vision whose most essential features survive intact in spite of the differences between each performance imposed by the introduction of the element of chance. However, it must be the kind of vision that will not basically be altered by the eventuality of certain notes, or even groups of notes, not always being played in the same order. Fortunately the fulfillment of this condition is possible thanks to our capacity for registering and memorizing sounds being limited. In those cases where we are able to perceive a certain rhythm, a certain sequence of sounds, or a certain harmony, our minds will also record any changes in the performance of the text. But if our text is composed in such a way that it is only the kind of rhythm, the kind of sound sequence, or the kind of harmony that is detectable, any changes in the course of performance may pass unnoticed in the perception of the whole passage and so prove immaterial.

When composing along these lines, I define the conditions to be fulfilled by each passage. In principle I should make allowance for all the possible versions that can arise out of my text as a result of the introduction of simultaneous *ad libitum* performance and compose the text in such a way that all the versions meet the planned requirements. It is usually impossible to visualize all the possible alternatives, but then it is not really necessary either. It is enough to compose just one version of a particular section of the form; this is the version which might be called the least advantageous from the point of view of the original intention. In other words, from all the possible situations that may arise from the combination of elements of my sound vision in *ad libitum* performance, I select the one that is at the greatest remove from my purpose. The combining elements are then, if necessary, subjected to whatever modifications are needed to see that, even in that least advantageous situation, they perform the role set them in the original design. As a result, I can be sure that in any other situation they will fulfill their purpose that much better. Of course, the requirements expected of the composed sound vision cannot be defined with absolute precision. Some examples will show that the precision of the requirements expected of our sound vision can, however, be fairly high, especially in comparison with the extreme instance described earlier. High enough, at any rate, to make all the possible versions of our passage seem identical to the listener.

Here is a simple illustration of such a passage (see *Paroles tissées*, part I, figure 4).

In this example we see two levels, each represented by three parts. Each of the instruments repeats its short phrase until the conductor's next sign, whereupon it completes the phrase and waits. All the performers play *ad libitum* from the conductor's first sign. This, together with the varying lengths of the repeated phrases in each part, makes it impossible to anticipate with any accuracy which sounds will occur together. In the upper three parts there are groups of short notes (demisemiquavers) played *piano* and longer notes played *crescendo*. As far as the rhythm is concerned, the least advantageous situation occurs if one of these two kinds of notes appears in all three parts at once. To forestall an undesirable sameness of rhythm in the parts, while at the same time preserving their similarity, the short note groups contain a different number in each of the parts: that is, three in the first, four in the second, and two in the third. The same applies to the longer notes played *crescendo*: the first part has two successive crotchets, the second single dotted crotchets, and the third single crotchets. Hence, even if there should be a fortuitous coincidence in, say, the short note group, it will be very brief on account of the difference in duration of these groups in each part.

As regards pitch, the section is organized very simply. All the sounds employed belong to a single chord composed of the five notes contained between the notes B4 and D5 sharp. The least advantageous situation arises if all the instruments meet at the same time in the same note. But even if this happens, prolonged simultaneity is avoided as a result of the differences in the duration of the notes in each part, although the interval progression is similar in all three upper parts. Balance in the intensity of each of the notes in the chord is maintained by confining the three lower parts solely to B4, C5 sharp, and D5 sharp while the other two notes of the five-note chord—C5 and D5—appear as longer notes played *crescendo* in the three upper parts. To avoid excessive differences in tempo between the individual parts, one bar conducted at 3/4 is played before the beginning of the passage.

The following excerpt has a slightly more complex structure (see *Jeux vénitiens* part I, initial structure of woodwinds in a frame).

There are seven woodwinds here, each of them playing a number of motifs divided by caesuras. Altogether there are nine such motifs. They appear in a different order in each of the instruments (the flute parts, for instance, playing A, B, C, D, E, F, G and H, C, B, F, A, D, respectively, the oboe part I, A, H, C, D, G, and so on). The least advantageous situation is when the same motif is played by all the instruments at once. But even should this

Example 1-26.

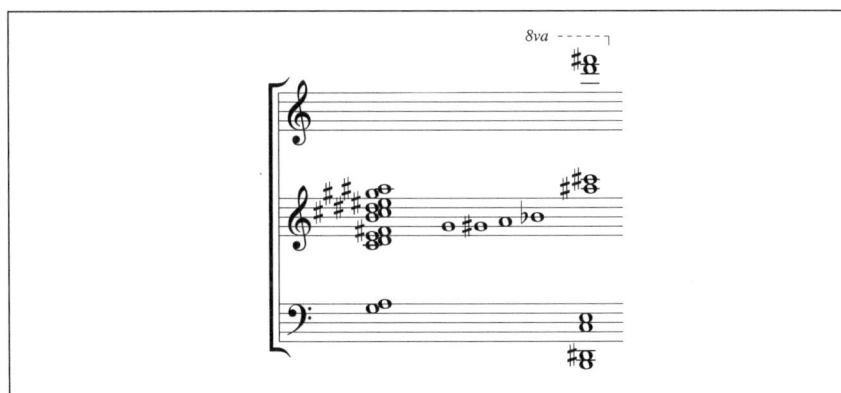

Example 1-27.

happen, there would be no sameness of rhythm because each of the motifs appears in various rhythmic variations, one version being reserved for each instrument. For instance, motif A appears in the rhythmic variations in the particular instrumental parts of example 1-26. Identical forms of the same motif appear only when their distance from one another makes the probability of concurrence very slight.

As in the preceding example, pitch is organized in a simple way. All the sounds belong to a single twelve-note chord, namely G, A, C4, D4, E4, F4 sharp, B4, C5 sharp, D5 sharp, E5 sharp, G5 sharp, and A5 sharp. This twelve-note chord is treated modally, that is to say, the order in which the intervals appear in each part is left open. (See example 1-27.)

In another section of the same movement of the same work, the section just described reappears as one of the four strands in the music, the others being represented by a group of three brass instruments, untuned kettledrums, and piano four hands. All the sounds played by the brass group are taken from a four-note chord of adjacent semitones lying between the middle notes of the previously mentioned twelve-note chord, that is G4, G4 sharp, A4, and B4 flat. The piano plays four-note chords placed at opposite ends of the scale above and below the first twelve-note chord. Each of these four-note chords is constructed of two major thirds a minor ninth apart. The four notes of the brass strand and the eight notes of the piano strand combine to form a twelve-note chord having no notes in common with the previous chord. In this way twelve-octave doublings are produced. These octaves are barely discernible to the listener. This is due to differences in the timbre and interval and rhythmic construction of the particular strands. In the perception of the whole passage there is what might be called a division into local harmonies, that is, disintegration of the perception of the harmonies into three separate strands and an elimination of the harmonies arising between the notes belonging to different strands (see *Jeux vénitiens,* part I, sections G–H).

At the end of this same work, four strands are played *ad libitum.* Each is constructed of notes belonging to a separate twelve-note chord. Here, too, because of the scattering of the notes, the differences in timbre, rhythm, and articulation, the octave doublings, numerous though they are, are almost inaudible. First and foremost, we register the local harmonies, that is, those occurring within particular levels and not between them.

The lowest level is constructed around a twelve-note chord composed of all notes between C3 and B3. The double-basses and cellos play C3, C3 sharp, F3, F3 sharp, G3, and B3, the other notes being taken by the harp. The next twelve-note chord is played by a motorless vibraphone and lies between G3 flat and F4. Its three top notes are also played by a group of three brass instruments.

The third chord has a different structure (see example 1-28). Its notes—B4, C5 sharp, F5, F5 sharp, G5, G5 sharp, A5 sharp, C6, D6, D6 sharp, E6, and A6—are played by a group of woodwinds and celesta. The highest chord is an eleven-note chord contained between B6 flat and A7. E7 is missing because of the quite distinctly audible E4 that occurs at the close of the French horn part. The highest eleven-note chord is played by three violins, three violas, and a piano. Each of the four levels has its own rhythmic physiognomy. On the other hand, there is a correspondence between the way in which the time density of the sounds varies in each of the levels. To begin with, it rises and reaches its peak about one-fifth of the way through each section, after which it tails off until the end of the section. Since the instrumental groups involved in each

Example 1-28.

of the levels do not enter simultaneously, but successively, the moments of the highest density of sound do not occur at the same time. The listener's attention, caught by these summits of density, is switched from one level to the next, and this also tends to make for a perception of local harmonies rather than of summing up of all the sounds into a single harmony (see *Jeux vénitiens*, part IV, sections I–M, pp. 44–49).

In the preceding examples, we saw an organization of pitch that consisted of a modal treatment of one or more twelve-note chords. From the harmonic point of view, therefore, each of the passages could be reduced to a single simple aggregate or one made up of a few strands lasting a certain time. Of course, not all the notes of this harmony are always present, but constant repetition plants it in the listener's mind almost as a chord in which all notes are played together. Thus the fruit of the procedure I have been describing is of a singularly static nature. This limitation is compensated for in part by the enormous freedom in the handling of time granted by the technique of ensemble *ad libitum*. No other technique can yield such a richness of rhythm and individual expression in the playing of each of the instruments. Nevertheless it is worth finding a way of at least partly reducing the static nature of this kind of music. The simplest method would, of course, be to relinquish all control over the harmonies in progress, which would mean a measure of chaos in the organization of pitch. In the process, the sound effect would forfeit certain invaluable qualities, so that this simple solution can only be practicable in a few cases.

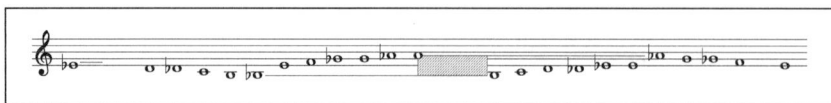

Example 1-29.

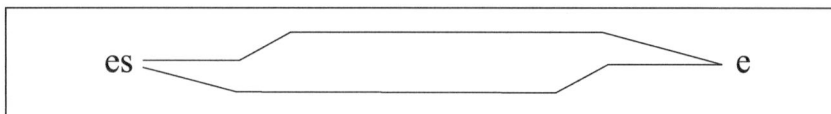

Example 1-30.

The next handful of examples will illustrate attempts to make the music less static without sacrificing all the advantages of the technique of ensemble *ad libitum.*

Example 1-29 is only marginally different from the preceding ones. Nonetheless, as regards pitch, it no longer forms a fixed, unchanging image. This relatively long section begins with an E4 flat unison, after which the number of notes in use gradually increases. The first additions are notes below E4 flat—D4, D4 flat, C4, B3, and B3 flat. Then come the ones above E4 flat, that is, E4, F4, G4 flat, G4, A4 flat, and A4. At this point twelve notes are in play, making up a chord of the twelve adjacent notes lying between B3 flat and A4. Shortly afterward, the sounds begin to fade. The first to go are, starting from the bottom, B3 flat, B3, C4, D4 flat, D4, and E4 flat, followed by, from the top, A4, A4 flat, G4, G4 flat, and F4. In this way the passage ends with another unison—this time E4.

Thus the whole passage runs, as regards the notes used, as shown in example 1-30. However, this formula is only a simplification. In actual fact, many other notes between the B3 flat and A4 are used, since all the instruments of the string quartet play glissando for almost the whole time. Thus the formula describes only the outer limits of the pitch of the notes used.

In passing, let us make a brief examination of the rhythmic structure of the passage. It is not so much a four-part polyphony as a bundle of four continually intertwining lines developing the same melodic and rhythmic substance. This substance can be divided into fifteen sections according to the formula: A B A C A D A E A F A G A H A, with A appearing in the whole passage in four rhythmic versions:

1. See example 1.31, that is, 3 + 1; 3 + 4 + 1; 4 + 1;
2. 4 + 1; 4 + 5 + 1; 5 + 1;
3. 5 + 1; 5 + 6 + 1; 6 + 1;
4. 6 + 1; 6 + 7 + 1; 7 + 1.

Example 1-31.

These versions are so distributed that at the same point, different instruments are always playing different variants. For instance:

$a^1 \; a^2 \; a^3 \; a^4 \; a^1 \; a^2$

$a^3 \; a^4 \; a^1 \; a^2 \; a^3 \; a^4$

$a^2 \; a^3 \; a^4 \; a^1 \; a^2 \; a^3$

$a^4 \; a^1 \; a^2 \; a^3 \; a^4 \; a^1$

etc.

Parts B, C, D, etc., are played in appropriately different variants by the four instruments. The rhythmic structure of each precludes an identity of rhythm in any pair of instruments (see String Quartet, part II—main movement, beginning, page 22).

Another way of reducing the static element in this technique is to divide the twelve different notes of our scale into two groups, one of which contains notes common to the whole ensemble, the other one or more notes assigned to particular instruments. In example 1-32, for instance, we have a group of four instruments: three flutes and celesta. The common notes are C5, C5 sharp, D5, D5 sharp, E5, F5, F5 sharp, and G5. Each of the remaining notes—A3 flat, A3, B3 flat, and B3—is assigned to one of the instruments.

Whereas the common notes must always remain in the same octave in order to avoid the undesirable appearance of octave doublings, the assigned notes can be played in as many octaves as the instrument permits, since each of them is performed by only a single instrument.

It is also worth drawing attention in this passage to the characteristic interval sequences wherever the common notes appear. These intervals are a fourth, a fifth, and a major second. The assigned notes contrast with these sequences by departing from this principle, which is further emphasized by a difference in dynamics: *forte* set against the *piano* of the common notes. In this passage there also appear five tom-toms which provide the bass part (see Symphony no. 2, figure 5).

In example 1-33, we have a group of five instruments: three clarinets, motorless vibraphone, and piano. The clarinets play only assigned notes, that is, two apiece: the first D and F, the second C sharp and E, the third C and E flat.

Since these are assigned notes, they can be played in various octaves. The piano and vibraphone play the common remainder of the notes: F4 sharp, G4,

Example 1-32.

Example 1-33.

G4 sharp, A4, A4 sharp, and B4, which form a chord of six adjacent notes. To avoid octaves, the notes common to the piano and vibraphone appear in only one position (see Symphony no. 2, figure 15).

The restriction of each of the clarinet parts to two notes is naturally a handicap, melodically speaking. To offset this, there is the greater variety of harmonies made possible by continual changes of the positions of the notes in these parts.

An extreme example of such melodic impoverishment in favor of harmonic variety is a passage in which each of twelve instruments has one note assigned to it, played in a number of octaves in succession. There are, of course, no common notes in this case. (See example 1-34.) The succeeding chords form a natural passage from a twelve-note chord embracing several registers: E2, B2, A3, F4 sharp, C5 sharp, G5 sharp, B5 flat, C6, E6 flat, F6, G6, D7 to one consisting only of adjacent minor seconds in the middle of the scale and finally to a minor second F4, F4 sharp (see *Paroles tissées*, Part IV, from figure 90 up to the end).

The smaller the number of notes assigned to an instrument, the less its melodic potential. However, even when assigned notes are used exclusively, it

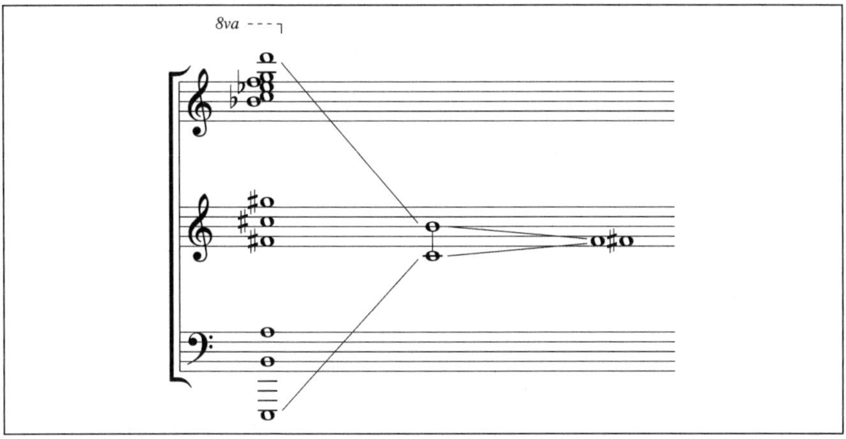

Example 1-34.

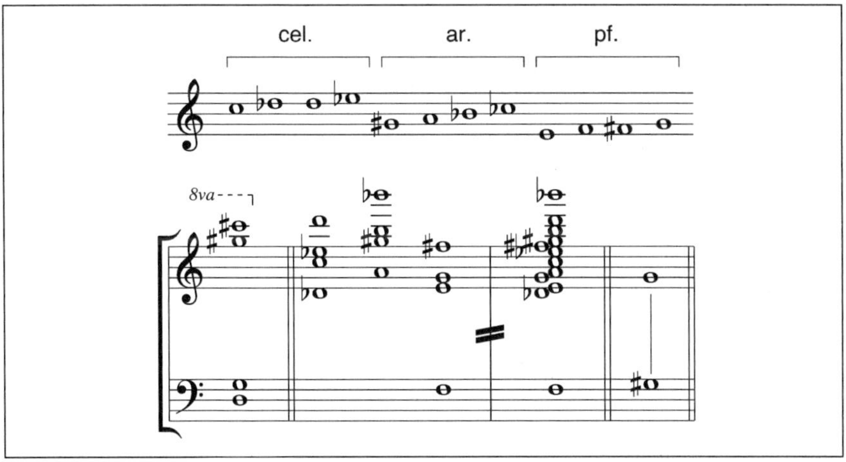

Example 1-35.

need not be as slight as it was in the foregoing example. It is enough to reduce the number of instruments and assign each of them a greater ration of notes.

In example 1-35, we have three instruments, each of which has been assigned four notes: the celesta C, D flat, D, E flat; the harp G sharp, A, B flat, C flat; and the piano E, F, F sharp, and G. These notes are employed such that the continually emerging twelve-note chords differ from each other not only in their scalar distribution but also in their intervallic structure.

Thus there is a gradual transformation of two remote chords consisting of six adjacent notes into a single expansive twelve-note chord with a structure based partially on thirds, which in its turn changes into another twelve-note chord, this time composed of semitones. I pass over the numerous transitional stages through which the chords run between these extreme points. The latter have three different shapes. For 1:

celesta: D3, E3 flat, C7, D7 flat
harp: G6 sharp, A6, B6 flat, C6 flat
piano: E3, F3, F3 sharp, G3—in other words two chords composed of six
    adjacent notes, D3–G3, and G6 sharp–D7 flat;

for 2:

celesta: D4 flat, C5, E5 flat, D6
harp: A4, G5 sharp, C6 flat, B6 flat
piano: F3, E4, G4, F5 sharp—in other words a twelve-note chord: F3, D4
    flat, E4, G4, A4, C5, E5 flat, F5 sharp, G5 sharp, C6 flat, D6, B6 flat;

and for 3:

celesta: C5, D5 flat, D5, E5 flat
harp: G4 sharp, A4, B4 flat, C5 flat
piano: E5, F5, F5 sharp, G5—in other words the twelve-note chord com-
    posed of semitones G4 sharp–G5 (see Symphony no. 2, figures 20–22).

Employment of assigned notes is only possible with a handful of performers. We saw that with a group of twelve instruments, each of which has only one note assigned to it, the melodic possibilities within each part become negligible. Accordingly, if we want to employ ensemble *ad libitum* with a large group, we must once again have recourse to a modal treatment of aggregates. To avoid the static element in this case, we can adopt yet another procedure: for example, we can lay down two chords for the whole section with a number of notes in common. The section is divided into three stages. In the first we use the first

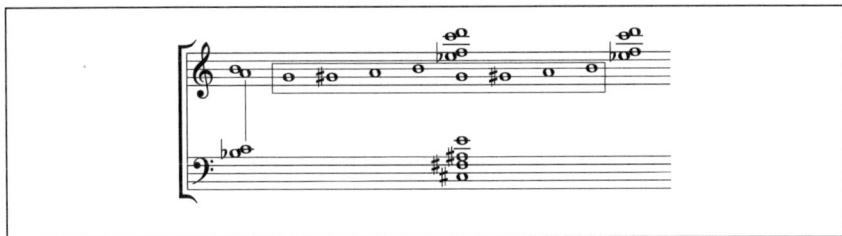

Example 1-36.

chord, which is treated modally, that is, all the parts are constructed around its notes, which are kept in the same position throughout. In the next stage we use only the notes that are common to both chords. In the third come all the notes of the second chord. The duration of the middle stage must be long enough to preclude notes from the first and second scale coinciding, since this would blur the harmonic picture and introduce undesirable octave doublings.

In example 1-36, the first chord consists of the twelve notes: B3 flat, C4, C4 sharp, D4, D4 sharp, E4, F4, F4 sharp, G4, G4 sharp, A4, and B4, while the second sharply contrasting chord is composed of C3 sharp, F3 sharp, A3 sharp, E4, G4, G4 sharp, A4, B4, E5 flat, F5, C6, and D6. The common notes used in the second stage are G4, G4 sharp, A4, and B4. Toward the end of the third stage, the number of notes played is reduced to four. These are the four upper notes of the second chord. In this particular example the performers are a string orchestra divided into twelve parts. In fact there are far more of them, since everything is played *ad libitum* and the performers assigned to each part do not, of course, play it identically. To steer clear of lengthy explanation I have omitted in this description the brief entries by a group of wind instruments (see Symphony no. 2, figure 123a).

My next two examples will be illustrations of ensemble *ad libitum* accompanied by music with a single common time division, in other words, with the same beat in all parts.

In the first example (1-37), the *ad libitum* strand is carried by a group of five soprano voices. The notes used here are C5, C5 sharp, D5, and F5 sharp, not counting the *glissandi* from F5 sharp to C5. In each part, the order in which the intervals occur is the same: F5 sharp–C5–D5–C5 sharp, but the arrangement of the approximate distances between these notes varies. The second level is formed by irregularly dispersed groups of short notes played by woodwinds. The ensemble is conducted by a separate conductor. The notes used in this

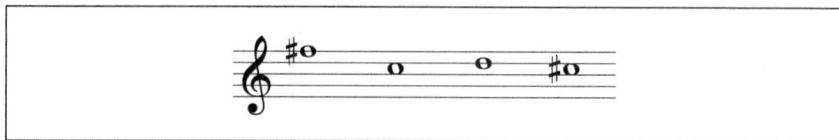

Example 1-37.

Example 1-38.

level, added to the previous ones, bring the number up to twelve. Unlike the four notes in the vocal part, the remaining ones played by the woodwinds appear in various positions forming kinds of constellations sliding around the scale (see *Trois poèmes d'Henri Michaux*, figures 46–60).

In the second example (1-38), the strand with a regular, common beat is formed by two solo parts: tenor voice and harp. The trunk of the form consists of seven sections, each of which is based on a few notes, 7, 5, 7, 5, 6, 5, and 7. The second level is an orchestral part divided into a much larger number of sections. Most of them are played *ad libitum* and organized in the various ways described earlier.

Characteristically, the dividing lines between the sections of the orchestra part do not coincide with the divisions between the sections of the solo parts. In consequence, when the divisions between the solo sections occur, the notes used in the orchestral sections can only be ones that do not appear in either of these adjoining sections or, at most, notes that are common to both. Otherwise octaves would ensue and here they would be undesirable. For instance, in one of the adjacent pairs of solo part sections we find the following two sets of notes: (1) C, D flat, F, B flat, B, and (2) C sharp, D, E flat, E, G, A, B. This leaves us with only two other notes: F sharp and G sharp, and these provide the material of the orchestra section that begins before and ends after the boundary between the solo part sections (see *Paroles tissées,* part 2, p. 11).

That brings me to the close of my illustrations of the various uses of the technique of ensemble *ad libitum.* I was particularly anxious to indicate the need for certain essential restraints in the employment of rhythm and the organization of pitch. The point of such discipline is to achieve the greatest possible measure of control over the results of the whole procedure.

From the examples I have shown, you will see that the technique of ensemble *ad libitum* can yield great advantages in the field of rhythm and lead to free, uninhibited expression in particular parts, while at the same time depriving the composed passage of harmonic variety. One of the reasons for this is that, to get the most out of this technique, it has to be employed over sufficiently long sections, since the attainment of complete freedom in *ad libitum* playing is a matter of time. A certain degree of harmonic mobility can be achieved by the use of what have been called assigned notes, but this impoverishes the particular parts melodically and in any case is only feasible in small instrumental or vocal groups. Another expedient is to combine the technique of ensemble *ad libitum* with music played at a common, regular beat. But this requires dividing the performers into groups and at times the presence of two conductors.

It will be apparent from these concluding remarks that although there are quite unmistakable advantages to be derived from the technique of ensemble *ad libitum,* one can hardly imagine it forming the sole basis for the construction of large scale forms.

Source

A lecture delivered in Polish during the first "Musical Encounters (*Ars nova—Ars antiqua*)" in Baranów Sandomierski, on September 9, 1976. This lecture was published in Polish, in *Muzyka w kontekście kultury* (Music in the Context of Culture), edited by Leszek Polony (Kraków: PWM, 1978), 76–87, and in English, in *Polish Musicological Studies 2* (Kraków: PWM, 1985), 37–53 (no translator is credited). Copyright for the English version—Polish Musical Edition, Kraków. Printed by permission.

Notes

1. See note 5 to the text "Aleatorism" in this chapter.
2. John Cage, *Composition as Process, II—Indeterminacy,* in *Silence* (Middletown, Conn.: Wesleyan University Press, 1961), 36. Lutosławski quoted the same, but slightly shortened passage in the text "About the Element of Chance in Music" in this chapter.

TONAL SYSTEM

The tonal system had as its base the seven-tone diatonic scales. By way of evolution, which consisted of a gradual introduction of sounds that did not belong to particular scales, this system developed first of all into so-called extended tonality and then ultimately went out of use in favor of the invented free atonality. This process opened up great prospects for the development of the sound world that have not been fully exploited to this day. The attempts at that so far have given rise to only fragmentary, narrow, and transient ways of using the twelve-tone scale. At the same time, tendencies emerged based on the assumption that both the particular sounds of this scale and their reciprocal relations (vertical and horizontal) are not intended to be perceived and identified as such. The goal of these endeavors is to create sound-complexes that are perceived to have a high level of independence not only from the scale used to construct them, but also from any other scale. These tendencies are a transitional stage leading to the creation of music not based on any scale, which today is achieved in totally different ways, and especially with the help of electro-acoustic equipment. At present there exists a clear division between music based on the twelve-note equally tempered scale and music totally independent of that scale. The latter type is most fully realized in electronic music studios and therefore it does not seem useful to continue the efforts to create it using traditional instruments performing in the realm of the traditional twelve-tone scale. I feel certain that this scale still has within it unused and unknown possibilities. To discover them and, possibly, to systematize them, is not a task that one man or even one generation would feel able to undertake. It should be the result of the efforts, experiences and, above all, the inspiration of many generations of composers just as happened with the tonal system. As a result, I am not of one mind with many of today's composers who consider that music (or any other art) is now approaching its inevitable end. One cannot exclude the prospect that the future will raise music to such a height as it reached in the past two centuries, although it is hard to imagine that this could happen in the next few years.

I started my considerations with a short reminder of what the tonal system was. We should also remember that its roots reach back to a remote past; and it could not have come into being without the existence of both the scales created by European antiquity and by the medieval and Renaissance polyphony.

A steady development of this system, measured in centuries, guaranteed its extremely solid foundations and a basic compatibility with the laws of acoustics, the physiology of hearing, and the psychology of perception. I do not share the view expressed by many, that this system can be seen as a totally arbitrary convention, which one could replace by any other one. This solid basis and the long process of the development of the tonal system make us realize the depth of the breakthrough that occurred in music at the end of the nineteenth and the beginning of the twentieth century. We are still the victims of the crisis this breakthrough caused in the world of sounds. We try to extricate ourselves from this crisis, everybody in his or her own way, while looking for a constructive, positive way out, neither destroying anything that was transmitted by the past, nor engaging in polemics with this past. The fact is that at the end of the twentieth century we found ourselves in a different situation from the composers who were active at its beginning. At that point, one of the main tasks undertaken by the pioneers was to liberate themselves from tonal laws, to oppose them, and to abolish them. It was a destructive process in many respects and, in any case, a polemical one, which was peculiarly dependent on the system against which it fought. Here, of course, we come, above all, to the case of Schoenberg. One of the aims of his doctrine, which he himself did not deny, was to avoid any tonal elements. The mechanism that made this possible is known to everybody. One cannot really say that this mechanism, which in itself was orientated destructively and even preventatively, was not a historically and psychologically justified attempt. The tonal system was so deeply rooted in the psyche of composers and listeners that the slightest allusion to it, one chord or one sound-sequence, awakened immediately an entire avalanche of associations that Schoenberg wanted very much to avoid. Yet he was dependent upon the system he strove against, and this dependence had a polemical character. This is the usual fate of the avant-garde of every revolution. Its pioneers are not predestined for constructing new systems.

Schoenberg did not resist the temptation to create such a system. His belief that he had found something that would change the image of all future music and would, according to his own words, "secure German music supremacy for the coming 100 years," is a symptom of a euphoria that should not astonish us, taking into consideration his achievements. However, it is beyond understanding how he could have imagined that one man, creating his own system, could replace the work of dozens of great composers over a period of several centuries. From the perspective of the almost sixty years that divide us from the rise of Schoenbergian dodecaphony, it is clearly seen that this doctrine—in spite of its crucial importance for the period that immediately followed—did not play the role foreseen by its author. The fact that it was taken over by a legion of third-rate composers unfortunately contributed to the creation of hundreds of works with no durable value. Today the Schoenbergian system is a dead letter and has no chance of a permanent, literal use. We consider its creator a very clever man because of his work and independently of whether people follow this doctrine, and whether they were composing before or after it originated. Schoenberg's oeuvre is only one source of tradition in twentieth-century music. It is my opinion that the oeuvre of Debussy, early Stravinsky, Bartók, and Varèse are more important and durable, with greater impact on the future. I believe that the direction pointed out by these composers has a better chance of leading to new, more universal conventions—without which a full flowering of musical creativity by seventeenth- and eighteenth-century standards does not seem possible.

In this essay I directed attention to just one aspect of the problem, that is, the organization of pitch. It was impossible to deal in one short text with the equally important aspects such as, first of all, the organization of time in a musical work. What I have touched upon here would require a broader consideration and more precise justification. Therefore, I treat my reasoning as a pretext for an exchange of thoughts rather than a credo.

Finally, I will make one last important remark. I have discussed the vicissitudes of the musical language over the centuries, crises we have witnessed, and perspectives for the future. This is not, however, what the history of music consists of. It is created by the works themselves, very often independently of the means their composers have at their disposal. Therefore, even if the present time does not favor a true full bloom of musical creativity, one cannot totally exclude the rise of works of lasting value that, in the era of crisis of our whole civilization, will be a bridge toward a better future.

Source

Manuscript in Polish. Copyright Witold Lutosławski Collection, Paul Sacher Foundation. All rights reserved. Printed by permission. This text was presented as a lecture during the Summer Courses for Young Composers in Poland, in Kazimierz nad Wisłą, at the beginning of September 1983.

SEMINAR ON INSTRUMENTATION

Introduction

The contemporary composer has no adequate instruments to fully realize his musical ideas. In order to make this statement clearer, let us remember some well-known facts about the instruments we have at our disposal nowadays.

Let us consider first the wind instruments. The so-called natural tones of the wind instruments are those of the harmonic series (natural series). The chromatic scale of a wind instrument is composed of a set of seven harmonic series. This creates a preference for diatonic and simple chromatic sequences of tones. They are easier to perform than the actual twelve-note ones.

The stringed instruments are built partly on the base of the Pythagorean scale, and the present state of the technique of playing violin, viola, etc., uses the diatonic scale as a starting point. Here again, the diatonic and simple chromatic sequences of tones are favored instead of nontonal ones.

Keyboard instruments are obviously diatonic because of the arrangements of the keys according to the C major scale. The same goes for the harp, which is tuned according to the C-flat major scale.

Except for xylophones and the like, the percussion instruments are perhaps the most loosely connected with the tonal system.

The contemporary composer is no more connected with the tonal system. His musical thinking is still based on the traditional twelve-note equally tempered scale. But he tends to introduce more and more elements that are totally independent of the traditional scale, and here he is hampered by the traditional instruments, which can satisfy his needs only to a limited extent.

It is true that in principle the violin family could offer the possibility of playing not only the actual twelve-note sequences, but also the sounds that don't belong to the twelve-note scale at all. But this would require the elaborating of a new method of training players that is obviously difficult to imagine now.

Apart from the construction of the traditional instruments, which makes them inadequate to serve the purposes of a contemporary composer, there is something in the very nature of these instruments that associates them in our mind with the past. Their sound is beautiful indeed, but old, as beautiful old furniture may be.

There are various ways of overcoming this obstacle. One of them is unusual ways of playing the old instruments: preparing pianos, striking violins, playing behind the bridge, etc. These are but marginal possibilities and they exhaust themselves very quickly. On the other hand those methods are noteworthy because they clearly support my statement about the inadequacy of the traditional instruments. The only way out of the crisis is probably the electronic and concrete music. But so far, their results are not comparable with the instrumental music as far as the richness and subtlety of sound is concerned. The need for new instruments has been beautifully expressed by Edgar Varèse. In 1936 he said:

"When new instruments will allow me to write music as I conceive it, the movement of sound-masses, of shifting planes, will be clearly perceived in my work, taking the place of the linear counterpoint. When these sound-masses collide, the phenomena of penetration or repulsion will seem to be projected onto other planes, moving at different speeds and at different angles. There will no longer be the old conception of melody or interplay of melodies. The entire work will be a melodic totality. The entire work will flow as a river flows."[1]

But so far we have no new instruments and we must learn to use the old ones in such a way that they can serve our purposes.

∞

The topic of this seminar is instrumentation. It would be more correct to call it the technique of composing for instruments or for orchestra. That is because instrumentation, as I understand it, is merely the composing of the orchestra version of a piece that has been composed previously either for another medium, as in the case of Ravel's version of Mussorgsky's *Pictures at an Exhibition*, or composed in an abstract way, without predetermining any particular medium, as in the case of Bach's *Kunst der Fuge*. The instrumentation, as understood in this way, is perhaps not as useful as is the technique of composing for the orchestra. The latter is certainly one of the most important elements of the contemporary composer's professional equipment. To achieve it, special training of our sound imagination is needed, so as to enable us to think instrumentally (so to speak), that is, to imagine sound structures not in an abstract way, but in their complete instrumental form, including the texture, articulation, and color peculiar to particular instruments and instrumental groups. The final purpose of such training is to allow the sound ideas offered us by our creative musical imagination to have not only their complete instrumental form, but also sometimes to include a special use of a group of instruments, a new unusual texture, a combining of different sorts of articulation, and so on. To make a little clearer what I have in mind, I shall give you some examples of purely instrumental musical ideas: The Wet-Nurses Dance of Stravinsky's *Petroushka* (figure 170), later repeated in a new version in the *Rite of Spring* (figure 29). Here the essence of the musical idea consists of the alternate use of grace notes in pair of instruments (or in two groups). Sometimes simply the choice of a specific instrument to play a given role may be a musical idea in itself as, for example, the use of 2 cl. in the last movement of Debussy's *Iberia* to play in unison in high register the quasi-folklore theme (after figure 57). The same goes for the major sevenths played *staccato* by the piano together with the glissandi going from the lower note to the higher and the other way round, played by violins *pp con cordino* in the slow movement of Bartók's *Music for Strings, Percussion, and Celesta* (two measures after figure 20).

Innumerable examples of that kind have nothing to do with the so-called instrumentation, their instrumental form being inseparably connected to their melodic and rhythmic shape or sometimes even conceived before the final choice of pitches and rhythms.

Another aspect of orchestral writing is the ease of playing particular parts as well as the ease of playing the given musical text. To simplify the problem we can say that the easier your text is to play, the better it sounds. But here some doubts immediately arise. The question is not so simple as to be solved at once. That is why I propose two extreme approaches to the problem. First, there is the rule: "I don't bother about the difficulty of my music; it is entirely the matter of the player, singer, or conductor." Or—second—"I always consider the natural possibilities of the instruments and the human mind." The disadvantage of the first: the difficulties or even impossibilities of attaining the adequate level of performance; the advantages of the second: the certainty of a good performance and the ability to attain a good sound. But, on the other hand, the first has its advantages. There would not have been any progress in the technique of playing instruments if we always and only thought of the natural possibilities of the instruments. What seems unnatural nowadays may become natural in the future. Certain twelve-tone passages that seem quite natural and are easy to play for a modern clarinet player may have seemed unnatural and were certainly difficult or even impossible to play for a clarinet player in the first half of the nineteenth century.

Usually the older orchestra players are resistant to any new kind of difficulty. However, there are those who are anxious to solve new technical and musical problems. You find them especially among great soloists and chamber music players (e.g., Rostropovich).

How far should we go when deciding the final level of difficulties in our score? I think here common sense ought to make the decision. Anyway, one thing is unquestionable: any difficulty must be justified by the final sound result, unnecessary difficulties should be totally excluded.

Your work sounds better when the players feel that their effort pays off. On the other hand, it sounds much worse when they can see clearly that the part is awkwardly written, and that the difficulties are unnecessary.

The crucial problem is perhaps not the sense of color, but the knowledge and experience of the instruments' dynamic possibilities and the capacity to create the balance between them.

One of the crucial problems of orchestra writing is the dynamic balance. The old Rimsky-Korsakov principle that in *p* we can treat (use) all instruments as equal, still holds good. (Obvious exceptions: ob., bn. ↑ , trb., cor. ↓.) Consequently there is no problem in orchestrating the *p* section, soloists, ensembles, etc. It is still possible to adjust dynamics. The problems are *f* and especially *tutti*. I have not much to say about general rules concerning this problem. We shall discuss particular fragments of scores in order to get some experience in this field. We shall see, for example, that in composing an *f* for the whole orchestra it is sometimes necessary to begin with brass instruments, because they don't blend with other kinds of instruments, and therefore must form a nearly independent element of the *tutti*. We shall also see that some percussion instruments played *ff* may entirely cover all the remaining ones. We shall examine many, many other particular examples of building up an orchestral *tutti*, which is indeed the most difficult part of that knowledge I have called orchestral writing.

But before we reach that stage of our work, I suggest that we look more closely at particular instruments and their characteristics. I assume that all of you have basic knowledge about instruments and it is not my task here to describe them fully. Nevertheless, I have decided to talk a little about each kind of instrument in a very informal and subjective way. I think it may stimulate your imagination, and help you to more easily find the way to my own orchestra writing, which will be the object of a great part of my analysis.

Flute

Melodic lines can be compared with those drawn with charcoal crayon (the lines of oboe with those drawn with pen). To produce sounds, the flute requires a relatively great amount of air, and therefore the rests for breathing can be shorter than in oboe and bassoon parts (where the player must have time to breathe out the air he had to hold in during playing). Agility in the whole scale. Dynamic possibilities according to different registers.

The use: Debussy: Prelude to *The Afternoon of a Faun*, Ravel: *Daphnis et Chloé*—sensual, voluptuous character.

Critical analysis of fragments of scores: Stravinsky: *The Nightingale* (figures 4 and 13)—giggles (a favorite trick of early Stravinsky); Mussorgsky-Ravel: *Pictures at an Exhibition* (figure 90); Stravinsky: *Firebird* (figure 18); Debussy: *Ibéria* (figure 46—*soutenu dans la douceur*).

Flute Piccolo

One octave higher than the flute minus the low register; strength; use in *p* instead of high register of the flute. An unconvincing example of 2 fl. picc. in octaves is in Varèse's *Intégrales*.

Flute Alto

Good—Stravinsky: *The Rite of Spring* (figures 6–10); doubtful—some places in Boulez's *Le marteau sans maître* (pitch).

Oboe

Melodic lines and isolated short notes may be compared to those drawn with a pen and can include a great variety of expression, from a tender cantilena to somehow sarcastic, ironical sharpness. Because of its construction, the oboe places special demands on the composer. The production of sound requires a small amount of air and therefore we must assure the player the rests not only to breathe in the air necessary to produce the sounds, but also to breathe out the rest of it after the preceding phrase.

The dynamic characteristics of the oboe are opposite those of the flute. The high register is rather delicate whereas the low is strong and powerful. That is why in *f* played by the full orchestra we use the oboe in its low register rather than in high. On the other hand, we can't require an average player to produce beautiful *p* notes in the low register.

Critical analysis: Brahms: Symphony no. 1, second movement (measures 38–43); Varèse: *Intégrales*, p. 4–5 (*pincé et mordant*); R. Strauss: *Don Juan*, p. 62—a model oboe cantilena (a little commonplace); Debussy: Prelude to *The Afternoon of a Faun*—the hero is the flute, but there are also oboe solos of incomparable beauty in figure 4 (second theme cantilena).

English Horn

To familiarize yourself with the nasal sound of the English horn, listen to Berlioz's *Roman Carnival, Andante sostenuto*, page 3. Special role in the context: Stravinsky: *Petroushka* (figure 149); Debussy: *Nuages*.

Clarinet

The melodic lines of the clarinet are less sharp than those of the oboe and sharper than the flute. The *breathing* is similar to that of flute and the clarinet has great technical possibilities and great agility. Here again the old principle of construction makes the diatonic and simple chromatic passages easier than twelve-tone ones. Sometimes it may be useful to consult on difficult passages with a clarinet player in order to avoid unnecessary difficulties.

Dynamics: only the middle register is relatively weak. The *f* is otherwise possible both in the high and low. The *pp* in the highest part of the scale is difficult and we can't depend on it from average players.

Special possibilities: glissando.

Fragments of scores to analyze or listen to: Brahms: Symphony no. 1, *Un poco allegretto e grazioso*—a sweet melody-instrument; Stravinsky: *Petroushka* (one measure after figure 188)—ludicrous, farcical; *Firebird, Petroushka, The Rite of Spring, The Nightingale*—examples of broken chords.

Clarinet Piccolo

R. Strauss: *Till Eulenspiegels lustige Streiche*—the ending is "entstellt"—defaced, disfigured; Varèse: *Intégrales*, begins similar to Stravinsky's *The Rite of Spring* (second measure after figure 9). Here the instrument is used in a one-sided way: in a grotesque, comical character. But Webern, for example, uses the piccolo clarinet as highly lyrical instrument to produce delicate, subtle sounds, as in op. 10 (*5 Stücke für Orchester*), second movement.

Bass Clarinet

Bass clarinet is mainly used to play solo parts. Generally, the technical possibilities of this instrument are the same as those of the clarinet, except for lessened agility. The high register is to be used rather exceptionally. If there is time (i.e., enough rests) to change the bass clarinet into an ordinary one it is better to do it.

Fragments to listen to: short solos in *The Rite of Spring* (figure 4, four measures after figure 8, three measures after figures 140–142), and in *Petroushka* (figure 125).

Bassoon

The agility is less than that of the oboe. The solo of two bassoons in Ravel's G major Concerto is very difficult (third movement). The variety of expression is very great, but the bassoon keeps it a little clownish. Breathing for the bassoon is similar to that with the oboe, so we must assure the rests to breathe out the air before breathing in. Dynamics are much the same as with oboe: the low register is much stronger than the high. It is difficult to play *p* in the lowest register.

Fragments to listen to: *The Rite of Spring* (the Introduction); R. Strauss: *Don Quixote* (measures 15–18 after figure 64).

Contrabassoon

Contrabassoon as solo instrument has always been used for ludicrous effects: *Petroushka* (figure 52), Dukas: *The Sorcerer's Apprentice*. There is still a possibility of finding some other role for this peculiar instrument. There is no sense in using the high register where an ordinary bassoon sounds much better.

Trumpet

The trumpet has great dynamic possibilities. One must reckon, however, with the considerable effort that is needed to produce high sounds. The low register is not very valuable in singing parts; it is especially suitable for some grotesque effects when sounding like a child pretending or imitating grown-up persons.

Fragments to use: *Pictures at an Exhibition* (*Samuel Goldenberg and Schmuÿle*, figure 58); *Fêtes* (traditional!—fanfare); *Petroushka* (figure 192—*legato*); *The Nightingale* (figures 4 and 13).

Horn

The horn is highly expressive in melodic parts. Used legato in a simple sequence of notes, it may have quite an unusual sound. One must not forget that the sound in the low register is not easy to produce *f*. The pitch is very often uncertain, that is why one must be very careful when using low notes. In practical terms, when using brass as a group in *f*, one must count that one horn is equal to a half of a trumpet or trombone (doubling).

Listen to the Prelude to *The Afternoon of a Faun*, page 28 (*un peu plus animé*) when the horn uses the simplest segments of notes that sound fresh.

Trombone

I believe that the trombone is the most similar to the human male voice from among all instruments. I have always felt a lack of low brass instruments in the standard orchestra. The tromboni cannot fill it up, they don't sound very well in the low when playing *f*. Of course, now the technique of playing instruments has developed, and what was difficult to achieve fifty years ago is now quite possible. Compare the traditional sound of the trombone in Wagner's music with one in the *Bolero*. I recommend studying this piece carefully to familiarize yourself with some unusual and highly expressive sounds of the trombone.

Tuba

Tuba is surprisingly expressive in some melodic parts, but it is very rarely used in this way. Listen to *Pictures at an Exhibition* (Mussorgsky-Ravel).

Percussion, Leather

This includes the tamburo piccolo (militare)—snare drum, side drum (and its variants: cassa rulante; tamburo rullante—parade drum). Most are seventeen to eighteen centimeters high, diameter approximately thirty-five centimeters.

Tuning is possible, but only within a major third at the most. To differentiate the appropriate pitch one constructs instruments of different height: bop, eight to ten centimeters; jazz, twelve to fourteen centimeters; concert, normal, sixteen to eighteen centimeters; rullante approximately twenty centimeters.

Tom-tom—trixon (tamburo)—eight sizes: five to be fastened to the bass drum (piccolo, soprano, alto, tenor I, tenor II), three to stand on legs (baritone, bass, c.-b.).

Timpani—E-d, A-f.

Percussion, Metal

Crotali (Prelude to *The Afternoon of a Faun*)—six to fifteen centimeters in diameter, two to three millimeters thick. They may be graduated according to the chromatic scale in the fourth octave. There are more than ten sizes, with diameters from twenty-five to sixty centimeters.

The tam-tam is 60 to 120 centimeters.

Campanelli (Glockenspiel)—written: C4–C6, sounds C6–C8.

With the vibrafono, the pitch sometimes depends on the kind of sticks. When they are hard, the first harmonic (one octave higher than the written notes) is more audible than the actual note.

Campane (chimes, bells) range from C3–F4; the pitch is sometimes difficult to define, as the harmonics are audible in different way, according to the register and to the way the player hits the tubes.

Concerning the xylophone, some authors say the compass (range) is C4–C7 and sounds as written. It depends on the construction of the instrument. I am inclined to consider the compass of the old type of xylophone (without pipes under the slabs) as one octave higher, that is, C5–C8.

∞

Many ways of notating percussion symbols by including explanations on the front page of the score don't help much. I am skeptical about conductors being willing and anxious to learn them by heart every time they conduct a new score. I always prefer the explanation above the notes in the score or in the footnotes.

There are many ways of using the percussion instruments of undefined pitch. Traditional composers don't bother with the acoustic spectrum of those instruments and use them as an addition to the notes or chords of defined pitch. There is, however, another way of handling them. Provided that we know at least approximately what a given instrument represents as far as the pitch is concerned, we may include its sounds in our vertical organization of a given section.

For example, Symphony no. 2, figures 4–6 (fl. above tom-toms), figures 120–121 woodwinds and brass ↑, tom-toms and drums ↓, then ↔; figures 121–122 woodwinds and trumpets ↑, tam-tam ↓. These examples are simple, as I have not studied the spectrum of the instruments before. It was not necessary. But if we want to develop this way of using the percussion instruments of undefined pitch, we should make some methodical tests of the acoustic characteristics of particular instruments.

Harp

The most elementary of acoustics—to produce a sound on the harp, the player must first touch (i.e., stop) a given string, as shown here:

$$(\, \text{♩} — \quad \text{♩} — \; = \text{always:} \; \text{♩} \, \text{,} \quad \text{♩} \,)$$

For example, Bartók's Violin Concerto (if there were two harps it would have sounded better and it would have been much easier to play). To hear an unusual use of harp: listen to the untuned harp in Boulez—*Pli selon pli*, first version. One can also tune a harp in a special way, for example, with quarter-tones, etc.

Strings

String instruments are quarter-tone instruments. In orchestra writing we cannot reckon on the quarter-notes as notes of full value (training) either between neighboring notes of the twelve-note scale or after neighboring notes belonging to the twelve-note scale; either sliding (notation) or playing with different figures (notation: fingering!).

For example, String Quartet: figures 1–2, 35–36, in which you can hear the use of quarter-tones without limitations—only in solo parts.

Source

Note

1. This quotation comes from the lecture "New Instruments and New Music," which Varèse delivered in Santa Fe, New Mexico, in 1936, and which was included in the compilation of Varèse texts edited by Chou Wen-Chung under the title *The Lib-*

eration of Sound. See Elliott Schwartz and Barney Childs, eds., *Contemporary Composers on Contemporary Music* (New York: Holt, Rinehart, and Winston, 1967), 196–208 (the quotation is on p. 197).

THEORY AND PRACTICE IN THE WORK OF THE COMPOSER

In 1961, I wrote an essay titled "Music in the 20th Century," which I used as an introduction to my lecture on Polish music at the first Music Biennale in Zagreb. Here is the text of this introduction:

If we want to understand the full significance of contemporary music at this point in its history, we must consider the course of musical history from its last classical period until the present day. The classical period embraces the seventeenth century until the beginning of the nineteenth, that is, the period of the so-called Viennese classics. In their music there is, indeed, such proportion and such harmonious blending of all elements that one is forced to admit that it hardly falls short of true perfection. But though I see this perfection in particular works, I nevertheless guard against the fallacy of thinking that it lies in the actual means of expression, that is, in the musical language itself. In point of fact, more than one musician, critic, and listener has been tempted into thinking just that. We often hear the erroneous contention that the iron logic of functional harmony, the effortless naturalness of diatonic melody, and the ideal balance of form constitute the chief virtues of classical works and guarantee their greatness. The fallacy of this becomes apparent when we realize what a vast number of works fulfill these conditions and yet are completely devoid of artistic value. All qualities of musical language are relative, and what in an authentic work of art we feel to be a virtue becomes in a commonplace one a vice: the logic of tonal harmony becomes mere slickness, the charm and the naturalness of diatonic melody—banality, and formal balance—tedious formalism. The truth is that perfection of language alone does not determine the worth of the Viennese classics, and yet it is no less true to say that probably no epoch in musical history has produced so many masterpieces as the one during which this musical language held sway.

The language of the classics, which has taken shape down the centuries and is the result of the endeavors of several generations of composers, is like some mighty building whose existence seems assured for all eternity. There are cultures, especially in Asia, which follow the same pattern of artistic conventions over thousands of years. Such could never be the case, though, in our own culture, in view of the peculiar restlessness and nervous energy that reside in the European character. The European, it would seem, is happier when he is striving after some goal than when he has attained it; he prefers the process of perfecting something to perfection itself, and the exploring of new possibilities gives him more satisfaction than does the subsequent exploitation of them. The consequence of this is evident in the history of our music from the time of the classics to the present day. In order to build something new, it was first necessary to demolish the vast edifice of which I have already spoken, namely that of the traditional language of the classics. The history of this demolition constitutes one aspect of the history of music during the last one hundred years.

Wassily Kandinsky wrote in 1923: "In the course of the last few decades creative artists in all fields have been analyzing their artistic stock-in-trade. With radical thoroughness they are reducing each aspect of their art to its elements, consciously or unconsciously, examining their appropriateness within a given framework. It is in fact an era of intense analysis, and on all sides we hear at the same time animated discussions about a grand synthesis. This breaking up into component parts is a necessary preliminary to reconstructing anew, dismantling—to assembling anew."[1] I entirely agree with Kandinsky, but find, forty years after these words were written, that, unfortunately, as far as a "grand synthesis" is concerned, we have still not got beyond the stage of "animated discussion" about it. I even surmise that this grand synthesis will continue to elude us for quite some time yet. For the time being, at least, the process of intense analysis or, as I expressed it earlier, of great dismantling, still continues, despite the fact that the beginnings of this process reach as far back into the past as the period of Romanticism. For it was the Romantic composers who delivered the first blow. Initially they confined their attack to classical form; later, however, the tonal system came under their fire to a certain extent. But it was Debussy who first seriously undermined this system, while Schoenberg, for his part, sought to liquidate it completely. Stravinsky abolished the rigidities of classical rhythm, while Webern did away with melody as an orderly succession of sounds in one part, breaking it up into small groups or single notes—a program his followers are carrying to its final conclusions. Concrete and electronic music leads to depriving pitched sounds of the chief role they have filled until now, while John Cage and his disciples are intent upon destroying the hitherto-held conception of a musical work as an organization of sounds following a definite course in time.

This picture I have just given you represents only one aspect of the problem; it is a short history of the process of wholesale demolition or dismantlement, or—as Kandinsky would say—of intense analysis. The character of this process is, in the final reckoning, only seemingly negative: if the future is to introduce new elements into our musical idiom, from which new artistic conventions are to evolve, then first of all it is necessary for the old conventions to be liquidated. This is a long process that is certainly not yet finished. And yet in the very speed of this large-scale liquidation, I already see positive signs, because the quicker the disintegration of the old type of musical texture takes place, the sooner a new one will arise. And from it, by means of synthesis, new, lasting conventions can be evolved, which will initiate a new classical period, which is, of course, what we all desire.

As I mentioned before, "wholesale demolition" is only one aspect of the history of music during the last hundred years. I am very far from believing that this period has contributed nothing to music beyond a gradual liquidation of the classical conventions. For this is, at the same time, a period in which a vast and hitherto unsuspected wealth of creative sound material as well as entirely unexpected possibilities in regard to the organization of time in music have been discovered.

The Romantic composers revealed to us the unsuspected riches of chromatic harmony. Debussy represents a theory of harmony, characteristic of his entire era; Schoenberg is the author of dodecaphonic technique; Stravinsky is discovering entirely new worlds with regard to rhythm; while Webern is the author of structure as a fundamental element of a new musical form that can be regarded as the prototype of the later *objet sonore.*[2] We are not yet in a position to foresee all the future possibilities of the most important sound invention of our time, namely concrete and electronic music. However we can already speak of the discovery of areas in the region of sound previously unknown and far exceeding the bounds of the former twelve-note scale. Finally, there is John Cage. He and his disciples have opened up entirely new perspectives with regard to the organization of time in music, and made possible the birth of a new style of music making itself.

In spite of these undeniable and immensely exciting achievements, I, nevertheless, cannot help feeling that the period of synthesis, which Kandinsky anticipated as early as 1923, is still far off. What makes me think this? Certainly, my opinion is not based exclusively on the study of the musical history of the last one hundred years, which I have just reviewed in an intentionally simplified and schematic way. There is one rather important circumstance that must be taken into consideration when one is forecasting the future, which is the fact that music of the seventeenth, eighteenth, and nineteenth centuries still comprises the main part of concert repertoires and radio programs throughout the world. Honegger's sarcastic remark "Bach is killing us" still holds good. A contemporary composer in the program of a subscription concerts feels, again—according to Honegger—just as if he were sitting at the table in a house to which he has not been invited. This situation does not really favor the creation of new styles and conventions, and so long as it lasts there is not much we can do. We can, however, trust that maybe the moment will come in which even the greatest masters of the preceding centuries will share the fate of their predecessors, when their works will slowly begin to change into museum specimens, of interest only to specialists. Only then can we imagine the true flowering of contemporary music.

These reflections might well seem to be but a futile excursion into the realms of fantasy, were it not that they make it possible for me to define my own position in the contemporary scene. Unattractive as is the role of the modern composer as pictured by Honegger, it nevertheless has purpose behind it, namely to foster the continuous development of art, even in the least favorable circumstances, and prepare for its new flowering in the era to come.

∾

Rereading today the above text, which was written a couple of years ago, I ask myself a question: did this very short account of the history of twentieth-century music help my compositional work in any way? (Although I did not do it for that purpose, by any means.) The answer to this question—as in many similar situations—must be equivocal.

Every effort to discover a hidden logic that governs the development of creative activity in the history of any branch of art, must stir the reflexes of skepticism in the so-called active artist. Hence, what strikes me in my essay is not only the cursoriness or ease with which I place particular occurrences in a continuous line. There is also something in it, which—as in all writing on this subject—awakes my dislike and even objection. It is the way the historical significance of works of art is allowed to outweigh their purely artistic meaning. When thinking "historically" about artistic phenomena, we lose sight—necessarily—of the individual properties of particular works, that is, of all that determines the characteristic physiognomy of each of them. We look for their common features, which unites them in bigger groups, currents, tendencies, etc. Yet the temperament of a creative artist balks at doing that, since he tries instinctively to defend the uniqueness, singularity, and the "personality" of every work of art worthy of the name. This uniqueness and singularity result from such features, which defy qualification, do not allow themselves to be described precisely, and remain forever within the language of art, which is untranslatable into words. If all that I am talking about did not exist, art itself would not exist and, if it still existed, it would not merit any interest. It would be enough to read its history. Fortunately art does not consist entirely in what could be *known* about it. I will say more: what could be known and written about it has not much in common with its destiny, that is, with its direct impact, which bypasses complete consciousness. This specific communication between people takes place only by means of the autonomous language proper to a given art. And what is even more important, the content communicated by this language is so closely connected with it that we are not sure whether we don't, in fact, have to do with a homogeneous phenomenon; with a somehow isolated entity, communing with which gives us a satisfaction impossible to experience otherwise.

Are my reflections an attack upon "historical thinking" about art? Not in the least. The history of art, or musicology, does not belong to the art itself, but to the human sciences and their output: domains of human activity that I hold in the greatest respect. My remarks express something different. They are a reaction of an active artist to the proposals of the theorist inside me. They are a composer's self-defensive reflex against assuming too great a distance in relation to his art. This is, in fact, what I am most afraid of. From too great a distance all faces seem alike, and all movements tend toward, so to speak, a common goal. We lose sight of the "uniqueness" and we see only the "collectivity," we can't "experience," but we can instead "denominate" and "classify." All these activities are in essence alien to the creative act, no matter which art. The creative act requires something totally contrary: that we approach a single, particular artistic vision and eliminate any distance from it, so that we become almost one with this vision. To speak more simply: in order to compose something I must forget everything which is not the work to be composed. And above all I must not allow myself any thought that would tend to "denominate" and "classify" the music composed, in other words to deprive me, while I work, of my conviction of the "uniqueness" and "singularity" of what I am writing, even if, in a moment, I myself might come to consider this conviction a total illusion. And although I sometimes observe quite clear connections relating my works both to one another and, of course, to various traditions, every new work of mine is always an individual experience for me, as though independent of anything else. This requires an extremely subjective attitude, which is the first condition of any artistic creation. An excess of consciousness does not facilitate this attitude, and it is no wonder that the composer in me reacts defensively against the aspirations of a random theorist.

If only things were so simple, how much easier the composer's life would be! Meanwhile, in reality, the participation of consciousness in my work is a necessity. What is this participation like in the light of what I have written above? It is not easy to explain it, but my experience brings me many instances of the usefulness, in my composing, of not only analyses of old and contemporary works, but also theoretical, historical, or aesthetic literature and, finally, my own investigations of these subjects, even to the modestly "scholarly" extent that I can manage. All these activities have certainly affected the direction of my purely compositional investigations and their concrete results, that is, my own works. This influence, however, can never be direct. The study of theory or aesthetics cannot alternate with composing in quick succession, since the direct impact of such studies on the mechanism that sets the creative imagination in motion is, as I have been trying to describe, paralyzing.

The necessity of assuming the mutually contradictory attitudes of composer and observer at the same time, a kind of psychic gymnastics that allows changing each of these attitudes into the other, giving the ability to switch off consciousness, that is to say, "forgetting to order"—these are examples of the by no means trifling problems I have to struggle with in my everyday work, as many other composers probably do, too. In the light of what I have written here, it is obvious that I cannot give myself a precise and unequivocal answer to the question I asked at the beginning of this commentary.

Source

"Teoria a praktyka w pracy kompozytora," *Studia Estetyczne* no. 2, (1965): 128–33. Copyright Marcin Bogusławski. All rights reserved. Printed by permission. This text is interpolated with the typescript *Music in the 20th Century*. Copyright Witold Lutosławski Collection, Paul Sacher Foundation. All rights reserved. Printed by permission. Lutosławski presented the latter text in French at the first Music Biennale in Zagreb in 1961, and later—in the English version (no translator is credited)—as the first of five lectures he delivered during the composition course at the Berkshire Music Center in Tanglewood, Massachusetts, in the summer of 1962.

Notes

1. K. C. Lindsay and P. Vergo, eds., *Kandinsky: Complete Writings on Art* (Boston: Da Capo, 1982), 505–506.

2. See Pierre Schaeffer, *A la recherche d'une musique concrète* (Paris: Éditions du Seuil, 1952), chapter XVI—*L'objet musical*, 142–56.

❦

REFLECTING UPON THE ART OF COMPOSING

All my works written in recent years are evidence of the long process I had to go through to write the first of them—*Jeux vénitiens*. At the time *Jeux vénitiens* was composed, only seven years had passed since the completion of the Concerto for Orchestra, but already it seemed to me to belong to the distant past. Did I realize when writing the Concerto that in seven years time it would become something so distant to me? Of course; even more than that, I wanted this to happen as soon as possible. I expressed this idea in one of the statements published at that time: "As the technical means I have mastered so far are not sufficient to let me compose in the way I would like to, I write in the way I am capable of." This would have sounded a little bit pessimistic had I not had long years of work on the technique I needed behind me.

The rule quoted above was to serve me well until I was ready to start composing in a way at least close to what I sought. Therefore, the method I used while writing the Concerto had nothing in common with "quietism." Quietism, as I understand it, takes the elements lacking in a composing technique directly from outside, from the current idiom of the so-called avant-garde. This would not have made any sense in my case, as the fundamental principle of that idiom then was serialism, a doctrine based on assumptions entirely alien to me.

Under the circumstances, I was compelled to make efforts, almost completely on my own, to work out a technique suitable for my purpose. Such an attempt could be regarded as insane or at least naïve. But I would rather be the victim of my own illusions than give up any attempt at solving this challenging task.

Can I say today that this effort was worthwhile, that I have found what I have been looking for? Whenever I try to answer these questions, various sad thoughts enter my mind.

Perhaps the mechanism of composing is so illusive that it arouses a permanent feeling of dissatisfaction, which stimulates the artist to continuous efforts aimed at enriching and improving his means of expression. If so, it is comforting that the artist exposed to such difficulty never goes back to the same point. So I willingly accept such a situation and, apart from working on new compositions, I regard the work of experimenting with sounds as my daily bread.

Starting this work many years ago, I had to accept several facts, two of which were and continue to be of crucial significance to me. Firstly, that there exists no system of organization of sound pitch that would fully suit my aims, and that neither dodecaphony nor tonalism are of any use to me. Secondly, that there is no sound combination—whether horizontal or vertical—that would be without impact from the point of view of expression. Quite the contrary. Every single sound combination exerts a definite influence upon the listener. The nature of such influence can be studied only on the basis of the experience of the composer when imagining himself as a listener.

Taking these two, and several other, assumptions as a starting point I began my work by studying extreme phenomena in the sphere of harmonics within the traditional twelve-tone scale. These extreme phenomena are consonances containing all twelve sounds of the scale. Five Songs to poems of Kazimiera Iłłakowicz written in the years 1956–1958, serves as an example of the use of such consonances and of their classification and expressive values.

Twelve-tone chords have since become the principal element of the organization of pitch in a number of my compositions. Only in the last few years, when I have mastered the practical use of twelve-tone chords (which have nothing in common with dodecaphony), has the time come for various experiments with simpler sets, containing less than twelve sounds, monody included. This has been reflected in such compositions as Concerto for Cello and Orchestra (Introduction), Preludes and Fugue, *Les espaces du sommeil*, and *Mi-parti*. I think there is a lot more in this sphere. The task is immensely difficult and it is a long way from its successful solution.

The emphasis I have put in this essay on the means of expression, or the organization of pitch, or otherwise on the elements of compositional techniques, does not mean that I regard this side of music to be the most important. I firmly believe that the idea or the message of a work of art is indescribable unless one is unafraid to enter into meaningless diversions that have nothing to do with reality. "Language" (the language of art) is the only element in music about which one can safely speak and write. In doing this, one must remember, however, that it only approaches the core of things and never touches the essence.

Source

Biuletyn Muzyczny Polskiego Radia i Telewizji (Musical Bulletin of the Polish Radio and Television), no. 5-6, (1977): 21–22. Copyright Marcin Bogusławski. All rights reserved. Printed by permission.

THE COMPOSER AND THE LISTENER

The main purpose of a piece of music is that it should be experienced by the listener. Consequently it follows that a work of art is a complex phenomenon, the main part of which—according to the design of its purpose—is to play on the human mind. (I am here excluding all subordinate problems connected with art, and limit myself to the actual process of creation and reception.)

As a result of recognizing the psychological aspect of art as paramount, I am opposed to all those who consider the existence of a work by itself, independent of its being perceived, as the main aim of its being created. The score or recording are quite certainly necessary for the existence of a piece of music. However, they are not in themselves the actual musical work but only a stage in its realization, which is fully achieved only when the work is experienced by the listener. I understand the process of composing above all as the creation of a definite complex of psychological experiences for my listener, the fulfillment of which is on the whole extended throughout the greater number of performances of the same work.

This attitude, which has always seemed to me obvious, has certain important consequences for composing itself. One such consequence is, for example, that the only thing that is important and pertinent in a musical work is that which can help to produce a definite result as it is perceived. Thus, for instance, all elaborate methods of organizing musical material can only be of value if they produce a particular experience for the listener, as intended by the composer, even if this is only achieved after the work has been heard many times. I must emphasize that I am speaking of the listener undergoing a direct experience and not of him becoming aware of the actual organization of the musical material. I am thus on my guard against all experiments that would lead to a purely mathematical beauty in the arrangement of elements of a musical work. This particular concept of beauty is known to all those who have ever come into contact with mathematics. I do not intend to negate its existence or to deplore the delight it may give. However, I consider it to be a misunderstanding to realize this form of beauty in music. I do not wish to hear anything but the sound effects that result from the mathematical and quasi-mathematical operations to which a composer of today must turn.

It seems to me quite extraneous to discern in numbers and their arrangement some factor of equal importance to the actual perception, and which might be supposed to have some value in itself even when it has no perceptible influence on the sound progress of the work. An example of this kabalistic faith in numbers to which I am opposed, and in the laws governing them, might be one of the early electronic pieces where the composer works from a great number of simple sounds of frequencies that have been ordered in some simple way. This material, however, undergoes a series of operations that entirely destroy the order accepted initially. Consequently this order has no influence on the ultimate sound progress of the work and assumes a value that is merely symbolic in the composition.

In opposing the significance of numbers being raised above everything else in music, I do not, however, consider all mathematical operations of no use whatsoever. On the contrary, I often turn to mathematics, or rather to certain simple mathematical processes, in my composing. However, in all such operations I try never to lose sight of my basic aim, which is to compose the particular aesthetic experiences of my listener.

The word *listener* has been used here a number of times. It is thus high time to define more precisely what I have in mind using this word. This is particularly important for me, because I am aware that in using the word *listener* without explaining it more precisely, I am leaving what I have to say open to misinterpretation.

Here listener has nothing to do with the "average listener" or with any particular listener, or even with any one type of listener. Here listener is the creation of my own imagination, modeled on the basis of my long and continually enriched experience in the field of listening to music. I am perfectly well aware that my imagined listener is no typical listener, and that he is even probably very particular. For my work, however, he has one invaluable advantage: he is the one listener about whom I really know something. As such, he is an element absolutely necessary for me in composing music, since it would be impossible for me to imagine this process other than in conjunction with a constantly imagined perceiver. In this way, creation and perception intermingle and are elements of the same complex phenomenon.

From what I have said, it follows that the listener in the usual sense of this word would be completely eliminated from my efforts at composing and would not play any role in them. It would be possible perhaps to call such an attitude egoistical and even antisocial. I could not agree with such an evaluation and—on the contrary—I believe that in taking this attitude I take the shortest way to that supreme aim of an artist's fulfillment of his ethical duty to society. On what are these convictions based? By obeying the voice of my imagined listener, who is in reality myself, I am certain that I am on the way to fulfilling the desires of at least this one listener. But I surely have the right to hope that, however particular this imagined listener of mine may be, he is at least similar to many other real or actual listeners. It is on this that I base my supposition that the music I compose can be of some value for the listener, even though it was not written for this immediate aim.

If I were to proceed otherwise, that is, if I were to resign from following the voice of my imagined listener and try to guess the desires of real or actual listeners, I would be running the risk of introducing complete confusion into my work. This would happen because firstly, I do not believe it is possible to know anything concrete about the aesthetic desires of another person; and secondly, I consider one's own aesthetic desires and needs to be the only real compass in the work of a fully conscious and mature artist. In condemning myself by my own free will to forfeit this compass in favor of a chimera such as guessing the tastes and desires of others, I would fall victim to the illusion that I were performing some service for my listeners. Such procedure would essentially amount to deceiving these listeners, for the product of methods in which the supreme and decisive factor is not the conscience of the creator can only be false.

My imagined listener is simply the personification of the artistic conscience, and I hope that in following its demands I come closer than would otherwise be possible to the most important aim in the work of an artist: to give the truest form to what he has to communicate to others.

Source

Lutosławski, edited by Ove Nordwall (Stockholm: Edition Wilhelm Hansen, 1968), 119–24, translated from Swedish by Christopher Gibbs. 1968

AB Nordiska Musikförlaget. Printed by permission of Ehrlingförlagen AB, Stockholm, Sweden.

✧

SOME THOUGHTS ON THE PERCEPTION OF MUSIC

Many of us were tormented in childhood by the question of whether, for instance, the color green looks the same in our eyes as it does in the eyes of another person. Does my colleague see green when I see red? Have perhaps the green objects only their name in common, yet in the eyes of everybody they have a different color? Is there a possibility of objectively defining subjective experiences? This general question goes far beyond the sphere of visual phenomena and it provokes a whole mass of detailed questions. First and foremost we are interested here in those questions that concern the aural phenomena, particularly music. We enter a complicated domain that has not been investigated sufficiently by scholars, but is essential for the art of music. I refer here to the perception of a musical work.

I am not familiar with the literature on this subject and I have only occasionally met people who were engaged in pioneering psychological research into the area of perception of sound, for example, Milton Babbitt of the Columbia University and Princeton University. He demonstrated to me the sound-tests that he designed and recorded on tape in order to examine the differences in the perception of sound by different people. But, as I have already mentioned, I am unacquainted with the state of research into the perception of a musical work. Therefore, I want to share with you some thoughts resulting from my own experiences as both composer and listener.

I come back to the questions I asked at the beginning, transferring them in the realm of music. Is it possible to examine to what extent, similarly or differently, various people perceive the same sound-phenomena? I give up straight away any attempt to answer the question myself as to whether everybody hears in an identical way the tone-color of particular musical instruments, and whether my neighbor at a concert hears the timbre of, say, the oboe just as I do. I give up because this question, which does not differ much from the one about the color red or green I asked initially, goes beyond the realm of things it is possible to investigate and belongs to philosophy rather than to the psychophysiology of hearing. There are, however, a whole series of questions that we can answer, thanks to the experience acquired during years of hearing music and talking to those who listen to music.

Superficial observations allow me to assert that even quite simple, elementary sound-phenomena can be perceived by various people in different ways.

I emphasize that I have in mind here not various interpretations of essentially the same experiences of individual people, but the differences in the very *perception* of a given sound-phenomenon. In other words, while listening to the same sound-phenomenon, the individual may simply *hear* something different. For example, Milton Babbitt recorded a sound repeated several times at a high speed. When asked "How many sounds do you hear?" individual listeners gave different answers. Similar tests can be multiplied endlessly, and one would suppose that they would all justify our assertion of diversity of hearing even the simplest sound-phenomena by individual people. This assertion is all the more justified in relation to more complex sound-phenomena, in particular to complete musical works.

The perceptional apparatus of a listener to music is not perfect, even in cases of supreme musicality. The awareness of the imperfection of this apparatus is greater in more experienced listeners, that is, by those who have had more occasions to be disappointed with this apparatus. From a larger experience in listening to music there comes a distrust of one's own experiences and impressions acquired during listening, particularly to an unknown musical work for the first time. An experienced listener is aware of facts like the various degrees of concentration involved when listening to music. We register some moments in a work with complete clarity, whereas others escape our notice. This means that the second time we hear the same work it seems slightly different from the first time. This is because some of its moments reached our awareness more acutely, whereas the others passed unnoticed. Only after we listen a great many times does the image of the perceived work start to be fixed in our memory, and only then can we expect that this work will not surprise us any more. I will not embark upon a discussion as to whether we gain greater pleasure when we know more or less of the work. It certainly depends on its value. My point here was only to demonstrate the variety of sensations while listening to one and the same work by one and the same listener. If we note the variety of sensations by one person, then the sensations of different people must be all the more diverse.

This talk up to now has been about the outermost layer of music, that is, purely of its sound-content. Even on this purely material level, which is the easiest to describe and examine objectively, music can be, as we see, perceived in different ways.

The variety of perception greatly increases when we start to penetrate deeper layers of a musical work. More precisely—the variety increases when we move away from the purely acoustic sphere, when we reflect on the psychological side of musical sensations (I mean here the psychological reactions to particular stimuli provided by a musical work), and when we penetrate the realm of associations, that is, the extramusical interpretations of sensations the work produces. The differences in the perception of music in this layer (if it exists at all) are, of course, the greatest, and even diametrically opposed. Sometimes we encounter amazingly inconsistent reactions, according to the personal characteristics of particular listeners, the kind of education they have had, and the circumstances in which they listen to music. To illustrate my point, I will use examples taken from my own practice. After hearing the first performance of my Symphony no. 1 (I would describe its ultimate undertone—if I had to do it in extramusical terms—as serene), one of the older listeners remarked to me: "What an immensity of suffering!" Another listener described my Cello Concerto as a risky satire, and it was the only way in which he could explain for himself the excessive, as he put it, emotionalism of this work. As for myself, I never supposed that my work could be understood in any other way than seriously and straightforwardly, without any satiric allusions. One very famous artist, not a musician, found in my String Quartet—to my uttermost wonder—moments indicating a sense of humor. I don't consider myself to be deprived of such an emotion, but the Quartet would be, I suppose, the last work in which I would want to express humor.

Obviously the result from these few examples shows that an attempt to interpret music in an extramusical way can lead one astray and, instead of bringing people closer together it separates them; instead of uniting—it divides. We must definitely assert that music is not an unequivocal art if one can attach to it so many different meanings. Because of this unequivocalness, it is better to consider music as an asemantic art. Its sense, content, or message must remain indefinable with the help of the terms taken out of the realm of music itself and, as undefined, they should rather be considered one of the elements of a musical work, but not as its main and ultimate goal. If the introduction of the word *content* into the considerations on music has any sense, we must, in any case, consider that the elements of content and form closely intertwine in a musical work, so that it is impossible to isolate something that could be defined as its content.

Considerations of the supposed existence of the extramusical content in music are probably not important. The interpretation of music as an expression of "vital feelings" (if we use the wording of Stanisław Ignacy Witkiewicz[1]) is characteristic, especially for those listeners who are less acquainted with music. They feel uncertain in the realm of music when they cannot associate it immediately with better-known areas, such as feelings or human experiences, images and visual representations, etc.

However, even if we ignore misunderstandings that result from an erroneous interpretation or from an unsuitable approach to music by less experienced listeners, it is still possible to claim that music is an art in which it is difficult to enter into contact with the recipient and arouse reactions corresponding to the intentions of its authors.

It might seem that the conclusions resulting from my considerations can only be pessimistic for a composer: that he can not count on a proper understanding, that he risks a multitude of false interpretations, and that contact with a greater number of listeners is an unrealizable dream, etc.

This state of affairs does not fill me with pessimism. I accept the risk of misunderstanding or of false interpretations. A lavish reward for them is the fact that I apparently appeal to some people once they can find in my music something for them and receive it in accordance with my intentions.

I hope that the thoughts of a composer that I have presented here may result in some helpful suggestions for those who educate young people and for writers on music. I am not a specialist in these areas and I am not able to formulate any conclusions today. If any of you consider my ideas to be correct, and my views worth discussion, I shall be delighted.

Source

Manuscript in Polish. Copyright Witold Lutosławski Collection, Paul Sacher Foundation. All rights reserved. Printed by permission.

Note

1. Stanisław Ignacy Witkiewicz, pseudonym Witkacy (1885–1939), Polish writer, painter, philosopher, theoretician of art. The author of the theory of "pure form" in art, theatre, and poetry; the main representative of catastrophism in Polish literature. Witkiewicz committed suicide when the Soviet Red Army, according to the secret pact Ribbentrop-Molotov, invaded Poland on September 17, 1939.

SOUND LANGUAGE

The term *sound language* was for a long time quite unnecessary, namely in the period of tonal music. The tonal system—the major-minor system, as others call it—is a phenomenal construction, the result of the endeavors and inspiration of generations of composers, a creation that can unhesitatingly be acknowledged as perfect. Yet some of the great composers of the tonal period such as Chopin, Liszt, or Wagner make us think that they sometimes wanted to go beyond the tonal system. In their music some fragments tend toward total chromaticism. As we all know, this was accomplished sometime during the first decades of our century when the problem of the sound language arose. Arnold Schoenberg believed that his twelve-tone technique would replace the tonal system. I can't understand how one could imagine that one single composer's creation, even one as ingenious as dodecaphony, could replace the inspiration of a number of musical geniuses. So it's no wonder that Schoenberg's prediction that his system would determine German music for the next hundred years hasn't come true. The situation is just the opposite: up until now there has been no single common convention for all composers of our time. On the other hand, the need for order has induced some composers to work out their own individual system. An extremely convincing example of such a system will finally result in a common convention, an indispensable convention for a new classical period to come into being in the future.

The topic of this text is to look at my work as an individual sound language.

As we know, a sound language can be divided in two parts: organization of pitch and organization of time. The first, in turn, may be divided further in two: vertical, that is, harmony, and horizontal, that is, melody. The organization of time may concern microtime, that is, rhythm, and macrotime, that is, form.

After the first performance of my First Symphony (1947), which was in some ways the sum of my youthful experience, I realized that the sound language I used in it had no future, no possibility for development, which means it could not accomplish what I wanted. The sound language of my First Symphony can be defined as posttonal. Here is the beginning of its slow movement (see *Poco adagio*, figure 39).

I decided to begin working on a sound language that would fit a vision (although rather vague) of my possible future works. There were no models that could help me in this work. I had to do it all myself. I began by studying the harmonic and melodic possibilities of eight-note scales. Some of them are rather unusual, for example, seven chromatic steps plus one minor third. Example 1-39 is the first theme of my Overture for Strings (1949).

I soon abandoned the work on scales, which brought no interesting results and I concentrated on harmony. I began working on twelve-note chords. I found a great variety of harmony among them when following a simple rule: the fewer kinds of intervals between the neighboring notes of the chord, the more characteristic the result is. For example, among the chords constructed of two kinds of intervals, there is a great variety enabling the creation of sharp contrasts. As an illustration, see the last of Five Songs to the poems of Kazimiera Iłłakowicz, which I wrote only in the late 1950s. The text is composed of two stanzas. In the first, mention is made of church bells that are singing, the second refers to church bells that are angry. The harmony of the whole song consists only of two twelve-note chords, according to the two contrasting stanzas of the text (see Five Songs, "Dzwony cerkiewne" [Orthodox Church Bells]).

Example 1-39.   Overture for Strings, Figs. 1–2. Copyright Polish Musical Edition, Kraków. Printed by permission.

This cycle of Five Songs was the first completed concert piece in which I used the results of my work on harmony. Up until then I had used them only in some of my incidental music for the theatre.

From 1945 to 1955 I wrote quite a number of works considered "functional music": easy pieces for piano for music schools, children's songs for radio broadcasts, pieces for small orchestras, etc. For my functional music, which was my marginal activity, I had to work out a special sound language, which had nothing to do with my main work. This functional language consists of simple diatonic melodies, sometimes taken from the folklore material, combined with some unconventional harmonies and sometimes nontonal counterpoints. This kind of language I used almost exclusively to compose functional music. Here is an example, one of the Dance Preludes for clarinet and piano (1954) I composed for music schools (see Third Dance Prelude).

In 1950 Witold Rowicki—the chief conductor of the newly organized Warsaw Philharmonic Orchestra—asked me to compose something for them. The sound language I was still working on was then far from being ready to be used. So I decided to use a piece of my functional language for the Warsaw Philharmonic. The Polish folklore tunes were used as the raw material to compose neo-Baroque music in a large-scale form. The work in question is my Concerto for Orchestra. In spite of the fact that it is probably the most often performed piece of mine, I always think of it as a marginal work: I composed it as I was then able to, and not as I should really like. That is why there is such a difference between the Concerto for Orchestra and for example, Five Songs. Here is a fragment of the final movement from the Concerto for Orchestra (see *Allegro giusto*—three measures after figure 61 up to figure 63).

The piece that can be placed between the Concerto for Orchestra and Five Songs and the following pieces is *Musique funèbre* for string orchestra, in which I used both new procedures, that is, the results of my work on the sound language and some elements of my functional technique, but the latter to a small extent. Although the piece is based on a twelve-tone row, it has nothing to do with Schoenberg's method (see *Musique funèbre*, Prologue, figures 1–15).

At the end of the 1950s, I began writing a cycle of pieces for symphony orchestra, which I called Postludes, as if pointing out the phenomenon of the declining years of the symphony orchestra. It did not mean that I had decided not to compose for a symphony orchestra any more. It was just the statement of the fact that the symphony orchestra is a rather anachronistic instrument. In spite of the fact that I am deeply attached to all orchestra instruments and I hardly imagine my work without them, I think of them rather like a collection of museum specimens.

The cycle of Postludes has never been completed, because in the course of the work on them, something happened that had importance to my possible future work. Every composer knows that we sometimes listen to music in a quite different way from other people. Music actually heard may be only an impulse to set in motion our imagination. We do not hear the music really played, but rather what is happening in our imagination. That was exactly my case when I heard on the radio a short fragment of John Cage's second Piano Concerto.[1] The use of the element of chance opened for me a way to use a lot of musical ideas, that were kept "in stock" in my imagination without any way to use them. It was not a direct influence of Cage's music, but the impulse, which enabled me to use my own possibilities. So I wrote to him that he was a spark thrown on a barrel of gunpowder inside me. In fact my music is not at all similar to Cage's. No wonder, bearing in mind my approach to the role of the element of chance in music, which is just the opposite of Cage's. In his music, the element of chance is partly the author of the work, the role of the composer being reduced to organizing the circumstances in which the element of chance is to act. I don't want to resign from the total authorship of my music. And the music composed by the element of chance does not interest me. So what is the element of chance in my music for? It is a factor that can considerably enrich the repertoire of the means of expression, especially in what I have called microtime, that is, rhythm. The rhythms that result from the introduction of the element of chance are very sophisticated and it is impossible to achieve them in any other way. And they are not difficult to perform. Another advantage of this kind of technique is the restoring of the pleasure of music making. The most complex textures and rhythms are achieved by the performers with no effort. The weakness of many works composed in the last decades is their difficulty, which alienates the performer from the composer and his music. The most important feature of my aleatoric music (i.e., my music with the element of chance) is the full control of the pitch organization, particularly over its harmony. To explain how this is possible would take too much time. Anyway, this control is for me a condition *sine qua non*. In other words, the music in which the harmony is left to chance does not interest me. Here are some examples of my music with the element of chance: (see Symphony no. 2, *Hésitant*, figures 1–2; *Livre pour orchestre*, *First Intermède*, figure 110).

In my music there is no improvisation. Everything is precisely written down and it is to be faithfully performed. The difference in playing such music compared with music with bar line and meter consists of the lack of the common division in time in particular parts of an ensemble. Every member of the ensemble performs his part as if alone.

Now a few sentences about the horizontal organization of pitch, that is, about melody. The work on melody was somewhat abandoned at the beginning of our century. It was the reaction against melody used and abused during the Romantic period. I see some positive results of this, for instance drawing the attention of composers to other elements of the sound language such as harmony, texture, rhythm, and color. Some composers made very important discoveries in these areas. Since then melody has been treated by composers with disdain. It may have been justified, but it lasted more than eighty years and, in my opinion, it is time to work on a new melody, which has always been a powerful element of music. I am not speaking of a possible return to old kind of melodies, that is, diatonic and tonal. I don't believe in going backward in the arts. I believe that there are plenty of ways to create new kinds of melodies within the chromatic totality. One of my methods of composing melodies now is to use a limited number of kinds of intervals between the notes of the melody. The character of a melody may depend in a large part on such a choice. The strongly contrasting pairs of intervals are for example, minor second—tritone and major second—perfect fourth or fifth. Here are the examples: the first pair (see the first theme of my Fugue from Preludes & Fugue for thirteen solo strings), the second pair (see a fragment of the second movement of *Chain 2* for violin and orchestra). It does not mean that I always compose my melodies in this way. It is only an example of one method.

Finally some thoughts about the macrotime, that is, the form. The large-scale closed forms have always been the object of my preoccupation. I have composed four symphonies, one concerto for orchestra, two concertos for solo instruments and orchestra, and other pieces in large-scale closed forms, for example, *Livre pour orchestre*. My concept of such a form is based on my experience as a listener. The large-scale form should have the right duration and the right portion of musical content. One example of such a form is all Haydn's symphonies. Each has only one main movement, namely the first. This movement requires more concentration when listening to it than the later movements, the last being often light, cheerful, lively music. It makes us think that Haydn composed especially for the listening capability of his audience. He composed his symphonies for the court. The listeners there were probably more attentive at the beginning of a symphony and less so toward the end of it. The duration of his symphonies and the portion of the musical substance were probably ideal for those circumstances. They are also ideal for my way of listening to music as far as the portion of the musical content is concerned. The symphonies of Brahms, on the other hand, always contain two main movements. In spite of the fact that I am a great fan of Brahms's music, I must avow that two main movements in a symphony make the work somewhat overloaded and exhaust my ability to perceive music afterwards. So I decided to compose my large-scale closed forms in two movements, the second being the main one. The first movement is just to prepare the listener for a more important experience, that is, the second movement. Thus, the first is composed of short episodes whose musical plot doesn't develop and doesn't lead to any climax. The result is that after a few such episodes, the listener may get impatient and expect that something important must finally happen. And this is the right moment to produce the main movement, whose perception requires a higher degree of concentration on the part of the listener. I can't demonstrate it by a recorded example, as it would require at least half an hour. Please listen to one of the episodes of the first movement of my Third Symphony (see third episode).

Source

Typescript in English. Copyright Witold Lutosławski Collection, Paul Sacher Foundation. All rights reserved. Printed by permission. The information on the file with Lutosławski's occasional speeches indicates that he presented this text during his visit in Japan in 1993 when he was receiving the Kyoto Prize.

Note

1. Concert for Piano and Orchestra (1957–1958).

· 2 ·

On His Own Works

❧

COMMENTS ON EARLY WORKS (1934–1954)

Sonata for Piano (1934)

This work was written during my studies with Maliszewski. A traditional sonata form is connected here with post-Impressionist harmony and texture. It is the composer's first larger work.

Symphonic Variations (1936–1938)

This is the work with which the author[1] (then twenty-six years old) made his début in 1939 at the musical festival in Kraków. The style of the work is, perhaps, far from being crystallized. Yet in spite of that, one could talk, on the evidence of the Symphonic Variations, about the artistic maturity of their young author, which is first and foremost thanks to a richly developed orchestral palette as well as a consistent and well-balanced architecture.

Variations on a Theme of Paganini for Two Pianos (1941)

This is a free paraphrase of the Twenty-fourth Caprice of Paganini. The virtuoso piano texture and colorful harmonies make this composition a typical, brilliant stage turn.

Trio for Oboe, Clarinet, and Bassoon (1945)

This is an attempt at a free atonal technique, a result of studies carried out during the war. Sharp, harsh harmonies, Neoclassical form, and rhythm characterize this work.

The Early Pieces for Young People

I wrote the first pieces for young people in 1945. This was a cycle of piano miniatures, *Melodie ludowe* (Folk Melodies), intended to be used at music schools. I wanted to make the rich melodies of Polish folklore accessible to the youngest performers. Such a piece did not exist in any of our Polish compositions. A cycle of twelve folk melodies from various regions of Poland was elaborated into an easy piano texture, principally for school use. Diatonic folk melodies, kept almost in their authentic form, are accompanied by a second, mostly nondiatonic melodic line or chords. The character of this elaboration is such as to introduce a young performer into the contemporary sound-world.

What surprised me was the fact that adult pianists started to play the Folk Melodies at concerts soon after they had been published. The first to include them in his repertoire was Prof. Drzewiecki and I know that the Folk Melodies are still played by other Polish and foreign pianists.

I started writing genuine music for children a bit later, with a cycle of songs that were intended to be sung by children. The poems of Julian Tuwim served as texts. The genuine charm and extraordinary artistry of their composition made an impression on me. Let us just read the first text of Tuwim's "Taniec" (Dance) in my collection of children's songs. In these eight lines we have a real drama in miniature, with its exposition, conflict, and denouement. I am emphasizing this so much in order to explain that while I was dealing with such small but accomplished Tuwim masterpieces, I could find my own way of writing music for children more easily.

In the following years I wrote many little songs for children and music for children's radio plays. Some of them are published, such as—for instance—*Słomkowy łańcuszek* (Chain of Straw) for voices, with the accompaniment of a small ensemble of brass instruments.

Słomkowy łańcuszek (Chain of Straw, 1951)

The title *Chain of Straw* refers, in fact, to the last one of my Eight Children's Pieces. The first seven are original songs ("W polu grusza stała" [A pear tree stood in the field] to the lyrics of Janina Porazińska, and "Rosła kalina" [A guelder-rose grew] to the words of Teofil Lenartowicz) or new arrangements of generally known melodies. The actual *Chain of Straw* was written in the form of a theme with variations to the words of Lucyna Krzemieniecka. Particular variations consist of stories of animals, plants, and objects that have to do with straw. Thus, in the introduction, which constitutes the theme of the variations, the children, who are busy cutting the chain of straw for a Christmas tree, answer a question about what the straw is used for. Then, in the succeeding variations: a little well, a rose bush, a dog, a little flower, and a cow speak. The entirety was written for the Children's Radio Theatre in Warsaw, where it was premiered under the composer's direction.

In my work for the radio I sometimes had the opportunity to be in touch with the work of Hanna Januszewska, today's winner of a literary prize for creativity for children. It was always a treat to write music to her words, which were full of true poetry.

My children's songs were most often performed on the radio by Janina Godlewska, and on the concert stages by Maria Drewniakówna. However, as far as the six children's songs to Tuwim's words are concerned, their best performers are the children themselves. On the occasion of Children's Day I was able to record these songs with a children's ensemble from one of Warsaw's primary schools.

Symphony No. 1 (1947)

This symphony distinguishes itself by its concise, rigorous construction based on clear, characteristic themes submitted to the classical rules of development. A rich instrumentation here serves somewhat constructivist, formal purposes, rather than as a virtuoso display.

The first ideas for this work date from before the war, although it was fully realized only eight years later (in 1947). An obvious obstacle for the author in composing it was the war and the difficult early postwar years. The musical language of this symphony consists of a development of the language of the Symphonic Variations toward a greater sharpness or bluntness of sound. Although the instrumental forces are not deprived, as in the Symphonic Variations, of certain spectacular features, they fall into line, to a much greater degree, with the formal construction of the whole. Some late "Neoclassical" elements of style in this work reveal influences from Roussel.

The first movement is written in sonata form with a slightly shortened recapitulation. The first, seemingly playful theme, the beginning of which is played by the trumpet against the background of the orchestra (see figures 1–2), contrasts with the second, more melodious theme, presented by the strings, which is an echo of Brahmsian themes (see figures 6–9). The elements of the first theme serve as material for elaboration, which initially has the form of a fugato (*p*) in the woodwind against the "cobweb" of the trills of strings and the figurations of piano, harp, and celesta. Later on, bigger orchestral groupings appear in order to precede the recapitulation with a short reminiscence of the beginning of the second theme in *ff* by the whole orchestra. The shortened recapitulation contains all the elements of the exposition, intensified in their dynamics and instrumentation, which stresses its closing character.

The slow, second movements starts with a melodious, yet serious and concentrated first theme kept in dark colors (horn against the strings, see figures
39–40) and contrasting with a sarcastic second theme (oboe against interrupted
pizzicato chords prolonged by trills of the strings and the tremolandos of a drum,
see figures 45–46), which brings to mind Prokofiev's moods. The side phrase of
the second theme (first violins against two horns, see figures 49–51) provides material for a developing, longer crescendo that leads to a recapitulation of the first
theme, which appears here in an extended form and is intoned by the strings.

Allegro misterioso has a form close to a classical scherzo (simplified as A B
A B C A B), although it is totally lacking a playful character and is kept, particularly at its beginning, in dark colors.

The Finale (*Allegro vivace*) has again a sonata form without elaboration.
Some elements of the latter appear in the recapitulation and in the coda. A
vivid, serene character prevails here; the themes are characterized by a liveliness and momentum that are typical of the finales of the symphonies from the
classical period.

Stefan Jarociński once described Symphony no. 1 as probably the only
example of a "fauvism" in Polish music.

Overture for Strings (1949)

The overture is a short piece based on a formal scheme close to the first movement of sonata form. In the exposition and in the recapitulation, the whole
musical material is based on eight-note rows treated modally. The middle
part—the development—is freely atonal.

Little Suite for Chamber Orchestra (1950)

This work was commissioned by Polish Radio for a small orchestra that had in
its repertoire elaborations of Polish musical folklore written particularly for this
orchestra. The printed score is the second version of this piece prepared for a
regular symphony orchestra. The author treated the original folk themes from
southern Poland freely, and gave them a harmonic and instrumental setting that
is not typical of the folk music. The movements are Pipe, Hurray Polka, Little
Song, and Dance.

Silesian Triptych (1951)

Three songs from southwestern Poland served the composer as material for free
paraphrasing. The harmonic and instrumental features show that here we are
concerned with a somewhat subjective, individual look at folklore rather than

with its faithful interpretation. The folk texts, full of genuine charm, describe the feelings of a jilted girl: in the first song—her anger, in the second—her sorrow, and in the third—her sneering at a boy who is marrying for money.

Bukoliki (Bucolics) for Piano (1952)

Five short pieces that developed, so to speak, out of the idea of Folk Melodies. The folk themes from the Kurpie region became freely transformed and elaborated here, as in the Folk Melodies. These miniatures are also written with young performers in mind.

Preludia taneczne (Dance Preludes) for Clarinet in B Flat and Piano (1954)

This piece, written originally for clarinet and piano, was subsequently arranged for clarinet and small orchestra (without wind instruments). It is the last piece of the "folkloristic" series. The folk themes (from western Poland) are treated with complete freedom and never appear in their original form. A characteristic feature of the construction of the Preludes is a "metrical dualism," that is, frequent separation of the time signature for the solo instrument and the orchestra.

Source

Manuscript in Polish. Copyright Witold Lutosławski Collection, Paul Sacher Foundation. All rights reserved. Printed by permission.

Note

1. Here, and in other similar instances, Lutosławski used the word "the author" referring to himself. He most probably meant this and other notes on his works to be published in concert programs or in interviews.

❧

CONCERTO FOR ORCHESTRA (1950–1954)

While writing Folk Melodies, a piano cycle for young people, the author started a series of works connected with Polish musical folklore (these consist of: Little Suite, *Silesian Triptych*, *Bucolics*, and others). The Concerto for Orchestra is a result of experiences acquired during this work. However, the use of folklore is different here from previous compositions. The folk motifs serve the author only as "bricks" for building a large form which, considered on its own, has nothing in common with folklore. A colorful orchestration rich in various combinations gives the orchestral ensemble the occasion for a versatile display. The name *concerto* is fully justified by this fact. The whole is divided into three movements: I. *Intrada*, II. *Capriccio notturno e Arioso*, III. *Passacaglia, toccata, e corale.*

Source

Manuscript in Polish. Copyright Witold Lutosławski Collection, Paul Sacher Foundation. All rights reserved. Printed by permission.

∽

In 1945 the Polish Music Publishing Company, which had just been established, asked me to compose a cycle of easy pieces based on Polish folk song and dance themes. I readily accepted this proposition and began for the first time to introduce elements of folk music into my work. Soon afterward I accepted several similar commissions and in this way I came to compose a series of works based on Polish folk tunes. Among these are my Little Suite for orchestra, *Bucolics* for piano, etc. I did not attach any greater importance to these works and treated them merely as a sideline to my real work as a composer. At this time I was busy working above all on my First Symphony and later on an Overture for Strings and on problems of compositional technique that were entirely unconnected with folk music. At the same time, however, the whole series of my functional pieces based on folk themes gave me the possibility of developing a style that, though narrow and limited, was nevertheless characteristic enough. This mainly involved blending simple diatonic motifs with chromatic atonal counterpoint, and with nonfunctional, multicolored, capricious harmonies. The rhythmic transformation of these motifs, and the polymetrical texture resulting from them, together with the accompanying elements, are a part of the characteristic style that I have mentioned. In doing all this, I thought at the time that this marginal style would not be entirely fruitless and that despite its having come into being while I was writing typical functional music, I could possibly make use of it in writing something more serious. A stable opportunity for putting this into practice soon turned up. This was in 1950. The director of the Warsaw Philharmonic Orchestra, Witold Rowicki, asked me to write something especially for his new ensemble. This was to be something not difficult, but which could, however, give the young orchestra an opportunity to show its qualities. I started to work on the new score, not realizing that I was to spend nearly four years on it. Folk music and all that follows, of which I have already spoken, were used in my new work. Folk music in this work, however, was merely a raw material used to build a large musical form of several movements that does not in the least originate either from folk songs or from folk dances. A work came into being that I could not help including among my most important works as a result of my episodic symbiosis with folk music and in a way that was somewhat unexpected for me. This work is the Concerto for Orchestra. It seems to me that my possibilities of making use of folk themes have been almost completely exhausted in this score. Since my Concerto I have only written one piece based on folk music—Dance Preludes for clarinet and orchestra. In my subsequent works: *Musique funèbre, Jeux vénitiens, Trois poèmes d'Henri Michaux*, String Quartet, etc., all that had long been the subject of my thought and study found expression, and this had nothing to do with folk music.

Source

Ove Nordwall, ed., *Lutosławski* (Stockholm: Edition Wilhelm Hansen, 1968), 31–35. Copyright 1968, AB Nordiska Musikförlaget. Printed by permission of Ehrlingförlagen AB, Stockholm, Sweden.

FIVE SONGS TO POEMS OF KAZIMIERA IŁŁAKOWICZ (1956–1957)

This work can be called a study in twelve tones. Indeed, the melodic line is always accompanied by moving harmonic backgrounds based on the chords that contain all twelve tones of the scale. The composer is modeling the structure of these chords and, consequently, their expressive qualities, in such a way as to obtain the impact he intended, which strictly results from the texts used. Hence the emphatic physiognomy of each of the Five Songs and the sharp contrasts between them.

Source

Manuscript in Polish. Copyright Witold Lutosławski Collection, Paul Sacher Foundation. All rights reserved. Printed by permission.

As far as I am concerned, it would be impossible to write even the smallest composition without carefully considering the purely sensual reaction to the vertical and horizontal arrangements of the sounds. It is for this reason that I greet skeptically the assertion that harmony as an element of musical creation has disappeared; what is more, I believe that it is only now that we are liberating ourselves from the conventions of the tonal system that we can comprehend all the wealth of harmonic possibilities available in the chromatic scale.

These problems (quite unpopular opinions today) preoccupied me particularly when I was writing the Five Songs. . . . I put aside everything else in this work to concentrate solely on the expressive and coloristic possibilities of twelve-tone chords in their manifold variations—whence the homophonic texture, the traditional, static rhythm, and finally the choice of "infantile" texts calling for a simplified, lapidary musical interpretation.

Source

Warsaw Autumn Festival 1960, Program Book (French version), 27–28. Quoted according to Steven Stucky, *Lutosławski and His Music* (Cambridge, UK: Cambridge University Press, 1981), 65–66. Reprinted by permission.

MUSIQUE FUNÈBRE (1954–1958): IMPROVISATIONS ON A GIVEN THEME

Witold Lutosławski sketched in the background to his musical style in a letter to the editor of the periodical Nutida musik.

Thank you for your agreeable suggestion that I should write an article for your periodical. I very much wanted to do this. However, you wish me to describe the current artistic situation from my own point of view, to formulate a program for a creative artist, and to describe my *Musique funèbre*. I must confess straight away that this is a task widely beyond my capabilities: I am neither a musicologist nor a theoretician, and I have no program that is sufficiently premeditated as to be publishable. Apart from this, I cannot help saying frankly that a composer who theorizes too much, who talks too much of artistic programs and of musical perspectives of the future, always seems to me somewhat ridiculous. Music must be able to fend for itself, and if it cannot, then so much the worse for its composer. But no program, no theories can save it. I think that there are rather too many loquacious composers today who only compose examples for use in polemical debates. I am rather tired of this situation, and what interests me most at present are the works that exist in their own right, independent of their theoretical or historical significance.

Of course, this does not mean that I do not reflect upon the musical problems of our time, and if you have no objection, I will write a few of my thoughts here.

As we all know, musical language has gone through an interesting process during recent decades. One could call it *a successive blockade of the aural factor* in the various elements of musical language. In the field of harmony it took place as early as Schoenberg, when he placed the sequence of notes, and above all the construction of vertical formations, under numerical laws, that is, by "serializing" them. The actual serialization of the melodic element did not take place until Webern, however.

Messiaen's well-known Study (*Mode de valeurs et d'intensités*, 1949) inspired the composers of the youngest generation to attack other musical elements in the same way: rhythm, dynamics, tone color, etc. Their subjection to numerical laws through the use of successive metamorphosis totally eliminates the leading role of the aural factor in the actual forming of this music. In other words, this subjection neutralizes all these elements for the ear successively, makes them apathetic, and—if I may express myself in this way—places the experience of a musical work outside the realm of human sensibility. It goes without saying that every musical work has an aural side. The question is, however, whether it is the result of a certain process outside of the work, or whether it constitutes one of the factors that direct the creative process. At present we are witnessing the overthrow of the actual concept of musical creativity, which up to now (at least in "learned" European music) has been regarded as a more or less unalterable and fixed phenomenon. This is the result of the introduction of the chance factor, which occasionally leads to a practically infinite number of versions of the same passage.

Some people are indignant or even horrified over this situation. They see in it nothing other than the tendency of art towards conscious self-destruction. Personally, I am neither sufficiently pessimistic nor puritanical to be able to share these feelings. I wonder all the same where this process will lead the music of our time, or at least those who are guiding it on this path. One of the avant-gardists said to me once that in his opinion neither music nor any other form of art would exist among men in the future. One has to admit that this attitude is consistent. Webern comes easily to mind in this context when he said that his music "is on the way towards silence." If this is really the case, then one cannot ignore the compositions that indicate this process, from Webern's first appearance up to today. These works lack greatness perhaps, but one would have to be suffering from an acute lack of sensibility not to recognize elements of real beauty in them.

Is this the only positive aspect of the music of our time? Are we to consider it otherwise doomed to final destruction?

Apart from electronic music, the appearance of which suddenly threw a ray of light across this rather somber picture, yet one more thing comes to mind. The process mentioned above concerns only one part of the music of our time. I cannot limit its history to the age of serialism, and look down upon everything else as the remnants of bygone epochs, as many people wish to do. Schoenberg-Debussy does not at all mean the same thing to me as the two opposite poles "future-past." These two names actually represent the births of two equally vital and essentially different traditions. On the other side of Schoenberg and the serialists, for example, there are names like Stravinsky, Bartók, Messiaen, and Varèse. In contrast to the serialists, these represent an understanding of music based on the aural factor. I attach an importance to this factor, which is still in the front rank (especially if one still remains in the field of the traditional twelve-tone scale), and I look upon the belittling of its significance merely as a passing phenomenon that has chiefly assisted an escape from the traditional scale.

In this scale we find, in fact, intervals that differ from one another not only in the number of semitones they cover, but also through quite specific qualities, independent of the question of dimensions. These qualities, which are undoubtedly closely connected with the construction of the ear, and probably with the nervous system too, allow me to differentiate a fifth from a third not only as "larger," but also above all as something "qualitatively" different. A few simple consequences of this are: the comprehension of note sequence and the vertical distribution of notes as chiefly psychical impulse networks, which differ qualitatively from one another, and not as the reproduction of numerical proportions. In my opinion, it is impossible to remove the qualitative differences from the intervals in the twelve-tone scale. It is for this reason that Schoenberg's idea of creating a technique that disregards these differences has always seemed to me to have something provisional about it. Today it is possible to produce all the scales one wants with the help of electronic generators, and consequently scales whose intervals do not differ qualitatively from each other. Hence my conviction that serialism (if only pitch is implied), despite its colossal significance in the history of music, is today a completed episode, and that a continuation of it—inside the twelve-tone scale framework at any rate—would be an anachronism.

Electronic music has helped us to bypass the traditional scale. It has also given us the hope of being able to solve the problem of the instrument. It gives us the possibility of creating a completely new tonal world and it also forces us to see the traditional scale in an entirely new light. This lies, in my opinion, in the observance of the qualitative differences between the intervals. This by no means implies that we have absolutely got to go back to a new way of refreshing and reviving tonality. On the contrary, I believe that we have arrived at a moment when everything is once again to be discovered within the scope of the twelve-tone scale, just as all still remains to be discovered outside this scale at the point to which the ideas behind serialism have indirectly brought us.

I am aware that I have been far from being able to answer any one single question with what I have written above. Regard my reflections rather as "improvisations on a given theme."

Source

W. Lutosławski, "Improvisations on a Given Theme" trans. by Christopher Gibbs, in Ove Nordwall, ed., *Lutosławski* (Stockholm: Edition Wilhelm Hansen, 1968), 49–56. Copyright 1968 AB Nordiska Musikförlaget. Printed by permission of Ehrlingförlagen AB, Stockholm, Sweden. This text was originally published in Swedish in *Nutida musik* 1959/1960.

∽

In dedicating my *Musique funèbre* to the memory of Béla Bartók, I have wished, within the limits of my capabilities, to honor the tenth anniversary of the death of the great composer. Whilst writing this piece I have not sought inspiration amongst Bartók's own music, and any eventual resemblances that may appear in *Musique funèbre* are unintentional. And if these resemblances do really exist, then this proves once again the undeniable fact that studying the works of Bartók has been one of the fundamental lessons to be taken by the majority of composers of my generation.

Musique funèbre is a work in one movement, composed of four successive sections: Prologue, Metamorphoses, Apogeum, and Epilogue. The Prologue, which is constructed in the form of alternating several-part canons (two, three, four, six, and eight-part), is based on the twelve-tone row. This series, which only includes two intervals, (tritone and minor second), guarantees the harmonic homogeneity of the work.

The Metamorphoses begin with the slow rhythm of the Prologue, but as they unfold, they attain a violent *presto*, due to the division of rhythmical values. The Apogeum, the culminating point of the work, is characteristic in its harmonic structure, based on chords comprising all the twelve-tones of the scale. The twelve parts are gradually drawn toward the middle register where they form a unison, and it is with this that the Epilogue commences, *fortissimo*.

This final section, in which the structure is analogous to that of the Prologue, returns to the initial slow rhythm. The canons appear here first in their most complex form (eight-part), and then simplify by degrees (becoming six, four, and two-part respectively), and finally leave the last word to a solo violoncello.

The work was written for a normal string orchestra (forty-four to sixty-six musicians) divided into ten sections: first, second, third, and fourth violins, first and second violas, first and second cellos, and first and second double basses.

Source

Ove Nordwall, ed., *Lutosławski* (Stockholm: Edition Wilhelm Hansen, 1968), 57. Copyright 1968 AB Nordiska Musikförlaget. Printed by permission of Ehrlingförlagen AB, Stockholm, Sweden.

❧

JEUX VÉNITIENS (1960–1961)

It is in my piece *Jeux vénitiens* that I made use of certain elements of aleatory technique. The loosening of time connections between sounds is not—as it may seem—a great innovation. And yet its consequences may have an enormous importance for the composer's work. I have in mind both the possibility of a great enrichment of the rhythmical side of the work without increasing the difficulties of performing, as well as facilitating free and individualized playing on the part of particular performers within the framework of an ensemble. These elements of aleatory technique have attracted me above all. They open up a way for me to realize quite a number of sound visions that otherwise would have remained forever in my imagination.

On the other hand, I am not interested in regarding the chance factor as the most important in determining the form of a composition, or even the element of surprise in regard to the listener, performer, and even the composer himself through every consecutive and unforeseeable version of the work.

In my composition, the composer still remains the leading factor, and the introduction of the chance element in a strictly fixed range is merely a way of proceeding and not an end in itself.

The manner of performance I intend for my new work suggested the word "jeux" in its title. I have called it "vénitiens" because its first performance took place in Venice during the festival of contemporary music in April 1961.

Source

Ove Nordwall, ed., *Lutosławski* (Stockholm: Edition Wilhelm Hansen, 1968), 67–69. Copyright 1968 AB Nordiska Musikförlaget. Printed by permission of Ehrlingförlagen AB, Stockholm, Sweden.

❦

TROIS POÈMES D'HENRI MICHAUX (1961–1963)

I chose these three poems after I had already made a general outline of the entire work. The texts of the chosen poems then influenced the detailed development of the musical form. The verse, its sense and construction, and even particular words, had to exert an influence on the music of my composition. This was, moreover, as I had intended. If I had proceeded otherwise, if the words of the text were merely one more sound-element of the music, this would be a misuse of the poetry and artistically false, and at any rate it would be a wrong approach.

As I have said, I had already made a general outline of my work when I chose the texts. On what did this choice depend, and what influenced me in choosing these texts? In order to find an answer to this question more easily let us examine the actual texts of Michaux's poems.

The first—"Pensées"—briefly considers the theme of human thought. It is dominated by a skeptical tone from the first line, "Penser, vivre, mer peu distincte" (To think, to live, an indiscernible sea), to the last, in which thoughts are compared to "dust" that only exists "poussières pour nous distraire et nous éparpiller la vie" (to distract us and to scatter our life). Only during a short passage in the middle verse are we momentarily animated by a vision of "pensées à la nage merveilleuse qui glissez en nous, entre nous, loin de nous" (thoughts of marvelous swimming that slides in us, between us, far from us).

The second movement of my work is in sharp contrast to this introductory and reflective part. This part, because of its violent character and fast development leading to a dramatic climax, fulfills a role within the entire composition that is similar to that played by the development of conflict and the catastrophe in classical tragedy. Michaux's grotesque and macabre poem "Le grand combat" (The Great Fight) provides the text for this movement. Certain words in this poem have been invented by the poet. These innovations are, however, entirely comprehensible, as they are placed among ordinary words. And the quality of their sounds suggests their meaning: "Il l'emparouille et l'endosque contre terre." The fight ends in bloodshed. The words "Fouille, dans la marmite de son ventre est un grand secret" (Excavate his belly, it holds a great secret) conjure up an image of the shouts of an enraged crowd that ruthlessly follows the course of "the great fight."

The third movement provides a complete relaxation of the tension. Here the text is provided by a poem of resignation and a seeming acceptance of human fate: "Repos dans le malheur" (Rest in sorrow). "Dans ta lumière,

dans ton ampleur, dans ton horreur, je m'abandonne" (In your light, in your
fullness, in your dread, I abandon myself)—these are the words with which
the poet ends his ambiguous apostrophe to sorrow. [Sorrow is not the right
word for *malheur*. On the other hand "misfortune" sounds a little "materialistic."—WL] He makes a pact with it and dedicates his entire self to pay the
price involved.

Here I will not enter into an analysis of the music of my composition.
Like every composer, I hope that the music will explain itself. I merely wish
to draw attention to three points: firstly, the vocal part includes other uses of
the human voice apart from singing, such as shrieks, speech, and whispering. Here the interpretation of each vocal part has been clearly foreseen and
notated. Secondly, I would like to draw attention to the freedom with which
the time-connections between sounds have been treated and which often
appear transformed into "aleatory technique." This means that in many places
the performers can treat their parts with considerable freedom, as regards
rhythmical values. This is to enable a very complicated rhythmical texture to
be sometimes achieved while involving the minimum technical difficulties
for the singers and musicians. The individual psychology of each performer
is here, therefore, a factor which I have tried to incorporate into the means
which the composer has at his disposal. This approach is contrary to a mechanical and abstract treatment of sound, and is aimed at reestablishing the
pleasure a performer experiences in interpreting a musical work. I have
therefore tried to bring the individual capabilities and the particular talent of
each performer into play, and have often demanded that they play or sing in
a large ensemble with the same ease as when singing or playing themselves.
The third and last point I would like to draw attention to is the use of two
conductors in my work. This was necessary in those places in which various
types of rhythms and even in which absolutely different principles of time-
organization, appear simultaneously.

Trois poèmes d'Henri Michaux was commissioned by the musical Biennale
in Zagreb. The first performance of the work took place there in 1963. The
score is published by the Polish Music Publishing Company, Kraków, in two
parts: a choral score with a summary of the orchestral parts, and an orchestral
score with a similar summary of the choral parts.

Source

Ove Nordwall, ed., *Lutosławski* (Stockholm: Edition Wilhelm Hansen, 1968),
71–79. Copyright 1968 AB Nordiska Musikförlaget. Printed by permission of
Ehrlingförlagen AB, Stockholm, Sweden. This text was written in 1965 as a
program note for the BBC.

STRING QUARTET (1964)

The overall form is a series of short episodes against a longer main movement—*Jeux vénitiens*, String Quartet, Symphony no. 2, *Livre pour orchestre*. The origin of this form is baroque with the "gay" ending of a concerto, the same as in Haydn and Mozart's symphonies. By the time of Beethoven, and especially Brahms, this principle began to degenerate. The finales are too substantial, massive, large, significant, and the first movement was still the most important or at least as important as the finale. One feels fed up, tired. I have found a satisfying solution for myself: a set of short movements that engage in play, but don't give satisfaction, or fulfillment, and there is only one longer important movement.

The introductory movement contains a monologue for the first violin, the short intervention of the second violin, viola, violoncello interrupted by the first violin, then the development of the monologue into the actual first episode. There are eight episodes of different kinds, some *ad libitum*, some not. The framework (octaves c–c). The shortening of the frameworks. The last one—the longest one. The octaves "degenerating" into D flat—C and D—B three times. The cello solo—echo of the first violin's solo. A monologue and a bridge to the main movement.

The common features of all episodes are no actual development of the ideas and every time, the octave framework intervenes as it were in the middle of a word. The result is a lack of satisfaction, since each episode does not actually fold up at the end, it is not completed but brusquely interrupted. This is the means of achieving the "uncompleted," "unsatisfactory" character of the whole introductory movement.

The main movement is a sharp contrast to the introductory movement: one single whole, in spite of some differences of tempo in the last stages of the form. The body ("torso") of the movement is violent, fast; the inscription—*furioso* leads without digressions to a climax.

A → figure 14
B pizz. figure 14 → figure 24
A$_1$ (a$_{1,2,3,4,5}$) figure 24 → figure 29

C hidden, lurking figure 29 → figure 34
D short display of energy before figure 35
E series of four short sections of rising tension: e$_1$, e$_2$, e$_3$, e$_{1+2+3}$, each of them interrupted by a pizz. vc. chord figure 35 → figure 39

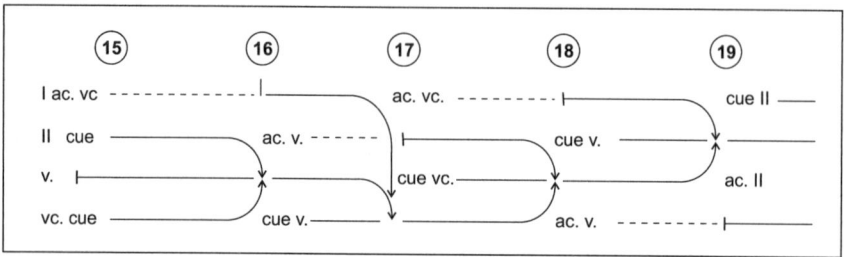

Example 2-1.

F the last interruption, rests, pizz. chords and apparent relaxation of tension. In reality only for a while (figure 40) is there a short raising of the tension → figure 42

G Appassionato (first climax) rising section and *sempre fff* (final climax) and discharge of the energy → figure 43 (description of the realization)

H Chorale figures 43–45
I Funèbre figures 45–46
J series of short "comments" on the event that has just happened figure 46 → figure 51 and a farewell, an exit.

It is important to know that many *ad libitum* sections are organized in such a way that one single twelve-note chord is used for a section in a modal way. That is why I have had to find means to avoid overlapping neighboring sections in an unusual way. (See example 2-1.)

Source

Manuscript in English. Copyright Witold Lutosławski Collection, Paul Sacher Foundation. All rights reserved. Printed by permission.

∞

At the beginning of my String Quartet I gave the following explanation: "The tempo is approximate as are all rhythmical values. Each performer should play his part as though he were alone. Changes of tempi (*acc.* and *rit.*) most often concern particular performers and should be treated separately. As the vertical result of the juxtaposition of the four parts of this work is not completely fixed, there can be no score. In exceptional places the full score appears in the parts."

When I was writing my *Jeux vénitiens* I came across a basic difficulty that arises when we want to score ensemble-music intended to be played *ad libitum*. This is because such music has no common rhythmic pulse, or common measures, or any other factors that would justify the notation of one part above another in one particular way and not in any other. The aim of a traditional score is, among other things, to show what is happening in the particular parts at any given moment of the work between its beginning and its end. This may be due to the fact that in traditional music there is full interdependence between all parts as regards the order of sound events in the course of time. This feature of traditional music is so obvious that it seems superfluous even to mention it. Consequently it has never been mentioned as long as there has only existed ensemble-music in which the full interdependence of all parts in time has been an absolute and binding principle. Now, however, when new works built on different principles are being created, we have to remind ourselves of these elementary principles, against this background, in order to realize precisely what the innovation consists of concerning the time manipulation in works in which the above principle of the interdependence of the parts no longer holds. My frequent contact with performers has confirmed the need for a clear and elementary explanation to these questions. Even distinguished performers may not realize the nature of changes that occur in music nowadays. Consequently they commit gross errors, for example, in trying to reduce all features of a musical work to the principles they know traditionally, which results in a completely wrong interpretation of the composer's intentions. The composer himself may give rise to such misunderstandings if he scores his work in the traditional way, giving no clear commentaries and expecting his music to be understood in some new untraditional way. Thus, because of this departure from the principle of the interdependence between the particular parts in time, the traditional scoring of such a work becomes simply its false image.

Example 2-2 is a simple example illustrating what I have said. The remark put at the beginning of the piece ("Each performer should play his part as if alone," etc.) is to be observed in the performance of this fragment. Here the score makes sense only with reference to the first note that begins in each part at the same moment. But the placing of the second note for each part precisely one above another is already a fallacy. This is because the duration of the first notes is not the same in each of the three parts. According to my first remark, pauses are to be interpreted by each member of the ensemble individually. If the performers were to arrange beforehand to treat the duration of the first notes as equal in all parts, they would act perhaps in accordance with what the score itself suggests, but against the composer's intentions as expressed in the first remark. Thus the placing of the first semiquavers vertically one above another has no sense. If I had not put them precisely on the same vertical line,

Example 2-2.

this would have suggested they should be played in some determined order, which would again be contrary to my intentions. The following part of the fragment gives rise to new obvious ambiguities. The fact that each member of the ensemble is supposed to interpret the *ritenuto* in his own way makes the placing of the subsequent notes in any fixed order absolutely unjustifiable. Consequently we must conclude that there is no way of notating this fragment in the manner of a traditional score. The most faithful way of notating this kind of music is to leave it in the form of separate parts, which is possible in this case, as there is no need for a conductor.

I have given here only one example illustrating that there is no possibility of notating my piece in the form of a score. My String Quartet consists mainly of music that involves analogous problems and that is why I shall have to work out some special form of scoring if I am not merely to publish the parts and let the matter rest at that. This would be most in line with my intentions and would perhaps not lead to gross misunderstandings. On the other hand it would make it more difficult for the performers to understand the work before rehearsing it.

When the reader has arrived at this point he will probably ask: What is all this for? What has the composer aimed at in this dissociating of the passage of time into independent courses?

I shall begin answering this question with some negative statements. It is not a question of diversity between performances; nor is it a question of the element of surprise; nor of freeing myself from a part of the responsibility for the work and placing it on the performers. The aim of my endeavors has been merely to attain a certain definite sound result. This result is impossible to attain in any other way, especially as regards rhythm and expression. I attach here a great importance to the influence of the musical text itself and explanatory notes for the performers. The remark saying that each performer should play his part as though he were alone is decisive. As we know, solo playing is quite different from chamber music. The mental activity of a solo performer is simply different, as is the actual sound result. In solo playing there is no necessity to submit agogic nuances to a common pulsation. This brings out the manifold rhythmical and expressive possibilities of the performer; it makes his playing supple, free, and individual. He can concentrate his whole attention on his playing and does not need to divide it in order to adapt himself to others. All this is perfectly well known from tradition, but only as far as solo playing is concerned. The idea behind "collective *ad libitum*" music is to transpose all the richness of solo playing into the field of ensemble music. My String Quartet is one of the pieces in which this transposition has been realized. The combination of a few players who think, feel, and decide independently of each other gives quite different results from those known from traditional ensemble music, in which particular parts are subordinated to one common time organization.

In performing this kind of ensemble music, somewhat different qualifications, and certainly a different approach from the one formed by long established tradition, are required of the interpreters. This new approach seems to involve the working out of a specific style of playing ensemble music that would enable the performers to display all their solo abilities and would prevent them from limiting these abilities through the habit of complying with a common pulsation.

Another question that may arise with these remarks is: how is the form of the piece organized as a whole? It is clear that this form does not consist of four independent parts, performed without any coordination from beginning to end. The independence of the parts holds good only for particular sections, the duration of which varies from a few seconds to two minutes. The transition from one section to another is realized in various ways, and sometimes requires a fairly complex system of signals. This system is especially important when the tempo is fast and when the shortest break would spoil the continuity of the music. Here is an example to illustrate one way of organizing the transition from one section to another in each of the four parts.

In the first violin part, it appears as shown in example 2-3. In the second violin part, it is as shown in example 2-4. In the viola part, it is like example 2-5. And in the cello part, it is like example 2-6. In a few short fragments I have introduced a notation in the form of a traditional score into the particular parts. This concerns passages in which time is organized in a traditional way.

Example 2-3.

Example 2-4.

Example 2-5.

Example 2-6.

The dissociation of time in music may give rise to one more problem that is by no means the least important: To what extent is the organization of pitch in my piece affected by such great freedom in the performing of the individual parts? Is this organization to some extent left to chance? If not—how does the composer avoid chaos? The performers should be fully aware of this state of affairs, otherwise they could not feel sufficiently free and unhampered to play their parts really independently of one another.

The answer to this question would involve a detailed explanation of the procedure I have applied in composing my piece, which may be called aleatory counterpoint. Here, however, I can only give an indication of this explanation, and my answer will be rather general. It may seem a little paradoxical, yet it corresponds with reality: quite simply, the element of chance does not play an important role as far as the organization of pitch is concerned. Of course, this does not mean that all possible performances of my piece must be quite identical. Nevertheless differences arising from the independent playing of particular members of the ensemble have no influence on the whole form or on its particular stages. In composing my piece I had to foresee all possibilities that could arise within the limits set beforehand. This, in fact, consisted of setting the limits themselves in such a way that even "the least desirable possibility" of execution, in a given fragment, should nevertheless be acceptable. This guarantees that everything that may happen within the previously set limits will fulfill my purpose.

Finally, some general information about the work: I composed my String Quartet in 1964 for Swedish Radio, to celebrate the tenth anniversary of the Nutida Musik Concert Series. The work consists of two movements, one of an introductory character and the main movement, and its total duration is about twenty minutes.

Source

Ove Nordwall, ed., *Lutosławski* (Stockholm: Edition Wilhelm Hansen, 1968), 81–88. Copyright 1968, AB Nordiska Musikförlaget. Printed by permission of Ehrlingförlagen AB, Stockholm, Sweden.

PAROLES TISSÉES (1965)

Paroles tissées (text by Jean-François Chabrun) for tenor and orchestra of twenty soloists (without winds) was composed in 1965 for the English tenor Peter Pears. The first performance, with Peter Pears as soloist and with the Philomusica of London orchestra conducted by the composer, was given on June 20, 1965 in England during the Aldeburgh Festival.

Source

Stefan Jarociński, *Witold Lutosławski. Materiały do monografii* (Materials for a Monograph) (Kraków: Polish Musical Edition, 1967), 54. Copyright Marcin Bogusławski. All rights reserved. Printed by permission.

❧

It is a composition in four movements (hence not a song cycle), which constitute one indissoluble whole. The binding element is not only the fact that the music is set to one four-part verse, but also that the music form corresponds to this basic design.

The first three movements are a graduation in tempo and tension. The third movement, dramatic in its nature, marks the culmination point of the composition. The broad melodic cantilena phrase comes to the fore in the elegiac fourth movement.

There is one specific feature to Chabrun's verse. One group of words reappears in each of the four stanzas of the poem. They evoke the same brief flashes of pictures. The pictures emerge in a different order each time as the words appear next to sentences that seem to belong to a kind of vestigial dramatic plot that is the framework of the composition. Actually, the plot is implied to a great degree, because nothing is actually explicit here. The pseudo-drama is told by a series of separate pictures that may be interpreted as dream visions.

Each time the group of words recurs in the stanza, it neighbors with a more advanced stage of the narrative, of the imagined drama, and assumes new meaning each time. In the musical interpretation of this extremely original poetic form, I tried to bring out the changing character of the same words and their groups. Thus, in the first movement, the words sound like unimpassioned information. In the second, they sound like a lullaby, and in the third like a dramatic shout, while in the fourth they assume the form of a sweeping melodic cantilena.

Source

Program note for the Warsaw Autumn Festival 1968, *Polish Music*, no. 3 (1968): 10–11. Copyright Marcin Bogusławski. All rights reserved. Printed by permission.

❧

Analyzing one's own procedures is a difficult task for a composer. However, there are some things that can be said about the subject, since a composer is ultimately prompted by something; he must have some general ideas in order to start working at all. I would like to formulate here some thoughts that seem important to me and some views to which I adhere in connection with composing music to a text. While saying "I adhere to them," I only mean practical guidelines for myself. I would simply like to be aware of my procedures, of my own attitude to the issue of composing music to a text.

So, my first guiding principle is as follows: the text is not, for me, purely one element of the sound, an unimportant or purely musical element. The text has its own content, which should be respected; it cannot only be a motivation. Therefore, what stimulates me most is to find a way of interpreting works with a text so that all the words reach the listener. The greatest singers are those who actually concentrate on the text, like—for instance—Fischer-Dieskau or Peter Pears. They present the text in their own way, but it is a way that does not leave the smallest doubt as to its content. The method of approach for them does not merely dwell on a group of sounds and the rules governing them, but also focuses on the text and, therefore, on the rules which govern it.

My method of working is usually as follows: initially there exists a general idea of a vocal-instrumental work. Then I start searching for a text to correspond to this first idea. After having chosen the text, I open myself to its influence. I try to be its interpreter, in the realm both of its structure and form and its content.

I refer you once again to *Five Iłłakowicz Songs*, since it is the earliest of my works that I can talk about. Here we observe very clearly the way in which the text has an effect on the elements of the musical material and, in the first place, on the form.

One question presents itself: What is a musical interpretation of a text? Are there any rules, general laws, or principles? Well, I proceed in the simplest way, which—at the same time—is the most difficult to explain. Music is not supposed to be an illustration of the text, nevertheless it is "married" to it, and so it has to be one.

The next question is the following: what is the connection between words and music if the latter is not just a naïve illustration? I cannot answer this question, since my procedures are impossible to describe or to analyze. It is an action similar to a device into which one throws something and eventually out comes a ready-made product. I simply find a text that makes an impression on me and in which I see musical potential. It affects my imagination and suggests ideas. Yet I never reflect on general rules governing this kind of relationship, and I would not want to do so.

I will now concentrate on certain details of my work that will perhaps throw some light on the issue of the relationship between music and words and the issue of music with a text. I will refer to particular examples, but not the *Iłłakowicz Songs* here, since they are a very basic example. The work that can provide good material for a commentary is *Paroles tissées* (Woven Words) to a surrealist text by Jean-François Chabrun.

The text consists of a series of utterances that are seemingly unconnected, although the title suggests the existence of some thread regarding content. It alludes to a known literary work, and its original title is *Quatres tapisseries pour la Châtelaine de Vergi* (Four Tapestries for the Lady of Vergi). It is known that the subject matter here is the love of the Lady of Vergi and the Duke of Burgundy, and the death of both lovers, but Chabrun does not mention it directly in his poem.

What struck me in this text was, first of all, the extraordinary finesse of its structure and, secondly, its specific value from a composer's point of view. Its form, constructed of four distinct parts, is not suitable for a song cycle, but it is ideal for a work in four sections.

The text of *Paroles tissées* is very unusual and unique. I do not know a similar text. Chabrun was never considered a poet of the first rank. I think, however, that this particular work is of exceptional quality.

In part 1 of the poem, which consists of three three-line verses, the poet has juxtaposed a series of disparate images, which have no perceptible connection with each other, but play an important role in the structure of the whole text:

> *Un chat qui s'émerveille*
> *une ombre l'ensorcelle*
> *blanche comme une oreille*
>
> *Le cri du bateleur et celui de la caille*
> *celui de la perdrix celui du ramoneur*
> *celui de l'arbre mort celui des bêtes prises*
>
> *Une ombre qui sommeille*
> *une herbe qui s'éveille*
> *un pas qui m'émerveille*

> *A cat that's wonder-struck*
> *a shadow bewitches her*
> *white as an ear*
>
> *The tumbler's cry and the quail's*
> *the partridge's and that of the chimney-sweep*
> *the cry of the dead tree, of captured beasts*
>
> *A shadow that sleeps*
> *grass which awakes*
> *a step to marvel at*

The next part starts with a new idea that has no connection with the preceding text: "Quand le jour a rouvert les branches du jardin" (When the day has reopened the branches of the garden), and then there appear those disconnected images, which—with some rearrangement—become a variant of the original version:

un chat qui s'émerveille
le cri du bateleur et celui de la caille
une herbe qui s'éveille
celui de la perdrix celui du ramoneur
une ombre l'ensorcelle
celui de l'arbre mort celui des bêtes prises

A cat that's wonder-struck
the tumbler's cry and the quail's
grass which awakes
the partridge's and that of the chimney-sweep
a shadow bewitches her
the cry of the dead tree, of captured beasts

Hence, the first line of this part—"Quand le jour a rouvert les branches du jardin"—is, so to speak, the beginning of a sentence, of a story, which is interrupted by these vague images. Two last lines of this part:

Au dire des merveilles
l'ombre en deux s'est déchirée

Speaking of miracles
the shadow is torn in two

constitute, in turn, separate material. Together with the first verse they are an embryo of one story. But there is no story. They are disconnected images intertwined with a germ of some possible action.

Part 3 includes more new elements, although the preceding ones also return. The content of the text, which consists of fragments of the material, suggests a certain violence of character, a dramatizing of the action:

Mille chevaux hors d'haleine
mille chevaux noirs portent ma peine
j'entends leurs sabots sourds
frapper la nuit au ventre
s'ils n'arrivent s'ils n'arrivent
avant le jour ah la peine perdue

It is an extremely dramatic cry:

A thousand horses out of breath
a thousand black horses bear my sorrow
I hear their heavy hoofs

strike the night's midriff
should they not come should they not come
till day ah the lost sorrow

It is worth noting that the word *la peine* appears in this text with several meanings: *portent ma peine* means "bear my sorrow" or "bear my suffering." At the end of the above quoted fragment, we have the expression *la peine perdue,* that is, "the lost sorrow."

We can presume that this cry refers to an action that does not actually take place. And here again images appear from part 1:

Le cri de la perdrix celui du ramoneur
au dire des merveilles une herbe qui s'éveille
celui de l'arbre mort celui des bêtes prises
mille coqs hurlent ma peine

The partridge's cry and the chimney-sweep's
speaking of miracles awaking grass
the cry of the dead tree, of captured beasts
a thousand cocks crow my sorrow

The last verse in the excerpt quoted introduces, however, a totally new idea ("a thousand cocks crow my sorrow"). The word *la peine* is used here in the sense of "sorrow," or "suffering." In the next lines the poet speaks again with images of a specific character:

Milles coqs blessées à mort
un à un à la lisière des faubourgs
pour battre le tambour de l'ombre
pour réveiller la mémoire des chemins
pour appeler une à une
s'ils vivent s'ils vivent
mille étoiles toutes mes peines

a thousand cocks wounded to death
one by one on the suburb's edge
to beat the shadow's drum
to wake the memory of the streets
to call one by one
if they live if they live
a thousand stars all my sorrows

It is a typically lyrical passage; it is also a cry, but from the point of view of meaning, we can't find anything here. We may only guess at some content on the grounds of the purely emotional impact of this image. Generally speaking, part 3 is distinguished by a relatively small use of the variants from part 1 (only three lines). Yet it introduces a larger number of new elements, the beginnings of some action.

Part 4 is constructed in such a way that the odd lines bring in new text, whereas the even ones contain images from part 1, in new combinations and new variants. The drama and the anger have already disappeared; only calm reigns. The first line reads:

> *Dormez cette pâleur nous est venue de loin*
> *Sleep: this pallor has reached us from far*

The second line brings disruptive images from part 1:

> *le cri du bateleur et celui de la caille*

The third line once again introduces a new idea:

> *dormez cette blancheur est chaque jour nouvelle*
> *sleep: this whiteness is each day new*

The fourth line again repeats images from part 1:

> *celui de la perdrix celui du ramoneur*

These are, as previously, separate images with no connection to the content of the even lines; they constitute a kind of insertion, decoration, an addition. The fifth line brings again a new, very important idea:

> *ceux qui s'aiment heureux s'endorment aussi pâles*
> *the lovers happy fall asleep so pale*

We see here a reference to a medieval romance, an allusion to the content of the poem, which we know from the original title. The sixth line repeats earlier images:

> *celui de l'arbre mort celui des bêtes prises*

And then the two final lines bring for the last time a new idea:

> *n'endormiront jamais cette chanson de peine*
> *que d'autres ont repris d'autres la reprendront*

> *will never put to sleep this song of sorrow*
> *till others have repeated others will repeat it*

Thus, this poem has no literal content, no story. It only contains an allusion in its title, a conjectural content that the poet, so to speak, never achieves, although he still has it in mind. In short, it is an extremely intriguing text from the point of view of its poetic intention.

The ways in which this poem could be used for a musical work are very diverse. The following questions came to my mind: should similar word groupings—for instance, the first text and its later variants—be musically coded and subsequently recalled, or should they have their separate leitmotifs, their musical counterparts?

Can the work, which does not actually contain any immediately comprehensible meaning, and only hints at a rational construction, be treated as if it had a specific meaning?

How did my process of composing music to Chabrun's poem develop? The point of departure was to treat each part separately. I accepted that each of them had its own physiognomy and its own character and, therefore, its own musical image. What became crucial for me were the new words that appeared in the consecutive parts. Of course, this does not apply to part 1, which presents material to be repeated later. Yet in part 2 the "germs" of a new content served to determine its character. The verse "Quand le jour a rouvert les branches du jardin," that is, the beginning of this quasi story, is articulated by the solo voice singing without any accompaniment. The music of part 3 takes its dramatic atmosphere and the element of violence from the text. In part 4, starting with the words "Dormez cette pâleur nous est venue de loin," I understand the word *paleur* (pallor) as a mortal pallor. I assume that this passage refers to the death of the supposed protagonists, as it alludes to the death of the Lady of Vergi and the Duke of Burgundy. Yet part 3, which I called "dramatic," is an outburst, as it were, and the tragic dénouement of the conflict.

This way of reading the text is entirely subjective. One could say that I wrote a musical work to a text that does not include the content that I read into it. However, what justifies my doing so is the poem's title and the allusions scattered in the whole text.

I treated the second layer of the poem, that is, those disparate images, as groups of words, taking no account of their semantic content. The music that accompanies them is supposed to be a commentary to a fragmentary action constructed from those few lines, or even just words, which gave me a pretext to create it. For instance, in part 2, which has a gentle character, the words "le cri du bateleur et celui de la caille" are sung calmly, like a lullaby, whereas the analogous words in the following fragment are treated as though they express an extremely dramatic idea. These disconnected images return once again in the final part. They follow in a long cantilena of the tenor voice, which is, so to speak, a threnody after the death of the lovers, and they assume an elegiac character. Thus, the same text at different times is lullaby-like, then dramatic, then elegiac. The words themselves cease to convey any meaning; they could even be sung in an incomprehensible language. Their content, although they actually don't display it, is determined by a concrete sense of the neighboring words of the poem that the music follows.

The compositional process discussed previously, those actual procedures that I might even have described as double dealing, were entirely conscious. I simply wrote music to a story that is absent in Chabrun's text. Hence there was a purposefulness in my method, but, at the same time, there was also an inconsistency in relation to what I said at the beginning: that I fully respect the content, that the text is and has to be important. I think, however, that what justifies my conduct is the fact that I use a semiabstract poem, which allows almost complete freedom in its musical interpretation. After all, I had the opportunity to meet the poet when he was already acquainted with my work and I know that he had not the slightest reservation about it. On the contrary, he accepted my interpretation, although I did not present him with the full details.

I hasten to add in conclusion, that the issue of the relationship between words and music is an ocean on which one can sail endlessly. I have focused on *Paroles tissées* while leaving my other compositions of this kind out of account, because, of all my works, it is a unique piece, quite distinct from all the others.

Source

Seminar on W. Lutosławski's vocal-instrumental works held at Baranów San-domierski in 1976. In *Spotkania muzyczne w Baranowie. Muzyka w kontekście kultury* (Musical encounters in Baranów. Music in the context of culture), ed. Leszek Polony (Kraków: Polish Musical Edition, 1978), 98–103. Copyright Marcin Bogusławski. All rights reserved. Printed by permission. In this text, the English translation of the Chabrun's poem was done by the staff of Aldeburgh Festival and published on the occasion of the first performance. Used by courtesy of the Britten-Pears Library.

SYMPHONY NO. 2 (1965–1967)

I am just completing a work that will be titled Second Symphony. The choice of this little old-fashioned title for my piece, whose form has nothing to do with the classical, romantic, or neoclassical symphony, is certainly not a pure fantasy. Neither is it the expression of a desire to draw attention to a work by simply calling it "Symphony" and not "Constructions," "Intentions," "Prohibitions," "Revocations," "Restrictions," or the like. No, my Symphony is to be an actual symphony, although there is no sonata movement in it.

The mere presence of two contrasting themes in a work, their development, recapitulation, and a coda, associates in my mind much less with the word *symphony* than does the very notion of a large-scale musical form applied to an orchestra work. The essential feature of such a form is the presence of a number of sections, whose functions are not only to express musical ideas, but also to determine the relationship of those ideas with other sections in the work or with the whole form. This makes the listener comprehend the performance of a large-scale work not as a sequence of sound phenomena, independent of each other, but rather as one single experience.

The process of listening to a large-scale form may be compared with following the action of a play, during which the spectator is supposed to integrate the episodes, which succeed one another, and to be able to recall the whole afterwards. Of course, we cannot remember every note of a composition, but, when listening to a large-scale work, we not only perceive the separate moments of it, but also remember what came before and may have an idea of that which is to come. Thus our listening to music becomes active: we feel engaged in the development of the composer's thoughts, which lead us from the beginning of the work to its final solution.

If the work is to be listened to in such a way, it is the task of the composer to impose this way of listening upon his audience. The ability to do this is the composer's sense of form. This ability is much more important, in the composing of large-scale forms, than the knowledge of putting together contrasting themes and developing them according to classical rules.

So, as far as the form itself is concerned, my new symphony will have relatively little in common with the classical idea of a symphony.

As for the instrumental ensemble, however, I have scored my work for a standard symphony orchestra, even though today the concept *standard symphony orchestra* is rather misleading. It makes us think immediately of standard symphony concerts. The contemporary composer is interested in these concerts only to a relatively slight degree. And if he is interested in them, then this is, in the main, an unrequited love.

Unfortunately Honegger's bitter remark is still true: the contemporary composer appearing in the program of a subscription concert feels like someone taking his place at a table to which he has not been invited. Indeed, there is no more regrettable situation for the contemporary composer than to find himself in a program between a Rossini overture and a Tchaikovsky concerto. He irritates those who come to listen to a famous pianist, and those who love his music are certainly not ready to put up with eighty minutes of music which they have long been bored with, in order to hear his ten-minute work. Consequently the contemporary composer feels more sure of himself when in the company of similar composers, and therefore in the program of such series of concerts as the Nutida Musik in Stockholm, Musik in der Zeit in Cologne, Das Neue Werk in Hamburg, and in the Zagreb, Palermo, or Warsaw festivals.

After such remarks, one might ask whether I can see any special reason for writing a "nontraditional" symphony for a "traditional" symphony orchestra. I shall try to answer this question.

I feel a respect for the traditional symphony orchestra similar to that which I have for works of art belonging to other epochs: pictures, antique furniture, etc. In the symphony orchestra I find far more that is connected with the past than with the future. In its present form, this orchestra is not a true expression of our time. It is an anachronism, even if only from the purely technical point of view. I do not want to compare the bassoon with the "Early Beard" but even in comparison with the contemporary piano it appears primitive and naïve—as an object from some remote epoch.

Consequently, I do not in the least feel at ease realizing my sound ideas by means of the symphony orchestra. And if, despite this, I still continue to compose orchestral works, it is because new means of sound production have not, until now, been able to compete with the old. I think that electronic and concrete music have a great future, and will eventually lead to the creation of a new rich instrumentarium. Today, however, the experimental studio is a somewhat primitive instrument and involves incredibly uphill work.

That is why I intend to go on and write several works for orchestra. In spite of the old instruments used in the orchestra, there is still something new to be discovered in it. The style of orchestra playing is today somewhat limited. This is based on an accepted convention, and involves the role of each individual musician being reduced to the most faithful expression of the conductor's will during the performance of the work. Today the actual performer of an orchestra work is the conductor, who is operating a complex mechanism of great precision; and the musician playing in the orchestra is merely a part of this mechanism. This convention, which I do not consider the only one possible, has been created by a long tradition.

In the works I am composing at present, I am trying to harness to my purpose an element hampered by this long tradition: the psychological capacity of each of the individual members of the orchestra. Thus I am trying to treat the orchestra not as a complex mechanism of great precision by which abstract sound visions are realized, but as a group of human individuals each of whom, in a work of mine, can have an opportunity to express himself. I am looking for means of liberating the energy latent in each of the performing musicians—an energy that has been smothered by the long established tradition of playing to the slightest movement of the conductor's baton. I am looking for means of stimulating the personal artistic initiative of each of the members of the orchestra in interpreting his own part—to a great extent—as a soloist. Perhaps my endeavors will contribute to restoring the pleasure that ought to belong to music making, and which is completely lost in many of the works of contemporary composers.

All this, of course, demands a special technique of composing far removed from the tradition of the past half century. One of the features of this new technique is that the way the composer treats the role of the conductor has changed. With such music, the conductor's role must become similar to that of the producer of a play. His role consists mainly of preparing the work at rehearsals and coordinating the individual roles of the particular members of the orchestra, as determined by the composer. During the actual performance, the conductor has considerably less to do: apart from the signals necessary for organizing music in time, he can remind the performers, by gestures, of the instructions given during rehearsals. Thus he sometimes plays a part analogous to the call-boy and prompter in the theatre.

What is new in this approach concerns only the actual means of music making. I believe, however, that the future will also bring new instruments. Then the face of the symphony orchestra will eventually change: it will come to correspond to the technical level of our epoch, but at the same time it will make use of an element that will not lose its significance as long as art itself exists; the element of a living human being, the artist and his individual talents.

Source

"The Composer on His Work. A New Approach to Orchestra," *The Christian Science Monitor,* June 24, 1968. Courtesy of *The Christian Science Monitor.*

∞

Is the symphony orchestra no more than a museum piece, a relic bequeathed to us by the generations that came before us? Or is it perhaps a living organism, showing no signs of age, with years of development still lying ahead of it? These questions cannot be answered by one general statement, for the simple reason that composers hold a diversity of views on the subject. The problem does not exist for composers whose musical language and sound ideas are inseparably bound up with tradition. Their creative inventiveness has been shaped to such an extent by the music of the past that conventional instruments and ensembles are to them an ideal tool for carrying out every musical idea. To others, the sound of old instruments evokes such strong feelings of tedium that they have banished them from their composing techniques forever and have found new resources that are capable of producing the desired sounds. In view of this wide diversity of views, I shall not attempt to provide an answer that would even pretend to be objective on the subject. Being one of the composers to whom the problem is not only real but also one of the most burning issues at hand, I seek to resolve it for my own purpose. I find that this is indispensable in my daily work and in the process of composing itself.

I must confess that I entertain greater respect than enthusiasm for the instruments that compose a symphony orchestra. True, we have not developed anything that can approach the rich and noble timbre of old instruments, yet the limitations the old instruments impose on the contemporary composer are gallingly restrictive. The strings and the wind instruments alike are, owing to their very construction, closely identified with music that is now a thing of the past. They are not even chromatic instruments in the true sense. It is more difficult to perform nondiatonic than diatonic sequences on the piano with its keyboard arrangement, on the harp with its tuning in the scale of C-flat major, or on the wind instruments based on the principle of harmonic series. Although it must be conceded that string instruments are capable of playing both diatonic and chromatic sequences, as well as sequences of tones that do not belong to the twelve-tone equally tempered scale, yet a completely new technique of playing would have to be devised to make this possible. Development of new techniques comes up against a twofold obstacle: the preponderant demand for performers of old music and the greater earnings possible in this profession. The situation is worsened by the absurd system of notation, where for the twelve-tones of an octave we have only seven positions on a five-line staff. This is a serious drawback to nontraditional music, which often looks unnatural and incomprehensible when written with these seven symbols.

For various reasons, therefore, the instruments of a symphony orchestra satisfy the requirements of my composing technique only in a limited sense. A great many composers find themselves in a similar predicament. Each one is compelled to look for a way to break the stalemate.

One way out is simply to ignore the limitations of the instruments, to idealize them, to treat them abstractly, in a manner unrelated to actual practice. This fact may lead to uncompromising, logically constructed scores that are not bound by the restrictions inherent in tradition. The bad thing about these compositions is that they are often difficult to perform. Much worse, however, is the fact that these difficulties are incomparably greater than the resultant effect would warrant. Consequently, I find this method entirely impractical to my purpose. Unlike composers who employ this particular method, I hold to the principle that compositions must be made as easy to perform as possible, despite the fact that this places an additional burden on the composer. For everyone knows how extremely difficult it is to write works easy to play without sacrificing something important. Nevertheless, I do try to write simply not only because I firmly believe that music that is easy to play sounds better than difficult music, but also because I hope to have some part in helping musicians recapture the sense of pleasure that playing music can provide. It is my contention that only the musician who derives pleasure out of playing can interpret a musical composition in the fullest sense. If, however, he is given a difficult and unrewarding text, if he is asked to perform functions that can better be required of a machine, it is ultimately the composer and his composition that are made to suffer.

Experimenting with new ways of playing old instruments is still another way of trying to find a solution to the problem under discussion. This method, like the preceding one, is of no use for my particular purpose. The prepared piano and use of strings and winds as if they were percussion instruments enlarges the range of these instruments by decidedly second-rate and marginal attributes. Furthermore, this particular treatment of musical instruments has a jarring effect on me. I find it exceedingly unnatural, at variance with the true designation of the instruments, but above all brutal in relation to these delicate objects, which are often great works of art in themselves. The sound of prepared instruments, their use as percussion instruments, is gross. The method may be compared to apings, parrotings, and mockery but never to natural speech. As such its uses are very limited indeed.

My critical remarks regarding some of the ways in which instruments are used have bearing solely in relation to the applicability of this method to my composition technique; they are not meant as criticism of the composers who employ these methods. The most ridiculous creative methods can be defended when they produce an outstanding work of art, just as the most convincing methods are compromised when they are used to produce a worthless piece of music.

Although the various methods of using instruments I have described are of no use to my particular purpose, the very existence of these methods strengthens me in my conviction that the instruments of a symphony orchestra are indeed obsolete and that the contemporary composer can make only limited use of them. Irrepressible is the thought that new instruments will be designed, that they will fully meet the demands of contemporary musical ideas. The new instruments will, so I like to imagine, retain all the fine qualities of conventional instruments, produce with equal facility all the sequences that lie within the twelve-tone scale of equal temperament as well as the sequences that lie beyond it, while producing noises and tone-mixtures, and finally— something that would improve music as a whole—produce tones of pitches that vary in a continuous manner. Experimental studios working on new ways of producing sound will, I feel, make this possible. Although the results so far

achieved cannot yet compete with traditional instruments concerning acoustical richness and expression, yet the fact that they can be expected to develop
in the future is definitely an advantage in their favor.

Since at present there are no new instruments that would fully meet the
new demands, and since I do not wish to use old instruments in a manner
inconsistent with their natural attributes, I must perforce seek other solutions
to the problem under discussion.

The experience acquired by employing the element of chance in musical
composition has afforded me the opportunity to achieve certain results in this
realm that may perhaps be far from perfect and not very lasting. In this very
restricted and strictly controlled aleatorism, old instruments do at times sound
in a fresh and stimulating way. I shall return to a lengthier description of my
experience in this area in another part of the essay. At present it may suffice
to state that this experience has enabled me to reach once again to what had
seemed like an exhausted store of sound contained in the symphony orchestra
without the slightest twitch of aversion or that dull sense of weariness and, I
may even venture to say, with a dash of enthusiasm.

My Symphony no. 2, another in the series of symphonic works I have
recently completed, is also another of my "farewells to the orchestra." My first
farewells were made in 1958 with a set of compositions for the orchestra. At that
time I had already realized that the symphony orchestra has no prospects for
further evolution, that its heyday had long since passed. This next of a series of
"farewells" is obviously not to be the last. New instruments, which must give at
least as wide as noble a range of tone as the instruments we now have and which
will at the same time faithfully mirror the sound ideas of contemporary composers, are a possibility only, I am afraid, in the dim and distant future ahead.

The term *symphony*, in the same manner as the terms *sonata, variations,* and
others, refers to the concept of a closed form. Such a form owes its existence to
the ability of the listener to remember the music he has heard and to integrate
its individual sections while he listens so that after he has heard the composition
to the end (no matter how many times) he is able of perceiving it as an idea
that, like a painting or sculpture, exists outside the limits of time. But to reduce
the idea of a closed form to a "timeless" existence would amount to simplification. Composing closed forms, we also take great advantage of the fact that
music is a form of art that takes place in time. Consequently, one of the reasons
why we compose music is to evoke in the listener a series of specific reactions
whose sequence and development in time is of essential importance to the final
result, that is, to the perception of the composition as a whole. In other words,
composing a closed form, we assume that in the course of its performance the
listener is led, so to speak, by the composer through the various stages of the
composition and to its final conclusion. (I have used the term *listener* in the

sense of an "ideal" listener rather than to denote a specific type or even an "average" listener.) In order to get a better idea of what is meant when we say that the composer "leads" the listener through the performance of his composition, we may recall the familiar stratagems and tricks, some of them infinitely subtle, that have been employed by the classic composers. One of them, to take an obvious example, is to break up a given motif, to repeat its fragments in various positions of the musical scale *ad nauseam* in order to prepare the listener for the introduction of a new musical theme. Without this preparation, in which a kind of "vacuum" is created by the weariness, or perhaps even impatience, generated by the tedious repetition of the same motive, the introduction of a new theme might have gone almost unobserved by the listener. It would not have been anticipated or expected with such impatience. Another typical stratagem employed by classic composers is to evoke in the listener—most frequently by harmonic means—the impression that the composition or one of its stages is drawing to a close, only to introduce slight changes that successfully annihilate the initial impression that the movement is ending and replace it with the certitude that no conclusion is to be expected at the given moment but that, on the contrary, the form will continue to unfold itself.

The examples provide evidence that there is a psychological aspect to the creation of musical forms. Account is taken of such listener attributes as musical memory, ability to foresee, and ability to react in the desired manner to the different densities of musical substance. Thus the closed form is a complex phenomenon, for it is based on the concept of a dual role that time can play in a musical composition. The composition evolves in a given period of time, it is true, but once it has been performed, it begins an independent existence of its own in the consciousness of the listener due to the faculties of memory and to the ability of the listener to integrate impressions. Unrestricted by time, the composition can be conceived in its entirety in one brief moment.

Open-form compositions do not possess this quality of timelessness. Before this form became the object of interest of contemporary composers who belong to our cultural sphere, it had existed in its primitive state in folk music and specifically in the music of primitive peoples. The object of this music quite often is to induce a state of excitement similar to the effects produced by certain stimulants. One cannot speak of a definite length of a musical composition in this case and even less so of an impression made by the composition as a whole after it has been performed. To simplify the problem somewhat, we might say that the closed-form composition is an "occurrence" while the open-form composition is a means of inducing a certain psychological "state" in the listener. The simplification applies primarily to the open form, because it is the object of interest of a large faction of composers and is now undergoing an exciting evolution. The closed forms, which were at their peak in the

Baroque and Classical periods, are today cultivated mostly in their ossified and degenerate form. Personally, I cannot see how or why the closed form, like the sonata, rondo, and others, should be revived. The principle of the closed form, however, is not, in my estimation, obsolescent in the least. Listening to music, I too react to it in the manner described here, that is, by involving my memory by integrating and responding to every impulse communicated by the composer, who is fully engaged in the process. Everything I have written so far is inseparably bound with the closed form. I feel that a long process of evolution may still lie ahead for the closed form.

My Symphony no. 2 is an expression of this conviction. In the light of what I have written here, it must be obvious that Symphony no. 2 has very little in common with the classical or the neoclassical symphonic form. The reason I decided to use the term *symphony* for my composition is that it is a work for a symphony orchestra composed in a large-scale closed form.

Symphony no. 2 is composed in two movements that are not separated from each other by a pause. The last phrase of the first movement still echoes when the second movement begins. The composition, therefore, constitutes an indivisible whole. There is a close interdependence between the two movements, though they stand in sharp contrast to each other in many respects. The first movement is composed in such a way as to prepare for the second movement while the second movement is a natural consequence of the first. To put it in the most general terms, the first movement is designed to involve the listener in the musical "action"; it is the kind of music that makes the listener receptive to the musical "occurrence" presented by the second movement. On the other hand, the second movement would not be a musical "occurrence" in the full sense if the first movement had not prepared us for it. Using a trivial comparison, if I may, the first movement is an appetizer before the main course.

The first movement performs its role in the following manner: it comprises a series of episodes performed by various instrumental groups. The introductory episode is played by the brass alone. The next five are played by:

1. Two flutes, five tom-toms, and a celesta (see example 2-7);
2. Four stopped horns, a side drum, a parade drum, a bass drum, and a harp;
3. Three clarinets, a vibraphone without a motor, and a piano;
4. Two cymbals, a tam-tam, a celesta, a harp, and a piano;
5. Three flutes, three clarinets, three horns, five tom-toms, a celesta, a harp, and a piano.

The last and slightly longer episode composed of several stages is played by a succession of various small groups, which finally give way to the percussion.

Example 2-7. Symphony No. 2, Hésitant, Fig. 6. (In this score accidentals affect only the notes to which they belong. Notes without accidentals are always to be understood as natural.)

All the episodes unfold in the same way: a short phrase emerges tentatively and then subsides for a brief moment. Only then does the true beginning of every episode follow. None of the episodes has an actual ending. The growing boldness and mounting momentum of the musical action is followed by a pause, as if the energy had been spent. Then a few tentative attempts are made to take up the episode again. All the attempts are in vain and the theme is abandoned. Despite the clear distinctions between them, the episodes are united by certain common traits: an analogous construction that invests each of them with something like diffidence or indecision (that is why the movement is called *Hésitant*); no single moment of "full expression"; the use of chamber groups and solo instruments, which inevitably give a defective, deliberately fragile sound; and finally a lively tempo.

Each of the episodes is followed by a slow, short refrain that is always played by three instruments. The refrain is heard in a slightly altered version every time it is repeated. It is played by instruments that do not take part in the episodes—for example, two oboes and an English horn, an oboe and English horn and a bassoon, three bassoons. As the refrain ends, a new group of instruments takes up a new episode. Always, however, the initial attempt seems tentative. It is followed by the central "musical action" of the episode.

The last episode is the pivotal point of the first movement of the Symphony no. 2. It is longer than the preceding ones, and the different instrumental groups are heard in succession. It seems to accumulate more momentum than the preceding episodes, but as it approaches the point that seems to bode the climax it stops abruptly. As in the preceding episodes, the pause is followed by an attempt to take up the theme once more. This time the role is assigned to the percussion. As before, the attempt to take up the theme is ineffective and the dying sounds of the percussion conclude the last episode. Thus the first movement of the Symphony does not have a climax and it therefore leaves one with a sense of unfulfillment. In this sense, the movement is intended as an introduction, involving the listener and building up for the central "occurrence"—the second movement. The incomplete nature of the first movement is further emphasized by the fact that the string orchestra does not take part in it, with the exception of three almost percussive *pizzicato* chords placed at specific moments of the form (e.g., to interrupt the introduction and the closing episodes).

The refrain is heard again after the last episode has been played. The final version is considerably developed, forming a bridge to the second movement. This time the trumpets, trombones, and a tuba join the oboes and the bassoons in the refrain. The last statements of the refrain are distinctive by their raw and deliberately ugly sound, which serves to heighten the contrast with the double-bass *arco pianissimo*, with a totally different subtle tone color as it comes in at the beginning of the second movement.

As I have already said, the second movement is intended as a contrast in many respects to the first movement. The listener is expected to accept it as a natural and anticipated consequence of the first movement. The second movement, unlike the first, unfolds continuously without any pauses. Individual musical ideas overlap one another frequently, creating uninterrupted discourse. This development heads straight for the final solution without any digressions. That is why this movement is called *Direct*. The sound of the string orchestra is heard here for the first time. The strings are joined soon afterward by other groups of instruments. The solo and chamber-group character is superseded by the full sound of a large-scale sound mass. The lively tempo and the prevalence of short notes in the episodes of the first movement give way to the slow, sustained, and at times lyrical melodic lines of the first stage of the second movement. In the most general outline, the form of the second movement corresponds with its agogic plan. The plan is simple in itself. It is composed of five successive evolutionary stages of the form. Sustained notes and a slow tempo prevail in the first stage already described. Individual melodic lines are tightly meshed, creating a thick, almost gummy, sound-mass. Due to the lengthened motion and mutual pervasion of sounds, the first stage appears massive, "languid" in character, unaffected by the sporadic moments of some liveliness or the sudden bursts of energy that finally lead to a broadly developed cantilena intoned by the mass of string instruments (see example 2-8).

The second stage is comprised of a superimposed cantilena of the string instruments begun earlier with initially short and then increasingly long interventions of instrumental groups playing in a fast tempo. The moment is significant

Example 2-8. Symphony No. 2, Direct, Fig. 123.

with regard to tempo because two contrasting kinds of tempo are manifest here simultaneously. The growing length of the interventions of instrumental groups playing a fast tempo, the briefer and briefer distances between the interventions, and the subsiding action of the strings—all these factors taken together give critical meaning to this stage of the form. The fast tempo triumphs ultimately, gaining full control of the situation. At this moment the form enters the third stage of its evolution: the fast tempo prevails, the tension mounts (see figures 125a–126). One small step takes us to the fourth evolutionary stage, with its fast tempo and steadily rising vehemence. The fourth stage is distinct by the fact that it is the only fragment of the composition in which the orchestra is conducted in the traditional manner. I shall explain this at greater length when I come to the subject of the rhythmical aspect of the composition. It is necessary for this part to be conducted because of the acceleration of tempo and the increasingly close succession of sound "occurrences." The steadily heightening tempo and tension resolve ultimately into an elementary and deliberately primitive result, that is, a persistent repetition of the same rhythmical values performed at an accelerating tempo. An abrupt pause and a brief "contest of forces" are followed

Example 2-9.   Symphony No. 2, Direct, Fig. 159f.

by the fifth stage, which marks the high point of the work. Here the primitive rhythm gives way abruptly to collective *ad libitum*, with the whole orchestra playing at full force. Then every instrument goes on to complete its culminating phase on its own. The three final accented notes constitute the culminating point for each instrument. Thus the sound of the culminating phrase is resolved into a series of independent solo parts and into a series of moments that succeed each other at irregular intervals. It takes the individual instruments some time to finish the culminating phrase. In the background for a long while now, the wind instruments have been conducting a soft and quick "babble," embracing a wide range of the musical scale, before the final instrument completes its culminating phrase. When this has been accomplished, the *pianissimo* "babble" runs on for a while, then gradually, by means of a few steps, is shifted to the middle register as it gains in force. What follows is an attempt of sorts to end the composition with a *fortissimo* accent. This attempt is "unsuccessful," for in the pauses between the repeated triumphal enunciation of the E-flat–F ninth by the entire orchestra, one can already hear four cellos and four double basses preparing the background for the epilogue that is to follow in a moment. Two double basses, playing solo, intone *pianissimo* a shy interrupted phrase (see example 2-9).

It ends with F–E-flat, the same notes that began the composition and which resounded a moment ago in the *tutti* by the full orchestra. When the two double basses complete the phrase, the background sounds begin to fade gradually and the composition draws to an end.

As in a few of my earlier compositions, so in my Symphony no. 2 the rhythmical physiognomy is closely bound with the technique called in general usage controlled or limited aleatorism. Without going into the pros and cons of the fitness of the term, I should like to explain what the term means to me. It signifies a composing technique in which the element of chance does play a certain role. The role it plays, however, is strictly limited by the composer so as not to allow the element of chance to affect in the slightest degree the architectural order of the composition or the pitch organization. This treatment of the element of chance consists above all of the abolition of the classical time division common to all the members of an ensemble. This is accomplished by having a certain, frequently large, number of performers playing *ad libitum* simultaneously. The sections constructed in this manner do not have the same pulse, the same meter, or even the same tempo for all the performers and cannot be conducted. It is evident from this very brief outline that the technique of controlled or limited aleatorism has nothing in common with improvisation. Nor do any of my compositions contain parts that may be improvised by the performers.

It may be assumed from the above that the technique described here has a decisive influence on the rhythmical physiognomy of the musical composition. We may distinguish two kinds of rhythms that appear simultaneously. One is the rhythm within each separate section performed *ad libitum*, which may be called *microrhythm*. It is often very complex, for it consists of many parts superimposed one upon the other, in that each of the parts is subject to fluctuations of tempo that remain independent of the other parts and allow individual treatment of the pauses and others (see example 2-10).

The second rhythm is produced by the sections as a whole, or rather by their beginnings. In contrast to the first, the rhythm of large sections, the macrorhythm, is extremely simple. It plays a singular role in the second movement of my symphony. Here the sections grow gradually shorter the closer we come to the end until finally we are but a short step from the kind of music where the tempo, meter, and pulse are the same for all the performers, the kind of music that has to be conducted in the traditional manner. From here on, the rhythm gradually grows simpler until it is reduced to the elementary, primitive form. This transition from highly complex structures, the result of ensemble playing *ad libitum*, to the primitive repetition of the same rhythmic values at an accelerating tempo, occurs slowly and almost imperceptibly during the long development of the second movement. A swing back to the ensemble playing *ad libitum* is abrupt, occurring at the culmination point of the composition. One common

Example 2-10.   Symphony No. 2, Hésitant, Fig. 15.

pulse does not emerge again to the end of the composition and, as logically follows, neither do we go back to traditional conducting.

It is apparent, therefore, that the rhythmical construction, or preferably the organization of time, is closely bound with the formal structure of the composition as a whole and plays an important role in shaping this structure.

The basic element of pitch organization in my symphony is the twelve-tone chord, or the simultaneity of twelve different tones, hence a harmonic creation. As in a number of my other compositions, so in my Symphony no. 2, the twelve-tone chords appear in a wide variety. The frequent use of elementary twelve-tone chords—that is, those whose structure is based on one, or at most two, kinds of intervals—enables me to make frequent use of sharp harmonic contrast. When the instrumental composition is reduced to a few one-part instruments, the twelve-tone chords appear in their defective forms and are completed within a certain sector of time. This "summing up" of the twelve-tone chord occurs in the mind of the listener. At such moments, however, the succession of intervals in time acquires greater importance. Consequently, depending on the density of the texture, the oscillation between hearing the "horizontal" and the "vertical" is a typical phenomenon on which the pitch organization in the composition is based.

In addition to tones of a definite pitch, percussion instruments of indefinite pitch take part in my symphony, as they do in every composition written for the traditional orchestra. I often try to treat them independently and in the same way as other instruments, as far as the position they occupy on the musical scale is concerned. In many instances, certain ranges of the musical scale are reserved exclusively for percussion instruments of indefinite pitch while other instruments are used in other ranges of the musical scale. At other moments the ranges may intersect, permeate each other, and so on. In this manner, the percussion instruments of indefinite pitch are promoted to the role of an element that cooperates in organizing pitch to the same degree as other instruments whose tones belong to the twelve-tone scale of equal temperament. In using the instruments that compose the traditional symphony orchestra, I was guided by the following principle: to make full use of the chief properties of the instruments according to the purpose for which they were constructed and with a view to the technical possibilities of performance and characteristic attributes of sound. The string parts are therefore not deprived of a clearly lyrical sound in the same way as the wind instruments are (to a certain extent). I tried to write the more lively sections for all instruments in such a way that they would be easy to perform. I was compelled to use certain simplifications regarding details of individual instrument parts. But I did this deliberately, and I do not feel that this will detract in any way from the composition. The ensemble *ad libitum* technique is distinctly helpful in making my composition easy to perform while at the same time enhancing its sound qualities. For the performer is able to play with an expressiveness that cannot be attained in music with a common time division for all the performers.

I have described here only one, the external, aspect of my composition. It is only a facade that hides the true life of this as it does of every other work. It is the inner life, however, which is the more important, the more essential part of the musical composition. What can I say about it? How would I describe it? What is it supposed to express? Fortunately, I cannot possibly have anything to say on the subject. Fortunately, for if the essence of music could be expressed in words, then the music would be unnecessary. One could simply take a few minutes to read the verbal description. Writing this essay, I was aware the whole time that I was only skimming the surface of a subject that the music alone can communicate fully.

I began to work on Symphony no. 2 in the summer of 1965 and completed the work in the spring of 1967. Happily, my decision to write a symphonic composition coincided almost precisely with the moment when the Norddeutscher Rundfunk asked me to compose a work to be performed in October, 1966, at the gala hundredth concert of the Das Neue Werk series devoted to contemporary music. Unfortunately, I was unable to complete the work on time. But desiring to meet my obligations to Norddeutscher Rundfunk, I had to relinquish the idea of having the complete composition performed at the hundredth concert of Das Neue Work and decided instead to have only the second, the principal movement of the Symphony, performed on October 18, 1966. *Direct*, as the movement is called, was then performed as an independent composition by the orchestra of the Norddeutscher Rundfunk of Hamburg, conducted by Pierre Boulez. The warm reception accorded the piece by the Hamburg audience and by those who had come to the gala concert from many parts did not however relieve my deep sense of regret that

I was able to present merely part, merely the torso, of my work and therefore did not give the audience a full picture of what I had undertaken to do. I am writing these words on the eve of the premiere of Symphony no. 2. Rehearsals are to start in a few days. The composition will be performed by the orchestra of the Polish Radio, which I shall conduct myself.[1]

Out of the series of questions addressed by the editor to the contributors to this volume,[2] one in particular seems important to me—the one that asks what suggestions the composer would give to the future performers regarding the interpretation of his work. The editor has given the composers a chance to express thoughts that may exert a decisive influence on the future of the compositions described by them. As we all know, the system of musical notation used currently is not precise. At best it expresses the composer's sound vision imperfectly and only approximately. In order to see this, one need do no more than contemplate for a moment the relativity of such terms as *ritenuto* and *più forte*. Even less exact are terms like *espressivo*, *appasionato*, and others. Yet, we must of necessity take recourse to these terms in order to provide at least a sketchy idea of the kind of interpretation we have in mind as we write the given work. Despite this, the composer always takes the risk that his score may be misinterpreted by a performer of small insights and no intuition. The risk is greater the farther the composer's style departs from tradition. Introduction of new techniques of conducting and of performance in an ensemble leads almost inevitably to misunderstandings. This problem has assumed a particularly acute form in my experience as a composer, mainly owing to the ensemble *ad libitum* technique here described. It is practically impossible to score music composed in this manner because of the cardinal principle in which notes placed in a vertical line on a score are understood as simultaneous. This rule does not hold in the case of music played *ad libitum*. Consequently, when writing this music in the form of a score, essential for the performance of an orchestral work, I fully realize that my system of notation must give a false impression of the music I have composed. It has been my experience that the score can be misconstrued by some conductors who add measures, meters, and other such things to the score. Needless to say, this distorts the composer's intention and reduces the work to a sad caricature. That is why, despite a certain reluctance, I am compelled to add numerous comments and explanations to my scores and even to give detailed instructions regarding interpretation. Symphony no. 2 has been annotated in the same manner as several of my earlier compositions.

Though it is true that my controlled aleatorism may meet with lack of understanding or even aversion on the part of certain conservative performers, this does not mean that this reaction is universal. I have the good fortune to belong to that group of composers whose ideas, even those that are most diverse from the accepted conventions, have captured the imagination of a number of performers and thus provided confirmation of the effectiveness of my experiments. Interpretations of my *Jeux vénitiens* and *Trois poèmes d'Henri Michaux* (the orchestra part) by the Polish conductor Jan Krenz and the interpretation of my String Quartet by the American La Salle Quartet display a profound understanding of my intentions. My experience of these interpretations is of immeasurable value, not only because it has provided me a more rewarding satisfaction than anything I have known, but also because it has stimulated me to carry on along the path of my choice.

Source

"New Work for Symphonic Orchestra (on Symphony no. 2)," in *The Orchestral Composer's Point of View. Essays on Twentieth-Century Music by Those Who Wrote It*, ed. Robert Stephan Hines (Norman: University of Oklahoma Press, 1970). All rights reserved. Reprinted by permission. Music examples are reprinted by permission of Polish Musical Edition, Kraków.

Notes

1. The first performance of the whole symphony, by the Great Symphony Orchestra of the Polish Radio and with the composer himself conducting, took place on June 9, 1967 in Katowice.

2. Other contributors to the volume were: Milton Babbitt, Elliott Carter, Ross Lee Finney, Peter Racine Fricker, Hans Werner Henze, Ernst Křenek, Frank Martin, Vincent Persichetti, Gunther Schuller, Michael Tippett, and Wladimir Vogel.

CELLO CONCERTO (1969–1970)

This work consists of four parts performed with no interruptions. The first part is an introduction played by the soloist without the participation of any orchestral instrument. It is a kind of monologue. A characteristic element of this introduction is what it starts with, namely the same note D repeated every few seconds. This is marked in the score as *indifferente*. This means that the notes are to be played without any expression. The same note, which is repeated *piano* from fifteen to twenty times without any expression, evokes the impression of stopping the flow of thought, and that is exactly my intention. When this state of indifference or blankness is suddenly interrupted, there appear brief motifs: jaunty or playful, sometimes slightly melodious, occasionally at times with the character of a march or dance. These short motifs, however, don't develop too widely and, suddenly, as though cutting somebody short, they are interrupted by the D repeated in the same way as at the beginning of the work. It is as though the performer had fallen into a state of numbness and, when this moment ends, as he suddenly returns to the thought that had previously been interrupted. Eventually, there comes a moment when the D is repeated as quite a long note, yet its indifferent character starts to change. The rhythm is the same, but there is a change of dynamic (one note *forte*, the second note *piano*) and later of articulation (*saltando*). This is how one and the same D is constantly diversified, in a quite primitive and intentionally naïve way. This makes an impression as though someone, who is deeply bored with a monotonous occupation, has tried to give variety to it, but a little thoughtlessly. Exactly at this moment the first intervention of the orchestral instruments takes place. Three trumpets play a C sharp *fortissimo*, interrupting in this way the repetition of the D by the cello. The C sharp is played *fortissimo*. It is just one short note.

This is the ending of the introduction, or, so to speak, its interruption. The idea of an interruption of the thread through the intervention of the brass is widely used in the whole Concerto. After the first intervention of the trumpets, the cello resumes the repetition of the same note, at which point other trumpets are heard and, in the end, all three play noisily and querulously in a phrase that can be figuratively called a "reprimand." The trumpets quiet down, they repeat a fragment of their phrase with a mute, and at this point the introduction ends. There follows the second part of the Concerto—the four episodes. They all have the same form; it is a kind of a dialogue between the cello and small groups of instruments. This form is maintained only for a short while. Later, the instruments start to play continuously without leaving the cello any space for solo playing. After a while there appears, in the cello part, a lively, almost dance motif, which ends each episode. This motif becomes somehow a provocation to the brass section, which intervenes and interrupts each episode as it did at the end of the first episode. For a short while the cello resumes the interrupted thread, but the three trumpets interrupt it, shouting their bad-tempered motif, but this time slightly changed.

All the "reprimands" consist of a series of motifs, which change during both the particular episodes and the entire work. The second episode is constructed identically to the previous one, and is kept in a similarly carefree, serene mood. There is no place here for stronger emotions; only the trumpets or—as in the second episodes, the trombones—adopt more violent accents. The third episode has a more virtuoso character than the preceding ones; it is less declamatory, more rushing. The last episode ends again with an intervention, this time by the trumpets and the trombones. This intervention is a bit longer and it takes us up to the moment when the cello replies. Now it is the cello which interrupts the intervention with its one *pizzicato-fortissimo* note. The instruments then calm down and, in a while, the cello repeats the *pizzicato-fortissimo*. At this point comes an unexpected moment: the remarkable energy of the solo part, which even allows it to interrupt the intervening trumpets and trombones, then suddenly gets lost and vanishes. There follows a numbness, as it were, that reminds us of the beginning of the Concerto. As at the beginning, the solo part of the cello repeats the D *indifferente*. This particular moment is as if it is being put out of countenance or losing the thread.

After several repetitions of the D, the cello regains its energy and enters with its *pizzicato-fortissimo*. In a while, for the first time in this work, the string instruments appear, namely the double basses playing *arco*. With every *pizzicato* stroke of the E there enters a new double bass, so that this sound is finally played by all of them. It is a background for the beginning of the third part of the Concerto—*Cantilena*. The cello plays a long, widely developing phrase with the accompaniment of a group of strings. It starts with the double basses, then the cellos enter, then the violas, then the second and the first violins and, when the whole string orchestra is playing, successive groups of solo instruments from among them accompany the cantilena of the cello solo in turn. All this goes *ad libitum*. Eventually, the *Cantilena* arrives at the moment that can be called the beginning of the culmination. The cello plays in a high register, the whole string orchestra converges from a widely spaced out twelve-tone chord to a unison G sharp, which becomes a background for the cello's repetition of the first phrase of the *Cantilena*, this time in its highest register. Finally, the cello meets with the whole string orchestra on one unison note and, as though leading the strings in faster and faster tempo, it brings them to the moment where we expect the *Cantilena's* culminating point to follow, but this does not happen. This unison phrase, which is played faster and faster and with even more vigor, is brutally interrupted by the brass *tutti* accompanied by the drum. Afterward, an "intervening" phrase follows, already known from previous episodes, but this time it is played by the whole brass, including the tuba. Here all the motifs are audible. Now, after this quite long "reprimand" phrase (played by the whole brass) there enters—with the same motif—the wind together with the violas and the cellos. As the wind becomes silent, the strings develop into a complete *tutti*, while developing the motif known as a "reprimand," and bring it up to their highest register. There follows a sudden intervention of the whole brass with the piano, then the second such intervention, and a very short passage played by the xylophone and the piano. And here it finally achieves a full orchestral *tutti*. All the instruments of the orchestra play the motifs, which are close to what I called a "reprimand"; eventually they play them *ad libitum*, that is without the conductor. The music here has a character nearing speech like a shout or scream (this happens, as a matter of fact, in all the places where the brass intervened, breaking the episodes). The whole passage—from the end of the *Cantilena* up to the place I am talking about—can be characterized as follows: the episodes were, as I said, rather carefree music so that three trumpets and a short, grumpy phrase were enough to break each of them. Yet it is different in the case of the *Cantilena*, because here the music reaches a much higher temperature, it develops much stronger tensions, there are moments at which we expect a real culmination. Therefore, the breaking of the musical flow cannot happen here with just the short intervention of a couple of instruments. This is why I originated this developed orchestral *tutti*; it was required by the dramatic situation of the work.

Thus, the *tutti* breaks all of a sudden and there follows a silence that lasts a few seconds. The cello's reaction to what happened a while before is unexpected: it resounds in a rhythm similar to what one could hear in the orchestra, in a very short phrase played *piano*, in a slower tempo. One can hardly resist here an analogy between the theatre or a situation among human beings. After this, as I said, the reprimand (this time very vehement) is also derisory, as it were, of what was "shouted out" by the orchestra a moment ago. The orchestra's reaction to that reply is a new, wild *fortissimo*. After this intervention the cello also starts to play *fortissimo*. There follows a noisy dialogue between the orchestra and the cello. Yet, all of a sudden, the solo part starts something completely new, namely a kind of fast escape. It is *presto* based on quarter-tone progressions; the cello is from time to time interrupted by small instrumental groups always in a violent manner. Now it comes to a trial of strength between the orchestra and the cello. The orchestral musicians and the soloist should play here in a way devoid of reciprocal coordination. Then follows the culmination of the work. The chords of the whole orchestra are repeated in similar intervals as at the beginning of the Concerto. After this, there comes a *tutti* chord from the orchestra that takes fifteen seconds. Afterward, to the background of the strings playing fast groups of notes, which create a buzzing and murmuring effect, we hear a mournful phrase on the cello. A characteristic of this phrase is the glissandi that lead from each note downward, and this is exactly what causes this wailing effect.

The work could actually end here, since one could say that this event brought it to a close. What actually follows is the final coda, taking place after the dramatic event that happened a moment ago. This coda leads the orchestra to a *fortissimo* that, after a while, remains only as a reverberation of the piano, the harp, and the tom-tom. Against the background of this reverberation, the cello plays an A in its highest register ten times, and this constitutes the ending of the composition.

From this partly literary description—at least from the use of such words as a "reprimand" or an "escape"—one could infer that the Cello Concerto has something in common with program, or even illustrative, music. Yet nothing is more alien to my intention. This work is a new example of an attempt to develop a musical form to larger dimensions. This attempt is based on the analogies that can occur between music and other arts, in this case—between music and drama.

Source

"Witold Lutosławski o swoim 'Koncercie wiolonczelowym'" (Witold Lutosławski on His Cello Concerto), *Ruch Muzyczny* no. 18 (1973): 3–5. Copyright Marcin Bogusławski. All rights reserved. Printed by permission.

❧

PRELUDES AND FUGUE (1970–1972)

I will start with a quotation from Lévi-Strauss, from his *Savage Mind*: "Non-representational painting adopts 'styles' as 'subjects.' . . . It is a school of academic painting in which each artist strives to represent the manner in which he would execute his pictures if by chance he were to paint any."[1] This rings much more true of music as it is today, than of abstract painting. The personal likes and dislikes of Lévi-Strauss encouraged him to formulate a thought that imposes itself irresistibly on the critical but impartial observer of the situation in music today, both in Poland and in the rest of the world. I would describe this situation as a state of "permanent revolution." Its essential feature is a negation of all that has been used in the past in the area of musical language, compositional technique, style, and means of expression. Hence, the motif of "permanent revolution" in the following statement: what was good yesterday is bad today, whereas what is good today will be bad tomorrow. Perhaps the words "yesterday," "today," and "tomorrow" here are meant symbolically, and should not be taken literally. Nevertheless, they are a sign of the unprecedented brevity of the periods of time in question.

Let us recall some facts. Almost 150 years elapsed between the first baroque music and the emergence of the rococo symphony. The first Romantics are separated from the first classical composers by decades, etc. Even in the uncertain first half of the twentieth century, certain styles, or mannerisms, were relatively long lasting: for instance, the Parisian neoclassicism of "Les Six" and Stravinsky's music of the years from *Pulcinella* (1920) to *Agon* (1957). The period of the Second World War coincides with the grafting of the ideas of the second Viennese school onto a Parisian rootstock, mainly thanks to the teaching of René Leibowitz who, apart from his direct contacts with the composers of the generation of Boulez and Serge Nigg, influenced them through his books (the first French books, in fact) devoted mainly to Schoenberg's work: *Schoenberg et son école*[2] and *Introduction à la musique de douze sons*.[3] The first results of this influence are seen in such compositions as Boulez's *Polyphonie X* of 1950. This time it was not long before the first works opposed to post-Webernism appeared; Xenakis's *Metastasis* followed only five years after Boulez's *Polyphonie X*, while Ligeti's *Apparitions* and *Atmosphères* took about ten years, as did Penderecki's *Dimensions of Time and Silence* and *Anaklasis*. Later on, events proceeded at greater and greater speed so that placing in time such styles as neosimplicité, which was a reaction to the growing complexity of texture, or attempts to date every tendency indicating a possible return to tonality, are pointless. A great number of attitudes, styles, and tendencies coexist, creating a real Tower of Babel. The prospects of some lasting style emerging, which would unite a greater number of artists, cannot be expected to happen quickly.

Some leading figures of today's musical scene manifest a particular impatience with the present state of affairs. Pierre Boulez, for instance, once expressed a view that all the music of the past should be destroyed in order to create conditions in which today's music (probably serial music, since all the other kinds, as he put it on another occasion, do not belong to our time as they are simply useless) could develop and shape the sensibility and taste of today's and future listeners in a natural way. This view moves the majority to indignation and disgust in the face of this composer's seemingly exceptional presumption and arrogance. One can, however, understand it quite differently, namely as an expression of weakness and lack of faith in the strength and importance of the music created today. If it is so feeble that it cannot withstand competition from the music of the past, if the past is so strong a threat to it that there are no prospects for the development and impact of today's music without destroying this past, then Boulez's view expresses a feeling of despair and panic rather than an excessively complacent belief in the strength and importance of the music he initiated.

However, let us not attach too great an importance to composers' verbal statements about their own or others' music. Rather, let us have a look at their own products, that is, the works themselves. As a whole, the musical production of today is characterized by an unprecedented variety of styles and artistic tendencies. This means that we cannot synthesize an enduring stylistic strategy, a lasting and uniform system of organizing sound. This variety greatly hinders the perception of music by a large number of listeners and it constantly prevents the likelihood that new music will reach listeners to the extent that it does in the music that constitutes the majority of the concert, radio, and recorded repertory, that is, the music of the two centuries from Vivaldi to Ravel. What makes the situation for new music worse is the fact that the older music that competes with it is—in essence—a selection of the most worthwhile items.

It has survived to our own time as the pick of the outstanding works chosen over the years, shedding all that proved unfit to survive. The music of our time is still undergoing that process and its merits are constantly obscured by the vast number of mediocre works that have no chance of survival. These works greatly contribute to the bad reputation the contemporary composer has acquired among the majority of listeners to seasons of concerts throughout the world. What aggravates this situation is the system of musical education, which still prefers the music of the past as its basic teaching material, and usually does not allow works composed more recently than several decades ago to be used in instrumental classes. Hence, there are no opportunities for any new rules, new ways of listening, or new hierarchies of sound-phenomena, to emerge naturally in the consciousness of a student at a school of music. All these phenomena are seen from the perspective of rules and principles applying to the music of the eighteenth and nineteenth centuries. We would not be far from the truth if we stated that the majority of works composed in the last dozen years is—from the standpoint of those eighteenth- and nineteenth-century rules—a total absurdity; although from the standpoint of the new rules (and this is how such works should be considered) they are by no means nonsense.

There are many reasons for the long-standing alienation between the art emerging today and the greater part of society, that is, between a composer and the majority of his listeners. This statement, however, should be treated with caution and with many reservations. We know from the relatively recent past that the state of affairs described here led some ideologues to quite false opinions and conclusions. As a remedy, a return to old principles and techniques, along with denigration of everything created in music after 1900, has been recommended. This is obvious nonsense and can only be based on complete ignorance of the issues concerning the rules of the development of art. This nonsense was eagerly adopted by those artists who could not offer anything that would reach higher, beyond eclecticism or simply imitation. The argument for such an ideology was the need for music for the masses. And these masses, their tastes, their liking, and the level of their familiarity with music, were to be a compulsory standard for composers. So the path spiraled downward, toward the lowest common denominator, in which the art of music was to find itself practically a caricature, supposedly crossing the current enormous divide between the composer and the listener. These attempts, which were not crowned with great success in our country, fortunately belong to the past. Nevertheless, they should not be forgotten, and those who were too young to experience them should be told about them.

If we think, however, that the alienation between the composer and the listener is a fact, and that the doctrine familiar to us from the years 1949 to 1955 is unacceptable, then the question arises as to whether any alternative, any remedy for this unhealthy situation in musical life exists. We called the present situation a state of permanent revolution, which is both a grotesque and sad phenomenon, since it degrades the achievements of contemporary music in the eyes of the listeners; it increases their aversion to it and weakens the hope for an early way out of this situation. This supposed "revolution" is an ongoing occurrence over a long period, which conflicts in principle with the essence of the very notion of revolution. What is being revolutionized needs this state of constant revolution. The most revolutionary, most courageous step today would be a style giving the lie to the principle that what was good yesterday is bad today, what is good today will be bad tomorrow. What may give the lie to this principle is to create works of a kind that have a chance of a long life; works that, while being *new* (I stress this particularly), do not proceed from mere novelty. For novelty is the feature of a work of art that grows old quickest of all. In other words: works should be created that represent values independent of the historical context, the values that allow a work to mature properly, just as the well-known masterpieces of the past do. It is certainly a difficult task and not everybody is in a position to undertake it. But every effort, even the most modest, to accomplish this makes a better contribution to progress than every now and again inventing new minor mannerisms and technical or stylistic tricks on a miniature scale in a permanent revolution.

I can already guess the kind of objection the leaders of the permanent revolution will raise to this argument. They could probably quote a dictum once formulated by Roman Haubenstock-Ramati: "Every composer invents a little philosophy for himself in order to justify his own conduct." Yet although I am anxious to make a contribution with my work in order to break the deadlock in the way I have described, I am not conceited enough to believe that I am actually doing this. The future will evaluate my efforts in this direction, and it will keep or reject the results.

∞

Now I would like to address the argument that I am about to present in a much more personal way than I have done so far. The matter under discussion here consists of my works in today's program, that is, the Overture for Strings, which I wrote in 1949, the Dance Preludes for clarinet in a version with string orchestra, piano, percussion, and harp, which I wrote in 1955, and the Preludes and Fugue for thirteen string instruments.[4]

I will start with a confession: in 1947, when I finished Symphony no. 1, I clearly realized that the language I had used in it would not lead me very far—at all events it would not lead me to where I wanted to go. I thought that in order to learn some way of using the traditional twelve-tone, equally tempered scale, I had to start from the very beginning. There existed nothing outside this that could be used in any way to gain the end I was then dreaming of. Neither the tonal and posttonal language (in which I wrote several works) nor dodecaphony could serve my purpose. Therefore, I decided to start almost from scratch, assuming only some axioms which were then obvious to me, such as that not even the simplest move in music, even an interval understood vertically or horizontally, a rhythm or a timbre, or the slightest musical element, is unimportant from the point of view of expression. This was all I knew with complete certainty, and very little else besides. Therefore I decided to try everything that would lead me to where I intuitively wanted to go.

One of the first of my timid and partial ventures of this kind was the Overture for Strings written in 1949. I will not spend long analyzing it; I only want to say that in this piece there are two ways of organizing the music in respect of pitch. The first is the use of two eight-note scales. The first of them consists of two equal four-note groups separated by a tritone, and the first theme is built on this scale (as the Overture is in sonata form with a reversed recapitulation). The second scale I used is made up of eight consecutive semitones, omitting the remainder of the octave. The whole second subject is written in this scale, yet in both cases the scale encompasses not only the themes themselves but also all the music, that is, everything that accompanies the themes. The middle section, which is the development, was written in a free atonal technique, although it is easy to find in it some regular features. Neither of the eight-note scales is present here, or in the initial part or in the part preceding the development.

This work is very impractical, since it needs a lot of work, yet takes only five minutes to play. Usually, after having listened to it, the audience is completely confused in spite of the fact that a long final chord crowns the "work." They seem to expect it to be longer. When Wisłocki[5] conducted the Overture in the National Philharmonic in Warsaw, there was no applause at the end. He did not know what to do; he just brought the orchestra to their feet and left the stage. The premiere took place in Prague with Fitelberg as the conductor.[6] His view of the Overture will interest you. Fitelberg was an enthusiast of my Symphony no. 1. His high opinion of this work meant a great deal to me; it encouraged me enormously. Yet he spoke reluctantly about the Overture, and even a little disparagingly: "It is like a homunculus in spirit." Nevertheless, he performed the Overture very carefully with the orchestra of Radio Prague. It was a public concert, and the work met with some success, with a lot of applause, etc. That's all I want to say about the Overture for Strings. I would only add what is obvious to every listener, that one hears in it echoes of Bartók. No wonder. Almost every composer of my generation when young was affected by this composer.

Dance Preludes. In the 1950s, Tadeusz Ochlewski proposed that I should write a cycle of easy works on folk themes for violin and piano for special academies attended by gifted children who might go on to a conservatory later. I started writing them. However, I could not make the music take shape for the violin, although I myself had played the violin for quite a long time. This being so, I decided to write pieces for the clarinet. They turned out to be good for young clarinetists, but quite difficult for their accompanists. Nevertheless, they were and still are played quite often in various schools, so that they serve their turn. Later on—I don't remember on which occasion—I wrote the version that will be performed today. Here is a funny little detail from the history of these small pieces: I did not manage to write *Paroles tisseés* for the Aldeburgh Festival which Peter Pears had asked me to write for him. Since my name had already been printed in the program, Britten decided to perform another work of mine. He chose the Dance Preludes without realizing the difficulties this version presented (the clarinet part was written in a meter different from the orchestral part), and rumor has it that he conducted it in a state of stage fright. Thus the first performers were Benjamin Britten at the head of the English Chamber Orchestra, and the first soloist was Gervase de Peyer, a famous English clarinetist.[7] There is no need to dwell at length on this work. It is similar to such compositions of mine as the *Bucolics* or the Folk Melodies.

Preludes and Fugue is a work on which a little more can be said. I do not want to bore you with detailed analyses. I will perhaps concentrate on the issues that are most essential in this composition. First of all, the very idea of writing a fugue today, in the 1970s, is strange enough. I am not tempted towards authenticity, so that this work, too, has no features of earlier music, at least I hope not. Nevertheless, I was interested in the form of the fugue, which I understood differently from what is traditionally known as the baroque fugue. I will explain why this happened. In the baroque fugue, as we all remember, there are two kinds of music from the harmonic point of view. One has a more static character, where the themes are present in the expositions and recapitulations, since the themes are always kept in one and the same tonality, at most having a modulation at the very end. Yet the transitional sections—the episodes—usually have more harmonic variety in the baroque fugue, that is, they modulate to some other tonality in which the theme reappears. And then there follows harmonically rather static music again. In the music I started writing in 1961, there are also two kinds of music from the point of view of harmony: one more static, the other more lively. The latter is written in a traditional way, that is, with a common division of time if conducted (if for orchestra), or with a common meter or common pulse, if unconducted. This allows for greater harmonic change no matter what the speed. On the other hand, music using so-called limited aleatorism cannot possess this liveliness when the composer wants to keep full control over pitch organization. Therefore, my aleatoric sections are static from the harmonic point of view.

These two types of music served me in terms of harmony as a pretext—or a reason—for writing a fugue today. The introduction—which precedes the appearance of the first theme—and all the episodes are written to be conducted. They are variable harmonically, that is, what changes is a kind of harmonic aggregate, and it changes relatively quickly. Yet all the passages in which the themes appear are aleatoric, and thus harmonically static. The differences between a baroque fugue and this work are quite substantial, consisting of two things in particular. Firstly, the episodes and, in this case, the introduction preceding the appearance of the first theme have no connection with the thematic material, which is never the case in a baroque fugue, since all its episodes are built on the thematic material. The second feature, which is perhaps more fundamental and in general makes this music different from any polyphony previously familiar to me, is the fact that individual parts of the fugal exposition do not appear as one melodic line, as happens in a baroque fugue (and in many later, even twentieth-century fugues), but in the form of a bundle of several lines, with a heterophonic character. Such a bundle is based on a marked trajectory on which all the lines of a given bundle move. Thus, it is a cycle of sounds and a cycle of the intervals between them. Only the rhythm is not identical, but it is similar. There is something like an indistinct view of the melodic line that constitutes a theme or one layer in the exposition. This is influenced not only by the rhythmic differences in the individual parts of the bundle, but also by the fact that the performers disregard whether their parts are coordinated in time or not. Though they perform all the written values, still they do not have either common meter, or any other common time division. This being so, the intervals present in this bundle play a double role. On the one hand they are obviously melodic intervals, but, on the other hand, one should also consider their vertical impact. In other words, if one instrument plays the first note and the second is already on the second note, the interval separating the first note from the second is not only a melodic interval of the two parts, but also a harmonic interval between both voices. There may be more of these intervals at one time if the bundle is composed of several melodic lines, and the displacement in time is bigger. Therefore, while writing the themes, I always had in mind the possibility of understanding the intervals placed at a certain distance from each other, which may be seen as possible harmonic aggregates. Paradoxically speaking, one could say that the meaning of each of these intervals is neither vertical, nor horizontal, but diagonal. This, of course, does not mean much, except that the intervals have some distinct significance. In the fugal expositions two, three, and even four parts may be found, and each of them consists of several heterophonic lines.

There are six themes. Their character is defined by the Italian markings added to each appearance of the theme: the first, *cantabile*; the second, *grazioso*; the third, *lamentoso*; the fourth, *misterioso*; the fifth, *estatico*; and the sixth, *furioso*. One can infer from this collection of adjectives that what occurs here is a kind of gradation, from a calm cantilena (*cantabile*) to a vehement music played by all the higher instruments, that is, by the violins and the violas in the theme marked *furioso*. These six themes are separated by the episodes that constitute a distinct thread and they are built of totally different intervals. The themes themselves are built on two intervals in different arrangements, that is, on a semitone and a tritone. They do not necessarily appear alternately; for instance, several semitones, which are separated from the next such group by a single tritone, may appear. Thus all the themes are based on these kinds of rows. Yet the introduction to the fugue and the episodes are characterized by totally different kind of intervals, namely by fourths and major seconds. It is a twenty-four-tone row or, more precisely, a twelve-tone row with its one variant in the form of a circle. A specific feature of this row is that it is divided into alternating two- and three-note parts. Inside each group there is also a possible alternation of particular notes. This is a technical detail, but also possibly a useful hint for those who will analyze this work sometime, since without considering this fact, the reconstruction of the row will be impossible.

After quite a lengthy exposition of the six themes separated by a distinct, connecting thread, which, according to how the themes themselves evolve, appears in more and more animated motion (initially in very slow crotchets, then in quavers and semiquavers at double the speed), there follows a long episode in a changing and capricious tempo, which is, as it were, a continuation or development of all the short previous episodes. It leads to what in a classical fugue is the development section. This fragment does not, however, resemble a classical development, since in fact it does not contain literal quotations from the themes. There are only allusions to them, appearing always in at least two layers, and they always unite two different themes. These allusions are easy to recognize, since the themes have their own very characteristic rhythms. They are easily perceptible despite the differences between the intervals and the succession of particular notes, which are not identical with the themes. It is quite a long part, played *pianissimo* the entire time, and it is like an echo of the materials already known from the exposition. Afterward there follows an even longer *ad libitum* section in which material analogous to the two last themes (*estatico* and *furioso*) emerges. This gives this episode a vehement character followed by the *stretto*. This *stretto* is not, as in a baroque fugue, easily recognizable. It is a juxtaposition of the six themes. Although it is impossible to hear all six themes there, we can still discern here and there the fragments or allusions to the themes already heard. This *stretto* appears twice.

Having constructed the core of the work so rigorously, I considered that it was simply necessary to introduce a completely irrational element. Hence, after the *fortissimo* unison, which appears after the second *stretto*, the instruments diverge upward and downward, and there follows the culmination of the whole fugue at the term *tutta forza*. It is a very violent and long moment. What makes it irrational is the fact that it has no connection with the themes or with the previous episodes. It is completely new music. Moreover, it is followed by the coda, which introduces a new theme repeated several times by various instruments. This theme takes a long time to disappear. It must indicate the ending of such a big form as a twenty-minute fugue. When everything becomes quieter, there follows a very short ending, only three measures, which clearly resembles the episode-thread, but definitely has a cadenza-like character. This is the description of my fugue. I would not like to probe deeper into matters concerning analysis of the pitch organization. The mere examination of the contrasting groups or pairs of intervals in the episodes and in the themes would be enough to convey some idea of the sound-character of this work as such.

Source

W. Lutosławski, *O muzyce dzisiaj; o własnych utworach* (On Music Today and on My Own Works). In *Zeszyty Naukowe Akademii Muzycznej w Krakowie* (Works of the Academy of Music in Kraków), ed. Leszek Polony (Kraków: Polish Musical Edition, 1985), 176–87. Copyright Marcin Bogusławski. All rights reserved. Printed by permission.

Notes

1. Claude Lévi-Straus, "The Science of the Concrete," in *Savage Mind* (Chicago: University of Chicago Press, 1966), 30.

2. R. Leibowitz, *Schoenberg et son école* (Paris: Janin, 1946).

3. R. Leibowitz, *Introduction à la musique de 12 sons* (Paris: L'Arche, 1949).

4. Lutosławski finished his Preludes and Fugue in August 1972.

5. Stanisław Wisłocki (1921–1998), famous Polish conductor.

6. The premiere of the Overture for Strings took place in Prague, on November 9, 1949, with the Prague Radio Symphony Orchestra and Grzegorz Fitelberg as the conductor.

7. This first public performance of the Dance Preludes (version for clarinet and chamber orchestra of 1955) took place in 1963 during the Aldeburgh Festival.

LES ESPACES DU SOMMEIL (1975)

The text of the work *Les espaces du sommeil* by Robert Desnos dates from the period when the author, together with a group of French poets, explored the subject of dreams. Desnos was a member of the surrealist movement. Later he abandoned this movement, returning to the neoclassical style in his poetry.

This text is charming, not only because of its structure, but also because of its content and its beauty. It is perfect for setting to music. My composition is in only one part, but it is not a song or a cycle. It is a symphonic poem in which the main role is given to a baritone. The poetic text starts with the words (see figure 2):

> *Dans la nuit il y a naturellement les sept merveilles*
> *du monde et la grandeur et le tragique et le charme*
>
> *In the night there are naturally the seven wonders*
> *of the world, and greatness and tragedy and charms.*

I draw attention to the words *dans la nuit*, which will be repeated and will play a fundamental role in the structure of the whole.

It is a work about dreams, about the "spaces of dreams" (*les espaces du sommeil*). An equally important role is played by the words *il y a toi*, that is, "there is you." The form of the statement is initially, so to speak, the author's story about what the night contains: that is, the content of dreams. At the same time the poet addresses a woman.

The first segment of my work consists of an introduction and four episodes. The sentence shown above, which opens the entire text, is the theme of the musical introduction. What follows is a kind of gentle *allegro*, sung almost as a whisper. Here is the text of the first episode (see figure 6):

> *Les forets s'y heurtent confusément avec des créatures*
> *de légendes cachées dans les fourrés.*
> *Il y a toi.*
>
> *The forests collide confusedly with legendary*
> *creatures hidden in the thickets.*
> *There is you.*

This refers to fantasies in the woods, in the background of which appears the woman referred to above. She is constantly present before the eyes of the dreamer.

The second episode describes a new group of images appearing to the poet in his dream (see figure 12):

> *Dans la nuit il y a le pas du promeneur et celui de*
> *l'assasin et celui du sergent de ville et la*

lumière du réverbère et celle de la lanterne du
chiffonier.
Il y a toi.

In the night there is the step of the stroller and that of
the assassin and that of the policeman and the
light of the street lamp and that of the light of
the ragman's lantern.
There is you.

The third episode consists of the following words (see figure 17):

Dans la nuit passent les trains et les bateaux
et le mirage des pays où il fait jour. Les derniers
souffles du crépuscule et les premiers frissons
de l'aube.
Il y a toi.

In the night there pass trains and boats
and the mirage of lands where it is day. The last
breaths of the twilight and the earliest tremors
of dawn.
There is you.

The fourth episode is an extremely subtle vision, which is very typical of dreams (see figure 22):

Un air de piano, un éclat de voix.
Une porte claque. Une horloge.
Et pas seulement les êtres et les choses et les
bruits matériels.
Mais encore moi qui me poursuis ou sans cesse me dépasse.

A strain from the piano, the sound of a voice,
A door bangs. A clock.
And not only the beings and the things and the
sounds of nature.
But also me who myself pursue or ceaselessly overtake.

Also, mention is made here of the dual personality of the sleeper. Then follow the words *il y a toi*. But this time they don't end the sentence, but start something new. A new segment of my work also begins here (see figure 28).

Il y a toi l'immolée, toi que j'attends.
There is you the sacrificed, you whom I await.

Thus, this woman is described in more detail in a poetic comment. Here again dream-like images appear:

> *Parfois d'étranges figures naissent à l'instant*
> *du sommeil et disparaissent.*
>
> *Sometimes strange shapes are born at the instant*
> *of sleep and disappear.*
>
> *Quand je ferme les yeux, des floraisons*
> *phosphorescentes apparaissent et se fanent et*
> *renaissent comme des feux d'artifice charnus.*
>
> *When I close my eyes phosphorescent*
> *flowers appear and wither and*
> *are reborn like fireworks of flesh.*

This is a strange combination of words, a strange description of the imagery of fireworks.

> *Des pays inconnus que je parcours en compagnie*
> *de créatures.*
> *Unknown lands which I traverse in the company*
> *of creatures.*

And once again the words *il y a toi* return, but with a new comment.

> *Il y a toi sans doute, ô belle et discrète*
> *espionne.*
>
> *There is you undoubtedly, discreet and beautiful*
> *spy.*

And then:

> *Et l'âme palpable de l'étendue*
> *And the palpable soul of the expanse.*

What a beautiful French expression! Then the poet enumerates various dream visions:

> *Et les parfums du ciel et des étoiles et le*
> *chant du coq d'il y a 2000 ans et le cri*
> *du paon dans des parcs en flammes et des baisers.*

> *And the scents of heaven and the stars and the*
> *cock crow from 2000 years back and the peacock's*
> *cry from the park aflame and kisses.*

The following image is remarkably gloomy but thrilling:

> *Des mains qui se serrent sinistrement dans*
> *une lumière blafarde et des essieux qui*
> *grincent sur des routes médusantes*

> *Hands clasped together ominously in*
> *a wan light and axles which*
> *grate on petrified roads.*

The word *médusantes* originates from *méduse*, that is, "medusa"; it means something that causes a stare of horror, which dumbfounds one.

This is the end of the second section of my work, and the next one begins with the return of the words *il y a toi* (see figure 82); they open a whole sequence of epithets to describe the person who again appears in the poet's dreams:

> *Il y a toi sans doute que je ne connais pas,*
> *que je connais au contraire*

> *There is you undoubtedly whom I do not know,*
> *whom I do know on the contrary,*

> *Mais qui, présente dans mes rêves, t'obstines*
> *a s'y laisser deviner sans y paraître.*

> *But who, present in my dreams, persist*
> *in leaving yourself to be guessed without appearing.*

> *Toi qui restes insaisissable dans la réalité et dans le rêve.*

> *You who remain elusive in reality and in dream.*

> *Toi qui m'appartiens de par ma volonté de te posséder*
> *en illusion, mais qui n'approches ton visage du mien*
> *que mes yeux clos aussi bien au rêve qu'à la réalité.*

> *You who belong to me because of my want to possess you*
> *in illusion, though you do not bring your face close to mine*
> *until my eyes closed as much to dreams as to reality.*

Toi qu'en dépit d'une rhétorique facile où la
flot meurt sur les plages, où la corneille vole
dans des usines en ruine, où le bois pourrit en
craquant sous un soleil de plomb.

You who despite a facile rhetoric, where the
wave dies on the sands, where the crow takes flight
in ruined factories, where wood rots,
cracking under a leaden sun.

Toi qui es à la base de mes rêves et qui secoues
mon esprit plein de métamorphoses et qui me laisse
ton gant quand je baise ta main.

You, the root of my dreams and who rouse
my spirit filled with metamorphoses and who leave
me your glove when I kiss your hand.

The whole part remains in the tempo of an *allegro*, contrary to the preceding one, which is a kind of *adagio*. Thus, all these enumerations and characteristics of the woman from the poet's dreams proceed in a hectic musical atmosphere, in a feverish "declamation," the latter in a metaphorical sense of this word, since it is not a true declamation, but singing.

There follows an approach to the culmination of the whole work, in words that bring the expressive tension in the poem to a climax (see figure 92):

Dans la nuit il y a les étoiles et le mouvement
ténébreux de la mer, des fleuves, des forêts, des
villes, des herbes, des poumons de millions et
millions d'êtres.

In the night there are stars and the dark
movement of the sea, of rivers, forests,
cities, weeds, of the lungs of millions and
millions of beings.

Here we have a crescendo and an orchestral *tutti* (see figures 102–103). After a long *fortissimo*, which leads this *tutti*, the voice enters again, *pianissimo*, on words with long durations. And some words from the beginning of the text return:

Dans la nuit il y a les merveilles du monde.

In the night there are the wonders of the world.

Dans la nuit il n'y a pas d'anges gardiens,
mais il y a le sommeil.

In the night there are no guardian angels,
but there is sleep.

The word *le sommeil* is intoned in a languid, undulating cantilena, and is repeated several times. Finally, there comes the moment in which the voice remains alone:

Dans la nuit il y a toi
In the night there is you

leading to the ultimate climax, which is for me not only an expression of supreme poetic mastery, but also something even deeper than the poetry itself:

dans le jour aussi
in the day also.

Thus, in the last line literally everything is inverted. In this way, after the whole vision, which is not devoid of nightmares, but is full of enchantment at the same time because of the presence of the woman, there follows an awakening. It is joyful, positive.

The general structure of *Les espaces du sommeil* presents itself as follows: short invocation, four fast but calm episodes, kept in low registers and separated by pauses, which constitute the first part, *Allegro*; after this part, with the words *il y a toi l'immolée*, there comes the slow movement, *Adagio*; and the last part, again *Allegro*, this time of a hectic, dynamic character.

And now a curiosity regarding the problems that face a composer who writes works of this kind. I think that it is unrealistic to make the music imitate specific sounds mentioned in the text, as for instance in the fourth episode:

Un air de piano, un éclat de voix
Une porte claque. Une horloge.

What should a composer do when he encounters such words as these? The simplest way, which is to imitate the sounds, leads to the slippery slope of banality, and that is out of question.

How have I treated this problem? It is by no means a secret—on the contrary, I consider that a potential listener should understand my intentions. So, this text is sung, and practically recited on one note in short values, and the individual phrases are separated by pauses. The soloist is accompanied by a static chord, forming a kind of background, in which nothing happens musically. We hear alternately the recited text and the silence.

My interpretation is as follows: the performer tells the listener his dream. Thus, the recited text is a narrative, it gives an account of things happening in the mind of the performer, whereas a pause—silence—is a moment when he listens intently to the sounds that are inaudible to others. However, neither he nor the listeners hear anything in a real sense—after all it is a dream—so that the symbol of the "inaudible" is here the static chord.

I think that the mechanism of my reasoning, although it is perhaps not obvious at first, becomes clear after listening to the work several times and reflecting on it. It depends to a great extent on the performer, who should—in this passage—act and somehow play the role of a man listening intently to something. This can be achieved by a suitable expression on his face or with a glance.

That is all I have to say on the interpretation of the text.

Source

Seminar on W. Lutosławski's vocal-instrumental works held at Baranów Sandomierski in 1976. In *Spotkania muzyczne w Baranowie. Muzyka w kontekście kultury* (Musical Encounters in Baranów. Music in the Context of Culture) ed. Leszek Polony (Kraków: Polish Musical Edition, 1978), 103–107. Copyright Marcin Bogusławski. All rights reserved. Printed by permission. In this text, the English translation of the Desnos's poem was by Paul Griffiths. Reprinted by permission.

SACHER VARIATION (1975)

I composed *Sacher Variation* for the seventieth birthday of Paul Sacher. On that occasion in 1976, a special concert took place in Zurich, during which Mstislav Rostropovich played several pieces for unaccompanied cello specially written by different composers. A few words about Paul Sacher. He is known above all as an outstanding Swiss conductor who founded two orchestras in his country: Bassler Kammerorchester in Basel and Collegium Musicum in Zurich. Besides that, he has been a great Maecenas of music and has played an important role in the history of music of our century. He has commissioned over two hundred works by different composers. To give the example of the importance of his activity it is enough to mention four works commissioned by Sacher: Music for Strings, Percussion, and Celesta by Bela Bartók as well as his *Divertimento for Strings*, and the Second Symphony for String and Trumpets by Arthur Honegger—to me the best work of that composer—and certainly the most beautiful work of Frank Martin—his *Petite symphonie concertante* for harpsichord, piano, harp, and two string orchestras. The idea of the cello pieces for Sacher's birthday was using the letters of his name as the basic material. In German S, A, C, H, and in Italian Re, which means E flat, A, C, B natural, and D were the notes in question. In my Sacher Variation there are two, so to speak, threads. One is based on the letters of Sacher's name and the other—on the remaining notes. Both threads alternate developing their respective musical ideas, leading to a climax on the notes of Sacher's name. The piece ends in a rather amusing way.

Source

Manuscript in English. Copyright Witold Lutosławski Collection, Paul Sacher Foundation. All rights reserved. Printed by permission.

MI-PARTI (1975–1976)

There are, as is well known, two sources of tradition in twentieth-century music, although not everybody wants to acknowledge them. The first one, obvious to everybody, is the Viennese School, the only one that has within itself something that may be called a system. This school has had a wide impact, since one can clearly point to musical phenomena that reflect its influence. If one accepts what Boulez says, one should recognize it as not just the main, but the only source of tradition. In this respect, however, I am unable to believe Boulez, since I think there also exists a second source, which is equally important but much more difficult to define. The figures standing for the two currents in the development of twentieth-century music are, on the one hand, Arnold Schoenberg and, on the other, Claude Debussy. What is distinctive about their attitudes?

To my mind, Schoenberg is a descendent of the composers of the tonal system. It sounds paradoxical, since the goal of his creative searching was, among other things, the invention of a system that would liberate him from tonalism [*sic*] and, at the same time, would be something constructive, providing possibilities for the future. The need to replace the previous system with something new, but still systematic, is very typical of the Germanic mentality. However, to regard this statement as an attempt to view the whole development from tonal music to the present day would be to exaggerate it. It is not so, and for me one fact is unquestionable, namely that a system, as such, is not an indispensable tool for the composer.

The proof of this is the work of Debussy and of a great number of composers I would venture to number among his followers. They are characterized by the lack of a unifying and unique system, specifying rules governing pitch and its organization. A system, as I have already mentioned, was indispensable for those whose imagination was shaped by the German way of thinking, perceiving, and creating music. Yet it was not a necessity for such a composer as Debussy, although that does not mean that Debussy was an improviser. On the contrary, I believe that he is one of the few composers whose music has perhaps no place in which a note is fortuitous. The consequence of this method is obvious to everyone. His technique is a collection of favorite procedures from which he eliminated everything he inherited from the past. In his early works we still observe traces of past times; at the end there is only Debussy himself. Of course, I am talking only about the technical, not the historical aspect of this issue.

This second current of tradition, which to me is indisputable, exists up to the present day in the early works of Stravinsky, Bartók, Varèse, Messiaen, and many other contemporary composers.

What characterizes the thinking of those belonging to this second stream of tradition is the lack of a need for a concrete, uniform system, either tonal or dodecaphonic. In its place, an individual, personal musical language arises out of various inspirations, that is, a language consisting of a number of procedures that do not reveal any perceptible and clear connections with each other. As the simplest example, I can point to Olivier Messiaen, whose very uniform musical language, as nobody would deny, springs from totally distinct elements. The first creative impulse is his fascination with, and a true personal feeling for, Indian music. The composer does not go deeply into its theoretical aspects, as he is not interested in transposing its rules or patterns. Bewitched by its originality and beauty, he builds his own version of Indian music. His second source of inspiration is birdsong. He writes it down in a way that defies scientific methods, but scientific precision is not essential when it is only a matter of stimulating one's imagination. Looking at the modal system he invented, that is, the modes with limited possibilities of transposition, and his theory of rhythm with added values (*valeurs ajoutées*), we observe highly differentiated elements that are not connected. On this basis, however, there emerges a work that in everybody's view constitutes an indivisible unity, identifiable after only a few moments of listening to the music.

So we may ask: what is the factor uniting these seemingly totally separate sources of inspiration? It is something impossible to define in a scholarly way and impossible to describe. To my mind it is, however, much more efficient than the clear and obvious logicality that characterizes other systems. It is extremely mysterious, but, when it exists, it guarantees much more unity and homogeneity in a work of a given composer than any logical system. It is the composer's personality. For it was nothing other than the composer's person- ality that enabled contradictory, or at least totally independent, elements to unite in Messiaen's work into an aesthetic whole. For my part, I believe in the primary importance of the personality. After all, Schoenberg himself said that his system did not imply any style. Also we know very well from the history of music that, although the tonal system used the same conventions in organiz- ing material, it did not establish uniformity in the work of a given composer. From this comes the simple conclusion that a system is a necessary factor for some composers, whereas for others—it is not. Now, does the lack of a system mean chaos? Of course not, provided that rules of another kind exist. A type of nonsystematic musical thinking is present in contemporary creativity, and I will cite one of my newest works as an instance of it.

Mi-parti is a one-movement composition, constructed from some strands that determine it as a whole. They seem independent from the point of view of their structure and sound-physiognomy. Nevertheless, without this appar- ent independence and these differences, the whole would not exist. So in this lecture, I would like to discuss some ways of organizing sounds. This will be an insight into the composer's workshop from only one point of view, namely pitch organization.

The first section of the work is relatively long; it starts on page 1 and goes on to page 15 of the score (up to figure 19). It becomes the first segment of the work (I call it conventionally A), in which the pitches are ordered according to the following twelve-note rows (see example 2-11).

I should explain that the distinguished sounds (those notes filled in with black ink) are those in a new position in relation to the preceding twelve-note row. The accidentals apply only to the notes to which they belong.

The next fragment—B (between figures 20 and 24)—is a new thread of the work that I would describe as two-layered. The compositional procedure used here consists of juxtaposing two multisegment layers in quite a specific way, so that the beginning of the section of the consecutive segments occurs in each layer at a different place.

For instance, at figure 20, the first segment of the first layer unfolds. Soon (with the entrance of the second violin), the first segment of the second layer is added, as though in counterpoint. While it lasts, its second segment ap- pears in the first layer (figure 21), and it continues like this alternately. The organization of the pitch has a loose connection with the Viennese tradition; it consists of using from time to time a pattern of twelve various sounds. The points of departure are vertical aggregations of those sounds, as well as their horizontal successions. The consequences, however, are different from those of the dodecaphonic technique. The main purpose of the latter was to ensure the homogeneity of the organization itself. One row was supposed to be a basis

Example 2-11.

for the entire form, the parts of the row constituted the elements, etc. In my case, this idea takes a different shape, since within the framework of the form I use many rows containing all twelve sounds, which sometimes transpose themselves automatically up to 144, or even 288. The horizontal row of the twelve tones of this section under discussion (reduced to one octave) presents itself as shown in example 2-12. Thread B, the double-layered structure of which is strictly connected with the organization of pitch, was built out of this material, as shown in example 2-13.

As I mentioned, the beginnings of the consecutive segments of this thread occur in layers in an unsynchronised way. In order to keep homogeneity inside the layers, I had to make a choice of sounds, such that each segment in every layer would be consonant with the two segments of the remaining layer. Hence, the horizontal ordering of sounds also has consequences in the realm of harmony.

I will explain this problem more precisely by referring to the preceding example. The beginning of the first layer (see upper stave) is built of the first five notes of the row. Together with them, but with some delay, comes the second layer (see lower stave) based on the notes from the ninth up to the twelfth, bound together, in turn, with the second segment of the first layer (the notes from the fourth to the eighth), which overlap the beginning of the second segment of the second layer (the notes from the twelfth to the third), etc. Each layer is then formed from segments of equal construction:

1. The first layer—the five-note segment, the initial two notes of which always repeat the last two notes of the preceding segment, and the three remaining notes are new ones;
2. The second layer—the four-note segment that starts with the repetition of the last note of the preceding segment.

Example 2-12.

Example 2-13.

Thus, the appropriate selection of pitches of the initial row and an adequate construction of the elements of each of the layers ensure there will never appear a combination in which I would lose control over the character of the resulting sound. Such a complicated technical process was necessary in this previously discussed fragment of the work, since it is an *ad libitum* section. What is created in it is an aleatoric counterpoint, which results from only partial regulation of the unfolding in time (in the score there are only arrows indicating when the action of a new segment starts). Thus, it should be foreseen how the pitches will be shaped inside each segment and the relationship between the layers in the encounters of particular segments.

The proposed twelve-tone row was used in this section in various ways, as shown in example 2-14. In the first segment (figure 20) the sound material is D, F sharp, G, A sharp, and B, which is repeated many times and has a highly melodic character. It is performed by various instruments, creating a heterophonic melody. The second segment of this layer (figure 21) has, in turn, a harmonic character. The sounds are E, G sharp, B, D sharp, and A sharp, played by the piano with the pedal to create a "crushed" five-note chord. Two further segments are again, alternately, melodic (the third segment: C, A, C sharp, G sharp, E; the piccolo part, figure 22) and harmonic (the fourth segment: D, F sharp, D flat, F, C, figure 23). The second layer of the thread under discussion was arranged according to similar guidelines (see example 2-14).

The third thread—C—starts on page 19 (figure 24). Its base is the twelve-tone row with a special construction that causes its transposition to be one whole tone lower (see example 2-15).

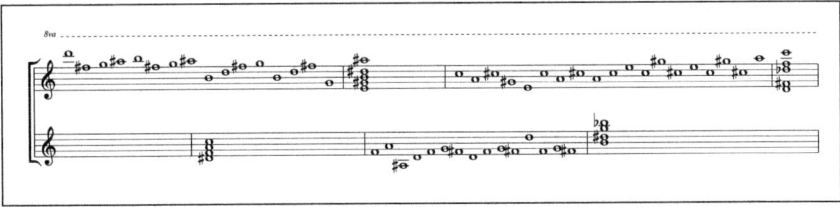

Example 2-14.

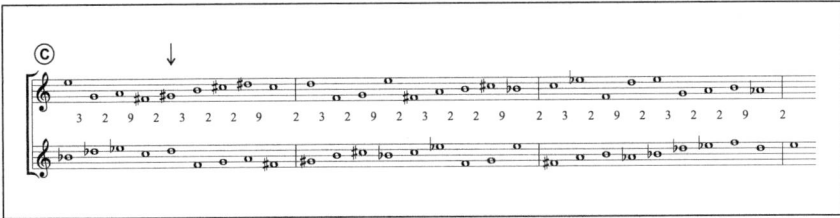

Example 2-15.

The previous example shows three versions of this row. In the work, how-ever, all the succeeding transpositions have been used. The progress of sounds created constitutes a trajectory pointing out the developmental course of the third thread. When this thread becomes interrupted in favor of the other, and when it returns, it starts with the note on which it ended, or with the next note (see example 2-16). This row and its composition are characteristic of the use of a particular kind of texture, in which the seemingly double-part texture in the horizontal dimension transforms itself into multisound aggregations. This effect is obtained by holding the sounds in particular instruments, while the action continues in the other instruments. In this way there arises, from the seemingly double-part texture, a pentachord in the second measure on the pause, a tetra-chord on the next pause, and so on. This is illustrated by the previous example. I would like to stress that, to make this clearer in this example, I reduced the pitches to one register and I took no account of the violin and piano parts, which accompany this particular thread as counterpoints or ornaments.

In the course of the work, the double-layered thread B is introduced again in a somewhat accelerated, multiplied, and more complex form. In conse-quence, the double-layered character of this thread at figure 29 acquires slightly different traits. First of all, the segments become shortened and their number increases. It is a clear intensification of the musical content, tending clearly to-ward the culmination of the whole work, which occurs between figures 39 and 40. It is filled by the section presenting a development of the double-layered

Example 2-16.

Example 2-17.

thread, which constitutes the core of the whole, fast movement.

After the culmination—one measure after figure 40, at the word *lento* and the metric sign 3/2—the way of organizing the pitch changes completely. A new kind of chord appears there, which becomes the basis of the construction of the succeeding section D (up to figure 43), as shown in example 2-17. It remains, or so it would seem, in the sharpest contrast in relation to the material of thread A and to the elements constituting the double-layered thread B.

When I wrote the program note, I described the above combination of sounds as "icy," being influenced, of course, only by my subjective impression. Is it in reality an "icy" one? I do not know, and I do not consider it to be essential. I think, however, that it is sometimes useful to create terms (at least from the realm of perceived impressions) in order to identify a phenomenon that does not have any specific name.

The process of shaping the final section consists of moving particular sounds by octave steps in a scarcely perceptible way toward the middle of the scale, so that at the end of this section (figure 43) the whole could close within a major seventh. Now a gradual passage from the mood of "iciness" toward something which could be called "warmth" takes place. This passage leads to the end of the work. Example 2-18 shows the basis of the development is the previously used row, which made a trajectory in the course of its action in the third thread (refer back to example 2-15, from the sound marked with an arrow). It appears in such a way that its parts, as the elements of aleatoric groupings, will create harmonies (in the example, they are marked with brackets of various length) built out of the successive sounds of this trajectory. The example shows that these groupings will contain—in the horizontal and in the vertical dimension—respectively: the first, six sounds; the second, five sounds; next, four sounds, three sounds, two sounds, and one sound. On the unison A, which is dynamically stressed, the culminating point of this section is reached. Next, in the passage up the scale, the groupings of three, five, and seven sounds lead to the final fading away on the unison C.

Hence, the physiognomy of the harmonies depends on the number of sounds used in each grouping, and a characteristic feature of their paths is the fluency of passing from one grouping to another. The passages between the segments of the sections take place by playing to the end of the repeated phrase, so that a grouping never starts simultaneously in all the instruments. As a result, the harmonies being formed fluently are obvious in their clear shape only after a while. Thus, a process of penetration and clarification of sounds is taking place alternately. It consequently tends toward a single note, which will appear twice: as a culminating point and as *finalis* of the work.

In this account I have presented some examples of the compositional procedures used in *Mi-parti*, and have tried to focus on one feature only, namely the organization of pitch. It was, one could say, a glance into the composer's "kitchen." As we well know, staying in the kitchen too long makes the cooked dish tasteless.

Therefore, I address myself to those who listen to my work with a request to be so good as to forget everything I have just said. I think that in a work and in its perception the emphasis is quite different. In saying all this, I only wanted to show how the composer takes pains with the things he wants to achieve, in what way he applies some rules, and how he creates them and uses them in order to discard them, if need be, in the future.

Source

W. Lutosławski, *Mi-parti*. In *Zeszyty Naukowe Zespołu Analizy i Interpretacji Muzyki* (Works of the Section of Analysis and Interpretation of Music). Vol. 3: *Z problemów muzyki współczesnej* (Problems of Contemporary Music), ed. Krzysztof Droba, Leszek Polony, and Krzysztof Szwajgier (Kraków: Akademia Muzyczna, 1978), 43–55. Copyright Marcin Bogusławski. All rights reserved. Printed by permission.

Example 2-18.

DOUBLE CONCERTO (1979–1980)

I wrote my Double Concerto for Oboe, Harp, and Chamber Orchestra in response to a commission from Paul Sacher. On several occasions in the past, the people who commissioned a work from me have chosen its first performers. The knowledge that the new piece would be baptized by a well-known ensemble or soloists, sometimes even by a great artist, was always an especially stimulating factor for me while I was composing it. It was like that when Swedish Radio asked me for a string quartet, to be performed first by the LaSalle Quartet. It was similar for *Paroles tissées*, written for Peter Pears; the Concerto for Cello and Orchestra, composed for the Royal Philharmonic Society in London and the cellist Rostropovich; and *Les espaces du sommeil*, which I composed in response to an invitation from Dietrich Fischer-Dieskau.

I felt the same kind of spur when confronting this double concerto, the premiere of which, in Lucerne, Paul Sacher had entrusted to Heinz and Ursula Holliger, oboist and harpist respectively. While I was working, it was a great help to me to think of how it would sound in performance by the Collegium Musicum Zurich, conducted by Paul Sacher, and two outstanding Swiss soloists. Heinz Holliger gave me valuable assistance in using the new multiphonic tones, which he himself performed on the oboe. He recorded them on tape for me, and showed me the notation he had worked out for them. These sounds with their bizarre character make an extraordinarily strong contrast to the noble sound of Holliger's playing in the classical repertory; they are most in evidence in the third episode of the march finale (marked *marciale e grotesco*). This episode is self-consciously different in its weird, caricature-like sonorities, verging on ugliness, from the other sections of the work with their lyrical, declamatory, or mocking characteristics.

The essential character of the three movements is captured to some extent by the performance markings: *rapsodico, dolente,* and *marciale e grotesco.* But these should not be taken too literally. Every attempt to define the expressive content of music with verbal, that is, nonmusical, means is open to misunderstanding and has no intrinsic objective value. I invented a saying, in connection with another piece, that I would like to repeat: Music per se means many things. It is precisely when one would like to state its meaning clearly that one realizes that it can also mean something quite different—exactly the opposite and simultaneously.

Source

Neue Zürcher Zeitung, no. 189 (August 1980): 57. Copyright Marcin Bogusławski. All rights reserved. Courtesy of *Neue Zürcher Zeitung.*

SYMPHONY NO. 3 (1972–1983)

Before I pass to the presentation of my work I would like to say that I am deeply moved and deeply grateful to the organizers of this meeting for their willingness to include the presentation of the recording of this work in the celebrations accompanying the anniversary of the Gdańsk Agreements.[1] It is for me an honor and a privilege and a reason for pride and joy. However, I also feel a kind of embarrassment. It is caused by the fact that, as a composer of a work deprived of a text or an implied meaning, or any literary program, I feel that my work is in no easy and noticeable way connected with the occasion.

Music is the most abstract of the arts and it was Debussy who said that music starts where the words end. In fact, each of the semantic arts, such as literature, poetry, or theatre, transmits some meaning and has more or less an unequivocal content. Joseph Conrad wrote in his preface to *The Nigger of "The Narcissus"* that the artist's task is to do the highest justice to the visible world.[2] This noble task is clearly fulfilled by semantic art, one that expresses something concrete and possible to translate into words. It is, unfortunately, not true in the case of music. I think that, as a composer, I am at odds with Joseph Conrad's definition of an artist's task. On the contrary, it seems to me that music belongs to those arts that are unable to do justice to the visible world, but rather can convey something of the invisible world, since what Conrad called a visible world was the one we live in. Music, I repeat, concerns the invisible world, the world of our desires, our dreams, the ideal world, and therefore the world we long for. This is how I imagine an ideal musical work, since, as I said, music is the most abstract of all arts, not transmitting any content that could be expressed in words.

As proof of this I would like to mention two examples of the reactions of people after having listened to my work, a recording of which you will hear in a moment. The first statement comes from one very famous, world-renowned conductor and a close friend of mine, who, after having heard the live, concert performance of this work, said this was deeply tragic music. Yet some days ago—and this is the second reaction—one of my younger composer colleagues, after having heard the same work, said: "for me it is a work full of vitality." So he considered this work to be an expression of optimism. As you see, music can be perceived in various ways by different people, and this is why it cannot be considered as an unequivocal art, even if we attribute to it an extramusical meaning.

Everything I have just said contributes to my feelings of embarrassment in participating with my work in a celebration with which this work is actually not directly connected. Is my embarrassment really 100 percent? I do—please allow me to tell you this in confidence—have some hope that this is perhaps not entirely so. What gives me the courage to say so? A very simple thing: a fact that a man has one soul, what we can otherwise call his psyche, but it makes no difference what we call it, since the point is not the terminology but the essence of the matter. In this particular psyche, various things happen. Therefore, in the creative act itself, in the very action of a composer's everyday work, all the things that happen in his psyche are involved. This is why I hope that everything we experience in this country affects what flows from my pen as a composer.

Let the confirmation of this hope be clarified in one sentence I read in a Chicago newspaper after the premiere of my Third Symphony. The critic wrote a comprehensive report, of which one sentence stuck in my memory and filled me with great joy. He wrote: "I understand that such a work can be created now and in Poland." I did not ask him what he meant by that, although I know him well. But this allows me to think with some optimism that perhaps all these experiences we all share (I am talking about all the Poles) influenced what flowed from my pen, although it was not my direct intention. What fills my heart with some optimism is also the fact that someone could sense in a musical work that the man who wrote it was not an alienated person, isolated from society, but that he was a member of it and felt very deeply and warmly his solidarity with society.

This is actually all I would like to say to you. However, allow me only one further remark of a technical nature. What is to be presented here is the recording of my Third Symphony as performed by the BBC Symphony Orchestra under my direction in March of this year.[3] I would like to draw your attention to an obvious fact: this will be, unfortunately, only a recording. A recording of a musical work can be compared with a colorless reproduction in relation to the original painting. Hearing it through a loudspeaker is not the best circumstances to get into touch with a work. After all, it is a work written for the orchestra, for living people, and only after having heard this work on the stage can one remember it properly when listening to the recording. However, the circumstances are such that we could not offer a live performance at this festival.

Source

Statement before the presentation of the recording of the Symphony no. 3 in Sopot, August 26, 1984, in St. Michael's Church during the Gdański Sierpień '84 festival (Gdańsk, August 1984). *Ruch Muzyczny* no. 21 (1984): 6–7. Copyright Marcin Bogusławski. All rights reserved. Printed by permission.

Notes

1. These agreements were made on August 31, 1980, in the shipyard in Gdańsk between the representatives of the communist regime and the shipyard-workers' committee under the guidance of Lech Wałęsa, which opened the way toward the foundation of the Solidarity Union.
2. See note 11 in the introductory text "Life and Music" in the present collection. The full passage Lutosławski referred to says: "A work that aspires, however humbly, to the condition of art should carry its justification in every line. And art itself may be defined as a single-minded attempt to render the highest kind of justice to the visible universe, by bringing to light the truth, manifold and one, underlying its every aspect." See: Joseph Conrad, *Typhoon, The Nigger of the "Narcissus," and Other Stories* (London: The Folio Society, 2000), 229.
3. The BBC Symphony Orchestra performed the Symphony no. 3 under Lutosławski's direction on March 23, 1984, in London (Royal Festival Hall, the Music of Eight Decades' Series).

∞

I wrote the last note of the score in January 1983, but I began writing it in the early 1970s, and the whole main movement of it, which is the nucleus of the whole piece, had been discarded. That means I had decided to put it into my drawer and I had never taken it out. I had to write another piece and in this way, two years' work was obliterated. It does not mean that in the meantime I did not compose other pieces. On the contrary, there were quite a number of them between the early 1970s and the end of the work on the Symphony. I composed, for instance, *Mi-parti* for orchestra, *Novelette* for orchestra, *Les espaces du sommeil* for baritone and orchestra, Double Concerto for oboe, harp, and small orchestra, and some minor pieces, but I did not want to be in a hurry when writing a piece such as the Symphony, because I thought that it would be better when it had matured and I think it is, in a way, a summary of my experiences in the last decades. Now I would like to say a few words about the form of this piece.

It is a typical form for pieces like my String Quartet and other pieces, like the Second Symphony. It is characteristic of those pieces—the form consists of two parts, two movements in which the main movement is not first, but the second and last. The first is a sort of introduction. What was the origin of this decision? It was based on my experience as a listener to music. To me, the composition of a large-scale closed form was ideally realized by the pre-Beethovenian classics. In those symphonies or in chamber works of Haydn and Mozart especially, the main movement is at the front, that is, the first. Then, as we all know, come other movements that are, perhaps, less important, requiring not as much concentration for the listener compared with the first movement. The final movement is mainly a light piece and very easy to listen to, and requiring less concentration. That was, from the psychological point of view, the right solution, ideal in a way, especially under the social circumstances when that music was being played mainly at court. But, of course, it could not last too long.

After Beethoven especially, and in Brahms's symphonies, to my mind, the composition of a large-scale form changed into something that consisted of two main movements, at the beginning and at the end of the form, with some perhaps less important movements in-between. When I say "less important," I mean something that requires less concentration, less tension, less attention. To my mind this solution, especially Brahmsian, was not terribly satisfactory, although I am a great lover of Brahms's music myself. Nevertheless, I always feel exhausted, so to speak, after hearing a symphony or a concerto of Brahms. I could not listen to any other music after listening to one of his symphonies or concertos because it is a little too much—I always feel "overfed," although, of course, I am enchanted by the music itself; that is quite a different matter. But I always think of a work of music as conditioned by the perception of it, that is, as a sort of an acoustical phenomenon in time, and just this, but also as impulses that form a whole from a purely psychological point of view, that is, a sequence of experiences corresponding to our psychological capacity to concentrate on the sound-process. And that is why the final result produced by a large-scale form, is extremely important to me.

I wanted to find a better solution, subjectively, as a result of my own personal experience as a listener to music. I wanted to find a solution that would be satisfactory to me and yet not follow the pre-Beethovenian classical pattern, which, to my mind, was not possible to follow today. I thought of a solution in the form of two movements in which the first is a sort of preparation for the main event, the second and last movement of the piece. That was the case, for instance, and very characteristically so, of my String Quartet. The first movement in such a two-movement form must consist of something that will engage the interest, involve, and provoke, but never satisfy the listener. That means there cannot be any climax in the first movement, no actual development, but rather some samples of something that may engage interest or involve the listener. It is very often abruptly interrupted, as in the form of my String Quartet, in which the octave passage separated particular episodes of the first movement. Those octaves abruptly interrupt each of the episodes, giving no possibility of development and leading to a climax. This is also a psychological trick in a way. In such introductory movements (such as in the Second Symphony, and also, to some extent, the Third Symphony) the psychological trick consists of creating an expectation of something that does not in fact happen. And finally, as a result of this, at the end of such a movement, we feel a sort of impatience. We want to hear something with more substance, something more important and something that would finally bring satisfaction. This is naturally provided by the main movement. One can compare the result of such a first movement of a large-scale piece to creating an appetite for something more substantial. For instance, it may be compared (although it may be a little dangerous to make such comparisons) to an appetizer in comparison with the main dish, or—in other words—creating low pressure that must be filled; and that is the role of the introductory movement. I think this was clear to everyone who listened to my String Quartet.

Almost the same construction exists in my Third Symphony. The only difference is that, following the main movement, there is an epilogue. That means that this third movement, which is pretty short (it is a separate movement, although played *attaca*), could be treated as a sort of commentary, as it was in the case of my String Quartet. All three parts are played without interruption. Yet the epilogue is a slow movement, contrasting with the main movement, which is fast, some conclusion to the work. After this slow *adagio* comes a short, fast coda, bringing in some motifs from the main movement. So the novelty, in comparison with former pieces, consists in the presence of this third movement (the epilogue).

The first part of the Symphony no. 3 is very similar to the first, introductory movement of the String Quartet, and also to the *Hésitant*—the first part of the Symphony no. 2, since it consists of several episodes separated by a sort of refrain that forms an independent plot, so to speak, a separate "action." The difference, however, is considerable, because in comparison with the String Quartet and Symphony no. 2, the episodes of this Third Symphony constitute much more development of the main idea of the first movement. In a way, it is a triplet piece, the first episode being a fast triplet piece, after which comes the second episode, composed of triplets but at half the speed.

The third episode is also in a ternary meter, but again twice as slow. Hence, the construction of this sequence of three episodes differs from the other pieces in which there were no developments whatsoever within particular episodes. Here, in the first movement, there is a moment at the end that introduces a sort of *adagio* that does not belong to any of the episodes, but separates the third episode from the refrain that comes next. After the refrain (the refrain is longer), and after the *adagio*, it is abruptly interrupted by a group of four notes. I would like to draw your attention to a very important feature in this Symphony whereby each episode is characterized by four notes repeated several times in the piece. The Symphony starts with those four Es, it ends with those four Es, and each episode is interrupted by those four Es. Finally, when, after the last refrain, this interruption comes, it marks the beginning of the main movement. Again, those four notes and their repetition are one of the motifs of the main movement.

The main movement itself is composed in a form that can be considered as a sort of allusion to the sonata form. Although I do not follow the classical pattern, there is, nevertheless, a group of motifs that is contrasted with another (this time not a group, but a theme), which is in a sharp contrast with the first group. Instead of a development, there is a large section, that is, the middle part of the form, in which new motifs are being introduced. On the other hand, there is a recapitulation in which all the motifs of the first group are repeated and then even pile up in a sort of *stretto* in *tutti* of the orchestra. The main movement of the symphony leads clearly to a climax, although this is not the final climax of the work, because that comes toward the end, within the last movement, which is the epilogue. I think that this will be all I will say about the Symphony regarding its construction and form.

I think that these few words could very well replace listening to my Third Symphony many times, during which we can finally get an idea of the construction of the piece. So I think it may be of use to you when listening to the music, but I should perhaps advise you not to remember too much of what I have just said but rather to listen to the recording with an open mind and without any preconceptions. But I think that during the performance you could possibly remember what I have just said about the construction; it may make it a little clearer, although my role here is just to present the recording of the piece. The recording was made last year (1984) in the BBC studios in London with the BBC Symphony Orchestra conducted by myself. I am afraid that the new recording that I made this year (1985) in August, because I was not terribly happy with the first one, is not ready yet. We made, of course, the recording in fragments and not as a whole. It will, however, be ready in a couple of months. So I regret being forced to present to you a recording that, to my mind, is not ideal.

Source

"W. Lutosławski's Presentation of His Third Symphony." In *From Idea to Sound. Proceedings of the International Musicological Symposium Held at Castle Nieborów in Poland. September 4–5 1985*, ed. by Anna Czekanowska, Zbigniew Skowron, and Miloš Velimirović (Kraków, 1993), 140–42. Copyright Marcin Bogusławski. All rights reserved. Printed by permission.

⚭

I began sketching my Third Symphony as early as 1972. In the following years I composed the main movement, but subsequently I discarded it completely. It took several years for the idea to become mature, and it was only in January 1983 that the whole score finally was ready. It is true, however, that during that period I composed several other works: *Les espaces du sommeil* for baritone and orchestra, *Mi-parti* for orchestra—which has already been performed by the Chicago Symphony Orchestra, *Novelette* for orchestra, and some smaller pieces.

When composing the Symphony I constantly had in mind the magnificent sound of the Chicago Symphony Orchestra, whose recordings are still in my working room. It was a tremendous stimulus for my imagination. But on the other hand, the weight of responsibility when writing a work for such an extraordinary ensemble made me especially exacting toward myself. That is probably why the work on the Symphony took such a long time.

The form of my Third Symphony is the result of my experience as a listener to music and particularly to such large-scale forms during a period of many years. Although the extraordinary strategy of Beethoven in this realm has always fascinated me and was a supreme lesson in musical architecture, the model of a perfectly balanced large-scale form has been for me the pre-Beethovenian symphony, particularly Haydn's. I confess I always feel exhausted after a performance of a Brahms's symphony, concerto, or even a sonata, probably because there are two main movements (first and last) in each of them.

These considerations made me search for other possibilities and, finally, I found a solution in a two-movement larger-scale form where the first movement prepares the main one which follows. The first is meant to interest, to attract, and to involve, but never to entirely satisfy the listener. In the course of the first movement, the listener is supposed to expect something more important to happen, he may even get impatient. This is exactly the situation when the second movement appears and presents the main idea of the work. This way of distributing the musical substance in time seems to me natural and is in conformity with the psychology of music perception. I have composed several works in such a form, the most characteristic being my String Quartet and the Symphony no. 2.

My Third Symphony is constructed in a similar form: after a short introduction comes the first movement, the "preparatory" one. The music here is never set in motion for very long. Many pauses interrupt the musical course. The movement consists of three episodes, the first being the fastest, the third—the slowest one. As a matter of fact, the tempo remains the same and the difference of speed is achieved only by the use of longer rhythmical values. A short slow section leads to the main movement.

The second movement is composed in a form that may be defined as "an allusion to sonata-allegro form" with its contrasting themes. Toward the end a series of *tutti* sections is followed by the climax of the whole work. A separate *adagio* passage, where dramatic recitatives of the strings alternate with a broad cantilena, forms the epilogue of the Symphony. A short, fast coda ends the work.

Source

Warsaw Autumn Festival 1988, Program Book (English version): 238–39. Copyright Marcin Bogusławski. All rights reserved. Printed by permission.

CHAIN 1 (1983)

The title *Chain 1* suggests both the form used in this work and the intention of composing more "Chains" in the future.[1] In a work composed in chain-form, the music is divided into two strands. Particular sections do not begin at the same moment in each strand, nor do they end together. In other words, in the middle of a section in one strand a new section begins in the other.

This principle has already been used in my previous compositions as a base for particular stages of the form or in whole movements, as in the *Passacaglia* of my Concerto for Orchestra. In *Chain 1* the principle of chain-form serves to construct the greater part of the piece. Toward the end, the texture becomes more complex and consists of several individual parts played *ad libitum*, which form a network of melodies to be played *cantabile*.

I have composed *Chain 1* for the fourteen principal players of the London Sinfonietta as a souvenir of our common music making.

Source

Warsaw Autumn Festival 1988, Program Book: 215. Copyright Marcin Bogusławski. All rights reserved. Printed by permission.

Note

1. *Chain 1* was written for and dedicated to Michael Vyner and the London Sinfonietta. The premiere took place on October 4, 1983, in London; it was performed by the London Sinfonietta with the composer conducting.

PARTITA (1984)

I composed the *Partita* for violin and piano in the autumn of 1984 on commission of the St. Paul Chamber Orchestra, Minnesota, for Pinchas Zukerman and Marc Neikrug. The work is composed of five movements, of which the main ones are the first (*Allegro giusto*), third (*Largo*), and fifth (*Presto*). The second and fourth movements are only short interludes played *ad libitum*. A short *ad libitum* section also appears before the end of the final movement. The three main movements refer, mainly in the aspect of rhythm, to the eighteenth-century tradition of instrumental music. It is, however, only a type of allusion. In the aspects of harmony and melody, *Partita* belongs to the same group of my recent compositions as Symphony no. 3 and *Chain 1*.

Source

Warsaw Autumn Festival 1988, Program Book (English version): 133. Copyright Marcin Bogusławski. All rights reserved. Printed by permission.

CHAIN 2 (1984–1985)

I composed *Chain 2* during the years 1984–1985. The title of work relates to its form. Over the last few years I have been working on a new type of musical form, which consists of two structurally independent strands. Sections within each strand therefore begin and end at different times. This is the premise on which the term "Chain" was selected.

I composed *Chain 1* for an ensemble of soloists, but this does not mean that the *Chains* form parts of a cycle. They are completely independent compositions,

Chain 2 for violin and orchestra (commissioned by and to Paul Sacher) is in four movements: (1) *ad libitum*, (2) *a battuta*, (3) *ad libitum*, and (4) *a battuta—ad libitum—a battuta*. In the *ad libitum* movements and in the *ad libitum* section of the fourth movement, the element of chance plays a part within fixed parameters. This has been a feature of my compositional style since 1960 and always offers new possibilities. However, in the last few years I have been particularly preoccupied by the shaping of pitch (i.e., melody, harmony, and polyphony). In my opinion, the traditional scale with its twelve notes has not yet been fully exploited in terms of harmony. I believe that there are still many possibilities to be discovered, independent of Schoenberg's twelve-tone technique.

Source

Warsaw Autumn Festival 1986, Program Book (English version): 241–42. Copyright Marcin Bogusławski. All rights reserved. Printed by permission.

PIANO CONCERTO (1987–1988)

My Piano Concerto consists of four movements played without a break, although each has a distinct ending.

The first movement is in four sections. In the first and third, the motifs used are rather negligent, light, sometimes somewhat capricious, never too serious. In contrast to the first and third, the second and fourth sections are filled with a broad cantilena that eventually leads to the climax of the whole movement.

The second movement is a kind of *moto perpetuo*—a rapid "chase" for the piano, against the background of the orchestra, which eventually calms down and prepares the third movement.

The third movement opens with a recitative for the solo piano, after which the soloist, again without orchestral accompaniment, intones a songlike *Largo* theme. The middle section, which begins with the orchestra's entry, differs from the first by its more forceful, in places dramatic, character. The unaccompanied cantilena returns at the end of this movement.

In its form, the fourth movement makes allusion to the baroque *chaconne*. The theme (always played by the orchestra) is built up from short notes interspersed with rests and not—as in the traditional *chaconne*—from chords. This theme, which is repeated over and over again, presents only one layer of the musical discourse. Against this background, the piano introduces one new episode after another. Both layers operate according to the principle of "chain form," that is, beginnings and ends of the piano episodes do not coincide with beginnings and ends of the theme. They occur together only once, toward the end of the work. The theme enters for the last time in a shortened form (without rests) and played by the orchestral *tutti* without the piano. A short recitative for the piano (*fortissimo*) follows against the background of the orchestra, and then a short coda (*presto*) concludes the work.

The element of chance plays a role in my Piano Concerto, though somewhat less than in other works. It is—as always—strictly subordinate to the principles of pitch organization (harmony, melody, etc.). I tried to explain how that is possible in an article published in 1969 in the periodical *Melos*.[1] I will not repeat here what I said there. Just one thing should be remembered: there is no improvisation in my music. Everything to be played is notated in detail and should be realized precisely by the performers—the members of the ensemble. The only, but fundamental, difference between the sections marked *ad libitum* (i.e., not conducted) and the sections in traditional notation (i.e., written in measures with a given meter) is the fact that in the former there is no unit of tempo common to all the players. In other words, each plays his part as if he was playing it alone and does not coordinate it with the other players. This results in a specific "supple" texture of rich, capricious rhythms, not to be achieved in any other way.

Everything said here concerns what is by no means the most important aspect, namely the means the composer uses to achieve his end. And what is his end? Only the music itself can answer that question. Fortunately, it cannot be expressed in words. If it was possible, if a piece of music could be narrated precisely in words, then music would be a totally superfluous art.

Source

Typescript in German. Copyright Witold Lutosławski Collection, Paul Sacher Foundation. All rights reserved. Printed by permission.

Note

1. W. Lutosławski, "Ein neuer Weg zum Orchester." *Melos*, no. 7-8 (1969), 297–99.

CHANTEFLEURS ET CHANTEFABLES (1989–1990)

The title of my recent work *Chantefleurs et chantefables* seems to be untranslatable since the words used by Robert Desnos to name his latest book were invented by him. The book contains eighty short pieces of poetry telling of flowers, animals, birds, and insects. The poetry is intended for children; I cannot say the same of the music of my cycle scored for soprano and orchestra. It sets to music nine texts selected from Desnos's book.[1] Still the fact that the book addresses the little ones is somehow reflected in the music I have written.

Source

Warsaw Autumn Festival 1991, Program Book (English version): 220. Copyright Marcin Bogusławski. All rights reserved. Printed by permission.

Note

1. The texts chosen are: (1) *La Belle-de-Nuit* (The Marvel of Peru); (2) *La Sauterelle* (The Grasshopper); (3) *La Véronique* (The Speedwell); (4) *L'Eglantine, l'Aubépine et la Glycine* (The Wild-Rose, the Hawthorn, and the Wisteria); (5) *La Tortue* (The Tortoise); (6) *La Rose* (The Rose); (7) *L'Alligator* (The Alligator); (8) *L'Angélique* (The Angelica); and (9) *Le Papillon* (The Butterfly).

• *3* •

On Composers and Musicians

&

ON J. S. BACH

$\mathcal{A}$rt is a special kind of human activity. The domain of art covers those things a human being can communicate to another individual only by those means appropriate for a given art. It is impossible, for instance, to put into words what the geniuses of music or painting have communicated to humanity through their works. Therefore, when we are asked to talk about art, we often encounter a total helplessness trying to find words.

This helplessness is especially painful when we want to put into words even a small part of such an immense phenomenon as Bach's oeuvre.

Let us then limit ourselves to one general reflection. When contemplating Bach's works, we are often amazed that he was able to liberate huge masses of psychic energy with such simplicity and naturalness. He did it in a way that brings to mind a notion of some kind of obviousness. This clarity of Bach's art is perhaps its greatest mystery. We sometimes try to reflect on this mystery. We compare then the clarity of Bach's art with our perception of the air, the soil, or the sunbeams. We do it because, just as the physical side of our being grows up basing itself on the elements of nature, so our spirit also formed and enriched itself, since our youthful years, on the heritage of geniuses, in our case apparently first of all, on Bach. Thus no wonder that he seems to us to be as obvious as the air or the sun.

We are privileged to also participate in what Bach had to communicate to people. Today we are so closely immersed in Bach's heritage that we can hardly imagine its lack. If we were ever, by some perfidious calamity, to be deprived of what has become innate in us, the work of the greatest geniuses of humanity, we would not be able to recognize ourselves in this devastation.

Source

Johann Sebastian Bach, 1750–1950:Almanach, ed. Zofia Lissa (Warsaw: Czytelnik, 1951), 143–44. Copyright Marcin Bogusławski. All rights reserved. Printed by permission.

ON W. A. MOZART

Everything that I might write about Mozart seems to me to be poor, pale, and awkward in comparison with the feeling I experience while listening to his music. These experiences can't be expressed in words and sentences. All adjectives, "pure," "crystalline," "perfect," etc., sound empty and naïve as soon as we hear the first bars of any symphony, concert, or quartet by Mozart. Therefore, on the anniversary we are just celebrating, instead of expressing in words some thoughts, I prefer to ponder for a while the peculiarity and, probably, the uniqueness of the phenomenon whose name is Wolfgang Amadeus Mozart, and to realize once again how happy we all are who are given the opportunity to commune with his art.

Source

Manuscript in Polish. Copyright Witold Lutosławski Collection, Paul Sacher Foundation. All rights reserved. Printed by permission.

ON BEETHOVEN AND BARTÓK

Here are two neighboring anniversaries: Beethoven's and Bartók's. The two are not only related by the proximity of their anniversaries but also, as I discovered today, there are parallels to be found in Beethoven's and Bartók's works. I notice them when I compare the sixteen Beethoven and six Bartók quartets or when I perceive the sonata forms in *Music for Strings, Percussion, and Celesta* or in the Sonata for Two Pianos and Percussion. The Beethoven effect manifests itself not only in the forms of Bartók's music, but also in its deeper aspects, which—for want of a better term—I will call the aspects of content.

Bartók for a long time was seen as first and foremost a great folklorist, who raised the "folk" to the level of the "universal." However I don't feel strongly about this opinion. It is true that scientific work on folklore was a passion of his life but, by chance, this has concealed from his listeners much deeper and more important parts of his activity. For me this is obvious. Therefore, while listening to Bartók's music, I forget the folk sources of his melodies or rhythms, just as I forget the Germanic folklore that abounds in the music of Beethoven, Mozart, or Schubert.

We are afraid to label in words what music communicates to us. For we know in advance that, instead of revealing a complex and mysterious phenomenon, we only skim over its surface or simply fall into triviality. Therefore, I hesitatingly put forward the thought that Bartók's music speaks to us about great things. Such an insight is certainly not obvious. In order to make it more comprehensible, let us listen with concentration, say, to the slow movement of the *Divertimento for Strings* or the last movement of the String Quartet no. 6. We will then forget Bartók's "folklorism" and his being Hungarian, and even the fact that he will remain one of the classics of our century. This music carries us into a place in time where there is a unity of feelings that has and always will bring people together.

Source

"Beethoven and Bartók Anniversary," typescript in Polish. Copyright Witold Lutosławski Collection, Paul Sacher Foundation. All rights reserved. Printed by permission. This text was probably written between 1977 (the 150th anniversary of Beethoven's death) and 1981 (the 100th anniversary of Bartók's birth). What prompted Lutosławski to write this text was certainly the proximity of two dates: March 25, 1881 (Bartók's birthday) and March 26, 1827 (Beethoven's death).

❧

ON MESSIAEN

I owe a lot to Olivier Messiaen's music. It never directly influenced me, but its characteristics and its concomitant greatness are facts of great significance for me.

There are two traditions to be distinguished in twentieth-century music. The first proceeds from Schoenberg and his school, the second (which to many is not as obvious) from Debussy and the manifold consequences of his discoveries. In my opinion, the second is the more important, and in every instance it comes closer to my own convictions. Debussy was an empiricist. His unusual ability to imagine sound gave him ideas that (it seems) were related to his experience, and his immediate reaction to sound phenomena. The primacy of immediate experience gives Debussy's work a firm foundation, the support for his compositional technique. It simultaneously argues for the rightness of such a technique and makes it possible to predict its future development. Messiaen's oeuvre, which obviously derives from the Debussy tradition, is eloquent proof of this. It clearly relates to the empirical response to sound phenomena. A characteristic example is the significant role Messiaen gives to harmony in his music. The harmonic factor is preeminent here, not subject to any other, ostensibly more important, element. Within this sphere, Messiaen created a powerful, ultra-rich sound-world, exceptionally characteristic of his personality. Here I confine myself to just this aspect of his music, and I will use it as an example. It is not my object to analyze the work of this great composer. All I want to do is draw attention to an element in his music with which I feel solidarity and which I myself try to follow in my compositions.

Source

Typescript in Polish. Copyright Witold Lutosławski Collection, Paul Sacher Foundation. All rights reserved. Printed by permission.

ON RAVEL

A work of art is a document that says much more about the potential of its creator at a given moment than about his ambitions. These ambitions—epitomized in the idea of a work and realized only partially—can be, however, visible to a penetrating eye. What are these ambitions in the case of my own musical productions? One is certainly novelty. If a composer's creativity does not contribute anything new to the common output of humanity, then he produces stillborn works. Novelty is not, however, my main aim; more importantly, it is not my *only* ambition. Works whose novelty is their only raison d'être are of doubtful value, for novelty is the feature of art that ages the quickest. Although I desire novelty avidly, I do admit that the durability of a work of art is much more important to me than its novelty. So, when writing musical works, I try to imagine how they will look in the future and what will they mean to me, not at the first, but at the twentieth, or even fiftieth performance. With such a test, I can appreciate them and think about them instead of polemics about the existing state of affairs. While longing for durability in my works, I have always had an eye for the music of those composers who were privileged to be able to achieve this durability. One of them, beyond a doubt, is Maurice Ravel. He seemed to display a certain indifference to the reforming tendencies in art, which prompted one famous French musician to see Ravel only as an "inexcusable consolidator" and even to reproach him with a "bourgeois conception of music," as opposed to those who represented courageous experimenters, breaking with inherited traditions—people like Beethoven, Wagner, Debussy, or Berlioz. This is a partial and short-sighted opinion about Ravel, just as partial and short-sighted as seeing Beethoven as first and foremost a courageous experimenter. I strive to discern in every work of art its unique physiognomy, independent of any historical context. Therefore I declare myself with another famous French musician who considers Ravel to be a classic composer, the Mozart of our century.

Reality and the predictions of some scientists, who warn humanity about a series of hard trials that await us within a few decades make us consider contemporary art differently than we could only ten years ago. This is why I consider it short sighted to see the value of a work of art only in terms of whether it has a reforming spirit. I hasten to add that in the light of the remark I have just made, I consider such an approach to be anachronistic and out of date.

Today the main concern of all those who are not indifferent to the fate of art should be what will happen to it in the near future: whether it will degenerate faster and faster, which is typical for periods preceding the closure of some cycle of development, or—on the contrary—whether it will strengthen itself, referring to what is great and timeless, which will allow it to survive the hardest tests and to transfer the baton in the relay race to future generations.

When we have such thoughts, we reflect on the immediate past in order to find durable and unquestionable values able to withstand the test of time and its adversities. Ravel's works surely belong to this category, and among the array of contradictory tendencies of his period, they shine as the purest diamond.

Source

Manuscript in Polish. Copyright Witold Lutosławski Collection, Paul Sacher Foundation. All rights reserved. Printed by permission.

ON ROUSSEL'S SYMPHONY NO. 3

I am not a musicologist, or a theoretician, or a critic. I am a composer, but also a listener to music, as everyone here among us is, I suppose. Now, as a listener I would like to share with you my impressions of a work that, to my mind, does not deserve its present fate. Albert Roussel's Symphony no. 3 (1929–1930) is rarely performed publicly, and it almost never appears in publications about music. Yet it is a work that, in my view, deserves to be recognized as one of the greatest achievements of our century. Needless to say, it is also the greatest achievement of the composer himself. This view was expressed by Harry Halbreich in his fine commentary accompanying the recording of all four of Roussel's symphonies, when writing about the Symphony no. 4 that "its only shortcoming was to have come *after* it."[1]

The aim of my presentation today is not an analysis of this work, and even less a rational explanation of its quality. I want to share with you my impressions evoked by Roussel's Symphony no. 3 and, possibly, encourage you to a greater interest in this work.

I am aware that the aesthetic direction and stylistic leanings characterizing this work are very far from the subjects that interest composers of recent decades. This symphony may represent a style that is not popular today, and that is even somewhat alien to the tastes of today's young composers. This style is sometimes called neoclassicism, although this term is far from being precise and unequivocal. I justify the use of the term in this case because Roussel adopted forms that are close to classical ones, especially the sonata form in the first movement of his symphony.

The lack of interest in neoclassicism and even neglect of its principles could be explained by what are seen currently as the disadvantages of this style, such as reliance on the models of Viennese classicism in constructing large forms, and the use of that period's characteristic rhythmic patterns, articulations, and, to some extent, types of expression. In other words, neoclassicism is blamed for borrowing too much from the past in proportion to what is totally new. Yet the very heart of it relies on an unconventional combination of a tradition borrowed from the Viennese classics with the sound language of the 1920s and the 1930s, which has nothing in common with the language inherited from the end of the eighteenth and the beginning of the nineteenth century. The strengths of neoclassicism are its thematic invention, solidly constructed large forms, and the special musical vigor so characteristic of the symphonies of Haydn, Mozart, or early Beethoven. The emergence of this style in the 1920s and the 1930s was a reaction to the state of music at the beginning of the twentieth century. That state was characterized by a trend away from traditional melody as in, for instance, Schoenberg's idea of athematicism, and by a shift of interest toward such musical elements as texture, rhythm, sound color, and, especially in France, harmony. This process contributed new or formerly undeveloped components to the means of expression, but, on the other hand, the music was relatively poor as far as its melodic content was concerned

(I mean here particularly the thematic role of melody as a formal factor). It also lacked a strong structure comparable to the large forms of the eighteenth and nineteenth century. The appearance of the neoclassical trend in such circumstances seems to me to be a natural reaction to the phenomena I have just described. The term *neoclassicism* is often associated with Stravinsky and with his hardly convincing maxim "retour à Bach." I consider this a mistake. We usually associate the term *neoclassicism* with the names of Haydn, Mozart, and Beethoven, rather than J. S. Bach. Apart from that, Stravinsky's supposed neoclassicism is hardly to be perceived as a reference to the past in a literal sense. Stravinsky's music of that period is a result of a satirical glance toward the past and, while looking back, he sometimes goes so far as to caricature it. This adds a special attractiveness to his music, but it is hard to discern in it any serious connection with the past. The neoclassicism of Hindemith or Honegger, or even Roussel appears much more "serious."

Here I will allow myself some words of a more personal nature: in my childhood and youth I was fascinated by French music from the beginning of our (twentieth) century, especially—it goes without saying—by Debussy and Ravel. Such elements as harmony and sound color seemed to me to be insufficiently exploited. I found it strange that both these leading composers almost wasted their talent on works that were not of the greatest value. I dreamed of large forms, comparable with the classic symphonies, created by the great French innovators using variegated harmony and orchestral colors. It was then that I heard Roussel's Symphony no. 3 for the first time. I have to admit that this work, although great by itself, fulfilled my expectations only to a small degree. Roussel's harmony, although original and rich, is not so "magical" as that of Ravel or Debussy. His use of the orchestra abounds with excellent ideas, which in certain moments evoke real emotions, but it also reveals some awkwardness or even lack of good taste. However, Roussel's symphony offers such extraordinary riches that all the criticism of its significance does not shake my faith in its worth.

∽

Let us briefly examine the thematic material on which the work is based. I will deliberately play its themes in a monodic form, in order to be able to concentrate on their melodic and rhythmic aspects. Here is a motto-theme that is present in all three movements of the symphony. I show it in the form in which it appears for the first time. It constitutes a culminating point of the development section, after two measures in which the tempo is slowing down (*poco meno allegro*), in the orchestral *tutti* marked with *fff* (except *ff* in the percussion) (see page 27 of the score).[2]

The first theme of the first movement draws attention by its length. It contains thirty-one measures preceded by three introductory measures. Its first fifteen measures are built of groups of three measures each. What is worth remembering is the motif that follows the first theme and appears in the development section, after the above-mentioned culminating point.

The second theme is presented in B-flat major, that is, in the corresponding major key, as in traditional sonata form. It contains only sixteen measures, which are divided untraditionally into: 4 + 5 + 3 + 4 (see page 10). Its first part includes a motif that later plays a less important role. The whole is constructed largely in accordance with the classical model of sonata form.

The second movement, *Adagio*, starts with the motto-theme (common for all three parts). This time it introduces a broad, melodious phrase that leads to a short motif that will play a significant role in the final section of the *Adagio* (see page 44). There, it will be repeated twice, as if insistent, leading to the culmination of the whole movement. Two other contrasting themes belong to the primary material on which the second movement is based. The first of them, while moving in the rhythm of a slow procession, attracts attention by its harmony, which hints at Ravel's harmony (see page 47). The second theme, which introduces a new, faster tempo and is constructed in the form of a fugato, begins again with the five notes of the motto-theme. This theme will appear just before the end of the second movement, initially in the flute part, then in the horn, and finally in the solo violin. These three entrances represent for me a particular, rare beauty.

The third movement is a scherzo written in a traditional triple rhythm. Two themes come to the fore. Here is the first of them, preceded by a kind of call to attention (see page 70). The second one, played by the oboe, has a prepossessing simplicity with a small hint of humor (see page 73). Also worthy of notice are the secondary motifs, such as the one on page 77 of the score, or an episodic one played by the trumpet (see page 84).

And here is the first theme of the last movement (see page 98). It is complemented by a contrasting motif, which will later play an important role in the final parts of the symphony. As though in answer to it, the violin plays a phrase worthy of attention (see page 105). Just before the recapitulation, the motto-theme appears again. This time it is played by the solo violin against a background of harmonies that are both simple and sophisticated, and it constitutes one of the most beautiful moments in the whole work.

The recapitulation ends with the motto-theme; this time in a solemn version, but free of any pomposity. It is a gorgeous completion of this extraordinary work.

☙

Except for the enumeration of the themes, what I have said is dictated by a subjective reaction and cannot in any case be an uncontestable truth. I decided to discuss Roussel's Symphony no. 3 not solely because I have a particular feeling for this work—which fifty years ago had an impact on my own development—but also for the more important reason that it seems there is an analogy between the role works of this kind played in their time and the present-day desire for art of great substance, full of content, transcending fashions and trends, and avoiding narrow-minded new technical or even stylistic tricks of no concern to the genuine listener. I trust that such an art, in spite of threats to our civilization, will come into being, since there are many people who strongly feel the need for it.

Source

Manuscript in Polish. Copyright Witold Lutosławski Collection, Paul Sacher Foundation. All rights reserved. Printed by permission. This text was written as a lecture for the Academy of Music in Basle, and was probably delivered in June 1970 during Lutosławski's visit to that city, where he participated in the festival of International Society for Contemporary Music.

Notes

1. That is, after the Symphony no. 3. See: H. Halbreich, "Commentary to the Recording of Roussel's Symphony No. 3 and No. 4," trans. Elizabeth Buzzard (ERATO ECD 88226).
2. This and the following references are made to this edition: Albert Roussel, *3e Symphonie en sol mineur* (Paris: Editions Durand & Cie, D. & F. 12149, 1971).

❦

ON SHOSTAKOVICH

I don't consider myself to be an expert on Shostakovich's music. Of course I know a number of his works, and many of them I frankly admire. But I don't have enough knowledge of him to enable me to express my opinion on this matter. But another Polish composer, my young and talented colleague, Krzysztof Meyer has such knowledge. He is the author of a book on Shostakovich;[1] he knew him well personally and was also on friendly terms with him during the final years of his life.

As for myself, I can only share a few impressions of my encounters with the music of this great Russian composer. I heard his music for the first time a very long time ago. When I was at the Lycée, a copy of some preludes printed in Moscow fell into my hands. These were probably the Preludes op. 2, and hence the works of the teenage Shostakovich. What struck me instantly was their originality, a very particular kind of lyricism, and often a good sense of humor. This was an indication of the humor I found much later in his suite from the ballet *The Golden Age*, which was performed before the war in Warsaw.[2] At the same time, I heard the Symphony no. 1 performed, and it was received with great admiration by Polish listeners.[3] It was immediately clear to me that we were looking at a talent of high caliber, with a very distinct personality. We all know how quickly this symphony conquered the whole world. I recently became aware that one of Shostakovich's admirers, and an enthusiastic promoter of his works in Europe and in America, was the great Polish conductor Artur Rodziński. When, after a break caused by the war, I had the occasion to be in touch with Shostakovich's music again, it was through a gramophone record of the Symphony no. 8 recorded by Rodziński. This powerful work, considered by many to be one of the best in Shostakovich's oeuvre, amazed me then by its seriousness and drama, elements that did not exist in his works I had known from before the war.

The postwar years brought, of course, many performances of Shostakovich's works in Poland. Only then could one be fully aware of the monumental character of his oeuvre. I understand that humor and the grotesque are secondary traits in Shostakovich's musical personality. Personally, I regret this, because it is just these elements that stand out in his works instead of other, perhaps even more important, ones. This is why I especially like his Symphony no. 9, which I consider a consummate masterpiece from the first to the last note.

In 1957, I had an occasion to meet Shostakovich over the course of a number of days at the Prague spring festival.[4] Unfortunately, there was no common language in which we could communicate. Hence, our contact was limited to an exchange of kindly glances and the simplest courtesies. I regret to this day that because of this I missed the opportunity of communicating with this great composer.

Source

"On Shostakovich for the Moscow TV," manuscript in Polish. Copyright Witold Lutosławski Collection, Paul Sacher Foundation. All rights reserved. Printed by permission.

Notes

1. Lutosławski meant Krzysztof Meyer's *Szostakowicz* (Shostakovich), published in 1973 by Polish Musical Edition in Kraków. The extended edition of this book (free from any censorship, which was abolished in Poland after 1989), entitled *Dymitr Szostakowicz i jego czasy* (Dmitri Shostakovich and His Time), was published in 1999 by Wydawnictwo Naukowe PWN in Warsaw.

2. The Suite from Shostakovich's ballet *The Golden Age* was performed by the Warsaw Philharmonic (with Julius Ehrich as conductor) on February 17, 1933.

3. Shostakovich's Symphony no. 1 was performed by the Warsaw Philharmonic twice before the war: in March 1929, conducted by Grzegorz Fitelberg, and in February 1936, conducted by Lovro Matacić.

4. No appointment with Shostakovich is noted in Lutosławski's pocket calendar of 1957. The sheets between May 12 and 31 are empty, and the only meeting noted is that with Prof. Smetaček on May 22.

ON SIBELIUS

The reputation of the works of Jean Sibelius is a unique, perhaps even unprecedented, phenomenon in the history of the music of our era. In his native Finland, as well as in Sweden, Norway, and Denmark, Sibelius is a kind of cult figure. His music is elevated above everything that has been created in recent times; it is considered as an embodiment of the most truthful account of human anxieties and aesthetic aspirations. It creates the most beautiful and the deepest emotions in both experienced listeners and the wider audience. In England, Sibelius is one of the most popular composers. In the United States, Sibelius's symphonies and symphonic poems belong to the core repertoire of the great orchestras and outstanding conductors. There is no doubt that this particular fondness for the music of Sibelius in the countries I have mentioned is sincere. Moreover, nobody should doubt that it is his due: the works of Sibelius show an undeniable musicianship, as can be seen by everyone who, through circumstances and their own competence, has been able to familiarize themselves sufficiently with the work of this great Finnish composer.

Does Sibelius enjoy the same popularity among audiences beyond the Scandinavian countries, England, and the United States? Is he similarly esteemed by musicians and music critics? One cannot, unfortunately, answer these questions definitively. The characteristic traits of Sibelius's work and individuality are known to the average listener from Central Europe only to a small extent. Those who are familiar only with the Violin Concerto, *Valse triste*,

Finlandia, or even his Symphony no. 1, certainly do not know the "real" Sibelius. The fact remains that the majority of the works that most clearly express
his personality (I have in mind here, first of all, his Symphony no. 4) remain
unknown to the average European listener. Furthermore, one cannot assume
with any certainty that the spread of knowledge of Sibelius to other countries
and hence the popularizing of the "real" Sibelius, is only a matter of time. We
should also not forget that Sibelius's last work was published in 1929, that is,
twenty-six years ago and that he was born in 1865, about the same time as
Richard Strauss, Glazunov, Granados, and Dukas[1]—those composers whose
works are always known and esteemed, which they deserve.

How do we account for the different approaches to the music of Sibelius
by people from northern Europe and the rest of his audience?

To solve this interesting and quite enigmatic question is not a task for the
present article. Joseph Conrad understood art as "the appeal of one temperament directed to all the other innumerable temperaments whose subtle and
resistless power endows passing events with their true meaning, and creates the
moral, the emotional atmosphere of the place and time."[2]

Perhaps special features of the temperament of both Scandinavians and
Anglo-Saxons, those features differentiating them from other people, have influenced the appreciation of the works of Sibelius until now, making them less
understandable, for instance, in Poland than in Denmark.

However, let us abandon these hypotheses, and content ourselves with
keeping in mind that this phenomenon is a mysterious one. Let us pass on to a
report of the festivities that took place in Helsinki in June of this year[3] on the
occasion of the ninetieth anniversary of Sibelius's birth.

∽

The so-called Sibelius Week, which in fact took ten days, started on the ninth
of June. The Finns tried their best to give the festivities great brilliance and
glamour. The president of the Republic was its patron. Four Finnish orchestras took part (one created especially for the festival), as well as five Finnish
conductors, a choir, a string quartet, and several soloists. Nonetheless, one
did not have to be content with only local musicians. Two first-rate soloists
with well-known names were engaged—Elizabeth Schwarzkopf and Yehudi
Menuhin—and the two final days of the festival were reserved, as far as performances were concerned, for the most attractive events: two appearances of
the Philadelphia Orchestra with Eugene Ormandy. Outstanding music critics
and composers from Belgium, England, the Soviet Union, Norway, Poland,
France, Sweden, Denmark, Czechoslovakia, the United States, and the German
Democratic Republic were invited.

During the festival, all seven Symphonies, the Violin Concerto, the most important symphonic and vocal-symphonic poems, the String Quartet, songs, and various small instrumental pieces were performed. In this way, the organizers attempted to give an overview of Sibelius's oeuvre in the best setting.

This beautiful and impressive event can be an example, or a model, for other countries. Incidentally, it made one reflect that Szymanowski's works as a whole also still remain unknown to Polish audiences.

◇

A week devoted to the work of one composer creates particularly favorable conditions for becoming more closely acquainted with his artistic personality. One remains longer in the atmosphere of his works, one has a chance to discern particular phases of his development, to compare them, and to identify the features common to all his works.

In spite of the favorable conditions for listening to Sibelius's work during the Helsinki week, it is by no means an easy task to obtain an overall grasp of it. We have here undoubtedly a very individualistic composer writing very personal music. Is it characterized by some easy to identify features? Has it some self-evident, characteristic harmonic, melodic, and instrumentation features that are apparent at first sight? While contact with, say, the music of Debussy or Schoenberg allows one to become aware of the musical language of these composers, unfortunately, the same is not true for Sibelius, whose characteristics are less easily identified. The essence of his musical language is deeply hidden. Giving in to the temptation of easy comparisons, one could say, however, that Sibelius's style is a continuation of Tchaikovsky's, and that here and there we find echoes of French impressionism. Indeed, the orchestration is based on Tchaikovsky at many points, and *The Swan of Tuonela*, *The Oceanides*, or some fragments of *Tapiola* do have common traits with Debussy's *Nuages* or Prelude to *The Afternoon of a Faun*. However, to confine oneself to such a formula would be unpardonable. So, let us abandon categorizing and labeling, and let us be content with an assertion that the music of Sibelius is highly individual, and that its individuality is not bound up with any noticeable details of technique; that—finally—this composer has a rare gift, which allows him, as Gabriel Fauré in France or Leoš Janáček in Czechoslovakia, to distinctly express his creative personality by seemingly well-known methods.

What I have said above justifies my use of some terms that do not belong to a purely musical vocabulary. Thus, the Symphony no. 4 (1911), a work that, among all the compositions performed during the festival, attracts my attention the most, is characterized by some "thrilling oddity." From beginning to end, we hear remarkably original music, the impact of which is extremely direct and strong. From a meditative *adagio* up to the last *allegro* (the most concentrated part of this work) the composer leads us, as though by the hand, along previously unknown paths on which we notice, every now and then, something new that intrigues us, moves us, seizes us as with a kind of fear and, sometimes—albeit rarely—make us rejoice. This work may be a lesson in talking simply about new things. There is nothing unnecessary or conventional in it. Finnish musicians consider the Symphony no. 4 to be the most "Sibeliusian" among the seven. Perhaps it is rather strange music for us. But this strangeness attracts and excites curiosity, as does the severe landscape of Finland, a country of sixty thousand lakes, of immense forests, and of a sun that never sets in the summer.

When emphasizing a certain trait or even an "oddity" in the Symphony no. 4, we want to call attention to the fact that this work epitomizes, perhaps most of all, the essence of the Sibelius style. This does not mean, however that we should criticize the other symphonies for a kind of conventionality. On the contrary, what deserves special attention is that none of Sibelius's symphonies is built totally on the model of the classical pattern. A certain liberty prevails in them, sometimes even a "rhapsodic" character in the way he developed a musical idea. In spite of that, each symphony is a perfectly constructed whole, a work complete in itself and providing a consummate, total artistic experience. These comments apply equally to the Symphony no. 2 with its pastoral start and somehow "ostentatious" ending; the one-movement Symphony no. 7; the well-known Warsaw Symphony no. 5, which is remembered mainly for its characteristic finale; and to the serene and modest Symphony no. 3.

This freedom with which Sibelius treats the classical scheme is perhaps connected with his fondness for the form of the symphonic poem. Apart from the symphony, it is the second characteristic form of Sibelius's works. The cycle of four legends from *Kalevala*, a Finnish national epic, is one of his best-known symphonic poems. The second part of this cycle is *The Swan of Tuonela*, a musical image full of dreamy moods, and is one of the most popular items in the repertoire of many symphony orchestras. If Debussy had been from the north, he would have had to compose similar music. Such thoughts revolve in one's head when one is listening to *The Swan of Tuonela*. However, his *Tapiola* composed in 1925 is one of the most intriguing of Sibelius's symphonic poems. Despite clear analogies with the impressionistic technique, we again encounter a characteristic Sibeliussian "peculiarity," of the kind that was so striking in Symphony no. 4.

Apart from the Violin Concerto, intimately known to many Polish listeners, Sibelius—formerly a violin soloist—is also the author of numerous smaller pieces for violin. A charming, serene, and beautifully constructed Sonatina in E major (1915) seems to be the most representative work of this part of his oeuvre.

I cannot cover everything in the festival's program. However, it allowed me to become acquainted with Sibelius as a composer for voice, the author of very subtle songs, sometimes full of strong dramatic spirit. Among these songs, *The Midnight* (op. 90) particularly leaves an impression of the rare charm that is a feature of the greatest song composers, such as Brahms, Wolf, or Henri Duparc.

∞

The program of the Sibelius Festival also included some works by other contemporary Finnish composers, but it is impossible to form an opinion of the whole of Finnish contemporary music on the basis of a few pieces. Nevertheless, it was easy to discern in the chosen works a great variety of stylistic tendencies: from a continuation of impressionism in its special, northern variant by Väinö Raitio (1891–1945), to the more modern—although far from pioneering—neoclassicism of Einar Englund (b. 1916). Englund's Cello Concerto is characterized by a gentle balance of form, steadiness of orchestral technique, and, a most valuable clarity and concreteness of melodic invention.

∞

Let us return for a while to Sibelius. The most moving moment of the Festival for a guest from abroad was the visit to the venerable maestro in his country abode. The wooden villa called Arinola has a snug interior, as though created for lonely meditations, with a view of a lake from the windows. The face of the ninety-year-old Sibelius lit up by a smile full of warmth, making us forget the characteristic frown from his photographs. He devoted a moment of sincere interest to each of the guests in turn, which made us recall once again the long-held conviction that simplicity is one of the privileges of truly great people.

Source

"90th Anniversary of Sibelius," manuscript in Polish. Copyright Witold Lutosławski Collection, Paul Sacher Foundation. All rights reserved. Printed by permission. This text was published in Polish as "Festival Sibeliusa w Helsinkach" in *Przegląd Kulturalny*, no. 28 (1955): 8.

Notes

1. On the reverse of this page (2) of his manuscript, Lutosławski wrote down the birthdates of Mahler, Debussy, Strauss, Glazunov, Dukas, Granados, and Roussel.
2. Joseph Conrad, *Typhoon, The Nigger of the "Narcissus," and Other Stories* (London: The Folio Society, 2000), 230.
3. It was 1955.

⚜

ON STRAVINSKY

Stravinsky's oeuvre is in itself such an immense part of what constitutes the musical content of his era that I sometimes think of and talk about "Stravinsky's era" as one thinks of and talks about Palestrina's, Beethoven's, or Debussy's era. When I contemplate a phenomenon of such dimensions, it is difficult not to resort to poetic comparisons: Stravinsky's creativity is like a mountain rising in the middle of the road that we all have to get past; there is no way to get round it. Surely, therefore, there is no composer of my generation who was not, at one time or another, subject, whether he wanted to or not, to the entrancing influence of Stravinsky's music.

Source

Manuscript in Polish. Copyright Witold Lutosławski Collection, Paul Sacher Foundation. All rights reserved. Printed by permission. This text was first published in German, in *Die Welt* of June 16, 1962, as a tribute on Stravinsky's eightieth birthday, appearing alongside statements from Hába, Carter, Boulez, Milhaud, Henze, and others. Its first Polish printed version appeared in Stefan Jarociński, *Witold Lutosławski. Materiały do monografii* (Materials for a Monograph) (Kraków: Polish Musical Edition, 1967), 39.

⚜

ON WEBERN

"A concise man inspires one to think deeply; a chatterer bores one." With these simple words, Edouard Manet once expressed a great truth, which, in spite of what it implies, has served only a few composers as a signpost. Anton Webern, as opposed to his imitators, belongs to this select group. Among many discoveries made by Webern, there is one that intrigues me particularly. It is the discovery of a sound world of microscopic dimensions, in which the shortest, instantaneous musical event may become a source of strong sensations.

    As is true for every great inventor, Webern's output has also experienced good and bad periods. I would call the present Webern period a "bad" one, since the wave of imitations, often inept, vulgar, and distorting his ideas, has not yet subsided, and we still drive "postwebernism" away like a tiresome fly. I believe, however, that just as Debussy recently liberated himself from "debussy-ism," so will Webern's oeuvre liberate itself from the imitations that blur his work and make it odious. It will then shine in its real and pure brightness.

Source

Stefan Jarociński, *Witold Lutosławski. Materiały do monografii* (Materials for a Monograph) (Kraków: Polish Musical Edition, 1967), 42. Copyright Marcin Bogusławski. All rights reserved. Printed by permission.

ON CHOPIN

Chopin's music stood, so to speak, at the threshold of my life. It is his music that made the strongest impression on me in my early childhood; an impression I was not then capable of comparing with anything else. I listened to the Scherzo in B minor, which was played by one of my music teachers while I sat under the table so that nobody would notice my reactions.

Later on, when I was "discovering" Bach, Beethoven, and other great composers and, particularly, when contemporary music first had an impact on me—with all its bewitching strength—through the Symphony no. 3 of Szymanowski (which happened when I was 11 years old[1]), then Chopin receded for a while into the background of my thoughts. He did come back soon, but not in the same way as in my childhood, not as that composer whose most intimate but simple-hearted experience wrung tears—diligently hidden—from my eyes. Chopin came back in all his power and beauty, played on a great stage: the Chopin of Józef Hofman, the Chopin of Brailovsky, Cortot, Orlov, and many others. At the same time, there appeared in my life a new Chopin, whose amazing face I was discovering at the keyboard, under my own fingers during my studies at the Conservatory. Yes, this was through my fingers, and not only through my ears and feelings, since this "keyboard" aspect of Chopin's works is one of his most mysterious properties. Unlike other works, I could practice Chopin's compositions for many hours without getting tired. This was, among other reasons, because for a pianist they have—along with their sound and spiritual side—an extremely advanced and unique, purely physical and tactile character. No composer in the whole history of music has created such strength and indissoluble cohesion, a mysterious connection of three elements: hand, keyboard, and the sensation of the music through sound. However, it was not only because of this aspect of Chopin's music that I could practice and listen to it for long periods without fatigue. Much later, I again experienced this effect, when for the first time in my life I was a member of the jury at the Chopin Competition in Warsaw. I had to listen to Chopin's music for many hours a day over several weeks, a crucial test of my feelings for this music. Yet in spite of performances by many participants at the first stage who "hurt" Chopin's music, and in spite of the necessity to listen several times a day to, for instance, the Sonata op. 58 in mediocre performances (it was not acceptable to be distracted by anything else), I remember today this period of such intensive contact with Chopin's music with great affection.

I stopped playing the piano in order to devote myself exclusively to composition well before the war (I don't count the period of the war, when piano playing was my source of income). This period moved me away from Chopin again, but not completely. To this day I come back to his music every now and again, when I play my favorite Etudes, Preludes, and Mazurkas as well as the bigger works. I read through them and study them, always discovering something new to me, something extraordinary, but—above all—always finding something extremely intimate to admire in them. This return to Chopin is especially dear to me in difficult moments of my life. His music gives me a shot in the arm and confirms my conviction that there exists an ideal, better world, a world of the imagination for creative artists. The world imagined in Chopin's works possesses countless, but also very particular, charms and riches. Despite all its fantasy it is, however, a deeply human world, in the sense that it conveys a fervent longing for the ideal.

Source

Manuscript and typescript in Polish titled "Powroty do Chopina" (Returns to Chopin). Copyright Witold Lutosławski Collection, Paul Sacher Foundation. All rights reserved. Printed by permission. This text, an answer in the interview "Chopin, Our Contemporary," was published as "Powroty" (Returns) in *Polska*, no. 9 (1970): 3–4.

Note

1. See note 2 to the text "Witold Lutosławski—Life and Music" in the present collection.

ON GRAŻYNA BACEWICZ

Grażyna Bacewicz is widely known for her musical and social activity, particularly in the period between the wars. This was when her extraordinary, exuberant, and versatile musical talent flowered; a period that, at the time of her unexpected death, seemed to be far from ending. This period of her life has already been explored in many publications and I have no doubt that we will soon see many more of them. Therefore, while recalling the prematurely terminated life of Grażyna, I want to dwell for a moment on a lesser-known period, namely the years preceding the Second World War.

Although we were of much the same age and had been studying at the same academy,[1] we actually were never colleagues. This was because Grażyna ended her studies in composition and violin playing when she was very young, whereas I entered the Conservatory relatively late—after the first year of my studies at Warsaw University.[2] Thus, while I was still a student at the Conservatory, Grażyna gave the first concert of her own works there. That evening remains clear in my memory because, as a student of Jerzy Lefeld,[3] I was turning the pages for him when he accompanied Grażyna on the piano. She played, among other things, her Violin Capriccios—compositions that were far ahead in their expression of the traditional sense of that virtuoso form. What particularly amazed me then, however, was a very beautiful miniature entitled *The Stained Glass*, woven of colorful sounds, as delicate as a butterfly's wing. During that concert she also played her piano works, and those were faultless, perfect performances. Since her first independent work, one could see in her a born, genuine musician, who combined—as did the great masters of the Baroque—the talents of a composer and a performer in one harmonious whole. Unfortunately I had few occasions to play with Grażyna, but the few popular Ormuz concerts[4] at which I had the chance to accompany her, I remember as an exceptional artistic experience. When playing with soloists who have a special, innate musical wisdom, the accompanist experiences a feeling of incomparable freedom and certainty. Every interpretative soloist's nuance seems to be obvious; any problems in forming a perfect partnership are solved in a few seconds. Grażyna probably brought her musical wisdom with her to this world. Every detail in her compositions has an accuracy and beauty that could only come from the instincts of a genuine musician.

The prewar years allowed me to keep in touch with Grażyna, who was at that time (not long ago), a "Wunderkind," playing skillfully on the violin, piano, and cello, and composing amazingly mature works. This eruption of talent at such a young age foreshadowed its subsequent splendid development. As a listener to Grażyna's music and a witness to the birth of particular works of hers, I especially recall those moments that moved me most. First of all, I recall the masterly Concerto for Strings from the 1940s. Its severe, rather ascetic texture always strikes me with its seriousness and authority, and I see certain moments of Stravinsky's *Symphony of Psalms* in this work.

Yet I particularly like the dense, slightly "bitter" harmonies that wreathe the secondary theme of the finale. Their effect is particularly marked in juxtaposition with the severe, "void" chords that predominate in that score. The Concerto for Strings is perhaps the highest point of the mature period of Grażyna's creativity, which the encyclopedias acknowledge with the flattering term of *neoclassicism*. Her style underwent various phases of development and, in the last period, in which we find the newest achievements of her compositional technique, she touched, as though unintentionally, a forgotten string, which had sounded before in the aforementioned, early piece, *The Stained Glass*. I can hear these achievements in the extremely subtle sound of the String Quartet no. 7, which is a testimony to many formerly unsuspected possibilities concealed within this seemingly well-known type of ensemble.[5] From Bartók on, few composers were as skilled as Grażyna at penetrating the mysteries of the string quartet's texture. Her String Quartet no. 7, one of the last of Grażyna's works, will certainly endure for a long time on the stages and in the studios of the entire world.

♋

These memories would be one-sided if I did not also express the feelings bound up with Grażyna as a friend, a colleague, and a person. A friend in need is a friend indeed, says an old proverb. Such an incomparable friend was Grażyna, who found it obvious to lend a hand to everybody who needed it. A talent, being a gift and a privilege, is at the same time always a heavy burden for an artist, absorbing thoughts and feelings, and creating many reasons to be egotistical. Grażyna was the negation of egoism. The beautiful features of her character were not spoiled in the slightest by the difficulties of creative work, which is still egocentric by its very nature.

The blow of Grażyna's death painfully struck the countless admirers of her talent, but is even more painful for those us who knew her as a person, a colleague, and an incomparable, well-tried friend. Let us take comfort in the fact of the existence of the imperishable works left by both her creative imagination and her warm heart.

Source

Typescript in Polish titled "Wspomnienie o Grażynie" (A Memory of Grażyna). Copyright Witold Lutosławski Collection, Paul Sacher Foundation. All rights reserved. Printed by permission. This text was published in *Ruch Muzyczny*, no. 7 (1969): 5 as a contribution to a special issue devoted to Grażyna Bacewicz following her death on January 17, 1969, in Warsaw.

Notes

1. The Warsaw Conservatory. Bacewicz finished her studies there in 1932, obtaining two diplomas: in violin playing (Józef Jarzębski's class) and in composition (Kazimierz Sikorski's class).
2. Lutosławski studied mathematics at the Warsaw University in 1931–1932.
3. Lutosławski studied piano in Lefeld's class in 1932–1936.
4. Ormuz was a Polish organization that popularized music before the war.
5. String Quartet no. 7, representing Bacewicz's later style, was composed in 1965.

❧

While reflecting upon the creative life of an artist, I often ask myself the following questions: With what did he or she come into this world? That is, what has nature endowed him with, and also, did he, by his effort, succeed in developing these inborn talents, taking advantage of them to the fullest, for the benefit of mankind? This last thought deserves special emphasis, because many creative artists treat their inherited talents as if they were their own to dispense with for their own personal aims, and not always in the noblest way. As I see it, the talent of an artist is a unique privilege, a gift, a distinction. As such, it carries with it commensurate obligations. Thus an artist with any moral sense whatsoever should know that, in developing his talents for the enrichment of mankind, he is only fulfilling his obligations, while that which he creates is only in small measure to his own credit.

My preceding reflections are the key to my remarks on Grażyna Bacewicz, a distinguished Polish composer of this century, whose premature departure has been an irreconcilable loss. There is no question in my mind that the answers to the above questions, as far as Grażyna Bacewicz is concerned, are positive ones. She was born with an incredible wealth of musical talent, which she brought to full flower through an almost fanatic zeal and unwavering faith in her mission. The intensity of her activities was so great that she managed, in such a cruelly shortened life, to give birth to treasures that any composer of her stature with a considerably longer life span could only envy.

I do not propose to discuss or dwell on the merits of her compositional legacy. To anyone who was privileged to be close to her creative activity, to become acquainted with and experience her creations, their great artistic value is obvious. To be sure, I have always been of the opinion that a true judgment of the creative ability of a composer does not belong to contemporary reviewers or artists, but to thousands of audiences over many decades, which may be referred to as the "jury of time." Based on the fact that many of her earliest works are still being performed throughout the world today, one can already predict that her music will survive this test of time. As examples, we can cite the Concerto for String Orchestra,[1] a favorite of this type of ensemble, and her String Quartet no. 3, which is marked by an exceptional polyphonic skill in addition to its masterly idiomatic writing for string quartet.[2]

To judge her works *only* in light of the compositional styles and rapidly changing artistic currents of her lifetime does not appear proper to me. Like so many other composers of larger compositional forms, she was to a great degree independent from the atmosphere surrounding her. Rather, it was her music that helped create that atmosphere and could be held up as an example to the younger generation of composers.

When I think of Grażyna Bacewicz, I cannot limit myself to her music alone. I was fortunate to belong to that group of people who were bound to her by virtue of professional friendship. Thus I was privileged to know her closely for many years. It allowed me to observe and admire her character firsthand—her integrity, honesty, compassion, and her willingness to share and sacrifice for others. This image of her as an artist and human being ought to be an inspiration to the succeeding generations of composers in Poland and throughout the world.

I wish to congratulate the Friends of Polish Music at the University of Southern California and Judith Rosen for their dedication and effort in acquainting the English-speaking world with Grażyna Bacewicz, one of the foremost women composers of all time.

Source

W. Lutosławski, "On Grażyna Bacewicz," in *Grażyna Bacewicz. Her Life and Works*, ed. Judith Rosen (Los Angeles: Polish Music History Series, 1984), 11–13 (preface). Published by the Friends of Polish Music, University of Southern California School of Music. Used by permission. The original Polish typescript of this text is kept at the Paul Sacher Foundation.

Notes

1. The Concerto for String Orchestra, one of the most representative of Bacewicz's neoclassical works, was composed in 1948.
2. The String Quartet no. 3 was composed in 1947.

ON GRZEGORZ FITELBERG

Much of the history of Polish music is bound up in the person of Grzegorz Fitelberg. Let us consider what characterized Polish music in the period preceding the appearance of the so-called Young Poland.[1] The leading figures at that time were Noskowski[2] and Żeleński.[3] The lack of stronger figures made it impossible to develop the Chopin tradition and aspire to create a national art. At best, this aspiration involved searching for inspiration in Polish romantic poetry or in adopting a "domestic" style, far from the genuine, pure sources of folk art. There was a complete isolation from European influences. The European "novelties" were Strauss, Reger, and Debussy. However, in Poland it was difficult to detect any influence from Wagner or Tchaikovsky. Our music still fed on the memories of Schumann and Mendelssohn, and reflected these composers tentatively and carefully *à la polonaise*.

Then, the wall separating our music from current European influences was suddenly broken, as though by a battering ram, when a group of talented and ambitious musicians, generally known as Young Poland, appeared on the scene. Despite the noticeable impact of Wagner, Strauss, and Reger, the individual style of these young composers was clearly taking shape. It was still difficult to foresee how the music of Szymanowski or Karłowicz[4] would develop in the way it did, but it is certain that these young musicians decided to break with the isolated Polish cultural situation in order to include those influences that animated the music of Europe at that time—in other words, to overcome the retarded development they had inherited from their predecessors. Moreover, it seems certain that these young people were realizing their goals with outstanding talent, vital momentum, solid education, and great ambition. The group's first concert, in 1906, showed us Grzegorz Fitelberg conducting the Berlin Orchestra and revealing for the first time his own works and those of his friends, Young Poland.

From the very beginning of his career, Grzegorz Fitelberg was concerned with what is most valuable, most vital, and most up-to-date in our music. He came across this way at the beginning of his musical career and he remained so throughout his life.

When Young Poland started its public activity, Grzegorz Fitelberg was first and foremost a composer. He had already studied with Roguski[5] and Noskowski. Among his works were Sonata for violin and piano (a prize winner at the Paderewski Competition in Leipzig in 1896), a trio, songs, a symphony, a poem "Song of the Falcon" (to Gorky), and other works.

These works were distinguished by their mastery of the *métier* in every way and by a great deal of imagination; they pointed to great possibilities for this young composer. However, the moment was approaching when Fitelberg would abandon his compositional plans and would dedicate himself to conducting. What stimulated this decision was his brilliant talent for conducting, which put in the shade even his undoubted compositional abilities. However, apart from this quite natural reason, we can suppose that Fitelberg's decision was also guided by a feeling of the mission he was to fulfill in the future development of Polish music. Fitelberg displayed an infallible intuition, particularly in relation to the early creative works of Szymanowski. This intuition allowed him to see in the twenty-year-old (actually, a bit more than twenty, but less than thirty) author of the Concert Overture,[6] the future great reviver of Polish music. Although it caused some detriment to his career as a conductor, Fitelberg decided very early on to assume this role, for which he was later given the title of an ambassador for Polish music.

Fitelberg was in fact such an ambassador for a long time after the first appearances of Young Poland. The schedule of his concerts was very intensive. He conducted in Berlin, Vienna, Leipzig, and Dresden. In 1912 he took up the appointment as chief conductor of the Opera in Vienna, in 1914–1919 he was the chief conductor of the operatic theatre "Muzykalnaya Drama" in Petrograd; he also conducted for the State Opera (in the former Mariinsky Theatre, nowadays the Kirov Theatre), and was nominated as the chief conductor of the State Orchestra (the former so-called court orchestra). In 1920 he obtained an appointment at the Bolshoi Theatre in Moscow. In 1921–1924 he was the leading conductor of the famous Diaghilev Ballet. He appeared in London, Paris, Monte Carlo, and in Spain and Belgium. Subsequently, Fitelberg made his appearance on the concert stages of Paris, London, Berlin, Zurich, Prague, Vienna, Budapest, Bucharest, Mexico City, Brussels, Copenhagen, Moscow, Leningrad, Luxembourg, Athens, and Stockholm. These are only the capitals and the biggest cities. To be comprehensive, one would have to add to this list at least three times the number of larger and smaller cities in Europe and America.

The world's concert audiences and critics thought highly of him as an interpreter of twentieth-century works. As an unparalleled interpreter of Strauss, he was invited to Moscow in order to conduct the cycle of symphonic poems by the composer of *Thus Spoke Zarathustra*. Diaghilev put him in charge of preparing and conducting the first staging of Stravinsky's *Mavra*. The premiere of the now world-famous Classical Symphony by Prokofiev took place in 1917, conducted by Fitelberg. One can safely say that Fitelberg belonged then to that exceptionally rare group of artists whose specialty and main object of interest was the music of his era. This was what first and foremost distinguished Fitelberg from the majority of other outstanding conductors who built up their reputation on brilliant interpretations of the then traditional repertoire. The inspiration of Fitelberg's life was, first of all, his own era and the music it created. This gave rise to his pioneering attitude, leading him to avoid always choosing what was easy and well known in relation to the audience, and he also avoided treating timorously what was new and progressive. His many travels abroad in the period between the wars did not completely fill Fitelberg's life. He spent longer periods in his homeland. In 1908 he became chief conductor of the

Warsaw Philharmonic, which he left in 1911, but he returned again to this position in 1924, this time for ten seasons. He also conducted for the radio. Unfortunately, the level of orchestral performance in Poland in the 1920s was poor. The only serious institution was the Warsaw Philharmonic, which was struggling with financial and organizational difficulties. The orchestra's working style was far from ideal. They sometimes used new untried conductors, often of a modest or low standard, there were few rehearsals (for instance, there was only one rehearsal for a morning or afternoon concert!), there were modest requirements on the part of both the musicians and the audience—all this presented a very unattractive environment for an artist of the quality of Grzegorz Fitelberg. Then, in the 1930s, we witnessed the birth of a new symphony orchestra organized on quite different lines from the Warsaw Philharmonic. The Polish Radio Symphony Orchestra, newly created on Fitelberg's initiative, was relatively small, but it was composed of excellent musicians, it worked regularly, it was subject to a firm artistic and organizational discipline, and it had a director who was able to transform this musical group into an artistically perfect whole. Fitelberg worked with great zeal and passion as the conductor of the new orchestra. The short existence of this orchestra, which was terminated by the war, was one of the few bright spots in the history of our musical life at that time. Radio programs, yearly Wawel-festivals,[7] public concerts in the Roma concert hall in Warsaw, all these things provided seminal interpretations, a series of Fitelberg's unforgettable creations, among which Polish music, mostly contemporary, always took a distinct and privileged place.

The interwar period of Fitelberg's activity in Warsaw contributed immense value to our musical life. It allowed us to participate in everything that was rich and vital in Europe at that time. Thanks to Fitelberg we became familiar with Ravel and Roussel, Prokofiev and Shostakovich, Stravinsky and Hindemith, Milhaud, Honegger and many other major and minor composers of that time. We owe to him the existence of a symphonic ensemble conforming to European standards. However, we should be most grateful to Fitelberg for all he did for the development of Polish music. Initially it was not an easy task to popularize Szymanowski's music, even in Poland. Yet due to Fitelberg's many years of persistent striving for this goal, as well as the strength of his talent, every new work of Szymanowski in the last years of his life was welcomed by the Polish audiences with impatience and excitement. Nonetheless, the greatness of Szymanowski did not blind Fitelberg to the creative endeavors of the growing generation of Polish composers. He treated every new score in which he observed signs of talent with curiosity, and often with enthusiasm. The majority of premieres of Polish works took place under the direction of Fitelberg. Moreover, one could say that it was thanks to him that many works were performed at all, in the face of a common dislike for new Polish music by other conductors, and often of their incompetence. Fitelberg's talent, his excellent knowledge of contemporary musical language, his enthusiasm for newly created works and for every genuine creative effort—all this was an enormous encouragement for young composers. Thus, in relation to young Polish music, Fitelberg played the role of a real publicity agent, without which the young composers could scarcely have developed their talents and have acquired the necessary experience. One can say without exaggeration that Fitelberg was a major influence on Polish compositional output at that time.

∽

The music of Poland, coming to life in 1945, was animated by great hopes and perspectives of unanticipated development. We saw the creation of philharmonic orchestras, broadcasting stations, and conservatories; and advances on a wide front were planned. Music became an object of interest to important social organizations, it absorbed the attention of high-ranking politicians and played a significant role in the nation's life, which had never occurred in Poland before. A fever of planning, stimulated as one might expect by unlimited possibilities for the arts, prompted us to turn a blind eye to all shortcomings, which one had to accept temporarily in this new musical life.

At that moment, the thoughts of many Polish musicians turned toward the question of who was to head the projected great musical institution—the National Philharmonic. Many of us asked: when would Fitelberg return to Poland? This moment eventually came in October 1946. Unfortunately, a devastated Warsaw was not in a position to even start organizing the National Philharmonic and we were forced to be satisfied with a provisional Philharmonic, which even the most courageous imagination would not associate with the person of Grzegorz Fitelberg. So, the institution which hired him was the Polish Radio. It had its own orchestra that, although young, was making fast progress under the direction of Witold Rowicki. The moment when Fitelberg took over the direction of the Symphony Orchestra of Polish Radio in Katowice was solemn one.[8] The orchestra welcomed a great artist, bound up with the Polish musical tradition, and Fitelberg himself was moved by the fact that he could start working with an ensemble that raised his best hopes.

From that moment on, Fitelberg gave his boundless resources of energy, knowledge, experience, and the treasures of his talent, to the work with the Great Symphonic Orchestra of Polish Radio. Every year, this ensemble became more and more precise in its performance capacities, it acquired vigor and developed its potential. In the initial years of conducting this Orchestra, Fitelberg traveled with it to give guest performances in Warsaw, Wrocław, and Kraków. Soon afterward he started a concert tour in Czechoslovakia. These early travels abroad for the young Orchestra were a great success for Fitelberg. This was especially significant when one considers the high demands of the Czechoslovakian audience and critics, accustomed for many years to a high standard of orchestral performance. His next trip took place in 1950, this time to Hungary and Romania. In the early years after his return to Poland, Fitelberg often made guest appearances in many European and American countries. He conducted successively in London, Edinburgh, Glasgow, Dublin, Rome, Venice, Copenhagen, Stockholm, Oslo, Paris, The Hague, again in London and Rome, Genoa, Bologna, Florence, Moscow and Leningrad, Utrecht, The Hague, Hilversum, Den Bosch, Buenos Aires, Berlin, again in Paris, Sofia, Budapest, Prague, again in Berlin, Leipzig, and Prague. Fitelberg often included contemporary Polish works in the concert programs, including works by Szymanowski and by composers of the younger generation.

The list of Fitelberg's appearances abroad from 1906 to 1953 included no less than 176 concerts with Polish works. Of that number, 121 programs consisted of only Polish music. Among others, there were 180 performances of Szymanowski's works, often several of them in one program. These numbers illustrate the extent of Fitelberg's work and enthusiasm invested in the dissemination of Polish music abroad; they also demonstrate his huge contribution in this area. One should be aware that it was only thanks to Fitelberg's activity that recent Polish music became known to the world. And one could doubt whether even Szymanowski's oeuvre would have found its way into the world's concert halls just by being published by the Universal Edition, were it not for the artistic skill and exposure of Fitelberg's performances on dozens of stages in Europe and America.

The work in his homeland absorbed Fitelberg more and more from year to year. Perfecting the playing of the Orchestra, performing newly created Polish works, and seminal recordings of a great repertoire, did not cover all his interests. Fitelberg also made an outstanding contribution in the field of the dissemination of musical culture among the working classes. He gave a series of concerts as the conductor of the Great Symphonic Orchestra of Polish Radio in mining and industrial centers such as Chorzów, Orzegowo (for the staff of the coal mine Karol), Jaworzno (for the distinguished staff of the coal mine Bierut), Sosnowiec (the House of the Miner), Gliwice, Bytom, and, of course, Katowice. He was also actively interested in the amateur musical movement, as evidenced by his becoming the patron of the Metallurgic Philharmonic in Chorzów in 1952.

In his later years, Fitelberg returned to the compositional work he had abandoned earlier. He prepared to print the works of Moniuszko, Karłowicz, and Szymanowski, bringing to the scores that he was preparing the wealth of his experience as both a musician and a conductor. He made a courageous attempt at realizing new accompaniments to Chopin's Concertos. He worked on adapting for performance a series of forgotten Polish works that, in their original form, were not suitable for performance, mostly because of their lacunae and imperfections. Thanks to Grzegorz Fitelberg developing them, they took a more attractive shape and sometimes they became, as in the case of the suite of Stefani's *Krakowiacy i Górale*, real masterpieces.

In this essay, I took a brief look at the activities of Grzegorz Fitelberg. The repetition of facts from somebody's life and works can only give a one-sided view of an artist. In order to fully understand who Grzegorz Fitelberg was and particularly to characterize his role in the history of our music, we should first and foremost deal with the essence of his art of conducting. This task, however, goes beyond what is possible for the author of this essay. Perhaps it is actually impossible to achieve. For it is not possible to account for all the factors involved, and, as in all true art, there may be no adequate words to describe the kind of phenomenon I have tried to examine here. Let us not attempt to answer the question of the essence of the enigma of Fitelberg's talent. Rather, let us try to cherish the memories of the vivid impressions from his recent concerts. Then we will experience the thrill of contact with truly great art.

Source

"O Grzegorzu Fitelbergu," *Muzyka*, no. 7–8 (1954): 26–33. Copyright Marcin Bogusławski. All rights reserved. Printed by permission.

Notes

1. Young Poland was a group of Polish composers (Karol Szymanowski, Ludomir Różycki, Grzegorz Fitelberg, and Apolinary Szeluto), active in the late nineteenth and early twentieth century under the influence of German neoromanticism (Wagner, Strauss, Wolf), and of Skryabin. Among their achievements were symphonic poems with extended orchestral means.

2. Zygmunt Noskowski (1846–1909), Polish composer, pedagogue, and conductor, active mostly in Warsaw.

3. Władysław Żeleński (1837–1921), Polish composer active in Warsaw and Kraków.

4. Mieczysław Karłowicz (1876–1909), Polish composer active in Warsaw, close to Young Poland. He was a leading representative of early twentieth-century Polish symphonic music and the author of several symphonic poems influenced by Wagner and Strauss. Karłowicz died in an avalanche in the Tatra Mountains near Zakopane. See: Alistair Wightman, *Karłowicz, Young Poland, and the Musical Fin-de-siècle* (Aldershot, UK: Scolar Press, 1996).

5. Gustaw Roguski (1839–1921), Polish composer, pedagogue and pianist, active in Warsaw.

6. Karol Szymanowski composed his Concert Overture E major op. 12 in 1904–1905.

7. Wawel is the name of the Royal Castle in Kraków.

8. Fitelberg became the director of the Great Symphonic Orchestra of Polish Radio in Katowice in 1947.

ON WITOLD MALISZEWSKI

I started my musical education as a six-year-old child, learning to play the piano at Mrs. Helena Hofman's, who was a pupil of Strobel. She was a very clever woman, since—apart from teaching me how to play the piano—she also played me a lot of music, which was extremely important for my musical development. Of course, she began with the classics and Chopin. Afterward I had many other teachers, but when I was eleven I became a pupil of Józef Śmidowicz, a very well-known pianist who was a student of Aleksander Michałowski. And although my studies with him only lasted one year, these were my first piano lessons in the proper sense of the word. Professor Śmidowicz, however, did not play anything for me, but instead required only my own playing. I had to play many pieces in order to develop my technical skills. It is only a pity that these lessons lasted for such a short time.

Later, when I was twelve, I started learning the violin and I was still playing the piano in an amateur way. My violin teacher was Lidia Kmitowa, a relatively unknown and underestimated violinist, an excellent teacher—a pupil of Ysaÿe and Joachim, with whom she mastered a fine technique of playing this instrument. I owe her not only for teaching me the proper position for my hand, but also the ability to phrase and interpret in the classical sense of these words. My studies with her went on for about six years. During this time I was able to become acquainted with quite a serious repertoire, such as, among other things, the solo sonatas of J. S. Bach and Mozart's concertos.

At approximately the same time, I started the study of composition, which I had actually indulged in as an amateur and a self-taught person since my childhood. Following the advice of Mrs. Kmitowa, I went to study composition with Witold Maliszewski, initially as his private student and later on as a student at the Warsaw Conservatory. Professor Maliszewski was, as a matter of fact, my sole teacher of composition. He originated from the excellent school of Rimsky-Korsakov and probably also attended lectures by Alexander Glazunov. Maliszewski set about teaching me very carefully: he imposed nothing on me but granted me as much freedom as possible. He quickly took me through all the theoretical subjects, including the fugue, which soon allowed me to enter the Conservatory. Unfortunately, Witold Maliszewski was an artist with clear conservative views. Nevertheless, I would like to stress his great artistic honesty. He never pretended that something was of interest to him if he really was not interested in it, and he never advised in matters in which he did not feel competent to do so. What illustrates his views most pointedly was his relationship with Szymanowski, whom he considered to have a splendid talent, which degenerated.

I always hold my professor in great esteem for his spotless honesty and morality, for his deep and versatile knowledge (apart from music, he did mathematical and medical studies). Thus, I felt the more strongly his total lack of understanding and disapproval of the contemporary music of the 1930s. I even tried to explain to him the aesthetics of such composers as Stravinsky, but I was not successful. Finally, it led to a situation in which I became aware that if I regularly attended his lessons during my last year of studies and presented my ongoing work on my diploma—composition—I would never have finished it, since my composition would never have been approved by my teacher.[1] Therefore, I stopped going to his lessons, but I was soon called to order: I had to put forward at least half of the score. This was a dramatic moment in my life, since my professor told me he simply did not understand the music I was writing. I tried to justify myself in his eyes, and prove that what I wrote was not an improvisation or something totally devoid of discipline. In other words, I did a detailed analysis of my work. Witold Maliszewski summed up the issue saying, "Now I understand you; we have found a common language, but what you have written does not cease in my view to be ugly." He also said that I had to show the exam committee a work for which he could be wholly responsible, which meant that I had to write something that would bear the features of the school from which he originated. I asked him whether I could present for my diploma exam a work that would correspond to the aesthetics of my earlier piano sonata, which he had accepted. I did not expect, for a moment, that he would want from me a purely academic work, as other Warsaw professors were accustomed to do. I wrote the fragments of *Requiem* he wanted,[2] and this was the basis for granting me my diploma. On that occasion, I heard my professor's characteristic words, which summed him up beautifully: "You must think about what you will do next, since if you wish to choose the way you began with that unfinished composition, I will not be able to give you any advice." Here once again the great honesty of this teacher and his responsibility for the fate of his pupil was revealed. A man with a smaller knowledge and narrower horizons would certainly have tried to protect a young, talented composer just to count him among the circle of his disciples. Fortunately, for Professor Maliszewski the artistic honesty of the composer's ethics took pride of place. Although in the last phase of my studies he could not be of any great help to me, because of his artistic principles, this was a beautiful lesson in the ethics of a creative artist, and of his fidelity to the beliefs he held.

Just a few words on what I owe to Witold Maliszewski from a purely professional point of view. I remember with particular thankfulness his lectures on musical forms, (not so much individual lessons of composition, although I do not deny that these also gave me a lot), since these lectures were a far cry from what had then been thought about this subject. These were his own considerations based on the traditions of the Russian method. Maliszewski called this method of analysis of a musical work a psychological one. It was not generally accepted and even ardently opposed, for instance, by the Germans. Personally, it deeply convinced me and, with carefully adaptation, it has continued to serve me during the preparation of my lectures for summer courses.

As I have already mentioned, I studied with Józef Śmidowicz for just one year, but my professor of composition insisted that I should recommence piano lessons. I was then a little out of patience with this instrument, because I had had a great many teachers, each one of whom considered that what I had learned with her or his predecessor was incorrect and bad, and therefore I always had to start anew. However, following the advice of Stefan Kisielewski, I decided to enter the piano class of Jerzy Lefeld, because I hoped that he would not ask me to learn from the beginning. I prepared for the exam on my own and, to my enormous amazement, I was admitted to the higher course. Professor Lefeld had nothing of the pompous fame of those teachers in vogue at the time, although he was an outstanding pianist. I studied with him for four years at the Conservatory and passed my diploma with him.[3] I did profit a great deal, since Jerzy Lefeld was something of a phenomenal musical institution. Of course, he could not teach me everything, as it is impossible to teach faultless and quick reading of notes and overcoming technical difficulties with no effort. Yet this professor's great musicality, his gentleness and cordial relations with his pupils guaranteed lessons without stress, which was a great advantage during my studies at the Warsaw Conservatory. I still maintain a great friendship with Jerzy Lefeld although we rarely see each other. He was a professor and, at the same time a friend who was always aware of a fact that he was not teaching a pianist, but a composer who wanted to know how to play the piano.

Let us come back for to my memories of Professor Maliszewski. Although we parted company at a certain moment, there was no conflict between us. We took leave of one another with friendly relations, especially because Professor Maliszewski, who was a great deal older than me, treated me almost like a son. I would like at this point to touch upon a problem of a more general nature. I sometimes reproach young people for some irrationality in their approach to their professors. I do it, of course, on the basis of my own experience and with a recognition that my advice is difficult to carry out. I think that a young person who is learning to be a creative artist should first study what her or his teacher knows best. For to learn something very well, even if it would not necessarily suit the individuality of a student, is the most valuable thing that can be learned. Therefore, I would urge young artists who are lucky enough to study with excellent musicians to start by imitating them, that is, with imitating what their teacher knows best of all. From the perspective of many years I regret terribly that I did not behave in this way, since I could have learned much more. I regret it now, but this is perhaps an issue one understands too late.

Source

"O Witoldzie Maliszewskim w ankiecie 'Mój nauczyciel' mówi W. Lutosławski" (On Witold Maliszewski in the interview "My Teacher" by W. Lutosławski), *Nurt*, no. 5 (1973): 5–7. Copyright Marcin Bogusławski. All rights reserved. Printed by permission.

Notes

1. Lutosławski means his Symphonic Variations, which he started writing at the Warsaw Conservatory, supposedly as his diploma-composition, but—because of Maliszewski's discontent with this project—put it aside and finished it much later, in 1938.
2. These fragments of *Requiem* included *Requiem aeternam* for choir and orchestra (later lost) and *Lacrimosa* for soprano, mixed choir, and orchestra, which was premiered in the autumn of 1938 in Warsaw, with Helena Warpechowska and Warsaw Philharmonic conducted by Tadeusz Wilczak.
3. Lutosławski's piano diploma recital in May 1936 included works by Bach, Mozart, Schumann, Liszt, Chopin, Debussy, and Maliszewski. He also played Beethoven's Piano Concerto no. 4 in G major, op. 58 and Variations from Prokofiev's Piano Concerto no. 3. See Charles Bodman Rae, *The Music of Lutosławski*, expanded 3rd ed. (London-New York-Sydney: Omnibus Press, 1999), 10.

ON CONSTANTIN REGAMEY

A tall man with dark hair, fascinating eyes and a penetrating gaze. The possessor of an unusual intelligence, which is difficult to convey exactly. His conversation was always (and still is) a genuine intellectual pleasure. His thoughts continually overtake and divine his interlocutor's ideas, skipping the intermediate stages; in terms of speed, comparing conversation with him and virtually anyone else is like comparing a flight in a jet plane with a ride in a taxicab. An authority on Sanskrit and Indian civilization, on which he used to lecture at Warsaw University, he knew more than a score of languages. His outstanding musical gifts enabled him to decipher any musical score you care to name at the keyboard, and he had no need to practice at the piano, because his fingers and his brain seemed to function with the same facility as if performing mundane actions. A brilliant music critic, whose verdicts were always astonishingly just, an experienced polemicist and advocate for musical thinking that looked toward new perspectives: that was the Constantin Regamey I got to know in Warsaw toward the end of the 1930s. It was only some years later, during the war, and still in Warsaw, that Regamey the composer revealed himself.

The revelation took place in out-of-the-ordinary circumstances, actually in a private apartment. Yet the audience consisted in part of Warsaw's musical élite, which lent the occasion an unusual significance. A few words are needed to explain the reasons for this: few people—especially in the West—know that in certain European countries under German occupation, between 1939 and 1945 musical life was completely banned. Poland was one of those countries. The only places where concerts could be given in public were the cafés. There the most celebrated Polish singers and instrumentalists gathered to give concerts, often with programs of wholly serious music; and Constantin Regamey was one of the artists who played in cafés. The circumstances obviously made it impossible to perform anything written under the occupation. The only way to present the premieres of new works was in clandestine concerts in private houses. It was in one such concert that a work by Regamey had its first performance: a piece that made an instantaneous sensation in the musical world, first in Warsaw, then throughout Poland. People recognized at once that what they were hearing was perfectly mature, extremely refined, and moreover totally independent of everything that constituted the style and methods of Polish music in the 1930s and 1940s. Not surprising: it was the first work heard in Poland to have been composed using dodecaphonic technique. (The first Polish twelve-note composer was actually József Koffler, resident in Lwów at the time; but his activities were almost unknown in Warsaw.) The technique in itself would not have been enough to make the performance of this work—it was the Quintet for violin, cello, clarinet, bassoon, and piano—such a sensation. There were several contributory factors, chief among them the composer's extraordinary imagination and his very personal way of using Schoenberg's methods.

The Quintet's success probably took the composer himself by surprise. Talking about it at the time when he was still writing it, Regamey adopted an almost jocular tone: "I'm going to see if, using twelve-note technique, it's possible to compose something that will sound like Richard Strauss," he told me in connection with the first movement. It is obvious to anyone who knows the work that this statement reveals a private psychological attitude of the composer toward himself, an attitude that had nothing to do with how the composition eventually turned out; no one will find the slightest trace of Strauss's music in the variations in the Quintet. "There is nothing like this in the whole of Polish chamber music," one of the players said to me after the concert. The statement is still valid, I may add, if the word "Polish" is omitted. The Quintet was a revelation to everyone who heard that first performance, even to those who had heard Regamey's previous work, *Chansons persanes* for baritone and chamber orchestra (1942), which contained no hint of the unprecedented character of the Quintet. The composer himself seemed rather disappointed with the first performance of *Chansons persanes*, because the orchestral part had to be played on two pianos. At the time he said of one of the sections of the work: "Those triplets should come over as no more than a murmur with an orchestra, whereas on the piano they sound like Chopin's B-flat minor Sonata." He must have been thinking of the last movement of Chopin's piece.

Only a few months after that momentous premiere, Regamey left Poland, his adopted country, and returned to Switzerland. There he produced a series of works that brought him an international reputation. The first of these works was *Études*, the extraordinarily beautiful cycle for female voice and piano or orchestra, first performed at the Donaueschingen Festival in 1955.

Despite his success and the many testimonies of admiration, Regamey remains a composer whose greatness is not sufficiently well recognized or appreciated as it deserves. He shares this fate with many of his predecessors, whose work had to wait a long time to achieve its proper place in the history of music: Webern, Varèse, and Ives, for example. Time will be the judge. I am convinced that it will do justice to the fascinating and very original musical personality of Constantin Regamey.

Source

"Fascynująca premiera—wspomnienie z 1944 r." (A Fascinating Premiere—a Memory from 1944), in *Oblicza polistylizmu. Materiały sympozjum poświęconego twórczości Konstantego Regameya. Warszawa 29–30 maja 1987* (The Faces of Polystylism. Materials of the Symposium Dedicated to the Work of Constantin Regamey. Warsaw, 29–30 May 1987), ed. Krystyna Tarnawska-Kaczorowska (Warsaw: Polish Composers' Union, 1988), 26–29. Copyright Marcin Bogusławski. All rights reserved. Printed by permission. The French version of this text, titled "Une création fascinante—souvenir de l'an 1944," was published in *Schweizerische Musikzeitung/Revue musicale Suisse*, no. 117 (1977): 69–70.

⤜⧓⤛

ON MICHAŁ SPISAK

It is difficult, indeed extremely difficult, to find words to talk about what is really beautiful, awaking admiration and attachment. This is why my hand trembles as I am to write about Michał Spisak—a splendid artist, a man of spotless integrity, and an incomparable friend. Since my first contact with him I have admired his mature music, full of a kind of severe beauty that is, at the same time, extremely transparent. As the years went by, I became closer to Michał Spisak—a man of an extraordinary kind-heartedness and also of a rare strength of character. This strength allowed him to withstand with a smile the suffering that always accompanied him in his life, while his kindness enabled him to feel for and very often help others. These character traits, along with a remarkable straightforwardness and a complete unselfishness, always elicited the admiration of those who knew him and a boundless affection from his friends.

In the program of one of the concerts of the Polish Society of Contemporary Music in the 1930s, Spisak's Quartet for wind instruments was performed. That was when I heard his music for the first time. What struck me was an unusual artistic maturity, an elegance of taste, a steady hand, which already characterized this early work. Shortly afterward I met Michał Spisak in Warsaw. He probably intended by that time to settle permanently in Paris. The years of war broke our contact and we only reestablished it in 1946 when I found myself in Paris for the first time. I immediately found that in this city, Michał Spisak was a real host to all his colleagues and friends arriving from Poland. He felt obligated to provide them with help and advice, always doing it with absolute simplicity, as though this obligation was natural for him. During my one and a half months' stay in Paris, we developed friendly relations that were soon transformed into a real and a very close friendship. In the 1940s, Michał Spisak began to visit Poland again. In 1949, Grzegorz Fitelberg was preparing a performance of Spisak's *Symphonie Concertante* no. 1,[1] undoubtedly one of Spisak's supreme achievements. In this Symphony there is a majestic, but slightly severe beauty. One of the stages of this monumentally planned form is the mysterious mood of the intermezzo, in which the solo piano part for four hands is accompanied by one note in the string quintet, which is split into a number of octaves. This idea is almost elementary in its simplicity, which few can manage. Spisak undoubtedly found it in a moment of a true inspiration.

Years passed, during which I saw Michał Spisak from time to time in Warsaw or in Paris and I developed an attachment for and admiration of this extraordinary man, whose attitude toward life and suffering became an incomparable and invigorating model for my whole life. I saw him for the last time in October 1964 in Paris. He was already conscious that his death was approaching. In the face of this he was a real hero. In spite of having to give up everything, especially his composing, he kept a smile on his face, a readiness for a light-hearted conversation, and even for keeping up the spirits of others.

We did not lose Michał Spisak, the composer. His music is alive in concert programs and speaks to the hearts of thousands of listeners. But we lost forever Michał Spisak, the man and the friend. Nobody will replace this splendid person whom we will always think and talk about with the highest reverence.

Source

"Jego muzyka żyje . . ." (His music is alive . . .), a memory of Michał Spisak following his death on January 29, 1965, in Paris. *Ruch Muzyczny*, no. 14 (1965): 6. Copyright Marcin Bogusławski. All rights reserved. Printed by permission.

Note

1. Spisak composed his *Symphonie Concertante* no. 1 in 1947.

ON KAROL SZYMANOWSKI

Observation of contemporary phenomena in the world of music brings to mind an irresistible, but exaggerated, comparison with the Tower of Babel. The proliferation of artistic directions, which sometimes reveals extreme differences between them, the reciprocal misunderstanding of intentions among composers, artists losing contact with the wider audience of listeners—all this corresponds to the confusion of languages in the biblical parable.

Today, this state of affairs surrounds a young artist and exerts a peculiar influence on him. A composer wastes a lot of creative energy today satisfying the constantly changing craving he senses for "novelty" or freshness. He is not capable of concentrating his efforts in one direction for any length of time; he creates more and more unconnected works, each of which breaks away radically from the preceding one. This blunts the composer's sensitivity—a valuable tool in creative work. In this way the *limited scale* of artistic endeavor—so characteristic of our time—finds expression even in a talented young composer. While defending himself against all that favors the dissipation of his own potential, the young artist looks for inspiration for the development of his talent. He wants to set his artistic actions against a stable, strong, and unquestionable base. In the chaos of contemporary musical life, he fixes his eye on something that could be called *the breath of greatness*, which one could search many schools or styles for in vain. For this breath comes only from the creativity of great individuals, and it is exactly what justifies—uniquely and best of all—every "ism" in art to which the great individuals adhere (constantly or temporarily).

In search of the breath of greatness, the eyes of a young Polish composer come across the powerful oeuvre of Karol Szymanowski and find in it the longed-for support.

Today's young Polish creativity does not follow the boundaries marked out by the great Deceased. Rather, it looks for relaxation after the over-sophistication of the *Myths*[1] or the fluency of the orchestral works. And after what is generally described as the "stifling atmosphere" of music from recent years, "air" or "space" is necessary *to talk* about music. One would expect that no young Polish composer will now imitate Szymanowski. Rather, he will oppose many of the currents that were bubbling in a composer so organically bound to the already defunct period of the Young Poland.[2] This opposition will be, however, an open one. In fact, it may be simply a form of reference to the strong and obvious attitude, which every Polish composer will see in the oeuvre of the great Deceased, when taking his first steps. The presence of such stability among the chaos of artistic phenomena surrounding us, and the long-awaited *breath of greatness* arising from it, allow us to look optimistically at the future of Polish music.

Source

"Tchnienie wielkości" (The Breath of Greatness), *Muzyka Polska*, no. 4 (April 1937): 169–170. An issue commemorating the death of Karol Szymanowski on March 29, 1937, in Lausanne, Switzerland. Copyright Marcin Bogusławski. All rights reserved. Printed by permission.

Notes

1. Szymanowski composed his *Myths* for violin and piano in 1915.
2. See note 1 to the text "On Grzegorz Fitelberg" in this chapter.

꼭

When I was eleven years old I first heard Szymanowski's Third Symphony and it was as if a gate had been opened into a fantastic garden previously unknown to me.[1] Afterward I ran home and spent days trying to recapture those sounds on the piano. It was as though I had been drugged and for several weeks I went around in a state of shock. This was my introduction to the world of contemporary music. This admiration of his music lasted for some considerable time, but, inevitably there came a reaction against the romantic aesthetic. I have no doubt that Szymanowski was a great composer and there are many of his works that will always hold a special place in my affections. I am thinking especially of the first Violin Concerto[2] and the song cycle *Słopiewnie*, setting to music poetry by our great national poet Tuwim,[3] and of course the *Stabat Mater*,[4] which is a masterpiece in my view. Unfortunately, I only met him once and that was very briefly, so I can offer no direct personal reminiscence, but the indirect effect of his influence on Polish musical life, including my own, was phenomenal.

Source

"Some Thoughts on Szymanowski," typescript in English. Copyright Witold Lutosławski Collection, Paul Sacher Foundation. All rights reserved. Printed by permission.

Notes

1. Szymanowski wrote his Symphony no. 3, *Pieśń o nocy* ("Song of the Night") in 1914–1916. See also note 2 to the text "Life and Music."
2. Concerto for Violin and Orchestra no. 1 was composed in 1916.
3. *Słopiewnie*—five songs to the poems of Julian Tuwim, was composed in 1921.
4. *Stabat Mater* for solo voices, mixed choir, and orchestra was composed in 1925–1926.

∞

Today, over forty years after Szymanowski's death, the greatness of his art is commonly acknowledged and admired in our country. This art, the extraordinary charm of which is obvious to every Polish music lover, is still underestimated in the rest of the world, and in some countries it simply remains undiscovered. Therefore, every Polish musician welcomes with joy the appearance of Nikolska's book.[1] It contains a lot of valuable material that allows us to know Szymanowski's art better and to bring it closer to readers in Russia, a country to which he was bound by various ties.

I share the joy at the appearance of this book with my colleagues—Polish musicians—in a particularly emotional way. Not everybody is aware today that Szymanowski's music played a very special role in the life of Polish composers of my generation. During our studies, Szymanowski was a symbol of all that was new, unknown, and full of a charm never sensed before. The word *charm* suggests itself when we consider such works as the first Violin Concerto, Symphony no. 3, *Demeter* or *Myths*. This mysterious and narcotic charm, as we may call it, inspired in me, at my very first hearing—at the age of eleven—a sensation of real psychic shock.[2] For several weeks I lived in a state of excitement that is not difficult to explain. This was, after all, a moment of great importance in my life: for the first time, music of the first decades of the twentieth century spoke to me and had an impact on me, demonstrating its enormous power, previously unknown to me, and opened up future possibilities I had never sensed before. This experience from my childhood left an indelible imprint in my memory and is connected to this very day in a very personal way with the music of this great Polish composer.

I was given the chance to attend some premieres in Warsaw of Szymanowski's works from the 1920s and the 1930s. One of these premieres caused not only in me, but also in several colleagues of mine, a completely unexpected reaction. The first performance of the Symphony no. 4 (*Symphonie Concertante*), in which the composer himself played the piano part and which was anticipated with great excitement, disappointed us.[3] It was very beautiful, but wholly tonal, a somewhat Straussian melody, which amazed us, as it was based on a repeated F major triad. At that time I was studying composition, and I worshipped Szymanowski as a pioneer and innovator, so I perceived this work as a kind of compromise in favor of popularity, almost a betrayal of the ideals he embodied. Today Szymanowski's *Symphonie Concertante* shines for us with its full brilliance as one of his outstanding works, and the circumstances of its premiere are no longer of any importance.

I have taken the liberty of mentioning some personal reminiscences of mine connected with Szymanowski's music, in order to explain its importance to all of us, as Polish composers and musicians. I am anxious that the power and beauty of this music should appeal to the greatest possible number of listeners. Nikolska's book, devoted to Szymanowski, will certainly further this desire. I am sure that all Polish musicians owe a feeling of deep gratitude to all who contributed to its publication.

Source

Manuscript in Polish written in the second half of the 1980s. Copyright Witold Lutosławski Collection, Paul Sacher Foundation. All rights reserved. Printed by permission. This text was published in Russian as a preface to Irina Nikolska's book on Szymanowski (see note 1 below).

Notes

1. Irina Nikolska, *Кароль Шимановский. Воспоминания. Статьи. Публикации* (Moscow: Советский Композитор, 1983).

2. See note 2 to the text "Witold Lutosławski—Life and Music" in the present collection.

3. This first performance of Szymanowski's Symphony no. 4 (*Symphonie Concertante*) for piano and orchestra, which was finished in 1932, took place in Warsaw on November 11, 1932, with the composer as soloist and the Warsaw Philharmonic conducted by Grzegorz Fitelberg.

ON HERMANN ABENDROTH

The news of Hermann Abendroth's death filled me with deep sorrow. I share this feeling with a multitude of Polish concertgoers who knew and admired the art of this outstanding musician and conductor. I remember Hermann Abendroth from the earliest years of my youth. Before the Second World War, he appeared as a guest conductor at the Warsaw Philharmonic at least once a season. I certainly remember his beautiful performances of Brahms and Beethoven, which were based on the best traditions. However, what has also stuck in my memory was his brilliant and vigorous performance of Hindemith's *Neues vom Tage*, as well as one of the symphonic poems of our own Karłowicz,[1] which, conducted by Abendroth, sounded richer and clearer than ever before.

These are all memories from my school and student years. When Abendroth came to Poland for the first time after the war, I was already a mature musician and I had the opportunity to get to know him personally. In 1954 he did me a great favor by including, in the program of his guest concert in Warsaw, my composition Little Suite for chamber orchestra. I anticipated this concert with great interest and I was keyed up for it, since I had not attended the rehearsals. I was particularly excited because Abendroth was an expert in classical and romantic German music and I imagined that my work belonged to an era unfamiliar to him. However, from the opening measures of my Suite, I could see that it was just the opposite. His performance demonstrated a masterly understanding of the material. From the beginning to the end, it was filled with a highly intensive expression and made a very strong impression on the listeners. The audience gave Abendroth a warm ovation, expressing their gratitude for such a beautiful performance of a work by a Polish composer. Today I remember that evening with affection as one of the loveliest moments of my life. After the performance of the Little Suite, Abendroth did not stop being interested in my work. He asked me to send him subsequent compositions that he intended to perform at his home in Weimar.

When my Concerto for Orchestra was recently published, I sent Abendroth the score. Only three weeks ago I received a letter written from the clinic in Jena, in which Abendroth confirmed the receipt of the score and expressed his thanks for the dedication in cordial terms. "Once I escape from the doctors' hands," he wrote, "I will start studying your score." I found this interest on the part of a gray-haired maestro a particularly valuable and moving experience for me. It was in this spirit that I wrote my answer to his letter. I don't know whether it reached Abendroth, for I read the news of his death in a newspaper the day before yesterday, which moved me deeply. An artist of great quality had passed away and one to whom Polish audiences owe many, many beautiful musical experiences. Personally, I am particularly affected by Abendroth's death, since he cared enough in his declining years to show me a lot of interest and kindness. I will always remember him with reverence and gratitude.

Source

"Śmierć Hermanna Abendrotha" (The Death of Hermann Abendroth), type-script in Polish. Copyright Witold Lutosławski Collection, Paul Sacher Foundation. All rights reserved. Printed by permission. This text was written as a memory following Abendroth's death on May 29, 1956.

Note

1. See note 4 to the text "On Grzegorz Fitelberg."

ON ANNE-SOPHIE MUTTER

The art of Anne-Sophie Mutter is one of the sources of inspiration for my compositional work. When I first heard her playing my *Chain 2*, it was a unique and unforgettable experience. I couldn't dream of my violin music sounding and being interpreted like this. The recollection of her playing always accompanies my thoughts about future music for violin. I am immensely grateful to her.

Source

Manuscript in English. Copyright Witold Lutosławski Collection, Paul Sacher Foundation. All rights reserved. Printed by permission.

Miscellaneous Items on Contemporary Music in Poland and Abroad

*O*ur meeting for the first time in a long while takes place in an atmosphere of real creative freedom. No one here will persecute anybody for so-called formalism; no one will try to prevent anybody else from expressing his aesthetic views, regardless of what individual composers may stand for.

When I look back today from the perspective of eight and a half years on the "famous" conference in Łagów in 1949, it gives me chills to remember the horrible experience of Polish musical creativity being openly attacked. In fact it is difficult to conceive of a more absurd hypothesis than that the achievements of the past several decades should be abandoned and one should return to the musical language of the nineteenth century. And yet they tried to convince us of this thesis. Not only that, they sometimes tried to launch epigonic, sterile works, while barring the way to the concert platform for original, creative efforts. We all know that what happened was caused by people to whom the very idea of beauty is utterly foreign, people who do not care about music unless one can pin to it some kind of little story or legend.

The period of which I speak may not have lasted long, for it passed a couple of years ago, but all the same it was long enough to do our music immense harm. The psyche of the creative artist is an incredibly delicate and precise instrument. Thus the attack on that instrument, the attempt to control it, caused not a few of us moments of severe depression. Being completely cut off from what was happening in the arts in the West likewise played a considerable role in that dreary experiment we were subjected to.

Have we shaken off our despondency? Do we have enough enthusiasm for new creative explorations? Certainly. Still, our situation is by no means an easy one. Each of us faces the problem of discovering his own place in that chaos the art of our era represents. The problem is sharply drawn for those of us who, after an interruption of several years, have renewed contact with Western European music. We don't all have here a clear view of what is happening in this music, of where it is leading. But I believe it is only a matter of time before we will not only acquire a clear view of the situation but also will play a positive and a not inconsiderable role in it.

I can feel optimistic because today we breathe an atmosphere of true creative freedom. And that is the first, the indispensable condition for the development of all art.

Source

"Zagajenie dyskusji na Walnym Zjeździe Związku Kompozytorów Polskich," *Ruch Muzyczny*, no. 1 (1957): 2–3. Copyright Marcin Bogusławski. All rights reserved. English version translated by Steven Stucky, *Lutosławski and His Music* (Cambridge, UK: Cambridge University Press, 1981), 63–64. Reprinted by permission.

Note

1. This assembly took place in Warsaw March 9, 1957, in the atmosphere of great political change after the so-called Polish October in 1956 that ended the postwar decade of Stalinism and its administratively imposed policy of socialist realism in Polish art.

REFLECTIONS ON THE ISCM FESTIVAL OF CONTEMPORARY MUSIC IN ROME (1959)

The Thirty-third Festival of the International Society of Contemporary Music took place in Rome in June 1959. This festival is held in a different country every year and is already an established tradition. Polish music has contributed considerably to this tradition. It is worth remembering some facts that illustrate this. For instance, over forty works by Polish composers have been performed at the Society's festivals, from 1923 onward. Szymanowski, whose name figures on the list of the Society's honorary members, has been performed seven times. Poles have served eleven times on the international jury made up of people whose task is to decide on the festival's program every year. Let us also remember that Poland organized the last ISCM festival before the war, in April 1939.

As a member of the jury of the Rome festival I had the chance to look through 111 scores sent from twenty-one countries. I was also present at the festival. For me this was an opportunity to look from a particular perspective at the current state of musical creativity. I don't deceive myself that I was making a very serious assessment. Rather, using the pretext of the festival in Rome, I allowed myself some reflections of a general nature. I had no intention of forcing myself to be objective, since I am not a theoretician or musicologist. As a composer, I prefer to submit to the natural inclination of looking at works of art subjectively, through the perspective of my own taste, preferences, and my own temperament. However, in order to make these personal reflections more understandable, it is sensible for me to start by looking back at the period that directly precedes the time we live in.

When I reflect on the history of the musical language of the past fifty years, I am always struck by a peculiar dichotomy. On the one hand I see Schoenberg, his school, and subsequent serialists, while on the other hand there are Debussy, Stravinsky, Bartók, Messiaen, and, finally, even Varèse. The question of the Viennese School is simple. What we see is a strictly formulated doctrine or, if one prefers, technique, its gradual transformation and its final stages, leading relatively quickly to the ultimate goal, which seems to me more and more clearly the disintegration of the traditional musical scale, or rather going beyond that scale.

The other tendency, which coexists with the Viennese School, is more difficult to define. Uniform doctrine is here out of the question and the techniques are very diverse. A clear question emerges as to whether the music of Debussy, Stravinsky, Bartók, Messiaen, and Varèse—if we are to persist with the same names—really has common characteristics that fundamentally differentiate it from Schoenberg and his followers. Many music writers and even composers themselves hold the view that all the music created recently, and independently of the Viennese School and its consequences, already belongs to the past, since it operates with the remnants of tonalism. I rather shy away from this view because of its tendentious character and also because of the obvious oversimplification on which it is based. Personally I am convinced that both the developmental currents of the music of our time have the possibility of thriving in the future, that they differ essentially from one another, and that they lead toward different results. Yet getting to the very essence of this difference is not easy. Certainly I touch here on a very subtle matter. The point is that there are probably two different ways of human reaction to sound. Without entering into detailed analyses, I will say broadly that for those who react in the first of these ways, the interval of the fifth in relation to the tritone presents, first of all, a totally different *quality*, whereas for the second group (I am thinking of the serialists) the point is rather a *quantitative* difference, that is, a difference of the number of semitones contained within these intervals. I deliberately illustrate my point here with elementary phenomena, but I nevertheless have in mind numerous and various consequences that result from this opposite point of view, chosen as an example. Thus I mean, for instance, a different role for chords and sequences of sounds that may be treated as configurations of qualitatively different psychological impulses, or as expressions of relations between numbers. Going further in generalizing this observation, one could talk about the preponderance of the sensual or intellectual element within these two ways of reacting to sound-phenomena. Giving priority to one of them or deciding on a supposed gradual elimination of the other does not attract me at all.

I have previously ventured to say that the whole of serial music from Schoenberg onward tends toward a frontier, the abandonment of the twelve-note equally tempered scale. One could set forth many arguments for this claim. Let us agree that one of the essential features of the chromatic scale is that it is based on a row of overtones, making use of the qualitative differences between the intervals. I have just set out briefly what I call the qualitative difference. I would add that this difference consists of everything that differentiates the intervals from one another, apart from their purely quantitative differences, such as the distance between particular pairs of sounds, that is, the difference in the number of semitones that divide the sounds of each pair. The quality of an interval corresponds, to some extent, to the level of complication of the arithmetic relationship of the frequencies of the two sounds. However, the qualitative differences between the intervals correspond, above all, to various reactions of our ear to these intervals. We should also keep in mind that our consciousness, in connection with each interval, registers some of its individual characteristics independent of its span. The serial system in its different phases tends toward suppression of the qualitative differences between intervals: for instance, through the use of the greatest number of different intervals in the smallest space. The ear then receives impulses that change so quickly that, for some time, it may react only to the distances between the sounds, and not to particular qualities. Another example of the same tendency is making use of the most arithmetically complicated of the frequency relations of particular sounds, which may, at some point, also blur qualitative differences. This is brought about by highlighting intervals, the pitches of which are in a complicated relationship to each other (for example, using the relation of a minor second or a tritone), and by avoiding the simplest intervals, such as the octave, the fifth, etc. The constant use of intervals in which the pitches are widely separated (a style deeply rooted in works of late serialism) is another way of blurring the qualitative differences. All these ways only partly achieve their goal, and it could be argued that complete suppression of the qualitative differences between intervals within our equally tempered scale is impossible.

Therefore I think that the direction taken by Schoenberg in the development of musical language aimed (among other things and perhaps unconsciously) to supersede the existing scale. And at least, if unable to do that, it aimed to establish changes within the old scale that would deprive it of its characteristic, fundamental traits and reduce the relationships between intervals to merely numerical ones. Today, thanks to synthesizers it is possible to create any scale, including one that would realize this goal of serialism in its ideal form. Therefore, continuing to compose music using the old scale is not justified. Moreover, today it is an anachronism, since it is always at variance with the very notion of a qualitative difference between intervals, that is, with the notion that—in my opinion—underlies the twelve-note scale. Does it follow that the role of the traditional scale based on a series of harmonics—the scale consisting of the division of the octave into twelve equal parts and qualitatively different intervals—is finished in the development of music?

It seems to me that it is possible to answer this question in the affirmative concerning only one of several currents in the development of music, that is, the direction taken by Schoenberg, which led, as we can already see, to the departure from the traditional scale. Let us not forget, however, that Schoenberg and the serialists represent only one of the developmental strands in the history of twentieth-century music; there is also the second, no less important strand, although it is much less frequently discussed by today's theoreticians and musicologists. This strand, based on the twelve-note, equally tempered scale, can be developed further in accordance with the scale's essential traits.

This does not mean at all that I would set any hopes on the development of the remnants of tonalism. Quite the contrary, and perhaps we find ourselves today at a point at which everything is to be discovered anew in the realm of the twelve-note equally tempered scale, but based on its fundamental features, and above all on the qualitative differences between the intervals. Everything beyond the twelve-note scale, that is, beyond that realm where serial technique, among other things, led us, is also still to be discovered.

It may seem now that by continuing and completing the vision described here, I could easily assign particular works to one or another developmental tendency; placing each of them in an appropriate historical moment, treating one as conservative and another as progressive. I have, however, not the slightest intention of yielding to this obviously dubious temptation. I am too aware of the heightened subjectivity of my views given here today. After all, it is only one personal view of the music of our time; one of many possible ones. And, apart from that, I also can't forget that works of art are, fortunately, not only music examples that illustrate the theoretical views of their composers. They also have their own, autonomous existence and, for the most part, they cannot be unequivocally classified.

It was from this point of view that I made the choice of works for today's broadcast. I chose those that, while I was listening to them, allowed me to forget their origins and the aesthetic they represent. It seemed to me a sufficient reason to classify them simply as music.

The first of them is *Ein irrender Sohn* (A Straying Son), a work for alto and instruments by the Swedish composer Bo Nilsson. It is interesting that the twenty-two-year-old Bo Nilsson is a complete autodidact; he started by imitating Stockhausen and Boulez without having studied any earlier compositional techniques.

The second work is *Samai* for chamber orchestra by the Japanese composer Yoritsune Matsudaira. Born in 1907 in Tokyo, Matsudaira studied composition in Europe. *Samai* is Matsudaira's fourth work performed at the festivals of the International Society of Contemporary Music. It is a five-movement suite inspired by an old Japanese court dance.

The name of Petrassi, a leading Italian composer of the middle-aged generation is known very well to everybody. His new work, *Serenada for Five Instruments*, was a surprise to many of us. It is as though there is a new Petrassi, who has had time to familiarize himself with the newest events in European music and to draw out of them quite individual consequences for his own works.

I chose the least known works as the most important items of the festival. In this year's program we see the names of twenty-seven composers and among them Stravinsky, Dallapiccola, Messiaen, Boulez, Nono, Henze, as well as two Poles, Baird and Szalonek.

Source

"Refleksje na marginesie festiwalu muzyki współczesnej SIMC w Rzymie," in *Horyzonty muzyki* (Horizons of Music), ed. Michał Bristiger, Stefan Jarociński, Józef Patkowski, and Mieczysław Tomaszewski (Kraków: PWM, 1970). Series *Res Facta* 1, no. 1 (radio broadcast of 14 October 1959). Copyright Marcin Bogusławski. All rights reserved. Printed by permission.

ABOUT RADIO (1959)

The radio can and partly does play the role of a powerful instrument for transferring cultural goods to great masses of people. And it is in this that I see the most important benefit of this invention. Unfortunately, the existence of the radio also has its weak points. The first of them is an excess of music listened to for hours by people who don't know how to make use of the radio. This leads to a depreciation of this art by overuse, and even becoming repellent. The second weak point is the violence perpetrated every day by millions of those radio users on their neighbors, and thus one of the nightmares and absurdities of our age is that people are forced, against their will, to listen to music.

Source

Statement on the occasion of the fifteenth anniversary of the postwar Polish Radio, *Radio i Telewizja*, no. 47 (1959): 24. Copyright Marcin Bogusławski. All rights reserved. Printed by permission.

REFLECTIONS ON BALLET (1962)

The beauty of the pose and the movement of the human body, the expression of gesture, the moving play of forms created by a dancing group—these are the element of the ballet spectacle. Everything that is supposed to be its plot, which a spectator should know in advance or understand while watching, is in principle alien to the essence of the ballet, and very often it is incomprehensible or ridiculous. I know that the tradition of many years is based on an opposite view, but even the most beautiful *Romeo and Juliet* or *Daphnis and Chloé* cannot reconcile me at this moment to that tradition.

Ballet is similar to music in this respect, in that, in its essence, it is an asemantic art. Although it employs elements that can signify or express something fully (for instance, particular gestures, mimicry, and even whole situations), the rule by which we link these elements to a larger context should not be borrowed from drama or other semantic arts, since it leads to an artistic falsehood, an incompleteness, or to the point of being ridiculous. A large form of a ballet spectacle should not be governed by the plot, an anecdote, or an action with its self-dependent content, but by a purely visual composition and its expressive flow. Ballet is composed of sufficiently independent means of expression for it not to have recourse to compromises from other kinds of stage art. In short: the ballet is only a pure kind of art when it directly *affects* and not when, apart from that, it also *represents* something.

In a ballet spectacle, the music may play a role equivalent to the dance. The music should not be crowded out by the role of a varying metronome enabling the dancers to perform their movements simultaneously and at the right time. The rhythm and the expression of what is taking place on the stage should not consist in projecting the rhythm and the expressiveness of music. The close connection between the music and the dance should sometimes act as a contrast and often in a kind of counterpoint, in which the gestures and events on the stage interact with the flow of the music, creating an inseparable composition. Obviously the rhythm and the visual part of such a composition must have precise notation, making up a part of the score. Will I ever succeed one day in creating such a work? First I would need to gain the cooperation of a choreographer and coauthor convinced of the rightness of my ideas.

Source

"Rozmyślając o balecie," in Stefan Jarociński, *Witold Lutosławski. Materiały do monografii* (Materials for a Monograph) (Kraków: Polish Musical Edition, 1967), 37–38. Copyright Marcin Bogusławski. All rights reserved. Printed by permission. The German version of this text ("Gedanken über das Ballet") was printed in *Opera Viva*, no. 3 (1962): 39.

IS THIS MUSIC? (1963)

Is this music? We often hear this question nowadays. It is asked not only by disoriented listeners or conservative critics, but also by musicians themselves, who are unaccustomed to the performance of sounds of this kind. Perplexed by such a question, we reach for the dictionary in order to find out what is meant by the word music. If we look up *Webster's New Practical Dictionary*, we are somewhat surprised to learn that music is "the art of combining tones in such a way that they are pleasing, expressive, or intelligible," and from the *Harvard Dictionary of Music*, we learn that a tone is "a sound of definite pitch and duration." From this it would seem that if a composer introduces percussion instruments producing sounds of indefinitive pitch into a work, he thereby renders that work unfit to be considered as music. The *Shorter Oxford Dictionary* proves to be more liberal; it defines music as "that one of the fine arts which is concerned with the combination of sounds, with a view to beauty of form and the expression of thought or feeling." This definition is more satisfying. The answer to our question depends here entirely on the interpretation given to such ideas as "beauty of form" or "the expression of thought or feeling." These concepts, being vague and subjective, are open to discussion and so allow us to defend our work and, in spite of everything, rate it as music.

When I hear the question "Is this music?" I am puzzled as to why it should be asked so frequently nowadays. Does the present work of the avant-garde composers really deviate to such an extent from what is regarded by the majority as music? Conscious as I am of some of the phenomena characterizing present-day music, I am compelled to answer this question affirmatively. As a matter of fact, the difference between certain recent works and, for example, the music of Webern, or even of his direct followers, seems greater, more fundamental than the difference between Webern's music and that of the Baroque period. I shall try to show the particular phenomena that, in my opinion, justify this assertion. These phenomena concern one of the most essential elements in music: the nature of the sounds used in its creation.

The sounds Webern used in his Cantata, or even Stockhausen in his *Kontra-Punkte*, are no different—as far as pitch is concerned—from those used by Bach in any of his compositions. All these sounds belong to the same relatively small collection we call the equally tempered twelve-note scale. From the eighty or so sounds of this collection have been composed such dissimilar works as, for example, Haydn's quartets, Tchaikovsky's symphonies, Debussy's *La Mer*, and Boulez's *II Sonata*. Techniques and forms, styles and tastes have undergone tremendous changes in the course of the last few centuries, yet the basic tonal material of music has always remained the same and has consisted of these eighty or so sounds.

That is probably why the equally tempered, twelve-note system has so firmly rooted itself in the human consciousness and habits. It is probably also the reason why so many of us identify this system with the very concept of the music itself, and why, as this system is being questioned and as works are appearing that have little in common with it, we hear the question: "is this music?" It is as if this system were indissolubly linked with the very essence of music itself. It is true, indeed, that certain of its elements are directly derived from physical and psychological laws, for example, the interval of an octave, or the intervals closely related to those of the harmonic series, such as the fifth, the fourth, etc.

On the other hand, the various nature sounds with which we are familiar very rarely have anything in common with the sounds belonging to the twelve-note scale; in fact it can be safely said, I think, that they practically never have anything in common with them. Take, for example, sounds such as the murmur of the sea, or the sound of the skylark. These are sounds that are commonly regarded as beautiful (in every sense of the word); sounds that the early romantic poets often refer to as music, and yet, from the point of view of their structure, they bear far less resemblance to the twelve-note scale than does many a daring product of our contemporary avant-garde composers.

This one consideration is already enough, I think, to make us realize how entirely natural is the present-day search for a new repertoire of sounds. I am only surprised that we did not begin this search sooner. Without going into the reasons for this, I should like to give you now a few examples taken from actual works that illustrate ways of transcending the bounds of the equally tempered twelve-note scale.

The presence in a piece of music of a certain number of sounds not belonging to the twelve-note scale is a phenomenon that has been known in music as long as the use of percussion instruments of indefinite pitch. But until now these sounds have played only a minor role: they have been an addition, an ornament, a kind of dressing to enhance the dish, and have never belonged to the basic elements of the musical language.

From this standpoint, Edgar Varèse's *Ionisation*, written in 1931, is a specific exception. The roles usually played in a piece of music by the two kinds of sounds are here inverted: the sounds belonging to the traditional musical scale are with Varèse only an additional element, and the main musical discourse is maintained by percussion instruments of an indefinite pitch. We can therefore regard Varèse as one of the precursors of a trend that is only now undergoing widespread development (sound illustration—fragment of Varèse's *Ionisation*).

Percussion instruments, however, set rather narrow bounds on a composer's imagination. That is why more recent research has been in a somewhat different direction. Composers have endeavored to make use of instruments such as the violin or the piano to produce new types of sounds. The possibility of playing glissando on string instruments, this short cut, so to speak, without regard to the well-trodden paths of the old musical scale, suggested to Iannis Xenakis a fascinating sound vision like this: (sound illustration—fragment of Xenakis's *Methastasis* or *Achorypsis*).

A rich catalogue of specific sounds unused so far, which can be produced by string instruments, has been worked out by Krzysztof Penderecki. They are sounds such as the highest sound of the instrument without defining its pitch, sounds played between the bridge and the tailpiece, sounds made when playing with the bow on the tailpiece, differentiated kinds of vibrato playing, etc. From the use of all these kinds of sounds in combination with those produced in the traditional manner *arco* or *pizzicato* arises an unusually colorful, singular, shimmering network (sound illustration—fragment of Penderecki's *Quartetto per archi*).

The piano has also become the object of similar experiments. John Cage, at the time a pioneer of the so-called prepared piano, draws out of this instrument a rich repertoire of new sounds that often do not belong to the traditional scale. He does this by means of various operations that make playing the piano similar to playing percussion instruments (sound illustration—fragment of Cage's *Sonatas and Interludes*).

In spite of the undoubted richness of the sounds resulting from these new ways of playing traditional instruments, the impression strongly persists, that all those possibilities lie outside the proper designation of these instruments. These are but their marginal possibilities. All the secrets of the art of violin are unnecessary when we play behind the bridge or strike the sound board with the fingers. For such purposes a cheap machine-made instrument would do. The same goes for the piano: it seems to be unnecessary luxury to use a new concert Steinway to play *pizzicato* or strike with the drumsticks.

All this is by no means an argument against composers. It only proves that traditional instruments are less and less suitable for the needs of the composer's imagination. This comes to light especially when a composer is trying to build his sound world outside the traditional twelve-note scale. Therefore, attempts to find new sound possibilities in a very old but longer-lived instrument seem to be more natural. That instrument is the human voice; in particular, considering that singing in the traditional sense is only one of the uses of the human voice and rather peculiar at that.

Speech, with its countless nuances of sound and expression, as well as every kind of call or shout seems a more natural human function than the singing of complicated sequences of sounds within the twelve-note scale. The human voice is, however, a very specific instrument and sets great limitation on the composer. There is no danger of the voice dropping out of use as traditional instruments are likely to in the future, but the voice will certainly not be able to serve all the musical needs of creative imagination.

That is why we now attach such strong hopes to a new instrument or to a whole complex of instruments and procedures that have been introduced into the world of music by the discovery of magnetic tape and later by the synthetic production of sound, and by all the operations to which we put the latter in experimental studios.

What has been produced in these studios seems poor and monotonous to all those who delight in the beauty of a Stradivarius's tone or in the finesse of the touch of great virtuoso pianists. It is true that synthetic sound will never replace that finesse. Nor will it ever replace the live performer, since its designation is neither to replace, nor—all the more—to dislodge anything. But the present day composer, fully aware of the imperfection or even crudity of synthetic music, can envisage its future development. In it he divines great potentialities and, above all, he expects that in the future through this medium he may realize the sound visions that impose themselves upon his imagination—visions that have long overstepped the boundaries set by the traditional scale and traditional instruments.

To complete these reflections you will hear the recordings of three pieces by contemporary Polish composers: Włodzimierz Kotoński's *Microstructures*,

Krzysztof Penderecki's *Quartetto per archi*, and the second movement of Witold Lutosławski's *Trois poèmes d'Henri Michaux* (*Le grand combat*). Each of these pieces may serve as an example of the search for new sound material independent of the traditional twelve-note scale.

The first is a piece produced synthetically in an experimental studio, the second—a piece in which old instruments are used in a new manner, the last is a piece in which human voices are employed in various and very natural ways that nevertheless exclude singing.

Source

Typescript in English. Copyright Witold Lutosławski Collection, Paul Sacher Foundation. All rights reserved. Printed by permission. This text served as a talk on BBC Radio, on May 24, 1964, and in the Polish version—"Czy to jest muzyka?"—on Polish Radio, on February 3, 1965. The Polish version was first printed in Stefan Jarociński, *Witold Lutosławski. Materiały do monografii* (Materials for a Monograph) (Kraków: Polish Musical Edition, 1967), 22–28.

Note

1. Lutosławski started his broadcast with an unidentified recorded music example, which he marked in his typescript as a collage.

SOUNDS IN NO MATTER WHAT SCALE (1971)

I don't like to think about the future of music and I almost never speak my mind publicly on this subject. In the history of Polish views on art we have, in fact, a futurologist, who stands out from what other writers have already said in this field, and probably from all that will be said in the near future. This eminent futurologist was Witkacy.[1] Independent of whether or not I share all his views, I consider his works to not only be the product of an incredible visionary gift, but also as the result of many years' profound consideration. Since I don't see any prophetic gift in myself, I rarely think about what awaits music in the future. Therefore, the result of this state of affairs may only be supposition without any thorough justification.

If, in spite of that, I decided to answer the questions in *Polityka*, I did it not in order to guess, but rather to express some thoughts about the kind of music I am longing for, and for which I work every day within the framework of my compositional workshop.

The sound-imagination of composers underwent a great transformation in the past decades. Concrete music (or *musique concrète*) and electronic music have already introduced a lot of previously unknown acoustic phenomena, enriching the means of expression, the value of which cannot be underestimated. The experiences in the realm of noises, of sounds with defined and undefined pitch, etc., developed the sound-imagination of even those composers who don't collaborate with experimental studios. Their imagination became so transformed that merely using traditional instruments no longer satisfies these composers. Hence, there emerged an urgent need to create new instruments on which live performers would play; instruments producing not only noises and sounds with defined pitch, but also "musical" sounds with no pitch and color, but belonging to freely constructed scales. Yet even in the future, I don't see any reason to totally give up the use of the twelve-tone equally tempered scale, for the possibilities of this have not yet been fully exploited. However, these possibilities can exist with one stipulation, namely that the sensibility of the human ear to the interplay of various sounds will be restored. This sensibility was for some time stifled, especially among those composers and listeners who were influenced by serialism.

Since I don't have any improved musical instruments that would totally suit my imagination, I must settle for the traditional instruments that I am acquainted with, and for "translating" into their language everything that stimulates my sound-invention. I also try to do my best, within the framework of the twelve-tone scale, to create a world of sounds and their sequences that do not offer the composer the serial technique.

In my composing I devote much effort to the equally fascinating issue of time in my musical works. This issue is connected, first and foremost, with all variants of limited (or partial) aleatorism, the possibilities of which are still hard to predict. I do not, however, see a future in the radical aleatorism with its presumption that chance itself should be the main author of my musical work.

If I said at the beginning that I don't like to think about the future of music it was also because its fate in the present day world makes me worried about its future. The omnipresence of music or, rather, of pseudomusic in everyday life—on the street, in the department store, on the beach, in the garden, in a taxi, on a ship, etc., and, what is worse, in one's own room coming through the wall—all this omnipresence must make one feel disgust at these sounds and, at best, indifferent to any music. I think sorrowfully about those people who listen to this pseudomusic for several hours a day. Will they ever be able to listen with concentration and satisfaction to a Beethoven symphony? I try to believe that this deadly swarm of sounds will die out in time, and will enable vivid, real music to have an impact on human souls. May it never lose what Joseph Conrad called its "magic insight."[2]

Source

"Dźwięki w dowolnej skali," *Polityka*, no. 1 (January 2, 1971): 6. Copyright Marcin Bogusławski. All rights reserved. Printed by permission.

Notes

1. Stanisław Ignacy Witkiewicz, see note 1 to the text "Some Thoughts on the Perception of Music" in chapter 1 of the present collection.
2. Joseph Conrad, *Typhoon, The Nigger of the "Narcissus," and Other Stories* (London: The Folio Society, 2000), 230.

REFLECTIONS ON THE FUTURE OF MUSIC (1972)

Much has been written and said about the degeneration of the arts in our times; about its disintegration; about its becoming stunted; or even about its path to self-annihilation. Here are a few thoughts on the subject that have occurred to me in the past few years.

In the field of music the process of "disintegration" began at the moment when Wagner wrote the first three measures of *Tristan and Isolde*. Thus, the first tiny crack was made in the granite of what seemed to be a sacrosanct and inviolate edifice. The phenomenal monument of musical construction, the major-minor scale system, which evolved over the centuries through the efforts and inspirations of countless generations of composers, starting with Perotin the Great, was indeed endangered.

Certainly neither Wagner himself, and even less those other rebels and violators of convention—"destroyers" and "devastators" if you will—such as Chopin and Liszt, could not have imagined or foreseen that what took centuries to develop could be brought down with such lightning speed and lead to something that may be called, with many reservations and qualifications, "antimusic."

The introduction of the notion of antimusic is full of the danger of misunderstanding, since everyone sees the dividing line between music and antimusic differently. It is not my intention to define it as I see it, nevertheless a classical composition belonging to antimusic is not an abstract notion to me. We see examples of such works, for instance, in the compositions of La Monte Young or June Paik. They are the end stages of evolution of the concept of a piece of music; and in the process of developing this concept, the ultimate goal is the elimination of music itself. Two questions arise:

1. Is the history of music in the last few decades limiting itself to, and only to, what would appear to be the path of "destruction" beginning with Wagner and proceeding to La Monte Young?
2. How should the organizers of musical life, that is, those who decide whether a piece should or should not be performed, deal with this antimusic?

I will consider the second question first. It is probably less important, but easier for me to answer. Very simply and nonetheless categorically: I am decidedly opposed to creating artificial barriers to the circulation of the products of art and denying the recipients, the public, access to them and justifying this action as being for the sake of aesthetic tendencies these products represent. It is not right to hide from the public the existing currents and tendencies in art, even though they may appear to be "antiart." The public has the absolute right to know everything that happens in art throughout the world and to have personal experience of it or an interrelationship with it. To deny the public any kind of composition immediately results in an unnatural situation. The suppressed authors grow into a stature of "persecuted heroes," a position they would possibly never have achieved had their creation been allowed to circulate freely. I believe that an antiart piece does not deserve to be endowed with the glamor and fascination of forbidden fruit.

As a coorganizer of the Warsaw Autumn festival programs, I shall always defend the institutions of Night Concerts, where the most radical compositions of those composers who broke with all known musical conventions are scheduled. The aesthetic value of these compositions is not *the only* criterion for selection, for who is in a position to precisely define these standards? Consideration has to be given, also, to whether they represent a manifestation in art that interests a certain number of people. An example of this phenomenon is what may be called, not in a strict sense, instrumental theatre, in other words—happenings.

Being opposed to all musical "taboos," I have yet another reason for this position, besides the one mentioned. It is my concern that some important, but at present difficult to recognize, manifestation in music could be overlooked or condemned to oblivion. This would preclude finding the hidden worth that may be found in even in the most "unconvincing" aesthetic, worth that may be discernible only by some future generation. Or that in some composition, the "purest" product of the last stage in the "process of destruction," there is contained some seeds for the future rebirth of music.

The first question I raised has no easy answer. The "process of destruction" is a phenomenon one would think evident to anyone who ponders for a moment and reflects on the future of music and the road it took, beginning with *Tristan and Isolde,* up to the hole made in a wall by a sufficient number of performers pushing a piano against it. (I am making here an allusion to a piece by La Monte Young, whose score reads: "Push a piano against a wall. If it resists, push more strongly.") Yet the changes taking place in the musical language, and even in the aesthetics itself, are only one side of the history of music of a particular era. The other side is the works themselves, created in a given period, and looked upon independent of historical context.

The fact that no new convention lasting at least a number of years has been able to replace the old classical one has not prevented the creation of a series of real masterpieces during our period. Making this statement may appear inconsistent, yet it only seems so. The value of principles and conventions, which form the basis of a given art cannot, per se, be used as a yardstick of the value of a piece of art, because in great measure it is independent of them. Principles and conventions may be justified by the value of a piece of art itself, for which they provide the foundation. Thus, with the help of the most "unconvincing" and even absurd principles and conventions, it is possible to create a masterpiece, whereas, on the other hand, even the most beautiful-in-itself principle serving as a basis cannot save kitsch from being what it is. Naturally, the question immediately arises, "What is a masterpiece and what is kitsch?"

I am an adherent of the opinion that there are no criteria for the value of a piece of art. The deciding factor in each case is the experience of the listener, and this is beyond the reach of objective categorization. The sum total of the experiences of thousands of listeners over a period of several decades, which is encompassed in the word "time," decides the value of a piece of art. The verdict of the audiences over the last several decades has been surprisingly positive. Thus, in spite of the "process of disintegration" of the classical conventions, brought to an absurd state today, musical works of undeniable value and power of appeal have been and continue to be created.

There is irrefutable evidence of the fact that the currently fragile and crumbling substance of music is subordinate to the human spirit, which is not in the least inclined to be drawn into the "process of disintegration." This spiritual strength, evident in many works, leads me to believe that the crisis of the *substance* of music, deeply alarming as it is, is after all a *passing* phenomenon. The greater freedom we ensure for the creation and propagation of the music composed today, no matter how radical, the sooner the renaissance of musical output will appear. Artificial barriers will only delay overcoming the crisis. I believe wholeheartedly and most confidently that this will be achieved and that art will not annihilate itself. Its ardent need has been so closely connected with humanity from its inception and it is such an essential attribute that I can only imagine the disappearance of art with the disappearance of humanity itself.

Source

Typescript in English. Copyright Witold Lutosławski Collection, Paul Sacher Foundation. All rights reserved. Printed by permission. This version was printed in *Polish Music*, no. 2 (1972): 3–6. The Polish version, titled "Z rozmyślań nad przyszłością muzyki," appeared in *Tygodnik Powszechny* on November 19, 1972.

TODAY'S MOMENT

The world of sounds that stimulates the composers' imagination (or which the imagination inhabits) is subject to constant changes over the course of time. However, there are exceptional short periods of balance in which the conventional means of expression correspond near enough to the composers' intentions, goals, and tastes, so that they remain in an unchanged form for some time. We usually call them classical periods, and they leave a legacy of their most perfect works to the following generations. In the classical works of every period of the history of music, we are often inclined to admire the beauty itself and the perfection of form. However, we immediately realize that this beauty does not unbalance the elements of a work but supports its higher purposes. The French differentiation between the notions of *message* and *language* helps us to understand this phenomenon more easily. In the classical works, the pre-eminence of *message* seems to be unquestionable, but, on the other hand, there is no great work of art in which the language is not sufficiently perfected so as to be the object of our admiration by itself.

Classical periods usually last only a short time. The balance of the elements becomes disturbed at a certain moment. It occurs mostly in the following way: the conventional means of expression lose their vitality, they become commonplace and cease to have any force; they become boring, which inevitably leads to their overexpansion. A composer, who is first and foremost absorbed by his need to refresh his technique, enriches his language and loses sight of what it should serve. The first signs of a disturbance to the balance of a work, which consist of an excessive growth of the formal elements of a work, cause an opposite reaction. There comes a generation of the so-called avant-garde, whose main goal is to destroy or, rather, to discredit existing art. This happens through a sudden retreat from the traditional, sometimes highly sophisticated technical means, replacing them with new, hitherto unknown ones, which are mostly primitive. Yet this primitiveness has the compensation of an invaluable advantage, which is its novelty. While proposing its new musical language, the avant-garde renders everyone an inestimable service, for they replace the old schemata, by new, formerly unknown ones; they liberate the art from a barren rhetoric and from a boring routine which the worn-out classics handed down to those who came after. The new means are, perhaps, far from being perfect, but they contain the germ of future development, and they hint at future glamor. In the course of time they are subject to selection, they strive for perfection and, ultimately, they may serve as a tool for a new classical period. Then the entire process starts again. Remembering such truisms as those I have mentioned helps us when we want to become more aware of the present situation in music.

While thinking about the process I have just discussed, let us ask a question: To which of the three stages should we allocate today's period of development? Is it a classical period, a period of degeneration of classicism, or a period of an aggressive avant-garde?

Source

"Moment dzisiejszy," manuscript in Polish, Copyright Witold Lutosławski Collection, Paul Sacher Foundation. All rights reserved. Printed by permission.

THE LONDON SINFONIETTA (1973)

From Mr. Witold Lutosławski:

Sir, I have just had the privilege of conducting the London Sinfonietta playing a program of my works in the Queen Elizabeth Hall. Working with this remarkable ensemble during the rehearsals and the concert itself provided me with the greatest artistic satisfaction.

The London Sinfonietta is one of the rare groups in the world, which, composed of first-class musicians, some of whom are really virtuoso players, devotes its efforts entirely to the promotion of music of the twentieth century. The admirable Sinfonietta's work is a great stimulus for the composers of our time and creates ideal circumstances for the promotion of their music.

It seems to me that the ensemble deserves special protection and encouragement. Yet I have learnt to my great concern that the London Sinfonietta is in financial trouble that threatens its very existence. It would be a great loss to the world music scene if such a group had to resign from its pioneer activity.

Yours sincerely,
Witold Lutosławski
Śmiała 39,
Warsaw 86, Poland

Source

The Times (London), February 16, 1973, 19 (letters page). Copyright Marcin Bogusławski. All rights reserved. Printed by permission. Quoted in full in E. M. Webster, "The London Sinfonietta. The Study in Survival," *Musical Opinion*, no. 96 (1972–1973): 409–11.

⚜

CONDUCTING THE LONDON SINFONIETTA (1973)

The words "London Sinfonietta" associate in my mind with two unforgettable experiences. The first was my first contact with the ensemble at the occasion of a gramophone recording of one of my pieces with Peter Pears as soloist. It was last September at Maltings Snape.[1] The second was a concert at the Queen Elizabeth Hall in London in January this year,[2] when I had the privilege of conducting the London Sinfonietta in a program of my works.

To appear for the first time in front of an orchestra one has never conducted before is very often an embarrassing situation for a composer. It is certainly a most valuable opportunity to convey the composer's interpretation of a work to the performers. But, on the other hand, it is rather a troublesome necessity to have to insist on the precise execution of the details of one's own work, and to have to introduce some new ways of making music, which need to be explained exactly.

From the first rehearsal with the London Sinfonietta, all my misgivings disappeared entirely. I felt very strongly that the only goal of those wonderful musicians was to achieve the best possible results; to respond as accurately as possible to the composer's suggestions; in other words—to help to realize his sound vision in the most faithful way.

A group of experienced first-class musicians, some of whom are really virtuoso players, who have such an interest and devotion for contemporary music, is an invaluable treasure for us—for contemporary composers. Arthur Honegger once wrote that a contemporary composer whose work was played in a subscription concert felt like a man sitting at a table to which he had not been invited. The London Sinfonietta's series of twentieth-century music concerts offers the participating composers just the contrary: the rare and incomparable feeling of being the right man in the right place.

The very existence of such a group and its pioneer mission of promoting the music of our time is a beautiful example to follow in other countries all over the world.

Source

Typescript in English. Copyright Witold Lutosławski Collection, Paul Sacher Foundation. All rights reserved. Printed by permission.

Notes

1. Lutosławski means September 25, 1972, when he recorded *Paroles tissées* with Peter Pears for Decca (HEAD 3, LP stereo); see also: Decca 448 258-2DF2 (CD, ADD).
2. This concert took place on January 20, 1973. Its program included *Musique funèbre*, *Paroles tissées* (with Peter Pears), *Jeux vénitiens*, and Preludes and Fugue.

ON THE OCCASION OF THE
TWENTIETH WARSAW AUTUMN (1976)

Poles are not universally considered a particularly musical people. They are, however, undeniably endowed with curiosity. They are curious about everything that is unusual and strange, about everything that they do not have at home. The trait may explain why the regular concerts that attract large audiences of seasonal ticket subscribers in many countries of Europe and in America are not especially popular in Poland. The major musical events, especially Warsaw Autumn, are something else again. The enormous crowds the festival concerts have drawn from the very beginning to this day may be explained by that typical Polish trait, by the public's love of the novel, the strange, and the unexpected. This trait should neither be shrugged off nor disdained, for the desire to learn about the new discoveries in music need not arise from superficial motives, nor does it necessarily reflect a giddy enthusiasm for every short-lived fad or craze. It may equally well express a deep need for the new and the creative and particularly for the prophetic. It is this last definition that I would use to designate the type of curiosity displayed by the Polish public and it, I might add, speaks in their favor. For the majority of season ticket holders to the vaunted concert halls of Europe and America have a taste for the same dozen or so symphonies and tolerate (but not always) the occasional stray work by a twentieth-century composer only for the sake of appearances.

    The Polish public's desire for novelty and their selfless curiosity deserved to be acknowledged now, twenty years after Tadeusz Baird[1] and Kazimierz Serocki[2] came up with the idea of organizing an annual festival of contemporary music in Warsaw.[3] At the time, the Polish public had long been isolated from the music that was being composed in the majority of other countries. Worse still, they had never heard the masterpieces of twentieth-century music that had become widely recognized as classics. They did not know Stravinsky's *The Rite of Spring* or *any* of the works of such composers as Webern, Varèse, and Ives.

It had therefore become a matter of utmost urgency to make up this glaring cultural deficiency as soon as possible. The first festivals were designed with this purpose in mind. The programs were devoted to the masterpieces of twentieth-century classics as well as to newer works that have since established a world reputation. Another aim of the festival was to present the widest possible selection of Polish works. It may be pointed out with some pride that Polish composers born after 1930, notably Penderecki and Górecki, were first brought to the attention of the world at the Warsaw Autumn festivals.

It was far easier to draw up programs for the early festivals—there was so much to be made up, so many works had not been performed and there was a host of fascinating new developments in the latest music that deserved presentation. The situation has now altered considerably. The Polish public have already heard nearly all the greatest works of twentieth-century composers. The only exceptions are the outstanding postwar compositions that could not be performed in Poland for technical or financial reasons.

While the festival offers the young and youngest Polish composers an excellent forum for their works, this very fact made the work of the Program Commission more difficult. Titles, names, and program ideas do not present themselves readily. It now takes far more time and effort to put together and carry out a festival program. In this difficult situation, one thing has not altered: the unfaltering—more, the growing—public interest. The interest and the expectations may be satisfied, it seems to me, in one way alone, that is, by a program that offers an honest presentation of the condition of music in the world as it is today. The Polish public not only desire, but they have every right to demand to hear the kinds of music that are presently written. The Polish public not only wish, but also are sufficiently discerning to choose between the compositions offered, to like what they choose and not to like what they reject. That the public may be trusted is due to twenty years of education, which they owe largely to the annual Warsaw Autumn festivals. Honest information about the music written today and its impartial presentation are the guiding principles of the work of the Program Commission. The great accomplishment of the Warsaw Autumn festivals over the past twenty years can hardly be overrated. The festivals have transformed Warsaw, which until then had not appeared large on the music map of the world, into one of the centers of contemporary music, of major significance not only to Poland, but also to all who are interested in music composed around the world today.

Source

Polish Music, no. 4 (1976): 6–7. Copyright Marcin Bogusławski. All rights reserved. Printed by permission.

Notes

1. Tadeusz Baird (1928–1981) was a representative of the of the so-called Polish School after 1945. In spite of his avant-garde innovations, his style reveals lyrical qualities inherited from the romantic tradition.
2. Kazimierz Serocki (1922–1981) was another representative of the postwar Polish School. His highly original innovations in the area of sound-colors and orchestral texture contributed to the Polish "sonorism" of the 1960s and the 1970s.
3. The first Warsaw Autumn Festival took place at the Warsaw Philharmonic in October 10–21, 1956.

THE PHILHARMONIA OF MY YOUTH (1976)

There are people in the world for whom music is an indispensable element in their spiritual life, just as essential for a human organism as is air or water. It is a strange and mysterious feature of the psyche of certain human beings. No one has discovered so far why this is so, although everyone who possesses it takes it for granted. In this world there are not very many people so closely bound to music. Yet they can be found throughout European culture and they are not lacking in our country as well. They are all listeners to music regardless of whether music is their profession or not. For listening to music, perceiving, and experiencing it, are also basic things for those who create and perform it. If they were not genuine listeners, at least during their youth, they could not compose or perform music.

Practicing and perfecting the technique of composition and playing instruments is a sad and sterile activity if it is not accompanied by a constant relationship with great works and great performances through listening to them in the concert hall.

I celebrate the jubilee of the Warsaw Philharmonic first and foremost as a listener. My thoughts wander back to all the most important moments I was able to experience in the hall at Jasna Street, realizing that they brought a richness into my life, and taught me to compose better than I would have, even if I had studied at the best music academy. The first of these moments was the first symphonic concert I ever attended, at the age of no more than seven: it was Beethoven's Ninth Symphony under the direction of Zdzisław Birnbaum.

After many morning, afternoon, and, only rarely, evening concerts came the second memorable moment for me. This was a concert devoted to the composers of the so-called Young Poland, at which—at the age of eleven—I first heard Szymanowski's Third Symphony.[1] His music introduced me to a totally new, magical world, the existence of which I had hardly imagined before. However, I must have been possessed by a kind of unconscious longing for this unique world, since a state of enchantment like a narcotic state, which overwhelmed me while listening to the Third Symphony, lasted for several weeks. During my studies my most beautiful "philharmonic" experiences were connected first of all with the appearances of great performers. Józef Hofman, Casadesus, Gieseking, Horowitz, Orlov, Huberman, Szigeti, Paweł Kochański, Bruno Walter, Ansermet, Klemperer, Kraus, Georgescu—are the names which give an idea of the intensity of the sensations which I experienced. A particular kind of strong emotion was evoked by the premieres of works by Szymanowski, such as *Harnasie, Symphonie Concertante* with the composer as soloist, *Stabat Mater*, and the Violin Concerto no. 2, which were anticipated with great excitement. Contemporary music, in spite of the pioneering initiatives of Fitelberg,[2] was at that time a weak part of the Philharmonic programs. We would look in vain in them for such milestones as Stravinsky's *The Rite of Spring* or Bartók's *Music for Strings, Percussion, and Celesta*. The exceptional events in this regard were guest appearances by Hindemith as the performer of his Viola Concerto,[3] of Ravel conducting his Piano Concerto with Marguerite Long as soloist,[4] and, most of all, five appearances of Sergei Prokofiev as a performer in his four Piano Concertos.[5]

The obvious lacunae in the programs, the uneven quality of the musicians in the Philharmonic orchestra, the often careless preparation of the concerts, the appearances of third class artists—all of this was still unable to change my boundless attachment to the institution that introduced me, from my early childhood, into a mysterious sound-world full of unexpected charms; an institution that was for me at that time a symbol of music itself.

This institution ceased to exist in 1939. The burned-down walls of the building in Jasna Street confirmed in me a conviction that something very important in my life had ended once and for all. I still believed that a new Philharmonic would come into being in the future, but I was fully aware that for me it would be something totally different.

And this is in fact what happened, despite the fact that, thanks to the affection many musicians felt toward the old Philharmonic, its building was reconstructed in a form very close to the original. Today, after thirty years, it does not seem to me that this decision—a result of strong feelings rather than careful consideration—was the happiest one. The building outside and inside feels somewhat like an artistic forgery, for the acoustics of the hall are not determined only by its dimensions, even when most precisely reconstructed. As a result no sound is heard in the new Philharmonic Hall exactly as it was in the prewar hall, which itself was not free of some imperfections, but was, however, famous for "beautifying" the sound.

A certain disappointment caused by the reconstructed building itself, which was re-created with an enormous expenditure of work and generosity, was however amply compensated for by what subsequently started to happen inside the Hall. One of the dreams of the young musicians of my generation was fulfilled: there came into being in the Warsaw Philharmonic a world class symphony orchestra, which was undeniably the work of its conductor—Witold Rowicki.[6] In order to fulfill another dream it was necessary to wait a couple of years. I have in mind Warsaw Autumn, thanks to which twentieth-century music was heard from the Warsaw Philharmonic, playing at its best, and thus Warsaw became one of the more important centers of contemporary music in the world.

These memories have such a personal character that I can hardly finish them without expressing the gratitude I feel toward the Warsaw Philharmonic. I owe it a lot. To artists, musicians, and the members of the orchestra and of the choir, I owe beautiful performances of my works and also unforgettable moments spent during the rehearsals. I am particularly grateful to Witold Rowicki for the priceless favor he did me in a difficult and rather sorrowful phase of my life as a composer. For various reasons I lived then in a state of complete lack of interest in composing. At the same time, Rowicki was creating in Warsaw a new Philharmonic orchestra that later was to become the orchestra known as the National Philharmonic. It was he who, by encouraging me to write a new work for the new orchestra, ensured that I set about working at a task, the result of which was the Concerto for Orchestra, later dedicated to him.

After the jubilee year,[7] the National Philharmonic faces new tasks and endeavors in which it will be accompanied by the best support and wishes of all those in our country for whom music is an indispensable need in their spiritual life.

Source

Typescript in Polish. Copyright Witold Lutosławski Collection, Paul Sacher Foundation. All rights reserved. Printed by permission. This text, titled "Filharmonia mojej młodości" was first published in *75 lat Filharmonii w Warszawie. 1901–1976* (Seventy-five Years of the Philharmonic in Warsaw. 1901–1976), Warsaw (1976): 11–13, and in the English version in *Polska*, no. 11 (1978): 58–59.

Notes

1. See note 2 to the text "Life and Music."
2. See the text "On Grzegorz Fitelberg" in chapter 3.
3. Paul Hindemith appeared with the Warsaw Philharmonic on December 2, 1932, as a soloist in Vivaldi's Concerto for viola d'amore and in the viola part of his own *Konzertmusik* op. 48 (1930). At this concert Grzegorz Filtelberg conducted Hindemith's overture to *Neues vom Tage*.
4. Lutosławski refers to the concert that took place on March 11, 1932, a special artistic event during the Second International Chopin Piano Competition. In the second half of that concert Ravel conducted his choreographic poem *La Valse*.
5. It is possible that Lutosławski associated four of Prokofiev's appearances in Warsaw as a soloist in his Piano Concertos with the number he mentioned. As a matter of fact, Prokofiev performed his Piano Concerto no. 3 twice—on January 15, 1925, and on May 23, 1930 (each time with Fitelberg conducting), Piano Concerto no. 2 on November 21, 1930, and Piano Concerto no. 5 on November 18, 1932 (with Fitelberg conducting). One week after his first concert with the Warsaw Philharmonic, on January 20, 1925, Prokofiev also gave a piano recital that included only his own works.
6. Witold Rowicki (1914–1989), an outstanding Polish conductor active in Katowice and Warsaw, where he created the National Philharmonic Orchestra and was its artistic director from 1950 to 1955 and 1958 to 1977.
7. The year 1976.

SPEECH AT THE TWENTY-FIRST GENERAL ASSEMBLY OF POLISH COMPOSERS' UNION (1981)

I would like to apologize, because what I want to talk about is irrelevant to the reports we are to discuss, but it seems to me that more general things should also be considered at our assembly, particularly in connection with what we experience today. I remember that I had an occasion to make such a speech on more general themes immediately after the events of 1956,[1] also at one of our general assemblies. I think this is a similar moment, in which we cannot keep silent about general subjects and discuss only things occurring within the Union.

Thus I go back in my thoughts to the period that preceded the events of summer last year. This period, which lasted quite a long time, can be considered extremely depressing. A deep pessimism entered people's minds, particularly people of my generation, but also the younger ones. We all know—I am repeating here well-known facts, but they should be repeated—that the great strain the shipyard workers at the sea coast underwent starting in September[2] had first and foremost for us a moral meaning. Gloom and pessimism, which permeated our former feelings, were combined with a fear that our nation was on the downward path to a precipice from which it would be difficult to retreat. Yet the events I call to mind here suddenly gave an impulse of very strong optimism. It became evident to all of us—pessimists or skeptics—that there were enormous reserves within the Poles, which would be revealed when the younger generation matured enough to make decisions. I see the primary importance of this event in its moral aspect. What guided these initiatives was the primacy of spiritual values over materialistic and consumer ones. It created obligations on all who were not involved directly in this struggle and it also created obligations for us, the composers.

What do I have in mind? We all know that the notion of "professional ethics" exists for artists and, in our case, for composers. What does this consist of? One could quote many examples of an unethical attitude toward one's own profession, but all that could be said on this subject can be related to how a creative artist confronts his task. In other words—how he manages the talents he was endowed with by nature. I would undoubtedly call unethical, conduct in which the use of these talents serves to gain some personal advantage, such as—for instance—fame or money. On the other hand, by ethical conduct I mean the fullest and the most honest use of the talents we possess in order that they may serve others.

In our discussions we are very often one-sided, in spite of the diversity of the subjects. For we focus our attention on what we expect from the external world, on what we would like to obtain, what we would like to take. However, is it not the vocation of an artist to give rather than to take and so to create works that can be useful to others? At this point I would like to call your attention to a very important aspect of this whole issue, namely that we are all important, quite independent of the level of ability and creative energy fate has given us. We are all important. I would also like to venture a statement, and here I will go further than my colleague Perkowski,[3] and say that we are all *equally* important.

Why do I say so? Because irrespective of whether there is a great fire in us or there only smolders a very small spark, the duty of learning from what we have is one and the same for every one of us. In the end, each product of our ability and talent becomes a common good, a particle of our common accomplishment that is our national culture. And it should be said that this fact has a great importance for us at the present moment. It has often happened that at difficult moments of history only the national culture was the basis of national identity, national existence, and survival.

This is actually all I want to say. It would be sad for me if anybody thought that what I am saying is a sign of my willingness to moralize or to lecture anyone. I assure all of you this is not the case. In these difficult moments full of tension I want to share my thoughts warmly with all those to whom I feel bound by the same duties, with all the members of the Polish Composers' Union.

To those who perhaps have found my words unpalatable, I ask for forgiveness. And I thank you all for your attention.

Source

"Na walnym zjeździe" (At the General Assembly), typescript in Polish. Copyright Witold Lutosławski Collection, Paul Sacher Foundation. All rights reserved. Printed by permission.

Notes

1. See the first text in this chapter.
2. The year 1980.
3. Piotr Perkowski (1901–1990), Polish contemporary composer. After his studies with Szymanowski and Roussel (1926–1928) he founded the Society of Young Polish Musicians in Paris. During the war he was as a member of the Polish underground cultural movement in Warsaw, and took part in the Warsaw Uprising in 1944. Later he was active in various fields of Polish musical life, including the reconstruction of the Warsaw Philharmonic Hall.

ABOUT THE ISSUE OF TRUTH IN A WORK OF ART (1981)

I am deeply grateful to the organizers of the Congress of Culture for having invited me to deliver this lecture.[1] This invitation is for me a honorable privilege. I feel all the more embarrassed by the fact that the theme of my address will be a banal topic, probably well known to everybody gathered here. Yet if I, in spite of it, decide to talk about this subject, it is because in discoursing on art one often admits that many things are generally known, and yet they are simply overlooked. The result is that one forgets the most important things and, when they are sometimes remembered, they may have the weight of a real discovery. I do not expect such an appreciation of my address but nevertheless I hope that these reminders of mine will be profitable.

The Congress has been organized by people from the arts and sciences. I will then start with a simple statement, that the supreme aim of art is beauty, as the supreme goal of science is truth. However, as in mathematics, astronomy and certainly in many other sciences one can perceive a kind of beauty, equally in the art we inevitably face the issue of truth.

Truth in relation to art is an equivocal notion. Roman Ingarden, in his work *On Various Understandings of "Truthfulness" in a Work of Art*,[2] discusses over a dozen meanings of this word. At this moment I am interested in the definition that refers, according to Ingarden, to "truthfulness" interpreted as the faithfulness of the author expressing his own ideas in his work. I am very particular here about the ethical aspect of this issue; about, for instance, whether the author, while creating his work, was true to his artistic conscience, whether he was acting in accordance with the aesthetic he professed, whether he respected the canons of art in which he believed, in a word—whether he remained faithful to his internal truth.

As we know, this does not always happen and there are various reasons for it. I would divide them roughly into internal and external ones. Internal reasons are those that relate to the psyche of the creative artist. It may happen that he has a weak character, that he is eager for success, fame, or money, and with a view to attaining his ends he is ready to compromise with various kinds of audiences or sponsors and to give up expressing his internal truth in his art. Yet while doing this he may not even be aware that he offers his listeners a false philosophy. It is, however, a deeply immoral attitude. For talent is, to my mind, not the exclusive and private property of the person endowed with it. It is certainly a gift, a privilege, but this privilege comes with many responsibilities.

If the artist feels the bonds that unite him with his potential listeners he realizes that it is exactly his internal truth that his listeners have the right to expect from him. Yet if this talent—which should not be considered as the private property of an artist, but rather held in trust—is used for private goals, which are foreign to his art, then such behavior should also be recognized as a kind of breach of trust. Thus, as we see, in order to voice his internal truth in the work of art, the artist must possess correct moral attributes.

But the truth I mentioned can be jeopardized not only by the lack of such attributes but also by the external factors, such as the pressure other people and whole institutions may put on the artist. An instance of what I have in mind may be the fate of Polish art in the period directly before 1956. I will not deal here with the arts that, perhaps, suffered then most painfully, that is, literature, theatre, or film. The vicissitudes of these arts are widely known and still discussed now, at least in connection with the new law on censorship. They will certainly be the object of discussion later on in this Congress. Thus, if I limit myself at this moment to consideration of music, it is not only because this is my domain, but also because the fate of this art is probably less well known, and its dire moments and unquestionable losses are partially forgotten. This happened because the official critique in relation to music lost its edge rather a long time ago, and not only was overt pressure on composers abandoned, but also the once so irritating moralizing. I have to admit that since that time, that is, almost since 1956, music in our country found itself, in comparison with the other arts, in a privileged situation. What contributed to it to some extent, was the successes of Polish music in the wider world, which gave our country some original features in this field, in comparison with other countries of Eastern Europe. One has, of course, to rejoice at this, but it should not conceal the sad truth of the years that preceded the year 1956, mainly because the blows struck at that time at musical creativity and the subsequent losses can still be felt today.

I will remind you in a few words what the fight against the so-called formalism, as this action was officially called, consisted of. One assumed that the twentieth century was subservient to the degeneration of art as a product of bourgeois culture. Thus, the works of Stravinsky, Bartók, Schoenberg, and Prokofiev of the interwar period, and many others, would be considered formalist, and one had to break with everything those works involved, to cross them out and to forget them. A return to a simple, nineteenth-century language based on the tonal system was the only way to create that era's music, accessible to the masses and expressing our time realistically. Vocal music, based on well-chosen propagandist texts was to have priority over instrumental works, etc., in a similar spirit.

The mere intellectual coarseness of such reasoning is perhaps less dangerous than the fact that we had the previously described rules thrust in front of us on the occasion of every discussion, every official meeting, by every critic, for a good many years. This perfidious, although primitive operation, which was a specific form of attack upon the truthfulness of art, had lamentable results. The necessity of shelving the most important works, the exclusion of performances of the composers' output, the falseness of the general situation in a musical world, and the persecution on the part of the critic of the smallest signs of individuality or stylistic and technical research—all this was for many of us a reason for anxiety and depression. It was a far-flung process of the devastation of social wealth as seen in the psyche of many talented people.

It makes me speculate as to the goal of this so-called struggle with formalism. For the mere writing of works accessible to large audiences, provided that it is a source of authentic creative satisfaction, is in itself not at all wrong or annoying. Thus one suspects that the goal lay in a totally different area.

To gain full power over a group of composers is difficult when in this group are present outstanding individuals who differ from other people, thanks to their talents, who possess the strength to win, and to divert attention with their works from the rules officially propagated. The way to neutralize the possible impact of such individuals was the struggle against formalism, which consisted, among other things, of condemnation of all originality, of all innovation, and all deviation from the officially accepted banality. However, this is not what was most important in this struggle. Unfortunately, in the artistic environment, as everywhere, one can encounter people of ill-will and, at the same time, of little talent. These people were natural allies of those who inveighed against formalism. The doctrine of antiformalism was the weapon delivered to them, which helped them get rid of potential competitors and was their only chance to survive in public life. Such an antagonized artistic community, deprived of the impact of more distinguished individuals and, so to speak, leveled down, is much easier to control.

Perhaps such a situation occurred less harshly in Poland than in other countries. However, the harm it caused here is obvious. Moreover, depression, dejection, and hopelessness were accompanied by an awareness of being totally off cut from the rest of the world, in which such extremely important things for every creative artist were happening. The impossibility of participating in them and the complete ignorance of them became, especially among the younger generation, a source of problems. It came to light with particular sharpness at the moment of opening the gates toward the vast world of music in 1956. The sudden contact with the wealth and variety of this world was a real shock for every young composer, and they could not find their own place in that new reality. So, it took a long time before young Polish music could let the world know of its existence.

Today the position of the Polish music in the world seems to be established. It is perhaps due to the traits that distinguish it favorably against a background of the general situation of the music of young generations of composers in today's world. This situation, at least recently, can be described as a state of permanent revolution. It would perhaps be better to call it a parody of revolution, since what characterizes this phenomenon could be presented briefly in the following way: what was composed yesterday is bad; only this that is composed today can be good. Yet if tomorrow's work will be good, then today's good music will already be bad. This intentionally simplified image tells us about a particular nervousness that characterizes the trends and, in fact, the changes of fashion in the music of past decades. These changes are of interest to only a few people and they certainly should not be of interest to authentic composers who have something to say for themselves.

Therefore, speaking slightly paradoxically, what I would consider the most revolutionary step in a situation of permanent revolution would be just to ignore it, to withdraw oneself from a dialogue with the external world, particularly with the world of those critics and promoters of music and those concert- and festival-goers who are interested first and foremost in the constantly changing trends and fashions. Instead, I would direct my efforts toward creating works that would have a chance of longer existence and of functioning independently in a direct historical context.

Such an attitude is another form of striving after the truth in a work of art and of a struggle with the external obstacles that stand in the way of obtaining it. This time it is a struggle with the pressure of opinions of those circles that are not interested in the rise of lasting works of art, but rather in those curiosities that offer a permanent minirevolution. It seems that a number of Polish composers display a high degree of independence from this kind of pressure, and this is, among other things, the source of their force and the source of constant interest in their music in the world, although the time has gone when Polish music was—so to speak—in fashion.

One can only presume with some sorrow that what is sometimes said to be the blossoming of Polish music could have happened much earlier, if the gloomy operation called the struggle with formalism, which prevented the Polish artists' contact with the outside world, had not happened at all. Today, provided no unexpected obstacles appear, we can look forward confidently into the future of Polish art, hoping that the liberty of its access to society will encompass all its areas, and will not remain a privilege of only one of them—music. However, every one of us—creative artists—will be in a position to enjoy a moral right to this liberty only when we can constantly be the advocates of truth in the work of art.

Source

50 lat Związku Kompozytorów Polskich (Warsaw: Polish Composers' Union, 1995), 139–42. Copyright Marcin Bogusławski. All rights reserved. Printed by permission.

Notes

1. Lutosławski delivered his speech at the Congress of Culture in Warsaw on December 11, 1981, just two days before martial law was introduced in the whole country. See notes 12 and 13 to the text "Witold Lutosławski—Life and Music."

2. Roman Ingarden, "O różnych rozumieniach 'prawdziwości' w dziele sztuki" (On Various Understandings of "Truthfulness" in a Work of Art), in Roman Ingarden, *Studia z estetyki* (Studies from Aesthetics), vol. 1, Warsaw 1957.

ONE HUNDREDTH ANNIVERSARY OF *PARSIFAL* (1982)

I am a bad opera-goer. The combination of conventional theatrical realism with music, so that the actors sing instead of speaking, strikes me as shocking, or at best derisory. That's why certain masterpieces, such as *La Traviata* or *La Bohème*, are completely closed books to me. But that is not the case with

Richard Wagner, who never resorted to theatrical realism. His characters are almost symbolic, his subject matter—legends. And so it is in complete safety that I can surrender myself entirely and without reservation to all the beauties of Wagner's music and his music theatre, of which he was a master without equal in his time.

Parsifal is one of two works by Wagner (the other is *Tristan* of course!) that I love the most. There are certain pages in the great works of the past to which I always return with the same ardor. (A composer's life would be inconceivable without contact with the pinnacles of existing music!) These favorite pages include, among others, the Prelude of *Parsifal*, the Flower Maidens' scene, the Good Friday enchantment, and the four-note motif of the bells. Curiously, this last is also found in César Franck's *Prélude, Choral et Fugue*, Mahler's First Symphony, and—a little earlier—in the finale of Brahms's Second Symphony.

Parsifal is celebrating its hundredth anniversary. Only a hundred! One could easily believe that this music has always existed.

Source

AN ANSWER TO YOUNG COMPOSERS (1987)

Sometimes my young colleagues—composers who have just finished their studies or who are still students—visit me. They show me their scores and we listen together to the recordings of their works. While talking with them I feel sometimes that they need some advice, answers to questions which concern them. Usually, all this is summarized by one basic question, which is both naïve and moving: "How should I now be composing"? My answer is extremely simple and always the same: "Write what you yourself would like to listen to." This, however, requires some clarification.

The word *now*, which is used in the above question, brings to mind immediately the interest of the young composer in adapting himself to some prevalent trend, orientation, or just to a particular fashion. Such an attitude is in fact a false one. Firstly because, while adopting it, the artist condemns himself voluntarily to the role of a satellite, not even believing that he himself can perhaps have something to communicate to others. Yet this is the only reason that justifies artistic creativity, irrespective of whether one has a lot to say or only a little. The second error in this naïve question is that it suggests a wish to obtain something through one's own creativity, for instance a respect for one's composition on the part of other people, and that it might be accepted as one of the fashionable trends, etc. These are things that are unworthy of even the smallest effort. What is worse, they lead to the distortion of the "instrument" of a creative artist, and may even have some implications for his professional ethics.

The attitude of a creative artist should be an attitude of someone giving, not taking. The frequent desire to "exist" in a certain musical world unfortunately hides the true vocation from the sight of a young composer. While advocating here a rather ascetic attitude, I can add, just to give some consolation, that an ascetic attitude leads to an "existence" more surely than an interest in the prevailing trends or fashions and especially in their imitation.

And just one more thing in connection with this naïve question of "how to write": I sense in it an interest, first and foremost, in the fate of a musical work after its first performance. After one year, or two, a young composer will already treat this work as an "old" one; he will claim that "now" one writes in a totally different way, etc. Yet the most important thing is the fate of works of art independent of what kind of reaction they evoke immediately after their creation. The real judgment of an artist's work comes from thousands of people over decades, that is, what we symbolically label with a word *time*. Instead of a reaction to the first performance, we should be much more interested in how our works are growing old. Are they likely to have a further life and to function in the musical world or are they doomed to oblivion?

Source

MUSIC YESTERDAY, TODAY, AND TOMORROW (1993)

The title of my lecture requires explanation. The history of the past, present, and potential future cannot be precisely divided into these three stages. Music created "yesterday" invariably belongs to the current concert repertoire, so it is a part of "music today." In turn, a part of music being created at present, that is, "music today" will hopefully belong to future concert programs, that is, to "music tomorrow."

Hence, when applying each of the three terms mentioned in the title, it will be necessary to realize each time how we understand the words "yesterday," "today," and "tomorrow": whether they defined music created or performed at one of these stages.

The music of "yesterday." Certainly, I will not attempt here to outline the history of music from its origins. We do not even know when and from what music sprang up. Speaking about "music of yesterday," I am in the first place interested in what has penetrated into today's concert programs and in a range of problems related to this phenomenon.

It is necessary to state that at so-called subscription concerts or at others that could be referred to as "regular," what is usually performed is the music of a relatively short period: more or less from Vivaldi to Ravel. It is a little more than two hundred years. The music of the previous five hundred years, starting with Perotinus, can be heard only at special concerts, which are of interest to a specific and not very large audience. It is difficult to say why this happens. However, what seems remarkable is an arrangement of the periods when particular composers worked and it is also important to realize that, for instance, between 1830 and 1847 lived and worked Mendelssohn, Schumann, Chopin, Liszt, Berlioz, Wagner, Verdi, and Rossini. Such a number of geniuses at one historical moment proves that the nineteenth century was characterized by a powerful accumulation of creative forces.

So, it is no wonder that the products of those forces have not been consumed yet and that they constantly find hundreds of thousands of recipients who prefer to commune with past art rather than art being created today. But the above remark does not give a convincing answer why it is so. After all, this situation does not correspond to any pattern handed over to us from the past. In the time of Bach, for example, only contemporary music was performed. As choirmaster of St. Thomas Church in Leipzig, Bach had to write new cantatas all the time. It would not have occurred to anyone to perform some of Palestrina's or Orlando di Lasso's works instead of those cantatas. Even the greatest masterpieces of the past were quickly forgotten and there was a constant need for new music, never heard before in churches and at court. Such a state of affairs survived till the beginning of the nineteenth century. It suffices to mention that it was only Mendelssohn who performed the long-forgotten *St. Matthew Passion* by Bach in Leipzig.

So, if the music of the two hundred years mentioned here occupies a leading place in concert programs, it may be worthwhile to consider which of its features have contributed to such a unique situation and its longevity.

As the first of these features, I mention tonality (understood as the tonal system), which is a basis for the organization of sound in all pieces of those times. It is a superb phenomenal construction with no parallel either before or after. It is a work of inspiration for numerous generations of creators and many of us realize that it cannot soon be replaced with anything else of a similar value.

The tonal system is distinguished by many advantages, a few of which are easily perceptible to everybody who loves listening to music, not necessarily only professionals. I will mention one of them: the system's universality.

The tonal system can be compared to a common language, understandable by millions of people. The fact that it is assimilated by a great number of listeners makes this system natural to those people, logical and impossible to be overthrown. Further history of music negates this, but I will talk about that later on.

Another trait of music, as we define it, from Vivaldi to Ravel, is its inventive and usually developed melodies. It is a powerful medium for influencing the listener's sensitivity and in the past it was probably the most important element of a musical piece. In particular, it refers to the period starting with Mozart's work. The melodic invention of composers of the time is a unique phenomenon that is entirely original in the whole history of music. It is enough to compare medieval music, Renaissance polyphony, or the music of the second half of the twentieth century, with what was characteristic of the period, of great melodies, as it could be called.

The development of sonata form at the beginning of the Classical period also favored the music of these two hundred years as a dominant part of the concert programs, which are still hard to imagine without the symphonies of Haydn, Mozart, Beethoven, Schubert, Schumann, Mendelssohn, Brahms, Bruckner, and Mahler, as well as Dvořák and Sibelius, even if we only confine ourselves to symphonic music.

The love for merely enumerated qualities of music of the period under discussion, and an almost slavish attachment to these qualities, is characteristic of the part of an audience who most willingly keep listening to the same works, revealing no interest in what can still happen within the realm of music, what is offered by new composers, and what can open a way to new, unknown worlds.

This peculiar inertia, even a lack of curiosity itself, brings to one's mind the personality of a child who wants to be told the same fairy tale all over again. This inertia, this lack of a need for any change was not shown by creators themselves. To illustrate this observation, let us stop at the issue of tonal system for a while. In the period of its primacy, that is, in the nineteenth century, certain signs expressing an urge to go beyond the limits of the tonal system were already distinctly visible.

The first blows at this edifice—seemingly indestructible—were inflicted by Chopin, Wagner, and Liszt. Basically all three of them worked within the tonal system, yet in their music we can find moments during which we suddenly detect a vision of the future development of the sound-system. Such a prophetic moment is, as all of us remember, demonstrated by the first measures of *Tristan and Isolde.* The less spectacular, although perhaps more unexpected moment is a modulation in the last Mazurka F minor op. 68 of Chopin, in which we find an identical harmonic progression as in the initial bars of *Tristan.* Unfortunately, it is known only from the handwritten copies of the piece, because a fragment of Chopin's manuscript, difficult to decipher, was never printed.[1] Equally surprising moments can be found in the last compositions of Liszt, which clearly presage Debussy and late Skryabin.

These examples are a result of a peculiar disquiet characteristic of European composers. A need for change, development, and the discovery of new possibilities stand in contrast to the art of the Far East, where the same patterns, styles, and aesthetics can last unchanged throughout the centuries.

Unfortunately, so far this creative disquiet has not led to the creation of a new system of sound arrangement, the system that could replace the declining tonality. The history of this decline and an attempt to find a way out of the resulting situation and also other accompanying phenomena form a very complex picture whose characteristics are worthy of attention. One of them could be described as "a joy of destruction."

This phenomenon lies in reacting against existing principles, as if only to violate them and offer nothing positive. That brings forth pieces that could be called in a simple way "tonal music with false notes." This mannerism was practiced for quite a long time and can still be traced in the late predodecaphonic pieces of Stravinsky (e.g., in *Orpheus*). It seems completely clear that no coherent, long-lasting system can come into being in this way. I want to stress that what I have in mind is only the very way of arranging sounds, which can have little or nothing in common with the value of particular pieces; its significant example is Stravinsky's *Orpheus* quoted above.

One of the traits of this trend is a specific lack of the composer's sensitivity toward vertical aggregations. They do not form a hierarchy in this music. The chords that contain a range of minor seconds or minor ninths are employed in common with triads without any differentiation of their impact on the listener's sensitivity.

In that, one can see the pursuit of equalizing all vertical aggregations, eliminating differences among them, including every possible chord in a language, so to say, "current." It is hard to resist an impression that it is a pauperization of the means of expression and also an action for the benefit of blunting the ear's sensitivity to harmony and, in this way, a destructive action.

The first decades of our century, however, are not only the period of "tonality with false notes." A need to replace the declining tonal system with something new was an obvious motive for the actions of those composers who bore in mind the future of music and the possibility of its development. The intuitive, so to speak, improvised atonality of the young Schoenberg did not satisfy its creator as he undertook a completely new way of arranging sound pitches. Apparently, he meant to create something that would replace the tonal system, which was seen as no longer useful for composers at that time. In such a way the twelve-tone technique was created, also defined as dodecaphony, which, according to its author, was to determine German music (that was exactly how he expressed it himself) "for the following one hundred years."

It is difficult to be surprised at Schoenberg's euphoric fascination with his discovery. Simultaneously, however, one cannot resist a reflection that it is evidence of a considerable naïveté to believe in the possibility of replacing the result of experiences and inspirations of generations of a few geniuses with the work of one composer. The history of dodecaphony confirms that this reflection is correct. This system has not survived the projected one hundred years as a composer's tool.

In my opinion, the more stable source of tradition in the music of the twentieth century is the work of Debussy. It is a view that certainly is not shared by many contemporary composers. I believe, however, that Debussy did much more for the future of music than Schoenberg and his dodecaphony. It seems that one of the aims to be fulfilled by Schoenberg's system was a protection against any, even the slightest, allusion to the tonal system. It was to be a radical change, a real revolution.

Debussy acted in an evolutionary way. He did not attempt to create any new, complete system. Nontonal fragments of his pieces had to come into being in an empirical way, in a permanent relation to experience, which probably came from an exploration of his own reaction to sound phenomena provided by his creative imagination.

Debussy's successors discovered more and more new possibilities in the realm of arranging sound pitches and, first of all, in harmony. It seems that it must have been created, as in the case of Debussy, in an empirical way. In Scriabin's work, early Stravinsky, Bartók, or Varèse there are no traces of any system that would take precedence over the experience of an earlier theoretical assumption.

Schoenberg's successors acted differently. For them, initial dodecaphony in the form presented by Schoenberg is an analogical tool, comparable with the tonal system, establishing a range of detailed obligatory rules. At a certain time it was a useful tool for those who approved of it, especially when taking into consideration the chaos and confusion in music. On the basis of dodecaphony, a number of outstanding pieces were composed. Beside Schoenberg's work, I, first of all, have in mind the pieces of Berg and Webern and also of other composers like Dallapiccola, Křenek, Apostel, Fortner, and Babbitt.

Unfortunately, Schoenberg's doctrine also brought about some negative phenomena. One of them is a great number of pieces without any particular value. It was enough to stick to detailed rules in order to produce a score that at first glance looked like a valuable musical piece, at least in professional terms.

The second, much more important negative phenomenon was a reduction of the role of harmony to a secondary element in a musical piece. As a result, with the twelve-tone technique there is not only a lack of any progress in this field but also worse: this leads on to blunting the listener's—and the composer's—sensitivity to vertical aggregations. What happens is a kind of equalization of all these aggregations and making them subject to some superior principle.

Another phase of dodecaphonic technique development is total serialism. Not only is sound pitch subject to the twelve-element series here, but also other elements like rhythmic values or dynamics. Even more than in the original dodecaphonic technique, serialism reduces the role of intuition, invention, and inspiration. Creation boils down almost to composing a series and realizing all resultant consequences, sometimes in a mechanical way.

The enthusiastic interest of the generations of young composers in a serial technique in the early postwar years can be explained in a different way. One of the reasons is that at the moment of the tonal system's decline, young composers must have felt helpless, having at their disposal no principle of arranging sounds that they could lean on. Serialism offered such a principle, hence its popularity. But this was not the only reason. Until the 1940s, Schoenberg and his successors were completely unknown in France. It was René Leibowitz who gathered a group of young people around him to acquaint them with the music of Schoenberg, Berg, and Webern, thus inspiring the creation of French serialism.

To a young generation of German and Austrian composers, the music of Schoenberg and his school, even though it was created in their native country, was also nearly unknown. It resulted from the cultural policy of Hitler's regime, which—among others—aimed at excluding from circulation everything that was officially regarded as "degenerate art" (*entartete Kunst*).

No wonder that for the young generation it was a real revelation to discover great German serialists. Yet this fascination with serialism did not last long. Today serialism already belongs to the past.

Today—what does music created today look like? One can notice a multitude of phenomena that do not represent a coherent wholeness. In the pieces of young composers there is a certain resentment toward too high a degree of complexity or complication of texture, which were characteristic of the previous period. Simplification proceeds here in a different way. Generally known American terms of *new simplicity* or *new romanticism* are typical of these tendencies. When communing with music of this kind, bad reflections come to one's mind. In the process of simplifying music, what can be seen is the composer's helplessness in the realm of harmony. This is a long-neglected realm that, as a result of its being simplified, is reduced to primitive loans from tonal music.

In pieces that belong to the aforementioned trends there is nothing that could be regarded as work done on new harmony, and even a need for such work.

Luckily, music created today is not restricted to the phenomena described above. Here and there one can see attempts to satisfy an increasing need for music whose purpose is not only a demonstration of new means of expression, more and more novel tricks, but something much more important; something that new means of expression would serve.

What is this "something"? One cannot answer this question precisely. Such words as *contents*, *message*, and *substance* do not say much about what music really is. And this is surely better. If the essence of music could be conveyed by words, music itself would lose its mystery, its "magic suggestiveness" according to Conrad,[2] and would become unnecessary. A decisive anticipation, a need for such music, is an optimistic forecast for the future of music, for "tomorrow's music."

I will not play at prophecies. "Tomorrow's music" is music of our dreams, our desires, our ideas about what music should eventually become. Its "message" ought to become strong enough, new and original enough, and perhaps primarily human, to be eventually an equal partner for the pieces of the previous two hundred years in concert programs.

New classicism, which many of us would like to live to see, will not become real until a coherent, sensible convention of arranging sounds is created, common to the largest range of listeners. At present it is not clear what this new convention would look like. It exists only in our desires and the pursuits of some of us, but not yet in reality.

I have been invited to give this lecture as a composer. I am neither a historian nor a musicologist. Therefore my considerations are probably of no objective value if they were to be understood as a description of real facts. They are rather a description of subjective reactions of one composer toward the facts that belong to the past and present and also a brief description of an even more subjective look at the future of music.

Source

Typescript in English. Copyright Witold Lutosławski Collection, Paul Sacher Foundation. All rights reserved. Printed by permission. Lutosławski presented this text as a lecture during the ceremony of receiving the Kyoto Prize in October 1993. The Polish version of this text was published in *Ruch Muzyczny*, no. 19 (1994): 1 and 4.

Notes

1. See: Hanna Wróblewska-Straus, ed., *F. Chopin, Mazurka in F minor [Op. 68 No. 4]*, facsimile edition from the collection of Chopin Museum in Warsaw with a critical commentary (Gdańsk-Warsaw: Romega, 2000).

2. Joseph Conrad, *Typhoon, The Nigger of the "Narcissus," and Other Stories* (London: The Folio Society, 2000), 230.

AN ATTITUDE TOWARD FRENCH CULTURE

When I am to answer a question about my attitude toward French culture, I am sorry that I am a composer and not a poet. For this question concerns in my case such warm and vivid feelings that, in order to express them, I would like to recall all the most beautiful words that exist. Unfortunately, I must content myself with a simple, unsophisticated speech of a man who, by virtue of his profession, is accustomed more to silence. In my justification I should note that my relations with French culture in its various aspects are not at all something extraordinary for me. On the contrary, these are everyday matters, deeply rooted customs, without which life would be difficult to imagine. I have in mind, first and foremost, reading and frequently returning to Montaigne, Flaubert, Proust, or Camus. But in this talk I must first speak of music. My first encounters with the music of Debussy and Ravel in early childhood were like opening a door on new worlds, never even sensed before. The shock to my imagination was probably very strong, since the recollection of it lives in my memory up to this day. Later on, during my piano studies, I was busy for hours on end studying the piano music of these two masters and the scores of their orchestral works that I heard at the Warsaw Philharmonic. This was itself an important lesson, one that will perhaps be useful for me to the end of my life. The following years allowed me to discover Albert Roussel for myself. Here I must acknowledge the direct influence of his music on my own creativity over several years. I have in mind particularly the symphony I wrote in the 1940s.[1] Among the decisive moments in my life I also include my first trip to France in 1946. This was like becoming closely acquainted with someone whom I had known previously only through correspondence. The fact remains that *Pelléas* does not sound as good anywhere else as it does at the Opéra Comique, notwithstanding the venues of the Louvre or the Jeu de Paume museum or even from the most beautifully recorded albums. Further visits to France followed and, along with them, came my much more extensive knowledge of French music, as well as a series of personal contacts with the French musical world.

Today I am in a phase of my life in which a tendency toward creation and recapitulation often predominates over the desire for absorbing new things. I am aware that of the two traditions that initiated twentieth-century music, that is, Schoenberg and Debussy, it is the latter that I feel prevails in my own compositional work.

Source

"Stosunek do kultury francuskiej," typescript in Polish. Copyright Witold Lutosławski Collection, Paul Sacher Foundation. All rights reserved. Printed by permission.

Note

1. Lutosławski was writing his Symphony no. 1 in 1941–1947. Its first performance took place in Katowice, on April 6, 1948 with Polish Radio Symphony Orchestra conducted by Grzegorz Fitelberg.

ON SILENCE

The human sense of hearing is a handicapped sense, since it is totally defenseless. We can close our eyes when we don't want to see, we can decide not to eat when something doesn't taste nice, we can decide not to touch when something scalds. However, it's no use stopping one's ears, and even sealing them up with wax, if we don't want to hear. The sound still reaches our ears through the skull. Our sense of hearing is vulnerable and, in that sense, we are the slaves of the world that surrounds us. It may seem odd that I repeat things that everybody knows. Yet the majority of people today act as though these quite obvious facts have not entered their consciousness. A motorcyclist does not care at all that, while driving through the empty streets at 3 a.m., he wakes up hundreds of people. The owner of a radio set, when he forces all his neighbors to listen to a radio program, sometimes for hours on end, cares even less about other people. I could give endless examples of our contemporary world which compel us to accept the sad fact that people are being deprived of one of their elementary rights—the right to have silence. This right is not protected by the law; it is not even respected by people in their everyday behavior.

Sometimes I dream of living in an era in which there will not be any noisy engines, but where inventions will exist to allow a person to create around him—whenever he or she may desire—a vacuum barrier through which no sound could force its way. I try, however, to avoid such dreams, since the return to reality is too painful.

An example of this is how, in summer, I must choke with heat and lack of air in my small study. This is because several hundred meters from me there is a man who is accustomed to turning on the radio with his window open. So if I open my window, my room is suddenly full of streams of so-called little music, and it immediately becomes not only impossible to work or to rest, but also to think, and in the end, any inclination to do anything disappears. What remains is only the irritation and sadness of a man whose privacy has been invaded. Some people may say that I am particularly sensitive. Certainly, for if I were not sensitive to sound, I could not be a composer. It is, however, an illusion that only musicians and composers are gifted with such sensitivity. It is much more common than it actually seems. Yet one's sensitivity grows blunt year by year as a result of the violation it suffers everyday from parts of contemporary life.

One of the forms of this violation is the constraint of being forced to listen to music. This constraint is nowadays present virtually everywhere. There is no way of liberating oneself from the radio playing through the wall of a neighboring flat, from a loud radio brought by an inconsiderate fan to the beach or on board a ship or in a restaurant. Even on the surface of a lake we cannot listen intently to the sounds of birds, because from the canoe being paddled nearby, a silly melody (of a hit) from a transistor radio is being pumped into our ears.

I am not at all an enemy of a popular music. Let it serve all those who find pleasure and relaxation in it. However, the habit of listening to it for hours and, most of all, of forcing a great number of people to listen to it, whether they like it or not, needs deeper examination. Scientific research should be undertaken in order to discover the impact of this phenomenon on the human psyche. It is easy to foresee that such an impact can hardly be positive.

I can already talk most certainly about one side of this issue. By this I mean the atrophy of musical sensitivity among people who have the habit of listening to so-called light music on every possible occasion, including the time devoted to intellectual work.

I would bet, ten to one, that a man listening several hours a day to so-called background music on the radio is, in the course of several years, sufficiently brainwashed into never experiencing the slightest emotion while listening to a Beethoven quartet or Debussy's prelude.

Source

"O ciszy," typescript in Polish. Copyright Witold Lutosławski Collection, Paul Sacher Foundation. All rights reserved. Printed by permission.

• 5 •

Occasional Speeches

❦

ON THE HUNDREDTH ANNIVERSARY OF THE GESELLSCHAFT
DER MUSIKFREUNDE IN VIENNA

In 1963 I had the honor to be distinguished with a prize at the competition organized by the Gesellschaft der Musikfreunde[1] and UNESCO. This event was in fact a competition in composition, although the works were sent in not by the composers, but by orchestras who had contemporary symphonic works in their repertoire. I owe my gratitude for this honorable distinction first of all to the Symphony Orchestra of the Danish Radio, which sent a recording of my Concerto for Orchestra to this Viennese competition. Nevertheless, this special and very pleasant event is associated in my memory with the institution that is just celebrating its jubilee, that is, the Gesellschaft der Musikfreunde in Vienna. For here the award was handed over, and also here the works that won prizes were brilliantly performed in a special concert by the Wiener Sinfoniker under the direction of Hans Schmidt-Isserstedt.

I am happy that the event I describe here links me somehow with the Gesellschaft der Musikfreunde and I feel therefore entitled to address these few words to this Society on the day of its jubilee.

A hundred years is a long time, long enough to change some aspects of the goals and work of any society. I imagine that a hundred years ago, the founders of the Gesellschaft der Musikfreunde must have been guided by just one principle: to make music and to disseminate a love for it. People then were either friends of music or they were indifferent to it. The friends organized concerts and frequented them or made music at home; the indifferent simply

273

had no interest in music. And thus many years passed, up to the moment when we all began to realize that as well as these two categories of people—the friends of music and the indifferent ones—there was in addition a third one: the enemies of music. These are, fortunately, in most cases the unconscious enemies, those people causing harm unintentionally, often even—as it would seem—quite good-naturedly. Nevertheless, their number and strength still increases, so that the real friends of music can't regard their activities indifferently. Whom do I mean when talking of the enemies of music? It is not difficult to answer this question, because there are a lot of them around. I count among them, for instance, a young man walking through a garden with a noisy rambunctious transistor radio in his hand; a taxi driver who "treats" his passenger—whether he wants it or not—to pop music transmitted through the radio; a director of a long-distance airline who does not allow his passengers to have a meal without idiotic pseudomusic being poured into their heads from loudspeakers; a hotel owner who does the same, adding music also in the lifts or elevators, on the terrace, in the bar, and in the swimming pool; directors of the majority of airlines who excel in the art of irritating their passengers by means of the loudspeakers placed right above their heads and active from the moment of taking one's seat in the airplane. Among the enemies of music I must also count, unfortunately, many simple inhabitants of cities and villages, who, by turning on the radio, CD player, gramophone, or tape recorder torture their neighbors by pressuring them to listen to music when they do not want it at all. With this last sentence I will stop enumerating the types of enemies of music, although this list has only just begun. I stop in order to call attention to one crucial word used in that sentence, that is, "pressure." Because what it is involved here is the fact—completely unknown not long ago, and even difficult to imagine—that the art of music, the origins and goals of which are always connected in our consciousness with what is most noble, can now be used to force people to hear it, which must be repugnant to everybody. The pressure to listen to music is a new phenomenon for all of us, and for genuine friends of music it is something very alarming. There are many questions related to it, for instance, will all those for whom real music matters a lot in their life always be condemned to have this pseudomusic, or sound-pap, poured into their ears in places and at times impossible to foresee? Is the only remedy to learn how to not listen to it (almost impossible!), and thus to agree voluntarily to dull one's own sensibility and, in consequence, to kill in oneself the ability to react to real music? And what will happen to the generation of people who grow up already accustomed to the omnipresence of pseudomusic? Will there be among them individuals able to concentrate on and to experience one of Beethoven's symphonies? The answer to these questions (and to many others), which occur today to real friends of music, is not the subject of this present speech. My goal was only to draw attention to a problem that, after one hundred years of existence of the Gesellschaft der Musikfreunde, caused a major change to the situation in which this society has to work and to develop. I am sure that in this society there are people present who are deeply convinced of the weight of the problem that I have touched upon, and that they will struggle with conviction and energy to deal with a matter common to all of us, that is the future fate of genuine, great music in the contemporary world.

May I be permitted on the verge of the second century of existence of the Gesellschaft der Musikfreunde to wish it many successes in achieving all its noble goals, including those I have already mentioned.

Source

Typescript in Polish. Copyright Witold Lutosławski Collection, Paul Sacher Foundation.

Note

1. The Gesellschaft der Musikfreunde in Vienna, the oldest musical society in the Austrian capital, was inaugurated in 1812 in order to revitalize Vienna's musical life after the Napoleonic War. The anniversary meant here refers to the year 1870, when the Musikverein built by T. Hansen was opened ceremonially in Karlsplatz. See: Franz Grasberger and Lothar Knessl, *Hundert Jahre Goldener Saal. Das Haus der Gesellschaft der Musikfreunde am Karlsplatz. Geschichte, Würdigung, Rückblicke* (Vienna: Gesellschaft der Musikfreunde, 1970).

TO THE FORTY-SIXTH GRADUATING CLASS OF THE CLEVELAND INSTITUTE OF MUSIC ON RECEIVING AN HONORARY DEGREE, JUNE 2, 1971

The Role of Today's Graduates in the Musical Arena for the Years Ahead

To receive the Honorary Doctor of Music Degree from the Cleveland Institute of Music is a very great honor. It is a distinction conferred by a conservatory that counts among its faculty many brilliant and world-famous musicians. That such an eminent body expresses appreciation of my work makes me proud and happy. I would like, first, to address those responsible for this decision and to ask them to accept my deepest gratitude.

The bonds that tie me to the Cleveland Institute of Music are no longer merely formal but from now on will acquire an emotional dimension. I shall always look with sincere interest upon what happens here and will be concerned with the fate of those young musicians who graduate and leave these friendly walls. It is to them that I offer the remarks that follow.

What kind of world will today's young musician enter to begin his independent exploration and to find a place for himself? The state of music and musicians today is complex, totally unlike that of the aspiring musicians of the Renaissance and of the Baroque. In those days, the young musician, finishing his apprenticeship, practiced his craft, fulfilling clearly defined duties in the church or at the court of a king or nobleman. There he played, sang, and composed music that had a defined role and a defined listener, producing music that conformed to defined aesthetic norms. To borrow from the language of economics, the balance between production and consumption was completely maintained: what was composed and performed satisfied concrete needs; no interest was wasted on works of the past, which were quickly forgotten after a few performances and were not accorded any status of permanence. The concept of contemporary music did not exist. Music that was not contemporary, had little, if any, relevance in practical life. I do not question whether this was good or bad. I want only to make the point that this picture (however superficial) of the past, differs fundamentally from the present. Today's musical life is characterized by a complete lack of balance between production and consumption. This is a phenomenon that merits close examination.

If we exclude the rather special case of popular music, we can say, generally, that the vast majority of today's music listeners derive their musical nourishment from compositions produced in the last two hundred years, roughly speaking, from Vivaldi to Ravel. However strange this state of affairs may seem, a look at concert and radio programs and a study of catalogs of recorded music corroborate this statement. A satisfactory explanation of this indisputable fact totally escapes me. On the other hand, it appears that the two centuries following the five hundred years of work by musical geniuses that began with Perotinus Magnus represent a peak in mankind's musical achievement: works created before Vivaldi and after Ravel simply do not seem to attain the standards of that exceptional period. On the other hand, I wonder if the quality of the music is the essential problem. Rather, what makes it impossible for today's subscription-concert audiences to appreciate the masterpieces of Guillaume de Machaut, Ockeghem, or Palestrina, is an unfamiliarity with the musical language of the pre-Baroque. Perhaps it is for a parallel reason that today's average concertgoer does not enjoy the most successful works of Stockhausen, Carter, or Ligeti (composers whose musical language constitutes an insurmountable barrier for people brought up on Mozart, Schubert, or Tchaikovsky). I am sometimes inclined to see the cause of this in the very essence of the conventions evolved through centuries, in the laws governing musical material that became stabilized in the Baroque and that lasted until the first years of our century. In accord with this view, works based upon such conventions and laws, in apparent harmony with man's congenital organic and psychic makeup, are ensured a lasting permanence.

There is some truth in all these explanations. None, however, is fully satisfactory. Without elaborating further, I will cite only the universally acknowledged fact that the music of 1700–1900 forms an integral part of the contemporary musical life, that it continues to exert an enormous influence, and that it clearly dominates concert and radio programs, as well as catalogs of recorded music. Even more important, perhaps, is the fact that young students in almost all the conservatories of the world are brought up on this music, a factor that seems to guarantee that the present musical climate will continue to be perpetuated for several decades to come.

The picture of the contemporary world of music or, more precisely, some of the aspects presented here, has serious, indeed far-reaching implications for the young performer today. For example, a young pianist will be well received by the world, provided he shows talent for and plays Beethoven's sonatas, Tchaikovsky's and Rachmaninoff's concerti, or solo works by Chopin and Liszt. No less sympathetic a reception awaits a talented opera singer enamored of Verdi and Puccini, or a violinist who is at his best in Tartini's *Trille du Diable*, Paganini's capriccios, or Ravel's *Tzigane*, as well as all those talented soloists and virtuosi whose dream it is to play the so-called grand repertoire with or within large symphony orchestras.

Greater difficulties await the smaller group of young musicians whose interests lie beyond the frontiers of the two magic centuries I have mentioned. I have in mind, for example, a singer who would like to give a recital of songs by Charles Ives, a vocal ensemble that specializes in Gesualdo's madrigals, or a pianist who plays from memory three sonatas by Boulez and eleven Stockhausen *Klavierstücke*. They will have to reconcile themselves to the fact that they will have a small audience. Since the interested listeners are scattered throughout the country, there is the geographic difficulty of getting them all into one concert hall on the same evening. A possible alternative is, of course, provided by radio programs devoted to this special kind of serious music.

Even allowing for these difficulties, which confront the contemporary performer striking out on his own, one may roughly assume that he can reasonably hope to attain, at some point in his life, a comfortable feeling of being the right man in the right place.

Unfortunately, the same cannot be said of the young contemporary composer. He will realize his predicament not without some chagrin. True, he cannot always justifiably complain that his works are not being performed. There are, after all, special concert series, even entire festivals, devoted to contemporary music. Radio networks are huge monsters devouring everything, including the most "contemporary" music. Even recording companies have started to produce albums of avant-garde music in order to "improve" their public image. Thus, admittedly, the situation is much better than it was, say, forty years ago. Yet, for all that, one must reach the inescapable conclusion that the contemporary composer is today relegated to a secondary, if not a marginal role. The giants of the past two hundred years still reign supreme and there are no convincing signs that they are likely to lose their dominant position in the near future. Nor is there a lack of people who openly declare themselves enemies of the contemporary composer, who say that contemporary music is deservedly rejected and that it has embarked upon a road from which it should turn before it is too late. Luckily the contemporary composer does not take these demagogic attacks too much to heart. He knows that what is new does not necessarily receive early recognition; that the advice to turn back from a so-called wrong road is a piece of naïveté characteristic of confirmed reactionaries incapable of understanding the laws governing the history of culture, laws that do not permit a regression into the past and a return to outworn, outlived artistic conventions.

Besides, the young contemporary composer has other concerns that propel his creative capacities and make everything pertaining to the fate of his completed works seem of secondary importance. His overriding preoccupation is with the act of composition itself, rather than with the immediate future of his works. For him, to compose, to learn, and to perfect his art is a different process from what it was in the times of Bach and Mozart. Then, it was sufficient for a composer to learn the laws and limitations of the language of music and, on that foundation, to go on developing his skills for the rest of his life, enriching it with new elements and thereby contributing to a great common cause—the period's artistic convention. For today's composer it is not so clear-cut, for he finds no single set of laws and limitations governing the organization of sound matter; no single convention that is shared by a majority of composers and which could be learned and developed. The young, mid-twentieth-century composer faces so many avenues of choice that he is compelled to cast frantically about in search of some restrictive criteria to reduce the practically infinite number of available possibilities, and help him to emerge from a darkness where "everything is possible." The search for these criteria is nothing but an attempt to erect the foundations of a new convention. Elaboration of such a convention is a gigantic task to be accomplished by the combined exertions and inspirations of several generations of creative artists. The thought that we are starting this process, assuming that it has begun at all, makes the head of the young contemporary composer swim. Impelled by a healthy reaction, he must rely on intuition and on the voice of his inspiration, at the same time trying to avoid involvement in an examination of this unprofitable subject, especially since this is not the main difficulty he encounters.

A much bigger problem today is presented by the instruments at his disposal. These instruments, inherited from past centuries, have little in common with our times and we acutely feel their limitations. Suffice it to recall that our best string instruments are two hundred or even three hundred years old; that the construction of wind instruments today is closely related to the harmonic scale; that the keyboards of piano, organ, and harpsichord, as well as the construction and tuning of the harp, are all directly derived from diatonic scales. It would be hard to maintain that these instruments are adequate for realization of the products of an imagination that regards the twelve-tone technique as a closed chapter of an historic era. To this we must add the problem of our generally accepted musical notation, which, from the point of view of present-day composition techniques, is nothing but absurd: for twelve different sounds it offers but seven places on the staff!

If, in these few remarks, I have drawn your attention to problems that exist in the musical life of today, it was not my intention to frighten or to disillusion you as to the rewards of the career you have chosen, the career that is—allow me to use this expression—your calling. I think it is always better to be aware of the difficulties and obstacles that await you. Naturally, the road you have chosen is not all difficulties and obstacles. You may look forward to experiences that will make all other satisfactions pale. Having tasted them, you will never want to turn from your chosen course. These experiences will be accessible not only to he who will perform Beethoven's Fifth Piano Concerto on a Steinway piano in Severance Hall with one of the best orchestras in the world, but also to he who, in the seclusion of his room, will be suddenly gripped by the mysterious beauty of a Bach solo Violin Sonata that takes weeks of arduous labor to learn; and also to he who, in the seventh chair of the second violin section of a large symphony orchestra, will, in a moment of truth, be struck by the greatness of the Passacaglia in Brahms's Symphony no. 4. Other, no less magnificent experiences, await those of you who, firmly believing in a colleague's talent, will, for the first time, perform his work in public—in front of a few dozen enthusiasts plus a couple of hundred more or less bewildered and invariably embarrassed regular concertgoers, and a few sardonically smiling critics.

And now, what about you, young contemporary composers? You are sure to begin by writing for months, or years, consciously or unconsciously, music "à la manière de —." This is quite natural and it is nothing to be ashamed of. But some day, if you have enough perseverance and talent, you will be visited, through means that defeat logical explanation, by a combination of a few imagined sounds which will be something of a wonder to you. For in this combination, you will discover vast possibilities for its application. And, what is more, this combination will in no way resemble anything that you had known before. It will be a significant moment—the birth of a composer, the emergence of a creative personality. It will also mark the beginning of a long process, sometimes lasting a lifetime, the discovery and development of your own personal technique. For technique of composition, in the sense of skill that can be learned, does not really exist. A technique of composition worthy of its name is born entirely of inspiration, while individual ideas that go into making it differ from other products of inspiration in that each single idea can be employed several times. Many such moments await the young contemporary composer, provided that he has talent and fulfills a number of conditions. Here are some of them: He must express truth, that is, his music must reflect what he himself believes in, since art is absolutely intolerant of sham; he must not use his music to win favors or to attain such goals as popular acclaim or wealth—goals incompatible with his true purpose—no matter how little they reflect on the purity of his artistic design; he must work hard and he must be ready at all times to hear the voice of inspiration that, to quote Tchaikovsky, never comes to he who is lazy; he must not rest contentedly with his finished works, since dissatisfaction with one's achievement and the desire to attain something better is forever part of the cruel mechanism of creation. These conditions, when suitable changes are made in their formulation, apply equally to performers.

I have briefly outlined what young musicians and composers, about to embark on a professional artistic career, can expect. I have mentioned the complex situation to be faced and the privilege of magnificent experiences to be shared. Let me add, in closing, yet another thought: we musicians derive joy from the conviction that, in our troubled and difficult world, where there is so much division, we are dedicated by declaration and by the choice of our career to that which unites people: Music. Music that, in the words of Joseph Conrad, through its "magic suggestiveness" becomes the "art of arts."[1]

Source

Notes of the Cleveland Institute of Music, no. 2 (1971): 1–4. Text used with permission from the Cleveland Institute of Music.

Note

1. Joseph Conrad, *Typhoon, The Nigger of the "Narcissus," and Other Stories* (London: The Folio Society, 2000), 230.

ON RECEIVING AN HONORARY DOCTORATE FROM WARSAW
UNIVERSITY, JUNE 30, 1973

Science and art are two areas of human activity, two products of the human spirit that, it would seem, are so utterly different from each other, yet have many traits in common. Although this is neither the time nor the place to expatiate upon the differences, I should, nevertheless, like to draw attention to one difference. I have in mind here the goal of science and the goal of art and the degree to which they can be defined. The goal of science is obvious to all of us, it can be defined by one word: knowledge. But whenever I try to define the goal of art, my thoughts encounter a cloud of mist beyond which nothing can be discerned clearly. No definition is satisfactory, all seem to miss the crux of the matter, all are imprecise and miss the essence of it. Yet the goal is obvious to all who are able to experience art and even more so to those who create it.

A great deal has been said, thought, and written on that subject. The goals of art are described in many ways, ranging from the definition offered by Debussy, which is not without a certain whimsy, who said that he composed to give pleasure, to the most elevated goal of art as seen by Stanisław Ignacy Witkiewicz, which he called "the metaphysical thrill." One would expect that these essential differences would become apparent in the works of scientists and artists. For indeed the role of a scientist is to investigate, probe, and bring reason to bear on all intellectual work and effort. The work of an artist has been generally associated with intuition, imagination, and emotion. And rightly so, for no one will deny that the results of ecstatic states—or in the popular idiom—moments of inspiration, are clearly evident in the greatest works of art. These moments may be described as a state of readiness in the creative imagination for signals that flow from some unknown source, whose result is the sudden emergence of something that has not existed a moment earlier. But, I believe that I am not wrong when I say that without inspiration there would be no knowledge in the world. The work of a scientist abounds in moments of inspiration. We, the people outside the world of science, are aware of this from the history of science, from the biographies of great scientists and from the history of scientific discoveries.

Nor could a creative artist be able to obtain outstanding results in his labor without possessing a certain degree of wisdom. Hence the artist's labor possesses similar elements to that of a scientist, namely, to investigate, probe, and reason. We are gathered today in this seat of learning and knowledge. A moment ago I experienced a great honor because I ventured to think that the

men of science sensed in the final fruits of my inspiration sufficient wisdom
to confer upon me this high distinction in the world of learning. This fills me
with great pride and joy. It is also a confirmation of the validity of my life's
achievement and gives me great encouragement to continue my efforts in the
future. May I be allowed to express my warmest gratitude for this remarkable
gift to His Eminence the Rector, to the professors, to the University Senate
and to my promoter (nominator).

Source

Polish Music, no. 3–4 (1973): 18–19. Copyright Marcin Bogusławski. All rights
reserved. Printed by permission.

⚜

ON RECEIVING HONORARY MEMBERSHIP IN THE ROYAL ACADEMY OF MUSIC, LONDON, 1976

Chairman, Dame Janet, Ladies and Gentlemen,
    Allow me, please, to begin with a quotation that will certainly sound too
sentimental for this occasion. But I can't help doing it, as these words are taken
from the text of a song that is one of the favorite records of my small collection,
namely a French song recital sung by Janet Baker. The words in question are:

> *Sur moi la nuit intense*
> *Plane comme un linceul*
> *Je chante ma romance*
> *Que le ciel entend seul!*

> *The immense night*
> *hovers above me like a shroud*
> *I sing my song*
> *That the sky alone hears!*

    Although a little sentimental in its form, these words describe—at least by
their content—the lot of the creative artist, which consists mainly of singing
for himself. Rare are the moments when he feels that his song is heard. One
of such moments in my life is right now. My song has been attentively listened
to and evidently considered not too bad. More than that: such a distinguished
circle as the Governing Body of the RAM has found "my song" good enough
to appoint me as an Honorary Member. It is a great honor to me, indeed. But it

also gives me an incomparable feeling, as if I were the fisherman in the Théophile Gautier text. I realize that my song has been heard not by the sky alone.

Chairman and Members of the Governing Body, for that feeling and for the honor you have so generously conferred on me, please accept my warmest thanks.

Source

Typescript in English. Copyright Witold Lutosławski Collection, Paul Sacher Foundation.

ON RECEIVING AN HONORARY DOCTORATE FROM NICOLAUS COPERNICUS UNIVERSITY IN TORUŃ, 1980

Rector, High Senate, Ladies and Gentlemen,

Giving me the title of an honorary doctorate of the Nicolaus Copernicus University in Toruń is for me a great honor, a great privilege, and a great distinction. I accept it with joy, but not without a certain embarrassment. This feeling has always accompanied me when I have received similar distinctions in the past. After all, they must be understood as an award for some merit, and in recompense for some hard work crowned with valuable results. What are the merits I would be entitled to ascribe to myself? Unfortunately, I do not see any such merits and I cannot acknowledge any as my own. Rather, it is quite the opposite, as, in the face of fate that gave me some talents, I feel that I am the debtor. I understand this debt as one I owe to people who have a right to expect from me—a man more privileged by nature than others—creations that could somehow be useful to them. Thus the mere talents that people possess I consider to be a distinction and a privilege, and not a personal merit. Perhaps one could discern some merit in the way the artist employs his talents. For the talents cannot only be used; they can also be wasted. But also here I don't see any reason to boast of anything, since—as for many colleagues of mine—a creative work, certainly connected with efforts of both reason and spirit, is first and foremost a vital passion. Without this work I can't imagine my existence in this world; I wouldn't have any right to consider it to be a sacrifice, and thus a merit.

I say all this in order to account for the feeling of embarrassment I mentioned initially. It does not, however, diminish a feeling of joy and pride in this award because of the distinction that has been conferred on me. I consider it not as reward for my supposed merits, but as one more gift, this time particularly valuable, since I receive it from scientists, and thus from people worthy of the highest respect and esteem.

Rector, High Senate, please accept my warmest thanks for this gift, which is a splendid encouragement to further work and efforts.

Source

Typescript in Polish. Copyright Witold Lutosławski Collection, Paul Sacher Foundation.

ON RECEIVING THE SIEMENS PRIZE FROM THE ERNST VON SIEMENS FOUNDATION, MUNICH, MARCH 28, 1983

Mr. von Siemens, Mr. Chairman, Ladies and Gentlemen, Dear Friends,

Granting me the Ernst von Siemens Music Prize for 1983 is an act of exceptional meaning in my life. What prompts me to make such a statement is the list of the previous winners of this prize, made up of some very famous artists of our time. Inscribing my name today on this list is a source of the highest satisfaction for me. I would also like to say that it fills me with pride. This, however, would be equal to ascribing to myself those merits that I have a right to consider to be my own, but only to a small degree. The work of a creative artist is, after all, the fruit of his abilities and talents with which he was born. Yet honesty in disposing of these talents is his basic duty. It is particularly so when, apart from the talents, he was given by nature an awareness that these talents are not his property alone, but rather an entrusted skill, which he should give back to other people in the shape of created works. However, an artist's task considered in such a way is not at all easy to fulfill. Every one of us experiences moments of faith and despair, of fervor and apathy, of an increase in creative energy and extreme exhaustion. Therefore, although it is difficult to accept the proofs of esteem coming from outside as an award for merit, they are an invaluable help, indeed. For they convince us that the efforts we make to dedicate our life to our work can somehow be useful for someone else. This help becomes particularly important today in this time of anxiety and threat. These feelings, although aroused in various ways and for various reasons, are common to all of us, inhabitants of the same planet. For this help and encouragement I would like to express to the founder of the Prize, to its Selection Committee, and to the author of the *Laudatio*, my warmest thanks.

Source

Typescript in Polish. Copyright Witold Lutosławski Collection, Paul Sacher Foundation.

Note

Lutosławski received the Siemens Prize in the seat of the Bavarian Academy of Fine Arts. After the ceremony there was a performance of his Dance Preludes for clarinet and piano (with Edward Brunner and Aloys Kontarsky) and *Grave* for cello and piano (with Edward Brunner, clarinet; Walter Grimmer, cello; and Aloys Kontarsky, piano).

❦

ON RECEIVING AN HONORARY DOCTORATE FROM JAGIELLONIAN UNIVERSITY, KRAKÓW, DECEMBER 6, 1984

Rector, Professors, Members of the Senate, Ladies and Gentlemen

I consider granting me the title of an honorary doctorate of the Jagiellonian University to be an exceptional honor. It certainly crowns all awards I have received from other universities and academies in Poland and in the world. This, which I am granted today, has the greatest value for me and is very dear to my heart, since I know very well that the Jagiellonian University is not only the oldest Polish university, but is also one of the oldest universities in Europe. What is also of particular importance for me, which I admit with all humility, is the fact that the same honor was granted to Pope John Paul the Second, and was accepted. I also remember with affection the granting of an honorary doctorate of the Jagiellonian University to Karol Szymanowski, who was a model and guide for my generation of composers during the years of our youth.

Therefore, the title I have been given today is a source of great satisfaction for me. It is, however, difficult not to admit that the situation I am in creates a feeling of intimidation. For I have been rewarded for something that I can only to a small degree consider to be my own merit. The value of musical works depends mainly on the value of the talent itself with which their composer has been endowed. Yet a talent is a privilege rather than a merit. A creative artist has no right to regard it as his own property. It is an entrusted skill, which is destined to be transmitted to other people in the shape of completed works, ready to be performed.

It is, of course, possible to discern the merits of a creative artist in his diligence or in the way in which he uses the skills entrusted to him. Here, however, new doubts immediately emerge. After all, the work, the overcoming of difficulties and all the possible endeavors connected with creativity are a vital passion for all of us, and do not require any victories over oneself.

There is another reason for my feeling nervous. I have in mind the fact that there are actually no criteria that allow a value judgment on a work of art. In my opinion, what decides the value of, for instance, a musical work, are thousands of people over decades, that is, what we symbolically call *time*. Nobody today is in a position to foresee the chances of music created today withstanding the destructive impact of time and thus proving its value.

I want to stress at this moment how very valuable is the honor I have received today. In the light of what I have already said, this award is not only a proof of recognition of the talents with which I was endowed by nature, but also an expression of confidence that my works are of some value, although it is too early to be completely sure of that. This certainty, particularly as a proof of the conviction of the members of the Senate of the Jagiellonian University, has a special value for me. It will be a help in the difficult moments that always abound in a composer's work. I have in mind the moments of uncertainty or despondency often resulting from the conditions in which I happened to live and work.

I want to express to the senate of the Jagiellonian University and to the rector my warmest gratitude for such a magnificent testimony of their confidence in the worth of my work and its results, and I wish to assure them that my gratitude will remain forever in my thoughts.

Source

Ruch Muzyczny, no. 2 (1985): 7. Copyright Marcin Bogusławski. All rights reserved. Printed by permission.

ON RECEIVING AN HONORARY DOCTORATE FROM THE WARSAW ACADEMY OF MUSIC, NOVEMBER 14, 1988

Rector, High Senate, Ladies and Gentlemen,

The granting of the honorary doctorate of the Academy of Music in Warsaw is a matter of great importance for me. This has—in comparison with other honors of this kind—a particular, unique meaning for me, for two reasons.

Firstly, the institution that has just honored me has Frederic Chopin as its patron. There is no need to repeat all the reasons, obvious to everybody, that make this a matter of great importance for me. Therefore, I limit myself to saying that in my personal, most intimate artistic experiences, the music of Chopin always had and still has a crucial role. I will not consider here the question of why this is so and how it arises. I hope that the echoes of my looking at or, rather, listening most intently to, Chopin's music, can be perceived in some works of mine by a number of listeners who know them.

Secondly, it is particularly valuable and deeply moving for me that I am granted this high award from that part of the Academy that is the successor to the Warsaw Conservatory where I studied and graduated. I will always feel warmly grateful to my teachers, professors Witold Maliszewski and Jerzy Lefeld. Now I offer my deepest gratitude to the rector and the high senate of the Warsaw Academy of Music for granting me this honorary doctorate. Through this fact, I am today closely bound to this Academy, which is for me a reason for both joy and hope. We live in a time when those people who are engaged in creating cultural works, have a particular extremely important role to play. For the future fate of the Polish nation, its identity, its recognizable existence, depends considerably on them. What evokes my feeling of joy is the fact that a community of leading Polish musicians, who share with me the same views and hopes, wanted, by granting me this high honor, to include me in this formal way into their inner circle.

Source

Typescript in Polish. Copyright Witold Lutosławski Collection, Paul Sacher Foundation.

⬥⬥⬥

ON RECEIVING THE POLAR MUSIC PRIZE IN STOCKHOLM, MAY 18, 1993

The great British writer Joseph Conrad, who—by the way—was a Pole, wrote in the preface to his novel *The Nigger of "The Narcissus"* of "the magic suggestiveness of music, which is the art of arts."[1] But we all know how low is the percentage of people for whom the so-called serious music is necessary, in spite of its being "the art of arts." In the light of this, the decision of the founder of the Polar Music Prize to create such an award for so-called serious composers deserves the highest appreciation.

The fact that I have been chosen to be awarded this prize makes me proud and happy. It is also an encouragement for my possible future work. I beg the founder of the Polar Music Prize and the members of its Committee to accept this expression of my most profound gratitude.

Source

Typescript in English. Copyright Witold Lutosławski Collection, Paul Sacher Foundation. The Polish version of this address was printed in *Ruch Muzyczny*, no. 13 (1993): 1.

Note

1. This quotation, to which Lutosławski returned several times, derives from the following passage of Conrad's novel: "All art, therefore, appeals primarily to the senses, and the artistic aim when expressing itself in written words must also make its special appeal through the senses, if its high desire is to reach the secret spring of responsive emotions. It must strenuously aspire to the plasticity of sculpture, to the colour of painting, and to the magic suggestiveness of music—which is the art of arts. And it is only through complete, unswerving devotion to the perfect blending of form and substance; it is only through an unremitting, never-discouraged care for the shape and ring of sentences, that an approach can be made to plasticity, to colour; and the light of magic suggestiveness may be brought to play for an evanescent instant over the commonplace surface of words: of the old, old words, worn thin, defaced by ages of careless usage." Joseph Conrad, *Typhoon, The Nigger of the "Narcissus," and Other Stories* (London: The Folio Society, 2000), 230.

ON RECEIVING THE KYOTO PRIZE, KYOTO, JAPAN, OCTOBER 1993

Your Imperial Highness, Chairman, Mr. President, Distinguished Guests,

The word *music* has more than one single meaning. It may signify something sublime, something producing the most noble sensations. With this meaning of the word *music* we associate what we experience when listening to—for example—works of Bach, Beethoven, Chopin, Debussy, etc. The great British writer, Joseph Conrad, who was in fact a Pole, certainly had this meaning of music in his mind when he wrote about "the magic suggestiveness of music which is the art of arts." But, on the other hand, music may signify something entirely different, a sound-pap, present everywhere: in the shops and on the beaches, in the streets, and in the hotels and many other places. This kind of quasi music destroys the natural sensitivity for the beauty of sounds in millions and millions of people. Music, in the first meaning of this word, needs to be defended and protected. A great contribution to this defense and protection comes from those who see in music an important factor in the work of improving the spiritual condition of mankind.

A magnificent example of an action aimed at this purpose is the Inamori Foundation and the Kyoto Prize in Creative Arts and Moral Sciences. For this work I have the greatest admiration. It is an inspiration to all those who are not indifferent to the fate of the arts on our planet.

President, Ladies and Gentlemen, to be selected as laureate of the Kyoto Prize in Creative Arts and Moral Sciences is a great honor. I am a very happy artist, indeed, whose work finds such a splendid proof of recognition. In the history of music, as we know, it was not always the case. This Prize is for me, not only an honor, but also a help and a stimulus. To all this I should like to add the fact that among the former laureates there was a composer of supreme importance, Olivier Messiaen, and a composer to whom I owe a very important moment in my development, John Cage. And also there is a personal friend of mine, my compatriot, and one of the leading filmmakers of our time: Andrzej Wajda. To join them now is an additional source of joy.

Mr. Inamori, please accept this expression of my most profound gratitude.

Source

Typescript in English. Copyright Witold Lutosławski Collection, Paul Sacher Foundation.

Note

See also the text "Music Yesterday, Today, and Tomorrow" (in chapter 4), which Lutosławski delivered as a lecture on that occasion.

· *6* ·

Notebook of Ideas, 1959–1984

22. I. 59

For a possible article on perspectives of contemporary music:

    a. two meanings of a musical work in the history of music:

    1. a "timeless" meaning = an "absolute" value; 2. a directed, evolutionary meaning = value for subsequent works, authors, generations, etc.

    Instances of mixing these meanings, combinations, e.g.:

    1) – 2)—every imitation
    1) – 2) + some works of the Mannheim School
    1) + 2) + *Tristan, Sacre*
    1) + 2)—Brahms, old Bach, Stravinsky in his period of "back to . . ."

29. I. 59

Title: "A glance at the music of our times"[1]

    b. The characteristics of a work can be presented as advantages or disadvantages (barley soup *versus* spinach). Often it is blamed, for instance, for "continuity" or "lack of continuity," and praised for precision or "lightness and the lack of pedantry," etc.

    In the end: what are the conclusions, what is the author's position in relation to the ~~avant-garde~~ the post-Webernists. Is he against? Does he deny their value? No. It was only an attempt to look at the phenomenon itself, to assess its role in the development, its "progressiveness" or "backwardness," "potential for development," or "blind alley." In every language, at every moment of development, works of value can be created. At the very edge of a precipice, and even at its foot, one can make a gesture full of beauty. No work is beautiful merely because of its "progressiveness," no beautiful work is less beautiful because of its "reactionary spirit," although a "progressive" work may arouse more interest by its "novelty." It is more difficult to acknowledge as beautiful those works which are not "new." Possibility of an inverted reasoning → relativity.

30. I. [59]

c. Today it is already obvious that twelve-tone serialism has not generated any specific form. It is an analyzing, partitioning, nonsynthesizing method. It ensures the homogeneity of material. And this is the only reason for its existence.

d. "Their" work is undoubtedly very useful: after the decline of the tonal system, in a moment of some chaos, "they" have ordered the material, given elements a name. The thing is, however, that they have gone too far, "their" conclusions can hardly be justified.

1. II. [59]

c. Total serialization resulted from "moving away" from a "repellent" pole, i.e., from tradition, the old elements of style. There was no attractive force, no goal. The evidence for this is the result of total serialization, i.e., the static character of music, "*der schwebende Zustand*," which is not satisfying, and Stockhausen himself, for instance, is looking for a remedy to escape this.[2] He claims that the only resort is spatiality, the possibility of spatial differentiation of the sound-sources. An illogicality. What governs the differentiation? A higher formal rule? What kind of rule? In order to be consistent one must also serialize the sound-sources, the result of which will again be a return to a stasis. No wonder, since spatiality is one of the basic elements of music, like pitch or rhythm. If spatiality is treated as a primary factor, it would be equally justified to choose another element to play this role and to "de-serialize" it. Searching for a formal rule for totally serialized material is something contradictory in itself. Black coffee and a sleeping-draught.

a. Webern's most important achievement was—of course—the disruption of continuity, pointillism.[3] It is something completely new, expressively and stylistically. Before it there were lines, but also points. After Webern there are only points.

b. Serializing an element is a way of eliminating its activity. Total serialism eliminates activity in general, that is, activity over a long span of time. It replaces activity by simple stasis.

This refers to spatial music *à la* "Gruppen."[4] The advantage of nonserialism applied to spatial differentiation unmasks a certain minimalism. The spatial differentiation can be nonserial, as a new element, which formerly didn't play any role. Hence, it can be nonserial without the risk of falling into an old convention. Hence, total serialization has, perhaps, a negative goal: a maximal "moving away from an old convention." Introducing a nonserial element of spatiality is a sign of ambiguity, inconsistency.

6. II. 59

c. It is only worthwhile "imitating" someone when what one does is better than the model. The examples are obvious: Mozart and the Mannheim composers, Bach, Pachelbel, Vivaldi, etc. One needs a lot of self-confidence to imitate. If one lacks it, one has to look for undiscovered things. Today there are no great "synthesizers," "blenders," there is nothing to repeat. The scouts are finding an insubstantial material, with which little can be done. Everyone has to look for their own nourishment, everyone is condemned to the "misery of avant-gardism." One has to be a paratrooper oneself, and then "occupy an area" by oneself as well.

21. II. 59

d. The next stage of using "spatiality" should be to serialize it, that is, "eliminate its activity." For spatiality is only one of such elements, like pitch, duration, sound-color, etc.

a. Rereading Wilde's *The Remarkable Rocket*—a subject for a one-act play, and—in any case—a good example of using the idea of a most advanced conventionality as the only outcome for an opera.

14. X. [59]

b. "Permutationism" = stasis, an equilibrium as in mechanics. Supremacy of one factor! disturbance of equilibrium, motion.

Two elements: "stasis" and "motion," i.e., "a whole" and "a part," i.e., "lack of contrast" and "contrast"—as the basis of construction.

17. X. [59]

c. The critic's most common defect: inability to realize that he doesn't know something.

19. X. [59]

d. I am interested mainly in those elements of technique which have prospects of a greater permanence and will not go out of date immediately.

Great monologues of contemporary drama: Beckett (Pozzo: *En attendant Godot*),[5] Ionesco (Béranger: *Tueur sans gages*).[6]

23. X. [59]

e. A composition teacher shows how to compose, when he does not feel any need to do it himself. I don't think this does anyone a favor. And all this leads moreover to multiplying the most perfectly useless objects there are—unsuccessful works of art.

24. X. [59]

f. To achieve something reasonable, one has to be totally independent of the outside world. Like Webern. Yet there is a fundamental difference between Webern and the Webernists, who are left with constant confrontations, and this is why none of them even tries to concentrate on something more enduring, consistent, long term. Engaging in an incessant dialogue with criticism is a kind of slavery.

7. XII. [59]

g. Those works of art whose main merit is their novelty are weak. It's the feature that ages fastest.

7. IV. 60

For the program introduction:
h. We all draw out of the same pot and the bottom is already in sight. The more ardent eager (Cage)[7] have already scraped the bottom. As for myself, I don't hurry forward toward this moment to which our history of music tends inevitably, that is, to the moment when there is no more music.

29 IV 60

For a possible note on the *Songs* (for the Festival program):[8]
It is possible that the endeavors of those few who scan music for a new approach to the Webernist tradition, are a mad enterprise. This is at least what I think of the leading "rhinoceroses" of Webernism. They even go much further. "Those," they say, "who never went through the Webernist school don't belong to our epoch at all." The future starts with Webern, and what does not have any connection with him belongs to the past. It is exactly as if the

impact of Webern is a kind of baptism, without which there is no orthodoxy in the new religion.

I totally reject all absolutism; and the utter certainty with which the dogmatic followers of Webern proclaim their own rights to dispose of the future awakens my reluctance and suspicion. Someone who is not modest enough to admit that he *doesn't know everything*, exposes himself, in fact, to the risk of *knowing nothing*. However, it is not only for this reason that I am unable to accept such an attitude.

Etc., etc., blah, blah.

We often hear today that the role of harmony is finished. This is the result of the enormous influence exerted on today's music by the Schoenbergian[9] concept of a sound world based, among other things, on the elimination of man's purely sensuous reaction to sounds and their connections. Personally, I could never write even the simplest work while disregarding this particular, sensuous reaction to the vertical or horizontal arrangements of sounds. Therefore I distrust the statement about the decline of harmony as an element of musical substance. Moreover, I even think that only now can we really start to embrace the whole abundance of the harmonic possibilities contained within the twelve-tone scale; especially now, when we are getting rid of the limitations of tonal thinking forever.

I was particularly interested in these issues, which are so unpopular today, when I was writing *Five Iłłakowicz Songs*.[10] Therefore, I tried to put everything else aside in this work and to concentrate only on the expressive and coloristic possibilities of the twelve tones in their diverse variants. Hence, a simple, homophonic texture which does not go beyond traditional rhythm; hence—ultimately—the choice of the "children's" texts which demand a simplified, concise musical interpretation.

It is obvious, however, that purely technical issues were not the only purpose of my project. Even while limiting my field of creative action so much, I found in the work on *Five Songs* a lot of the kind of satisfaction that generally comes from writing music. What certainly helped me was the particular poetic charm of Iłłakowicz's *Children's Rhymes*,[11] from which I took the texts for my work.

23. IX. 60

It seems to me that rhythm (in its broadest sense as a division of time in which the action of a musical work takes place) is the most indestructible element of music.

One is tempted by the idea of the "eternity" of this element. Instead of "melody" and "harmony" there is a new element (perhaps not completely new in essence, but new in use, i.e., an *objet sonore* (sound-object).[12]

19. X. 60

Re: technique based on "objects":

Object = collection of sounds in which there is a closer relation between each of these sounds and those which belong to another object. This closer relation guarantees, first of all, connection in time.

However, it can also involve a similarity of tone-color, rhythm, articulation, harmonic profile, choice of intervals, etc.

Hence two rhythmic flows in a work:

1. local rhythm, a "small" one—inside the object;
2. general rhythm, a "big" one—i.e., a rhythm of the succession of objects.

25. X. 60

For a possible program note:

These works show how far I have traveled in recent years. It seems to me today that my Concerto for Orchestra, written only six years ago, between 1950 and 1954, is the distant past, something like a memory from another incarnation.[13] Was I aware then that I would depart so far from the technique and aesthetic which this work presents? Certainly yes. And even more: I fervently desired that this would happen as soon as possible. In one of my published statements at that time I expressed this thought as follows: since I don't possess at present any of the elaborate means which would allow me to write as I would like to do, I write as I am capable of doing now. A certain resignation showing through that statement is, however, far from any quietism. This was my decision for one or at most a couple of works.

This very quietism always seemed to me to be a matter of helping myself to the elements of compositional technique that I lacked "from elsewhere," that is from the current language of the so-called avant-garde. The more so because the basis of that language was serialism, a doctrine deriving from the premises which were basically alien to me. In this situation I had to rely almost entirely on myself in working out a network of means which could be useful for me.

Such an intention could be called crazy or—at least—naïve. I prefer, however, to surrender to my own illusions rather than give up at once every attempts to resolve this, at any rate, seductive task.

Can I say today that those efforts were worthwhile, that I found what I was searching for? When I try to answer such a question, various gloomy thoughts come to mind. Perhaps the mechanism of creation is so perfidious that it relies on constantly feeling an unsatisfied need? Even if it is so, one can console oneself with the unquestionable fact that while making the moves that resulted from that mechanism, one never returns to the same initial point.

25. XII. 60

There are countless ways of perceiving works of art and of reacting to them. Two totally opposite standpoints are: to perceive a work in complete isolation from everything else as a phenomenon per se, or—contrariwise—to consider its significance only from the point of view of the historical development of a given art. These extremes are, of course, unattainable in practice, but the predominance of one over the other is quite frequent. Thus, there exist works, the significance of which consist first of all in the "newness" that they represent in every respect (and so not only in the technique, compositional means, etc., but also just in their "content," type of expression, etc.). If the new, embedded in the work, is of little concern and if it carries us away first and foremost by its "otherness," then such a work is not an independent phenomenon; it does not have its own existence, it exists only as an element of a game with a given set of rules. And in the future it is condemned to play only the role of a historical curiosity. However, while severely criticizing such a work "in itself," while seeing in it few possibilities for an independent existence, detached from the moment in which it appeared, we may still be overcome by the charm of the "newness" which it contains. This dual reaction is rare among most "professionals." They are first and foremost blasé, having overindulged; they react mostly to a work as an "element of the game." They are in fact blind to more enduring values in a work of art. Amateurs—conversely—are not affected by "the game," they search for an authentic aesthetic experience. Yet their weakness is often an inability to distinguish the authentic from an imitation. Here, one delicate difference: the values of the work and those of an artist. Theoretically: plagiarism, a skillful imitation, may have the value of a masterpiece, if the piece is considered in isolation from everything else. If it is not considered like that, it is because in practice we cannot completely isolate an object in that way. We associate a work with the person of the author and we cannot treat these two things separately. Yet the issue is simple: an imitation can be a masterpiece, but then it is only to a small degree a creation of the author whose name it bears.

25. XII. 60

As far as the notation of dynamics is concerned, there exist two meanings of the dynamic signs in ensemble music:

1. the range of individual instruments;
2. the common level of an ensemble.

In 1., e.g., f on a trombone is different from f on a celesta; in 2., in order to obtain f, a trombone must play almost p, etc.

One can notate in individual voices: 1. normally, but the common level, i.e., 2., in brackets.

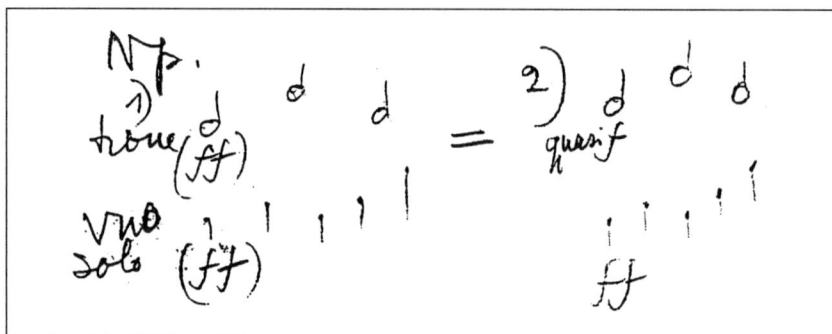

22. I. [61]

On explaining the issue of "accommodation"—a good expression: to blind oneself, i.e., to become desensitized to a variety of sound-stimuli, in particular structures, "classes."

12. II. [61]

The period I have been living through for quite a long time (a couple of years) is uninteresting. It is a period of intensive searching for means of expression which are appropriate for me. This leads inevitably to the state of using, more often than not, means which are badly devised, unfamiliar. One loses in this state the steadiness of one's hand, one loses accuracy of aim, authoritativeness and full responsibility for a work. What's more, the search proceeds slowly and brings few lasting achievements. The result is that the works of this period (orchestral works from 1959–1960[14] and also a work for chamber orchestra of 1961[15]) certainly stand lower, as far as their intrinsic value is concerned, than some of my previous works (Concerto for Orchestra, *Musique funèbre, Five Iłłakowicz Songs*). For me personally, however, they have greater value than the other works, since they lead towards something, they prepare something, they offer the facilities for doing something that will be much more my own. I will be able to write those works when I have mastered and come to understand the means I am exploring now, and made them as flexible as "late tonality" in the Concerto for Orchestra.[16]

11. III. 61

New instruments or a direction in which they should be researched:
    1. The piano enriched with various tone colors (those produced up to

now by "preparation" and the like) obtained with the help of mechanically moved objects placed on the strings, etc., and with percussive effects;[17]

2. instruments which combine traditional resources with electro-acoustic ones, such as—for instance—double bass, electric guitar, etc.

Stereotyped techniques and all the other aesthetic things are a sign of the degeneration of a given period: Signac[18]—stereotyped impressionist techniques were the final fatal blow for him.

12. III. [61]

Technique in art consists, among other things, of an ability to accomplish the most difficult tasks using a series of familiar operations, as well as simple ones in which deciding what to do doesn't present any difficulties.

Art in Poland was often regarded by artists themselves in an infantile way: "me too ...," "being equal ...," "a Polish variant of a current ...," "national traits ...," "Polish Picasso, Polish Bartók, Polish Salvador Dali...." Imitating adults, that's all. The characteristic of an authentic artist is the ability *to assume some responsibility* for the physiognomy and the fate of the art of a given epoch. Only thus may one achieve something. Even the most modest talent, if he is able to assume even a little bit of that responsibility, has his place in the history of art. The rest are parasites, rabble-rousers, a tiresome mob.

13. III. [61]

For the thousandth time: music doesn't express any specific feelings, it only constitutes the formal framework in which, while listening, everyone experiences their own emotions, according to their own personality. So a very easy explanation for the tears of the Gestapo listening to Mozart.

One could say that the influences of electronic music can be seen in the works I am now writing. Perhaps. One thing is obvious to me: that electronic music and "*musique concrète*"[19] realize to some extent those timbral and rhythmic effects which have been infiltrating my imagination for a long time.

19. III. 61

In order to justify the classical rhythmic formulae, it has been argued that this rhythm (i.e., "a harmonic one," based on a regular pulse) originates in nature: walking, the heartbeat. Yet it is not justified to say that other rhythms have no correspondence in nature. In fact, natural phenomena mainly proceed in irregular rhythms. Example: the rhythm of the drops when it's starting to rain. (*pizz.*, in m. 67 *presto* (II) of *Jeux vénitiens*).[20]

6. IV. [61]

I often see in my finished works only poor caricatures of what their first conceptions were like.

31. V. 61

Modesty is a luxury which immature people cannot afford.

4 VIII 61

In the dark one walks with a torch in order to avoid a broken nose. . . . Today we cannot afford the luxury of improvisation as in the time of the "peripheries of tonalism" [sic], when the ample resources of old conventions always protected our imagination from complete chaos. Today there are indispensable new codes, constraints, conventions to be adopted "for a while" or for longer. These conventions are young, they are not fixed sufficiently in the imagination to be taken for granted. They are as indispensable as a torch in the dark or plaster for an almost mended fracture.

9. VIII. 61

One's own compositional technique is like alcohol in the veins of a habitual drunkard. Three glasses are enough to make him drunk—little invention is needed to compose a work.

10. XI. [61]

What is characteristic and substantial in art nowadays is the creation of individual ways of expression, i.e., of languages, contrary to past periods (such as Baroque) in which there existed more or less common, generally accepted methods of expressing oneself. Today, in this era of an intentionally created Tower of Babel, treating one's individual achievement in the realm of language as a common property is not only borrowing, imitation or plagiarism; it is—when all's said and done—*an anachronism*, a transference of an old way of thinking about these issues into an era in which this method is irrelevant. "Eclecticism" is a notion which applies only in our age and was unnecessary in the past. Practices which were natural in Bach's time (let alone the transcriptions of Vivaldi's works Bach published under his own name) seem unthinkable today. And yet . . . how many young composer-copyists are there who don't understand this and stubbornly transfer the old customs into our time!

11. XI. [61]

With my new technique, the role of the conductor becomes more and more similar to the role of director and stage manager in one, and the role of the orchestral musicians is similar to the roles of actors and extras. The old school of orchestral playing was more like exercising, a mechanical process in which there was no place for a musician's individual initiative in the interpretation of the text and its expression.

17. XI. [61]

Everything in a musical work must be the result of "invention" or "inspiration"—if you like. In the end it must be so. And although the results of elaborating a piece of music are necessarily connected with a composer's technique, all the elements of the latter, all an authentic composer's "ways" of operating with sounds, are only a product of inspiration, and may be applied several times. In a word: technique is the fruit of inspiration.

13. XII. [61]

Analekta (plur.) lat. *analecta*, gr. *analekta* = "things collected" from *analigo* = "I collect":
    A collection of fragments chosen from one or several authors.
    [dictionary of foreign words]

20. XII. [61]

Notes for a lecture on musical characters,[21] analysis of the first movement of Beethoven's Sonata[22] and therefore its formal applications in the music of today.
    The beginning: "nothing is known," axioms, a gradual approach to twelve tones
        twelve-tones
        instrumentation?[23]
        alea[24]
        practical analyses *Musique funèbre, Five Songs.*
        Jeux vénitiens IV
        analyses of the works of other composers (Brahms, Piano Concerto no. 1?)
            history of twentieth-century music (Zagřeb,[25] *Horyzonty muzyki,*[26] letter to Wallner[27])

Presentations of works, for example representatives of the young generation in Europe:
Nilsson,[28] Penderecki, Bussotti.[29]
Themes from this notebook
Preparing a lecture
1. elaborate each theme separately, without regard to length;
2. estimate time taken for each theme and allocate them to parts of
the lecture;
3. arrange the parts so that they constitute a whole;
4. evaluate the whole, possible supplements and changes.

20. XII. [61]

All the most inventive and attractive ways of performing works (*Transition II*,[30]
Kagel,[31] Cage, Bussotti, etc.) have only one value, which can be ascertained at
one performance. This value depends on the fact that a certain sound-image
can only be obtained in a specific way.

25. XII. [61]

A man who stops to confess to himself that he does not understand something
is totally lost (numerous examples!).

2. I. 62

"Provincialism" as a state of mind consists, among other things, in forever seeking to "create a self-image."

3. I. [62]

Schoenberg treated equally all sounds which had certain assumed pitches. This
is a great oversimplification, and even a mistake. In any group of sounds there
are those which stand out either for *greater dynamics* (*f* on the background of *p*
etc.), or for *longer duration* (as perceived!).

7. I. [62]

A striking similarity between verse and prose, and between "the pulse" and
"*ad lib.*"[32] It is our epoch—the second half of the twentieth century—which
discovers "prose" for the second time.

8. II. [62] On criticism

Artistic criticism is just one *kind of literature*. It is a type of parasitic activity, since the subject of a critical text is not created by a critic, but by the author of the work of art under discussion. There is no substantial reason why criticism should be regarded as different from literature. There is, however, a social reason. It is a convention, deeply rooted in listeners' habits, which consists of assigning to a critic the role of a judge of works of art, a sort of superior agent in relation to the creative artist. This convention is as unfair as it is absurd, since there are no reasons why this self-appointed critic's right to judge should not be considered usurpation. In reality, critics do not have any authority to express their judgments. In order to decide to be a critic one must have repulsive traits in one's character; a predilection for writing articles which bring people much harm and personal pain, while not having anybody's authorization to do such things.

To me, the critic is both odious and ridiculous, and sometimes I feel embarrassed for the author of a review. I wrote all this not out of personal ill-feeling, but after having read Kijowski's statement on Polish literature in *Przegląd Kulturalny*.[33]

15. III. 62 Attention: alea[34]

Two terms: "small-scale aleatorism"—concerns detail, *ad libitum* performance, approximate treatment of rhythm, ways of organizing an A section, etc.; "large-scale aleatorism"—chance as a rule to construct form, alternate sections, and even whole movements (Boulez's Third Sonata, [Stockhausen's] *Klavierstück XI*,[35] etc.).

On "large-scale aleatorism": this may be noticed only at the second performance of a work, because one performance does not reveal any difference between an aleatoric and a nonaleatoric work (in its sound, in perception). Thus, an aleatoric work is a collection of similar works, only one of which is performed each time. It is a dubious raison d'être for such a work.

On the other hand: "large-scale aleatorism" can be a point of departure for another method of constructing form.

I take some elements, the order of which is arbitrary. I treat them all together as one big element which appears *several times* in one form. And these elements go directly one after the other or are separated by something else! I make the order of the smaller elements within the big element dependent upon the performer (or upon chance), while demanding only that a different order is chosen each time. For instance, the big element is A, the small ones are a_1 a_2 a_3 a_4 a_5.

In the form A B A C A etc., one of the possibilities will be: $a_2\,a_5\,a_4\,a_3\,a_1$ B $a_2\,a_1\,a_5\,a_4\,a_3$ C etc., whereas in the form A A A B etc.: $a_1\,a_5\,a_4\,a_3\,a_2\,a_1\,a_2\,a_5$ $a_3\,a_4\,a_5\,a_4\,a_3\,a_1\,a_2$ B etc.

Then I obtain the same result through several performances of an aleatoric work, "forcing"—so to speak—a repeat performance of my fragment. Obviously, it is interesting when we assume that the small elements overlap in time (as in the coda of *Jeux vénitiens*) and occupy separate places in space:

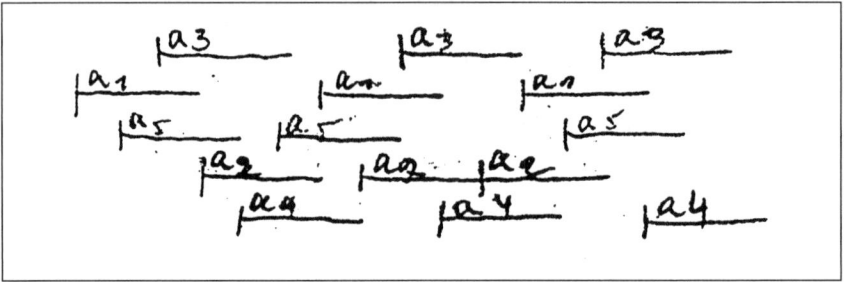

23. IV. 62

For an article on Debussy?[36]

The style, musical language and technique of a musical work can arouse positive or negative reactions. Yet it is the deeper level (?) of a work, i.e., something which is distinct from the style itself, the language or the technique, which determines this reaction.

An interesting fact: it is not because X was the first in his time to create a different style, language, or technique that his music causes our positive reaction, despite his style, language, and technique being old, out-of-date, and "out of fashion" today. This does not trouble us at all, since the deeper levels of X's music appeal to us so strongly that we completely forget the "antiquity" of his dated style. And even more: Y would have been quite unable to create his style, language, and technique. Y could be described in his time as an eclectic, but—in spite of that—his music, because of its value at deeper levels, awoke positive reactions in his day, and still does in our time, although his style, language, and technique have *never*, at any moment of their existence, been the "height of fashion."

On the other hand, A was an imitator and follower of X and adapted his style, language, and technique and, since he did not bring anything especially valuable into the "deeper levels" of his music, in his lifetime he was considered an imitator and follower, and after his death was forgotten. Even when his music is performed it irritates by its out-of-date, old-fashioned style, and by its "antiquated" technique. Something better happened to B. He belonged to those composers whose style, language, and technique were adopted by Y in his time. Yet B was only inventive in the realm of style, language, and technique, thanks to which he entered into history as one of the pioneers of our era. His oeuvre as a whole, however, did not present any greater value and therefore we listen to his music today as a historical curiosity. His music irritates us, in fact, by its outmoded style, as was also the case with A, an undisputed imitator.

Yes, novelty is one of the features of a work of art which ages very quickly, and even though it is a beautiful frill, it cannot be a lasting basis for the work's value.

Now I will illustrate my point by substituting real names for the letters: (to be continued!).[37]

26. IV. 62

Boredom, weariness, indifference, insensitivity to stimuli—these are the reasons for the perpetual evolution of language. Not only of musical language, but also of verbal language. It is out of boredom that people try to use a word to express something which it did not express before. There is a phase in which this new use of the word seems "original"; it attracts attention, gives the speaker a certain minuscule pleasure. This is how certain words used in their new meanings are brought into fashion. With time this new use of a word becomes commonplace, starts to be boring, its new meaning loses its "novelty," "attractiveness," and it enters into the official vocabulary. This is the origin of the litany of supplementary meanings which accompany many words in the dictionaries.

10. X. 62

Novelty is the feature of a work of art that grows old quickest of all. The goal of my search in the area of musical language is not novelty for its own sake. I look for the kind of technical solutions which can be employed many times and endure in a new repertoire of expressive ideas. Overall, I search for lasting values which do not expire immediately.

Some composers jealously protect their technical, textural, and even notational ideas. This is evidence of the poverty of their individuality. Individuality in art relies less on technical inventiveness. A striking sound or a textural trick are very superficial traits of musical individuality. I esteem an individuality which is difficult to grasp and remains hidden beneath its seemingly conventional appearance much more than one which relies on the effects of language.

The artist endowed with this kind of individuality does not care about the authorship of this or that technical trick. Tricks may be stolen, but nobody can steal individuality. The authorship of a trick is a fiction. Nobody remembers who was the first to use the Neapolitan sixth. The unquestionable individuality of Beethoven's Symphony no. 5 does not consist of technical ideas which could be immediately deciphered.

Nonetheless, the creativity within the language itself is necessary, and each of us cultivates it to a lesser or greater extent, etc.!

30. XII. 62

One should stop citing Honegger. The modesty which he wants to impose upon the contemporary composer (composition = *douce manie)*, is only a coquettish mask, a way of soliciting compliments.[38]

2. I. 1963

The carpenter Cymer said: a man is learning all his life, and yet still dies stupid.
   → For Zagreb[39]: Ionesco (*Notes et contrenotes)*,[40] Vallas—critics on Debussy.[41]

8. XI. 63

A term to describe many tendencies nowadays: "polytechnization" of music.

9. XI. 63

Possibly in Stockholm[42]: (*"exposé"*) against "polytechnization" of music:
   [1] music is a psychological act; conceiving music independently of perception—a kind of deceptive metaphysics. Even if a musical work was not conceived as an object to be perceived, it is not—perhaps—without value, but it is still totally useless.

What is a substantial part of a work and cannot be perceived by listening to it, even many times, is not music. Sophisticated ways of organizing material have their raison d'être only when they have their equivalent in perception.

   [3] Against "mechanization of performance," *restitution* of the satisfaction of playing and singing, the pleasure of making music (etc.). The time for saying this has come because of the rise of electronic music.

   [4] Against all "preparation," taking into consideration its marginalism, limitation, lack of perspectives. It has meaning only for as long as electronic music is so primitive.

[8] Last point: *beware of general principles*: the aim of all that has been said is only to specify the direction of my interests, it is meant to serve my practical goals, to facilitate composing, to bring order into my thinking and my intentions, and should not be considered as a criterion in evaluation. No such criterion exists, it may be found alongside features which can be perceived, described, etc. All the same, it is a *superior* criterion with regard to everything subjected to description and musicological analysis (impartiality). The value of a work ("talent," etc.) justifies the use of even the most nonsensical means. Consideration of Stockhausen *independently of* the higher levels of organization of material in his works, consideration of little Krzysztof,[43] despite the indubitable *decadence* (lack of perspectives in the development of his technique).

[7] For the earlier part of the lecture: the crisis of instruments, notation.

27. XI. 63

Possibly for Stockholm: music and text. Personal interpretation of the *meaning* (necessary for any realization of a work with text). Interpretation, because poetry is most frequently a polysemantic art, allowing various readings. This polysemantic character is subject to limitations, which vary according to the type of text (give examples: realist and symbolist poetry—Mallarmé?), so that if a composer bypasses this limitation it is a mistake, an erroneous interpretation, an artistic abuse, an act of piracy.

A question: Is it a personal interpretation?

25. XII. 63

Possibly for Stockholm[44] and Dartington.[45] Reconsideration of the resources of contemporary musical instruments.

26. XII. 63

Possibly for Stockholm: collect "assumptions" ("axioms"), including some of those under the date 9. XI., even perhaps in the text about ISCM in Rome?[46]

22. IV. 64

For *a survey of contemporary music* (possibly Dartington?)

Ligeti:[47] his recent works amount to a *form* of psychological test (example in *Nutida musik*).[48] It is, however, only pure form. The tests have probably no other goal than to provide psychic experiences, or to engage in an abstract mind game.

8. VIII. 64

It is dangerous to like composing music, since it leads directly to graphomania. Truly good music originates because of a radical boredom with what one has listened to and is hearing. It originates out of a longing for something which can deliver us from ennui.

This longing is the source of ideas, and these—in turn—of new works!

27. VIII. 64

One has to be very careful with "experienced" performers. What is experience? Most frequently it is the sum of knowledge acquired on the basis of the music of the past. A performer is proud of his experience. He knows better than the composer what is possible and what is not. But he does not know that everything invented by the greatest artists of the past, was not invented "once and for all"; that a composer is unwilling to use the same conventions all the time, and that, therefore, even the most "experienced" performer is less use to him than a young and inexperienced one. For lack of experience often goes hand in hand with lack of prejudices. The "inexperienced" does not fear something new, since everything is equally new for him. The "experienced" person is distrustful and reluctant to accept anything new, since his "experience" can't be of use to him. Faced with the new and unknown, he is again "inexperienced." Only a few, the greatest among the "experienced" ones, have enough courage and enough "experience" itself not to trust it unreservedly but to keep an open mind and heart all their lives to everything that requires constant revision of their knowledge and competence.

28. IX. 64

For the lecture on instrumental theatre:

Reaction to instrumental theatre: Ratz:[49] Austria will resign from the ISCM because of Raabe.[50]

Humiliation (Lachert[51])—a man deals seriously with people and they make a fool of him. (Here—explain that it is desirable that the principal genres or even styles should be separated in concert programs. It is a question of taste. Styles should not be mixed (e.g., putting a Beethoven concerto next to Offenbach in a program), just as one should not pour chocolate sauce over steak tartare.

"Can this be taken at all seriously?" It depends on us. Everything can be taken seriously. By this I mean everyone's desire to understand every phenomenon at first sight, even the most unconvincing.

Let us beware of ruling anything out too quickly, since that is precisely the result of "not taking seriously."

Many people will ask why. First of all, those of us who are interested in music's side effects (?) at every stage up to the "fun" element as the end result of an action.

Major problem: inquire whether behind all the appearances of organizing "fun" there is not something totally different; something which, in fact, can be significant for the development of music.

Cage: appearances of "fun"; perhaps not only appearances, perhaps they have something of a conscious intention. However, in the ultimate goals, and certainly in the actual action in Cage's Piano Concerto,[52] the appearances of "fun" contain hidden things which only those who have experienced their impact can really describe. Cage has had quite strange effects on the brains of dozens of composers. This operation, as it turned out, was beneficial in its effects. (Describe what it consisted of ?)

3. XI. 64

The true avant-garde are those who become bored earlier than others with current music. Eventually, the majority (the rest) also come to a similar state of boredom. It is precisely then that "harbingers" can be discerned. (I wrote this after I'd seen the play *Kurka wodna* by Witkiewicz in the National Theatre.)[53]

9. XI. 64

Paraphrase of Schoenberg's saying: "there is still plenty of good music to be written in C major" applied to the current situation: "there is still plenty of music to be written using the twelve-tone, equally tempered scale." It is only a pity that Schoenberg's idea was false!

20. XII. 64

On *prepared* instruments:

I feel the urge to protest, whenever inappropriate objects are used to achieve a particular aim. What is played on a prepared violin or piano could be achieved much better on instruments constructed specifically for these goals. There is another aspect of preparation which makes me dislike it. The fact, for instance, that one uses precisely the piano in order to obtain from it sounds (often very pretty in themselves) in a perverse way becomes the trump card of these contrivances. It may be a manifestation of an attitude towards the traditions of this instrument, by way of a kind of "flirting," "teasing," but also overt "sneering" or "iconoclasm." These are all peripheral, extra-artistic phenomena.

The use of the prepared piano in music—the opposite process to using objects which serve another purpose (Schwitters,[54] Kemeny,[55] etc.) in the fine arts. The piano—immense possibilities discarded, degraded to the role of a percussive and, in fact, rather poor instrument with limited possibilities (in comparison with its sophisticated construction!). Unimportant objects (nail, tram ticket, etc.)—*elevated* to the role of an element in a work of art.

28. XII. 64

On time organization:
Breath is necessary not only in singing and in playing wind instruments. There is something like a "breath of the brain" in the perception of music. One should take the listener's capacity for concentration into consideration, and, accordingly, foresee moments of rest, or "breathing," in a composition. Otherwise, one has to allow for a slackening of the listener's attention.[56]

On "negativity" and "positivity":
Few twentieth-century composers can assume an attitude toward their task which would be "positive" in *every* respect. They are all, to some extent, "wreckers" in one or another aspect of their work. It is a compromising, conformist, minimalist attitude, which lacks the broad gesture of the classics. It is a program for dwarfs, for people with the temperament of flesh-eating worms. It is hard to express how fed up I am with it all! But even worse than the "wreckers" are the false classicists, "positive heroes," who imagine that they will arrive somewhere while going backwards (Shostakovich,[57] etc.). Those "splendid," "monumental" paper sculptures are sad.

9. V. 65

Conceit, megalomania of the contemporary artist: 1. Presumptuous faith in one's own "individual" devices, in the infallibility of one's own reactions is in fact slovenliness (unfortunately: *a propos* many Picasso creations); 2. Novelty at any price; the race to be the first to invent something: "I invented this, nobody did it before me"—a characteristic attitude nowadays. Yet the "great masters of the past" envisaged first of all creating something attractive and not necessarily drawing attention to themselves: they blended, learned from others, had no other ambitions than to improve their own *métier*, which was what all musicians wanted.

22. VIII. 65

It is much easier to compose something amazing, shocking, terrifying, astonishing than something beautiful. That is why hardly anybody is composing anything beautiful.

People like Boulez make a dangerous mistake: they engage in a "dialogue with the history of music." The result is a situation in which every movement of the little finger must first be viewed in relation to the future, the present, and the past, which amounts to paralyzing the creative imagination.

As for me, I simply do the opposite: for a long time I have tried to eliminate from my music everything which does not directly serve my private, personal pleasure. Of course, the word "pleasure" is used here to stand for the whole rich, enlarged world of feeling and should not by any means imply a hedonistic attitude toward life and art!

12. IX. 65

For the interview:

What is my attitude toward the avant-garde? First of all, I have a fellow-feeling for it. However, in spite of the basic role the avant-garde plays in the development of every art, I also see something sad about it. There is always a tinge of resignation in the stance of an avant-gardist, since it consists of expecting elements that are of no real importance in themselves to perform the function of a finished work of art.

An avant-gardist bends his efforts first and foremost to polemics about the existing situation. His creativity is mainly a dialogue with other composers, therefore its significance is limited. In saying this I have, of course, in mind the attitude of an out-and-out avant-gardist. I consider myself a progressive composer and nobody would deny that some avant-garde elements may be found in my music. But the elements and their main purpose are two different things. The principal purpose of my creative activity is not a dialogue with other composers or an argument with the status quo. It is something completely different: to express as exactly as possible what penetrates my creative imagination and what corresponds to my personal desires and tastes. In order to achieve this, it is essential to work constantly on extending and renewing my own musical language. Quietism or attachment to the old forms of expression, no matter how perfect they might seem, do not belong at all in my nature. On the contrary: I constantly feel bored with everything in present day music which smells too strongly of even the recent past. This is what causes my constant yearning for a new, unknown sound-world; this is what stimulates my constant search.

17. X. 65

Once an aphorism on these lines occurred to me: one should take the great as one's models and "borrow" from the small. Yesterday I read a quotation from T. S. Eliot: "Bad poets imitate, good poets steal."[58]

11. III. 66

People who speak and write on art by virtue of their profession (critics, commentators, historians, theorists, etc.) can, of course, fulfill very useful and important missions. Yet they are also a danger to art: they smother it with words and overwhelm it with their accompanying thoughts. Critical editions of works of art, articles about concerts, anthologies, etc., are blurred, oppressed, stifled by the multitude of words. The commentators do not allow art itself to speak, they force themselves between the work and the listener, they talk him down, they order the artist to hold his tongue and to wait until their chatter stops.

27. III. 66

Often, nowadays, we hear from the mouths of critics the hypocritical claim that they express the opinions of an "average listener." This is obviously not true. A critic cannot voice the opinion of an "average" listener, or of any kind of listener, for a very simple reason: listeners go to concerts for their own pleasure, critics to earn their living. Hence a critic's relation to music is bound to be distorted. Often critics have "overindulged" in music, since they have to listen to it constantly. After some years they fall into a state of complete indifference to music, and they listen to it only as material for their columns.

30. VIII. 66

The news of a discovery of six hundred canvasses by an unknown painter, Lauvray,[59] friend and follower of Monet. He hated dealers and did not let them into his house. He could afford that, since he was rich. At the same time he was totally free of any craving for fame. A totally obvious attitude, as it would seem, but so rarely found in so pure a form. Even the hope that "future generations will judge my work" is nothing but a disguised form of yielding to the most dangerous tyrant for an artist, which is the desire for success.

2. X. 66

For the introduction of a lecture in Darmstadt[60]:
     Lectures and seminars will sometimes include pseudophilosophical digressions. "Pseudo," since the only area in which I feel professional is composing music. ~~I dislike dilettantism in everything I do, but~~ The profession of composer is, however, quite complex ~~among other things it must touch upon many other areas,~~ and it includes, among other things, amateurish philosophizing. By itself it may have no value, but it is sometimes unavoidable as a

supplementary factor in composing music. I have to refer to it at times in spite of all my dislike for dilettantism.

Ligeti's analysis of the process of atomization of the notion of form (form → structure → parameter), which I read in a summary in the Darmstadt 1965 brochure,[61] is probably clear-sighted and correct. Ligeti describes the disintegration of the notion of form, even going as far as questioning the possibility of its existence in music. Ligeti is a known catastrophist and he takes delight in analyzing the phenomena which confirm his vision of our time and reflect this vision in those processes to which art is subjected today. As for myself, I do not deny the reasons for taking a catastrophic view of our epoch. But the conclusions I draw from the possibility of the annihilation of our civilization and their instinctive expression in my music are not identical with the processes analyzed by Ligeti. Perhaps he does not develop his aesthetic views on the basis of a catastrophic view of the world. Therefore, I will adhere to my own observations. As follows: even if our civilization is to perish soon, and the disintegration of art expresses this, I don't feel personally interested to give in my works in joining in. The thought of annihilation arouses in me a totally opposite reaction. Not: "I perish, all is perishing, let us express it," but: "perhaps all is perishing, let us express something which would have a chance of survival." Therefore an instinctive search for what seems to be immortal in music. Among other things—a search for a form which would be something more than a result of disintegration.

28. II. 69

On thinking about possible returns to the past in writing music: if I did it, this would not be because it gave me any pleasure. Cherishing antiquity is not to my taste. It would be like a visit to a place abandoned long ago, in order to collect something one had forgotten.

9. IV. 69

If I accept an invitation to conduct my own works, I don't do it out of conceit. On the contrary, out of modesty. I am not convinced enough that the most famous conductors will ever look at my recent works (after *Musique funèbre*), and even if they do, I do not imagine they will have enough time, willingness, or independence from their own habits to conduct them well. Naturally there is an exception here; Janek Krenz.[62] But he rarely has an opportunity nowadays to conduct my works. It is surprising that—in spite of what I wrote at the start—serious conductors became interested so quickly in my Symphony no. 2 (Skrowaczewski,[63] Bour[64]). Perhaps there is really no need for me to discover for myself and prove to others that, for instance, the Symphony no. 2 could and should be conducted as its notation indicates and not as Boulez did in some places.[65]

[?] V. 1971

~~For Cleveland~~

Novelty—sine qua non (there is no reason for the existence of a work which does not offer something new, which repeats what already existed in a somewhat altered version). It is a necessary feature, but not a sufficient one. What decides on the value of a work is what it represents by itself when it stops being new. I am interested in how my work will age. This is what I try to imagine when I am composing it. I try to write something that will survive after its fiftieth performance.

20. X. 71

On learning to conduct my own works:

The decisive moment for overcoming difficulties is the moment at which one becomes aware of what one still has to learn.

24. III. 72

All kinds of motives trigger artistic creation. Among the more common or quite shallow is the artist's wish to attract attention, to become popular, to earn money and the like. (Poverty!) In my work I am mainly motivated by the wish to give as faithful a demonstration as possible of the world existing within me and continually developing, and to render it in a "material" form. This is combined with my passion for the entire world of music: mysterious, independent, and yet intimately connected with man and the human condition. Is my attitude purely introverted? Am I only concerned with what goes on inside me and nothing else? Certainly not. I feel an ardent wish to communicate with people through art all the time. Yet I do not exert myself to win over as many listeners and ad-vocates as possible. I do not want to win people over, I want to find those who, deep down, feel the way I do. How to achieve this goal? Through the utmost sincerity of artistic expression at all levels, from technical details to the most se-cret and intimate depths. I am aware that an attitude like this straightaway deters a large number of potential listeners for my works. Yet those who will stay are an invaluable treasure. They are people dear to me though I have never met them. Artistic creation may be thus viewed as a hunt for human souls resulting in a cure for the most acute of human sufferings, a sense of loneliness.

11. II. 73

What do I think about my critics? (possible question from a journalist)

Answer: The vocation of the critic is to mediate between art and the public. Some critics consider it their duty to express their judgment on artists and their work. This is a misunderstanding. The judgment on a work of art is pronounced by thousands of people over dozens of years. The results of this long-lasting process are impossible to foresee at that moment when a new work appears or a young artist has his or her first performance. Time decides both the value of the work and the value of the critic's opinion.

19. III. 73

(Once again the same, but a bit differently formulated.)

What is new today, will be old tomorrow. (Even the most dogged Schaeffer[66] will ultimately be an old academic.) And what then? Then it will become apparent whether the output of a given artist is a pile of old trash, or a fresh, vivid, original work of art, free at last from all nonsensical comparisons, and from its historical context. A lesson for the young and inexperienced: first and foremost, say what you really have in your heart; do not try to imitate someone who you are not, do not trouble your head about the question whether "perhaps you are not sufficiently avant-garde" (horror!). In other words—try to liberate yourself from "the slavery of your own reflection of someone else."

9. IX. 73

I don't take part in the dialogue with history, which has lasted for a long time, with Debussy reacting against Wagner, Stravinsky against Debussy, Schoenberg, etc. against Stravinsky, Xenakis and Krzysio[67] against Boulez and Stockhausen, whereas Riley reacted against the whole complexity of music as he saw it. I don't join in. And is it perhaps by not taking part, by searching for "timeless" music that I respond in my own way to the very existence of the dialogue with history?

3. X. 73

On interpretation:

After Fischer-Dieskau's concert (with Richter):[68] he is like a gigantic glass, magnifying the composer's work. How many there are, unfortunately, even among the great, who are only a distorting mirror.

28. II. 1974

For a possible article:

Terrorized by the fans. The existence of the Christian Diors (and others) of music: "this is how one writes now." I exhort all colleagues to boycott this kind of thing, take a look into their own depths, and realize what kind of music they would most of all like to hear. A genuine triad is better than a cluster imposed by fashion. Real iron is better than false gold.

25. XI. 74

Lévi-Strauss: "Non-representational painting adopts 'styles' as 'subjects.' . . . It is a school of academic painting in which each artist strives to represent the manner in which he would execute his pictures if by chance he were to paint any."[69]

26. VIII. 79

Theoretical analysis of a musical work consists not only in discovering and describing its actual methods, but first and foremost in choosing those which are significant for the construction of the work, and rejecting those which are present by chance. (Schaeffer's analysis of *Musique funèbre* provides an example of not conforming to this rule.) The result: an erroneous analysis.[70]

20. IX. 79

A statement by a famous composer that he creates for "future generations" is unbounded megalomania. The musical scene nowadays is full of such megalomaniacs. They search for an excuse for their failures, which result more from their own weaknesses than from "alleged" misunderstanding on the part of their contemporaries.

21. IX. 79

Unfortunately, it is impossible to justify all the processes of a musical work with words. They are governed by an internal logic, which, for the most part, is hidden from the power of the mind. We perceive it directly by *feeling* only, and not by *understanding* in what it consists. Therefore, when analyzing particular technical procedures used by a composer, at a certain point, we come to a complete halt. This state of affairs unfortunately generates a large area of misinterpretation, both on the part of the composer and his listeners or critics.

"This is how I feel" one tells the other, and although listening to these words may produce protests, nothing can be rebutted.

19. X. 79

After reading Boulez's "speech of thanks" (Munich, Siemens Price):[71]
   Still make a revolution today? There is nothing to be revolutionized. Everything is falling to pieces, disintegrating. Everything is waiting for synthesis, for durability, for substance. A revolution out of season is a way of evading a much more difficult task, namely the creation of works that will endure for a long time (timelessly?). Revolution is an escape from this task. Revolution means a safe existence, preparing for something great and enduring, without taking responsibility for the future of art. Yet the revolution was accomplished long ago. Those who still want to prolong it apparently fear a much more difficult task, which is to learn a lesson from it and start building. It is easier to destroy than to build.

24. XI. 79

Continuing from the above idea: one should deprecate, discredit, permanent revolution in art. One should have something to destroy when one wants "to revolutionize." In the time of "permanent revolution" everything new has to be immediately destroyed. Anything greater, any more enduring tradition, cannot come into being, since the smallest "shoot" must at once be considered "old" and fall victim to this quasi revolution. Therefore it proceeds on an even smaller scale. These are the wars of very small worms.

24. XI. 79

The lack of gravitation to any center (in the melodic and harmonic dimension), the state of permanent variability can be called a kind of "weightlessness."[72]

10. I. 84

As becomes a megalomaniac I am a modest man. For indeed, only someone convinced of his own gifts can afford modesty. Showing off often hides the conviction that one's own value is small. ("One's *own*?" Rather: a value given in trust!)[73]

[a separate fragment without date]

Sometimes I used to ask myself the question "what is music and what actually is a composer?" Kazimiera Iłłakowicz[74] once said in an interview for a journal that she considered "writing poetry to be a rather stupid occupation." This statement by a great poet (yes, I don't hesitate to say "great" because she is the author of a poem of which Słowacki[75] could be proud of, if he lived in our time) is full of admirable modesty. It is also packed with skepticism toward poetry in general and, as such, it forces a composer to reflect on the significance of music and on the purpose of his composing.

In France, when one is asked a question in an office about one's profession and the answer is: "*compositeur*," a second question is immediately asked—"*compositeur de quoi?*" Nobody would think that this word refers to a compositor (*compositeur*), rather than a composer (*compositeur de musique*). The owner of a little country shop in Norway once asked me if it was true that I was a painter. When I answered that I was a composer, there elapsed an embarrassed silence. I noticed that I was not understood at all, and I tried to explain what my profession involved. The reaction to this was a little giggle, and that was the end of the conversation about my profession.

~~This and similar events come to mind in those moments when I am in doubt about the purpose of art in general and of music in particular. I then regret that it was not my good fortune to have become, for example, a doctor. Is not bringing relief to human suffering the finest vocation?~~

This and similar events impel me sometimes to ask myself questions to which there are no satisfactory answers, such as, for instance, what proportion of people needs music at all. (I mean here, of course, a true need for genuine music, and not a silly desire for "background music," which accompanies thoughtless and usually insensitive people in their various everyday activities.) Now, if we found only a "quantitative" answer to this question, it would probably strike a musician as rather depressing. However, if we used an appropriate coefficient for the "quality" of a musical need, namely for how much this relatively small group of people needs music, the thing would perhaps not look so bad. Let us do a small mental experiment. As is well known, Pierre Boulez stated that all music created before Schoenberg should be destroyed. Only then could contemporary music develop in a natural way. I know another composer who would gladly destroy all contemporary music. The efforts of these two men would wipe all music from the face of the earth. Let us try now to imagine how the world would then seem not only to us—the musicians—but also to those nonmusicians who need music for whatever reason. It would certainly be a gloomy prospect for them.

Source

Notes

1. This is the title of a planned article, perhaps an early version of the text "Music in the 20th Century" originally presented in French at the first Music Biennale in Zagreb in 1961.

2. In his many works and artistic manifestos from the 1950s and the 1960s, Stockhausen revolutionized the traditional notion of a musical work, its material and structure, as well as its pitch and rhythmic patterns. Initially, his works were guided by the idea of a strict sound-order that he realized through the total serialization of all musical parameters. Later on, in the 1960s, under the influence of John Cage's aesthetics, Stockhausen turned toward aleatoric, improvised, and intuitive music. In his Diary, Lutosławski refers several times to Stockhausen's early solutions, discussing his concept of total serialization of the elements of a musical work. In the above entry he refers to the concept of musical space that Stockhausen presented in his text *Musik in Raum*, in his *Texte zur elektronischen und instrumentalen Musik. Aufsätze zur Theorie des Komponierens. 1952–1962* (Cologne, Germany: M. DuMont Schauberg, 1963), 152–175.

3. Lutosławski's attitude toward Webern can be described as ambivalent. On the one hand it reveals his great esteem for the novelty of Webern's ideas, yet, on the other hand, a deep belief that Webern went too far in disintegrating the tonal system and the rules of construction of a musical work related to it. Particularly, in Lutosławski's reflection on Webern's work, the thought returns constantly that he disintegrated the concept of melody inherited from the classical and romantic eras.

4. Lutosławski refers to Karlheinz Stockhausen's *Gruppen für 3 Orchester* (1955–1957)—the first large-scale work in the twentieth century that was based on a new, multidimensional concept of the sound space. It consisted of placing three orchestras around the audience; each of these orchestras required its own conductor. See the composer's comments on that work in K. Stockhausen, *Texte zu eigenen Werken, zur Kunst Anderer, Aktuelles. Aufsätze 1952–1962 zur musikalischen Praxis* (Cologne, Germany: M. DuMont Schauberg, 1964), 71–72.

5. Samuel Becket's *Waiting for Godot*, which was originally written in French in 1948 with the title *En attendant Godot*, became a radically new achievement in the history of twentieth-century drama, and it established the reputation of its author as a leading representative of the postwar theatrical avant-garde. The monologue Lutosławski mentions is delivered in the first act by Pozzo, one of the four characters in this play.

6. Lutosławski was impressed by the theatre of Ionesco, whose plays, such as *Rhinoceros*, were often staged in Polish theatres at the beginning of the 1960s, as well as others in the Dramatic Theatre in Warsaw in 1961. The existential anxieties on the threshold of the "atomic era" expressed by Ionesco were close to Lutosławski's heart, as is shown by his entry of 2 X 1966. Bérenger, mentioned in the entry of 19 X 1959, is a character who appears in several of Ionesco's plays: *Killer* (1959), *Rhinoceros* (1960), *A Stroll in the Air* (1962), and *Exit the King* (1962). The above entry refers to the first of them—*Killer* (its original title is *Tuer sans gages*) in which Bérenger delivers a great, final monologue in the third act.

7. Lutosławski, as his writings show, came across Cage's music almost by chance, while listening to his Concert for Piano and Orchestra (1957–1958) on the radio. Although it is difficult to determine the exact date of this event, it most probably took place in 1960, when he was composing *Jeux vénitiens*. Steven Stucky mentioned in his monograph another version of Cage's impact on Lutosławski: "A competing story, that Lutosławski met Cage in Darmstadt in 1961 and was impressed by what he heard there, stems from an inaccurate quotation in a newspaper interview: Howard Klein, "Notes from Underground," *New York Times*, August 7, 1966, sec. 2, p. 13. In fact neither Cage nor Lutosławski was in Darmstadt in 1961." See S. Stucky, *Lutosławski and His Music* (Cambridge, UK: Cambridge University Press, 1981), 242.

8. This entry concerns Lutosławski's note on his *Five Iłłakowicz Songs* for the booklet of the fourth Warsaw Autumn Festival in 1960.

9. Reflections on Schoenberg and his role in the history of twentieth-century music were quite a frequent motif in Lutosławski's statements, yet a critical tone dominated his attitude toward this composer. What he criticized was the destructive, as he believed, role of the twelve-tone technique in the traditionally understood structuring of a musical work, particularly in its melodic and harmonic dimension. In one of his conversations he stated: "What is alien to me in Schoenberg is the pre-eminence of the system over listening to the music. The latter is of course also present in his music, after all Schoenberg was an outstanding musician. However, the system in his art assumes universal significance, and determines the composition of not just one work but a whole series of works. That never occurs in my case. I always work out new elements of a system for every new work which stimulates my musical imagination." See Bálint András Varga, *Lutosławski Profile* (London: J. & W. Chester/Edition Wilhelm Hansen, 1976), 17.

10. *Five Iłłakowicz Songs* for mezzo-soprano and piano was composed in 1956–1957; in 1958 Lutosławski wrote a version for mezzo-soprano and chamber orchestra.

11. Kazimiera Iłłakowicz (1892–1983), a famous Polish poet, wrote her *Children's Rhymes* in 1923. Lutosławski used the following verses from that cycle in his *Five Songs*: "Morze" (The Sea), "Wiatr" (The Wind), "Zima" (Winter), "Rycerze" (Knights), and "Dzwony cerkiewne" (Orthodox Church Bells).

12. The notion of *objet sonore* was introduced by Pierre Schaeffer, one of the first creators of concrete music (*musique concrète*), in his work *A la recherche d'une musique concrète* of 1952 (Paris: Éditions du Seuil). This notion resulted from a totally new approach to the sound material. Schaeffer treated the acoustic effects from the surrounding world equally with instrumental sounds with a defined pitch. The novelty of his concept did not consist only in a radical extension of the range of sound qualities. Apart from the quantitative aspect, Schaeffer's concept had also a new, *qualitative* aspect. The latter resulted from the fact that both instrumental sounds and acoustic effects of nature and civilization (as previously registered on tape) constituted material for further electro-acoustic elaboration, thus offering new creative possibilities.

13. This opinion on the Concerto for Orchestra, in which Lutosławski distanced himself from this work, certainly resulted from his state of mind in 1960, when he reached a turning point in his style and compositional technique. It was no wonder that

in a passionate period of creative searching he wanted to distance himself from those compositions that represented his style from the early 1950s, along with those elements of neoclassicism and folklorism.

14. The works in question are Three Postludes (1958–1960, revised 1963) for orchestra. This cycle, which was planned as a four-movement work, has a special place in Lutosławski's output, as a composition from his transitional phase between *Musique funèbre* and *Jeux vénitiens*, since it shows both traces of his idiom from the 1950s and the features of a new language from the following decade. This dual stylistic status of the Postludes was described convincingly by S. Stucky: "The Three Postludes are altogether a less satisfactory work than the Iłłakowicz Songs or *Musique funèbre*; indeed they reveal rather clearly the sort of stylistic problems which caused the composer to abandon the fourth movement in 1960. Postlude No. 1 is performed occasionally; the second and third are almost never heard. Lutosławski has called the cycle a 'farewell' to the orchestra.... But the Postludes are certainly retrospective in character. Each movement is somehow connected with an earlier work: the first with *Morze* from the Five Songs, the second with the 'blurred toccata' style of the *Capriccio notturno* in the Concerto for Orchestra, the third perhaps with the First Symphony, especially the first episode of the postlude with the transition music of the symphony's finale. But there are many signs pointing to the future as well. The blurred toccata style of the Postlude No. 2 develops that of the Concerto for Orchestra in the direction of the second movement of *Jeux vénitiens*; the association of small groups of instruments with characteristic intervals in the Postlude No. 1 presages the first movement of the Second Symphony; the formal experiment in the Postlude No. 3 points the way to the finales of *Jeux vénitiens* and *Livre pour orchestre*." See S. Stucky, *Lutosławski and His Music* (Cambridge, UK: Cambridge University Press, 1981), 79–80.

15. *Jeux vénitiens* (1960–1961) for chamber orchestra. Characteristically enough, Lutosławski did not rate this work equally with the earlier compositions he mentioned, although there is no question that *Jeux vénitiens* marked a turning point on his creative journey, foreshadowing such works as the String Quartet and the Symphony no. 2. This understated evaluation resulted, perhaps, from the fact that Lutosławski's faith in his new language *in statu nascendi*, was still uncertain.

16. See note 13.

17. Here Lutosławski certainly had in mind John Cage's concept of the prepared piano, realized in such works by him as *Bacchanale* (1940), *Totem Ancestor* (1942), *Our Spring Will Come* (1943), *A Book of Music* (1944), *Music for Marcel Duchamp* (1947), and particularly the cycle *Sonatas and Interludes* (1946–1948).

18. Paul Signac (1863–1935), a French painter and graphic designer; one of the leading representatives and theoreticians of neoimpressionism. It seems that Lutosławski found in the innovations of Signac, which led to a liberation of color, an analogy to what he himself described as a "demolition" of the traditional musical language, especially in the sphere of tonal relations (see the text "Theory and Practice in the Work of the Composer" in part 1 of the present collection).

19. It seems that Lutosławski got to know concrete and electronic music only after 1956 when it started to reach Poland from such centers in the West as the studios in

Paris and Cologne. He also witnessed the creation of the Experimental Studio of the Polish Radio in Warsaw in 1957, and the first electronic works of such Polish composers as Włodzimierz Kotoński, Zbigniew Wiszniewski, Krzysztof Penderecki, and Bogusław Schaeffer, which revealed to him new creative perspectives of this new vogue. Yet in spite of his initial interest in concrete and electronic music, Lutosławski never used the studio technique and the sound effects it offered in any of his works.

20. It is very rare, as far as Lutosławski is concerned, to make a reference to the phenomena of nature in order to justify the irregularity of his musical process. It is well known that he treated with reserve any relationship between music and extramusical areas and practically never used them as sources of inspiration. An exception in this regard was his allusions to the rules governing a stage performance as related to the construction of great forms, such as String Quartet (1964) and Cello Concerto (1969–1970).

21. The sketchy character of this entry is connected with Lutosławski's preparation for the cycle of lectures he was going to deliver during his first visit to the United States, in the summer of 1962, at the Berkshire Music Center in Tanglewood, to which he was invited by Aaron Copland. He referred to the issue of musical "characters" in his lecture titled "Problems of Musical Form," where he enumerated four characters in classical music: "narrative, transitional, introductory, and terminative" (see part 1 of the present collection).

22. The exact data on this Beethoven Sonata are not specified.

23. Among Lutosławski's writings kept in the Paul Sacher Archive there is a text on instrumentation (see part 1 of the present collection). There is, however, no exact data that would allow us to establish whether and where this text was presented. One can only suppose that it was another lecture he delivered in Tanglewood in 1962.

24. This word is perhaps an allusion to the text by Pierre Boulez entitled *Aléa* (*La nouvelle revue Française*, no. 59 [1975]) in which he presented his opinions, not without a critical tone, on the use of chance in composing and in performing a musical work. This text was later published in the volume of Boulez's writings *Relevés d'apprenti* (Paris: Éditions du Seuil, 1966), 41–55.

25. Lutosławski is referring to his text *Music in the 20th Century*, which he presented at the first Music Biennale in Zagreb in 1961. See also note 1.

26. *Horyzonty muzyki* (Horizons of Music) is the title of a publication edited by Józef Patkowski and Anna Skrzyńska, printed in 1970 by the Polish Musical Edition in Kraków as the first volume of the series Res Facta. It contains the texts of fifty-six programs about various new music issues that were broadcast by Polish Radio in 1959–1968. Among the authors of these texts were not only critics and musicologists, but also outstanding composers of new music, such as Cornelius Cardew, Franco Evangelisti, György Ligeti, Luigi Nono, Bogusław Schaeffer, Pierre Schaeffer, and Iannis Xenakis. Among them was also Lutosławski—as the author of "Reflections on the Occasion of the ISCM Festival of Contemporary Music in Rome" (broadcast October 14, 1959), and "Is This Music?" (broadcast February 3, 1965). Both texts are included in part 4 of the present volume.

27. Bo Wallner (b. 1923), a Swedish journalist and musicologist specializing in new music, and editor-in-chief of the periodical *Nutida musik*; in 1956–1974 he was musical

adviser to Swedish Radio. Since 1962 he has taught at the Stockholm Conservatory where he was awarded a professorship in 1970. Wallner was keenly interested in the transformation in Polish music after 1956, which was shown by a "Polish issue" of *Nutida musik* (1959, no. 2), a broadcast on Swedish Radio devoted to Polish music, and by including in one of the concerts in Stockholm (on November 13, 1959) Lutosławski's *Musique funèbre* together with Bartók's Piano Concerto no. 3, Petrassi's *Coro di morti*, and Schoenberg's Five Pieces for Orchestra op. 16 (the Stockholm Symphony Orchestra at that time was conducted by Hans Schmidt-Isserstedt). The contacts between Wallner and Lutosławski date from the summer of 1959. In the Archive of Paul Sacher Stiftung in Basel there are four manuscripts and typescript copies of Lutosławski's letters to Wallner written in French. In one of them, dated August 28, 1959, Lutosławski presented his views, which Wallner published in *Nutida musik*, no. 2 (1959–1960) under the title "Improvisationer på ett givet thema." This text, which is included in the present volume, was first published in English in the collection *Lutosławski*, edited by Ove Nordvall (Stockholm: Wilhelm Hansen, 1968) under the title "Improvisation on a Given Theme."

28. Bo Nilsson (b. 1937), one of the outstanding representatives of Swedish new music. Nilson's avant-garde works from the late 1950s and the 1960s, such as *20 Gruppen* for piccolo flute, oboe, and clarinet, *Déjà vu* for wind quintet, *Attraktionen* for string quartet, *Versuchungen* for orchestra, *Litanei über das verlorene Schlagzeug* for orchestra, and *Revue* for orchestra, are marked by new sound effects (especially percussive ones) combined with melodic lines in high registers. His sonoristic innovations go hand in hand with precise structures (perhaps under the influence of early Stockhausen works, for example *Kontra-Punkte*), and with an expressive, aphoristic style reminiscent of the Darmstadt school, although Nilson distanced himself from it.

29. Sylvano Bussotti (b. 1931), a composer and an eminent representative of the Italian postwar avant-garde. He studied with Luigi Dallapiccola in Florence, and in 1956–1958 with Pierre Boulez in Paris. After having met John Cage in Darmstadt, Bussotti abandoned serialism and became interested in graphic music. He proposed original notations in such works as, among others, *Five Pieces for David Tudor* for piano (1959), and also introduced unusual vocal effects (for example in his *voix de femme* for voice and piano), which were combinations of vocal techniques and the spoken voice to texts with a wide semantic range.

30. Original spelling—*Transición II*. This is a composition by Mauricio Kagel for piano, percussion and two tapes, which was performed by Aloys Kontarsky (piano) and Christoph Caskel (percussion) on September 22, 1961, at the fifth Warsaw Autumn Festival.

31. Lutosławski came into contact with Kagel's music for the first time at the beginning of the 1960s, as a member of the repertoire committee of the Warsaw Autumn Festival. He then acquainted himself with Kagel's *Transición II* (see note 30).

32. Lutosławski refers here to his characteristic *ad libitum* sections, whose rhythm, which is only roughly delineated, has in fact a free character, resulting from the decisions of the performers who act according to the composer's indications in the score. The presence of such sections in a work, as opposed to the sections *a battuta*, is the main premise of Lutosławski's concept of a "limited aleatorism." This concept aims

at obtaining very subtle rhythmic effects, which are impossible to notate, and which include the performers in the creation of a work, while keeping control over its pitch dimension and, especially, of its harmonic structures.

33. Lutosławski is referring to the article published in *Przegląd Kulturalny* (Cultural Review) on February 8, 1962 (no. 6/493: 1 and 4). This was a transcript of a conversation in which the Polish writers Kazimierz Brandys, Jarosław Iwaszkiewicz, Wilhelm Mach, and Andrzej Kijowski took part. It was especially the negative opinions of Andrzej Kijowski, taken as a point of departure for this discussion, that outraged Lutosławski. According to these views, Polish contemporary literature was in a state of depression because it was not socially engaged, it did not harmonize sufficiently with world literature, and it had broken the ties with its own traditions.

34. See note 24.

35. Karlheinz Stockhausen's *Klavierstück XI* (1956) was, like the Third Sonata of Boulez, an example of aleatorism of form based on a haphazard arrangement of the sequence of its nineteen parts or "groups" by the performer. See the description of this work in K. Stockhausen, *Texte zur zur elektronischen und instrumentalen Musik. Aufsätze zur Theorie des Komponierens. 1952–1962* (Cologne, Germany: M. DuMont Schauberg, 1963), 69–70.

36. Although Lutosławski often quoted Claude Debussy as one of the main points of reference for his own creativity, he never wrote the article on this composer that he apparently planned. One of the most valuable, early references to his praise of both Debussy's oeuvre and his role in the history of twentieth-century music, is in an unpublished Lutosławski text "Pitch, the Interval and Harmonic Aggregate," which is included in chapter 1 of the present collection.

37. In spite of this remark, Lutosławski did not continue this entry in the following part of his Notebook, which is extra proof that he did not write the article on Debussy.

38. This entry shows that Lutosławski knew of the original edition of a small autobiography of Arthur Honegger entitled *Je suis compositeur* (Paris: Editions du Conquistador, 1951). It is based mostly on Honegger's conversations with Bernard Gavoty, a French critic, musical writer, and organist. The description of composing as *douce manie* (gentle mania), which Lutosławski quoted, appears at the beginning of this book. See also Arthur Honegger, *Ecrits*, ed. Huguette Calmel (Paris: Librairie Champion, 1992).

39. Lutosławski refers here to his preparations for the second Musical Biennale in Zagreb in 1963, at which (on May 6) his *Trois poèmes d'Henri Michaux* were premiered. This was the more important to him because he appeared for the first time on the stage as a conductor, guiding the orchestra in this work while the choir was led by Slavko Zlatić. Dragotin Cvetko presented criticisms of that concert in his article "Yugoslavia: Picture in Depth" (*Musical America*, no. 83 [196]: 16), and Nol Goodwin in the text "Commentary Zagreb. A Composer to Welcome" *Music and Musicians*, no. 11 (1963): 16–17.

40. Eugène Ionesco's *Notes et contre-notes* (Paris: Éditions Gallimard, 1962) are a collection of texts by the author himself and of various critics writing about him. The topics in this collection included the theatrical experiences of Ionesco, his aesthetic program (texts: "Discours sur l'avant-garde," "Toujours sur l'avant-garde," "Propos sur mon théâtre," "Mes critiques et moi"), the controversies among the London critics,

interviews, aesthetic manifestos, descriptions of plays, and the notes of 1953–1961. It seems that Ionesco's observations on the avant-garde and its attitude could have been particularly close to Lutosławski's heart, especially as they coincided with his own search for a new musical language in such works as *Jeux vénitiens.* The title of Ionesco's *Rhinoceros* could perhaps have inspired Lutosławski's later epithet "the rhinoceroses of Webernism" (see the entry of April 29, 1960).

41. Léon Vallas (1879–1956), an outstanding French musicologist and an expert on Debussy's music. In the period between the wars he lectured in Paris (Sorbonne, 1928–1930) and in the United States (1930–1931). Among his works on Debussy are: *Debussy, 1862–1918* (Paris: Librairie Plon, 1926); *Les idées de Claude Debussy, musicien français* (Paris: Librairie de France, 1927); *Claude Debussy et son temps* (Paris: Félix Alcan, 1932); *Achille-Claude Debussy* (Paris: Presses universitaires de France, 1944).

42. Lutosławski is probably referring to his preparation for a lecture he was to deliver at the Royal Academy of Music in Stockholm following his election as a member of this Academy in December 1962 (the ceremony of granting him a membership diploma took place in the Swedish Embassy in Warsaw). The lecture, which, as one would expect, was planned well in advance, was delivered in March 1965 on the occasion of the premiere of the String Quartet, and was later published under the title "About the Element of Chance in Music" (see part 1 of the present collection).

43. Krzysztof Penderecki.

44. See note 42.

45. Lutosławski was at that time preparing a series of lectures to be delivered during three week summer courses at Dartington (Great Britain), which were chaired by a musical director of the BBC, William Glock. Lutosławski lectured twice at these courses, in 1963 and 1964.

46. This text, titled "Reflections on the Occasion of the ISCM Festival of Contemporary Music in Rome" (1959) was published in Polish in *Horyzonty muzyki* in 1970 (see note 26 and also part 4 of the present collection).

47. György Ligeti's works, such as *Artikulation* for tape and *Apparitions* for orchestra, were performed in the late 1950s and in the 1960s at the Warsaw Autumn Festivals, so that his music was well known to Lutosławski, who was also interested in Ligeti's views on form in new music. Lutosławski held some late works of Ligeti in great esteem, including *Études—premier livre* for piano (1985).

48. A bimonthly devoted to new music, published since 1957 by Swedish Radio, whose editor-in-chief was Bo Wallner (see note 27). The recent Ligeti work that Lutosławski mentioned in this context could be the *Requiem* that was reviewed in an article by Harald Kaufmann—"Död och förnyelse," *Nutida musik*, no. 5–6 (1964–1965): 154–159.

49. Erwin Ratz (1898–1973), an Austrian musicologist. He studied with Guido Adler at the University of Vienna, and with Arnold Schoenberg. In 1953–1968 he was a chairman of the Austrian section of the International Society for Contemporary Music. Among his most important works are: *Erkenntnis und Erlebnis des musikalischen Kunstwerks* (Vienna: Österreichische Musizeitschrift, 1951) and *Einführung in die musikalische Formenlehre* (Vienna: Universal Edition, third edition, 1973).

50. Lutosławski probably refers here to Peter Raabe (1872–1945) and the repercussions of his relations with the cultural policy of the NSDAP (National Socialist German Workers Party, the Nazi Party). In 1935 he became the president of Allgemeiner Deutscher Musikverein, replacing Richard Strauss in the position of President of Reichsmusikkammer. Raabe held this post up to the end of his life.

51. Unidentified name or word.

52. The work in question is John Cage's Concert for Piano and Orchestra (1957–1958), which was often mistaken for another of Cage's works—Concerto for prepared piano and chamber orchestra (1950–1951). Lutosławski has many times noted the significance for him of hearing by chance on the radio Cage's Concert during the period when he was composing *Jeux vénitiens*, and therefore at the time when he radically changed his musical language by including the elements of chance and developing his concept of "limited" or "controlled" aleatorism (see note 32). This is how Lutosławski described this experience in his conversation with B. A. Varga: "It was in that year [1960—Z. S.] that I heard an excerpt from his *Piano Concerto* [*sic*] and those few minutes were to change my life decisively. It was a strange moment, but I can explain what happened.

Composers often do not hear the music that is being played; it only serves as a stimulus for something quite different—for the creation of music that only lives in their imagination. It is a sort of schizophrenia—we are listening to something and at the same time creating something else.

That is how it happened with Cage's *Piano Concerto*. While listening to it I suddenly realised that I could compose music differently from the way I had in the past. That I could progress toward the whole not from the minute detail but the other way round—I should start from chaos and gradually create order in it." See B. A. Varga, *Lutosławski Profile*, (London: J. & W. Chester/Edition Wilhelm Hansen, 1976), p. 12.

Lutosławski confirmed this influence in a letter to Cage written in Warsaw, on June 11, 1966 (now in a collection "Notations" of the Northwestern University, Chicago) in which, while responding positively to his invitation to participate in the collection of manuscript fragments from the scores of various contemporary composers (see John Cage, *Notations* (West Glover, Vt.: Something Else Press, 1969) he said that he was also sending the whole manuscript of *Jeux vénitiens* to him. On this occasion he wrote: "Perhaps you will be surprised to learn that I was influenced by one of your works when composing the last movement of my *Jeux vénitiens*. So is an especial pleasure for me to send this score to you."

53. The National Theatre in Warsaw staged *Kurka wodna* (The Water Hen) of Stanisław Ignacy Witkiewicz in 1964.

54. Kurt Schwitters (1887–1948), a German painter, sculptor, designer, and poet, and a leading representative of Dadaism.

55. Zoltan Kemeny (1907–1965), a Swiss sculptor, painter, and a fashion designer of Hungarian descent.

56. This short entry refers to a very important creative premise of Lutosławski's, which consists of considering a listener's response to the composed sound-structures. He explained it many times in his commentaries as, for example, in the following

fragment of his conversations with Irina Nikolska: "The bulk of contemporary music is being written as a succession of certain sonic phenomena which create a particular form. *My* method of approach to the very process of composing a piece of music is quite different. I don't 'linearise' sound structure events on an abstract basis, I don't just arrange them in sequence: I sort of compose sonic phenomena as they are to be *perceived.* That is to say, I conceive of music as it might be heard by me. (And this is absolutely indispensable to me.) Therefore, the actual piece of music turns out to be, so to speak, a record of perception, a perceptional process written down." See I. Nikolska, *Conversations with Witold Lutosławski*, trans. Valeri Yerokhin (Stockholm: Melos En Musiktidskrift, 1994), 106.

57. Lutosławski was aware of the situation in which Shostakovich was composing in the former USSR and, although he fully understood Shostakovich's creative choices made under the pressure of the official ideology, he apparently was not an enthusiast of the artistic value of their results.

58. Lutosławski quotes Eliot's phrase slightly altered, as it appears in various sources when being quoted secondhand. This phrase originates from the essay "Philip Massinger" included in a collection of Eliot's works—*The Sacred Wood: Essays on Poetry and Criticism* (1922). It is worthwhile, perhaps, to quote this sentence in a broader context, for it allows us to better understand its meaning: "Immature poets imitate; mature poets steal; bad poets deface what they take, and good poets make it into something better, or at least something different. The good poet welds his theft into a whole of feeling which is unique, utterly different from that from which it was torn; the bad poet throws it into something which has no cohesion. A good poet will usually borrow from authors remote in time, or alien in language, or diverse in interest."

59. Abel Lauvray (1870–1950), a French painter, and a representative of postimpressionism. His canvases (mostly mood landscapes) which he did not need to sell in order to maintain a comfortable standard of living, remained unknown until the death of their creator. They were brought to light by the critic Claude Roger-Marx and, since then, have started to appear in galleries and are sold at auctions. See: Gérard Schurr, *1820–1920. Les petits maîtres de la peinture. Valeur de demain* (Paris: Editions de la Gazette, 1972).

60. This entry relates to Lutosławski's preparation for the twenty-second Summer Courses of New Music at Darmstadt, which took place between August 22 and September 3, 1967. The preliminary program includes one of Lutosławski's lectures titled "Das kompositorische Prozess," but—for some unknown reason—he withdrew it shortly before the courses began.

61. The full version of Ligeti's text appeared under the title "Über Form in der Neuen Musik" in *Darmstädter Beiträge zur Neuen Musik* 1966, 35–50 (the whole issue was devoted to the problem of form in new music). The abbreviated version referred to by Lutosławski was included into Heinz Oepen's brochure prepared for the Darmstadt Courses in 1965, which contained abstracts of the papers for the accompanying congress *Form in der neuen Musik*.

62. Jan Krenz (b. 1926), a Polish conductor and composer, and the artistic director and first conductor of the Great Symphonic Orchestra of Polish Radio and

Television in Katowice in 1953–1967. He conducted the performances of many of Lutosławski's works at the Warsaw Autumn Festivals, such as *Musique funèbre* (1958), *Five Iłłakowicz Songs* (1960), *Trois poèmes d'Henri Michaux* (1963, Polish premiere—together with Lutosławski), and *Livre pour orchestre* (1969, Polish premiere). All these performances enhanced Lutosławski's reputation.

63. Stanisław Skrowaczewski (b. 1923), an outstanding Polish conductor and composer. In 1969, among other works, he conducted two performances of Lutosławski's Symphony no. 2 with the Minnesota Symphony Orchestra—on February 21 in the Northrop Auditorium at Minneapolis and on March 3 at Carnegie Hall in New York.

64. Ernest Bour (b. 1913), a French conductor and an outstanding performer of contemporary music. He conducted Lutosławski's Symphony no. 2 with the Sinfonie Orchester des Südwestfunks in the summer of 1968 in Baden-Baden. This was the world premiere of the complete work, after a performance of its second movement—*Direct*—on October 18, 1966 in Hamburg by the Sinfonie Orchester des Norddeutschen Rundfunks conducted by Pierre Boulez. Bour recorded the Symphony no. 2 on Wergo 60044 (LP mono-stereo). See Wolfgang Schwinger, "Lutosławski's zweite Sinfonie. Deutsche Entaufführung unter Ernest Bour" *Neue Zeitschrift für Musik*, 129 no. 10 (1968): 415–16.

65. Symphony no. 2 was commissioned by the Norddeutschen Rundfunk in Hamburg for the hundredth concert in a series of contemporary music, *Das neue Werk*. See note 64. The Polish premiere of this symphony took place on June 9, 1967 in Katowice, with the Great Symphonic Orchestra of the Polish Radio conducted by Lutosławski.

66. Bogusław Schaeffer (b. 1929), a Polish composer, theoretician, and playwright; an outstanding representative of avant-garde music. One of his most important theoretical texts is *Nowa muzyka. Problemy współczesnej techniki kompozytorskiej* (The New Music. Problems of Contemporary Compositional Technique) (Kraków: Polish Musical Edition, 1958, 2nd ed. 1969). In the late 1950s and in the 1960s, this book was the only Polish source of knowledge on the main currents in Western new music.

67. Krzysztof Penderecki.

68. Lutosławski wrote this the day after he heard a recital of Hugo Wolf's *Lieder* from the cycle *Gedichte von Eduard Mörike*, performed by Dietrich Fischer-Dieskau and Sviatolav Richter in the Warsaw Philharmonic Hall on October 2, 1973. Fischer-Dieskau, whom Lutosławski met after the recital, suggested to him that he might write a vocal-instrumental piece. The result of this proposal was *Les espaces du sommeil* to the words of Robert Desnos for baritone and orchestra, which was finished in 1975 and dedicated to Fischer-Dieskau.

69. Claude Lévi-Strauss's: *The Savage Mind*, in *The Science of the Concrete* (Chicago: University of Chicago Press, 1966), 30. Lutosławski started his essay titled "Preludes and Fugue" with this quotation (see part 2 of the present collection).

70. Lutosławski refers here to the analysis of *Musique funèbre* by Bogusław Schaeffer in his book *Klasycy dodekafonii* (The Classics of Dodecaphony) (Kraków: Polish Musical Edition, 1964), vol. 1, pp. 157–58 and vol. 2, p. 264. Lutosławski distanced himself from this analysis, which allowed him to sustain his belief that the dodecaphonic character of the fragment of *Musique funèbre* identified by Schaeffer was not essential to the

complete structure of *Musique funèbre*. Lutosławski's relations to dodecaphony remain still an analytical challenge. In spite of the fact that he constantly declared his *votum separatum* toward the twelve-tone technique, this is not totally confirmed in his music, even in those works from the 1940s that remain in manuscript. The most advanced research in this field was done by Martina Homma in her text "Lutosławski's Studies in Twelve-Tone Rows." See, *Lutosławski Studies*, ed. Zbigniew Skowron (Oxford: Oxford University Press, 2001), 194–209.

71. Pierre Boulez delivered this speech on the occasion of his receiving the Siemens Prize in Munich, on April 20, 1979. Its title was "Géometrie courbe de l'utopie" and it was published in the original version in a collection of Boulez's writings titled *Points de repère*, ed. Jacques Nattiez (Paris: Éditions du Seuil, 1985), 575–77. Its English version, titled "The Elliptical Geometry of Utopia," appeared in the volume *Orientations*, ed. Jacques Nattiez, trans. Martin Cooper (London and Boston: Faber, 1986), 525–27.

72. A similar thought appeared in Boulez's text of 1954 titled *Recherches maintenant*. Writing on the serialization of all parameters of a musical work, and considering its result, Boulez described it as "an impression of weightlessness" (*une impression de "non-pesanteur"*). See P. Boulez, *Recherches maintenant*, in: *Relevés d'apprenti* (Paris: Éditions du Seuil, 1966), 29.

73. A similar theme can be seen in Lutosławski's speech delivered at the Congress of Culture in Warsaw, on December 12, 1981. See the text "On the Issue of Truth in Works of Art" in part 4 of the present collection.

74. See note 11.

75. Juliusz Słowacki (1809–1849), a Polish poet, living since 1831 in exile in Paris, Switzerland, and Italy; one of the outstanding representatives of Polish Romantic literature.

Bibliography

Astriab, Jan, Maciej Jabłoński, and Jan Stęszewski, eds. *Witold Lutosławski. Człowiek i dzieło w perspektywie kultury muzycznej XX wieku* [Witold Lutosławski: The Man and His Work in the Perspective of the Musical Culture of the 20th Century]. Poznań: Poznańskie Towarzystwo Przyjaciół Nauk, 1999.

Aubigny, Benoît. "Poetic and Dramatic Schemes in Lutosławski's Vocal-Instrumental Works." In *Lutosławski Studies,* edited by Zbigniew Skowron, 57–95. Oxford: Oxford University Press, 2001.

Baculewski, Krzysztof. "Lutosławski: jedna technika, jeden styl?" [Lutosławski: One Technique, One Style?], *Muzyka* 1–2 (1995): 25–40.

Balázs, István. "Macht und Ohnmacht der Musik. Witold Lutosławski's Cellokonzert und seine gesellschaftlichen Zusammenhänge." *Neue Zeitschrift für Musik* 7–8 (1986): 40–47.

Będkowski, Stanisław, and Stanisław Hrabia. *Witold Lutosławski: A Bio-Bibliography.* Westport, Conn.: Greenwood Press, 2001.

Bietti, Giovanni, "La communicazione nella musica di Lutosławski." *Nuova Rivista* 29/1 (1995): 31–48.

Błaszkiewicz, Teresa. *Aleatoryzm w twórczości Witolda Lutosławskiego* [Aleatorism in the Music of Witold Lutosławski]. Gdańsk, 1973.

Brennecke, Wilfried. "*Die Trauermusik* von Witold Lutosławski." In *Festschrift Friedrich Blume zum 70. Geburtstag,* edited by A. A. Abert and W. Pfannkuch, 60–73. Kassel: Bärenreiter, 1963.

Casken, John. "Transition and Transformation in the Music of Witold Lutosławski." *Contact* 12 (Autumn 1975): 3–12.

———. Review of *Lutosławski and His Music,* by Steven Stucky. *Musical Times* 122 (December 1981): 822–23.

———. "The Visionary and the Dramatic in the Music of Lutosławski." In *Lutosławski Studies,* edited by Zbigniew Skowron, 36–56. Oxford: Oxford University Press, 2001.

———. "Programme Note [*Livre pour orchestre*]." http://www.chester- novello.com/work/8463/main.html (accessed July 7, 2005).

Chłopecki, Andrzej. "The Structure of a Crystal, and All for Sale. On Witold Lutosławski's and Krzysztof Penderecki's Works." *Polish Art Studies* 3 (1982): 261–66.

———. "*Tombeau* einer Epoche. Witold Lutosławski—eine Würdigung." *MusikTexte* 54 (June 1994): 47–50.

———. "Zeugnis zerfallender Werte. Witold Lutosławskis Abschied von der Moderne." *MusikTexte* 42 (November 1991): 45–50.

Couchoud, Jean-Paul. *La musique polonaise et Witold Lutosławski*. Paris: Stock, 1981.

Cowie, Edward. "Mobiles of Sound." *Music and Musicians* 20/2 (October 1971): 24–26, 38–40.

Dufallo, Richard. "Witold Lutosławski." In *Trackings: Composers Speak with Richard Dufallo*, 393–404. Oxford: Oxford University Press, 1989.

Gantchoula, Philippe. "La 3ème Symphonie de Lutosławski: Synthèse d'un itinéraire créateur." *Analyse musicale* 10 (January 1988): 68–74.

Gieraczyński, Bogdan. "Witold Lutosławski in Interview." *Tempo* 170 (September 1989): 9–16.

Guzowska, Marzenna, ed. *Lutosławski homagium*. Warsaw: Wydawnictwo Galerii Zachęta, 1996.

Gwizdalanka, Danuta, and Krzysztof Meyer. *Postscriptum*. Warsaw: Fundacja Zeszytów Literackich, 1999.

———. *Lutosławski*, 2 vols. Kraków: Polish Musical Edition, 2003; 2004.

Harley, James. "Considerations of Symphonic Form in the Music of Witold Lutosławski." In *Lutosławski Studies*, edited by Zbigniew Skowron, 163–193. Oxford: Oxford University Press, 2001.

Harley, James, Martina Homma, and Maja Trochimczyk. "Witold Lutosławski: Bibliography." *Polish Music Journal* 5/1 (Summer 2002): www.usc.edu/dept/polish_music/PMJ/issue/5.1.02/lutoslawskibbl.html (accessed May 13, 2004).

Homma, Martina. "Witold Lutosławski: *Mi-parti*." *Melos* 47 (1985/3): 22–57.

———. "Horizontal-vertikal. Zur Organisation der Tonhöhe bei Witold Lutosławski" and "Materialen zur Arbeit von Witold Lutosławski." *Neuland-Jahrbuch* V (1985): 91–112.

———. "Unerhörtes Pathos. Witold Lutosławski: III Sinfonie." *MusikTexte* 13 (1986): 7–12.

———. "Chronologisches Werkverzeichnis. Auswahlbibliographie. Auswahldiskographie." *Musik-Konzepte* 71/72/73, (1991): 198–223.

———. "Nostalgie des Aufbruchs? Witold Lutosławskis Klavierkonzert—ein Spätwerk." *MusikTexte* 42 (1991): 27–34.

———. "'Vogelperspektive' und 'Schlüsselideen.' Über einige Aspekte der Kompositionstechnik Lutosławskis anhand kompositorischer Skizzen." *Musik-Konzepte* 71/72/73 (1991): 33–51.

———. "Zwölftonharmonik und Präkomposition des Materials. Überlegungen zu Konkretisierungsgraden in Witold Lutosławskis Cellokonzert." In *Zwölf Komponisten des 20. Jahrhunderts*, edited by Felix Meyer 205–32. Winterthur: Amadeus, 1993.

———. "Gleichzeitigkeit des Ungleichartigen. Witold Lutosławskis Vierte Sinfonie—Synthese seines Schaffens." *MusikTexte* 54 (1994): 51–56.

————. "Przestrzeń muzyczna w harmonice dwunastotonowej Witolda Lutosławskiego" [Musical Space in Witold Lutosławski's Twelve-Note Harmony] *Muzyka* 1–2 (1995): 85–110.

————. "Witold Lutosławski's *Trois poèmes d'Henri Michaux*: The Sketches and the Work." *Polish Music Journal* 3/2 (Winter 2000). Also available at www.usc.edu/dept/polish_music/ PMJ/issue/3.2.00/homma.html (accessed August 1, 2005).

————. *Witold Lutosławski: Zwölfton-Harmonik, Formbildung, "aleatorische Kontrapunkt"; Studien zum Gesamtwerk unter Einbeziehung der Skizzen.* Cologne: Bela Verlag, 1996.

————. "The Twelve-Note Chord: Towards a New Definition of Twelve-Tone Music." In *Witold Lutosławski. Człowiek i dzieło w perspektywie kultury muzycznej XX wieku* [Witold Lutosławski: The Man and His Work in the Perspective of the Musical Culture of the Twentieth Century], edited by Jan Astriab, Maciej Jabłoński, and Jan Stęszewski, 110–129. Poznań: Poznańskie Towarzystwo Przyjaciół Nauk, 1999.

————. "Lutosławski's Studies in Twelve-Tone Rows." In *Lutosławski Studies*, edited by Zbigniew Skowron, 194–210. Oxford: Oxford University Press, 2001.

Huber, Alfred. "Witold Lutosławski: Cellokonzert." *Melos* 4 (1973): 229–36.

Jack, Adrian. "Composers." *Music and Musicians* 21 (April 1973): 64, 66.

————. "Broken Promises." *The Independent* (16 August 2001). www.enjoyment.independent.co.uk/music/reviews/article210302.ece (accessed July 7, 2005)

Jacobson, Bernard. *A Polish Renaissance.* London: Phaidon Press, 1996.

Jarociński, Stefan. *Witold Lutosławski. Materiały do monografii* [Materials for a Monograph]. Kraków: Polish Musical Editionde, 1967.

Jarzębska, Alicja. "Problem kształtowania kontinuum formy w IV Symfonii Witolda Lutosławskiego" [The Problem of Building a Form Continuum in the Fourth Symphony by Witold Lutosławski]. *Muzyka* 1–2 (1995): 135–54.

Kaczyński, Tadeusz. *Lutosławski. Życie i muzyka* [Lutosławski. Life and Music]. Warsaw: Sutkowski Edition, 1994.

————. *Conversations with Witold Lutosławski*, 2nd ed. Translated by Yolanta May and Charles Bodman Rae. London: Chester Music, 1995.

————. "Witold Lutosławski vu à travers sa correspondance." *Mitteilungen der Paul Sacher Stiftung* 9 (March 1996): 11–13.

Klein, Michael. "A Theoretical Study of the Late Music of Witold Lutosławski: New Interactions of Pitch, Rhythm, and Form." PhD diss., State University of New York, Buffalo, 1995.

————. "Texture, Register, and Their Formal Roles in the Music of Witold Lutosławski." *Indiana Theory Review* 20/1 (Spring 1999): 37–70.

————. *Intertextuality in Western Art Music.* Bloomington: Indiana University Press, 2004.

Kniese, Horst. "Lutosławski schreibt für Hagen ein Meisterwerk." *Melos* 36 (1969): 22.

Krawczyk, Dorota. "Koncepcja czasu Witolda Lutosławskiego" [Witold Lutosławski's Conception of Time]. *Muzyka* 1–2 (1995): 111–33.

Lidholm, Ingvar, György Ligeti, and Witold Lutosławski. *Three Aspects of New Music.* Stockholm: Nordiska Musikförlaget, 1968.

Ligeti, György. "Ligeti über Lutosławski." *Musica* 22 (1968/6): 453.

Marek, Tadeusz. *"Livre pour orchestre* by Witold Lutosławski." *Polish Music* 4/1 (1969): 9–12.

———. "Cello Concerto by Witold Lutosławski." *Polish Music* 6/3 (1971): 3–9.

———. "Composer's Workshop Witold Lutosławski *Preludes and Fugue.*" *Polish Music* 7/3 (1972): 18–22.

———. "Witold Lutosławski: *Mi-parti.*" *Polish Music* 2 (1977): 3–4.

Meyer, Krzysztof. "Kilka uwag na temat organizacji wysokości dźwięków w muzyce Witolda Lutosławskiego." [Some Remarks on the Pitch Organization in the Music of Witold Lutosławski]. *Muzyka* 1–2 (1995): 3–23.

Michaely, Aloyse. "Lutosławskis III. Sinfonie." *Musik-Konzepte* 71/72/73 (1991): 52–197.

Michalski, Grzegorz. "An Interview with Witold Lutosławski" [particularly concerning the Piano Concerto]. *Polish Music* 2–3 (1988): 3–22.

Möller, Hartmut. "Französich-deutsche Traditionsbezüge in Witold Lutosławskis Grave für Violoncello und Klavier." In *Deutsche Musik im Wegkreuz zwischen Polen und Frankreich. Zum Problem musikalischer Wechselbeziehungen im 19. und 20. Jahrhundert. Bericht der Tagung am Musikwissenschaftlichen Institut der Johannes Gutenberg-Universität Mainz 20.11–24.11.1988,* edited by Christoph-Hellmut Mahling and Kristina Pfarr, 175–92. Tutzing: H. Schneider, 1996.

Morawska, Katarzyna, ed. "Witold Lutosławski 25 I 1913—7 II 1994," commemorative issue of *Muzyka* 1–2 (1995). Includes articles by: Krzysztof Baculewski, Charles Bodman Rae, Martina Homma, Jadwiga Paja-Stach and Maria Stanilewicz-Kamionka, Krzysztof Meyer, Irina Nikolska, Dorota Krawczyk, Alicja Jarzębska. Also contains two reviews: by Zbigniew Skowron (on *The Music of Lutosławski,* by Charles Bodman Rae), and Dorota Krawczyk (on *Conversations with Witold Lutosławski,* by Irina Nikolska).

Nikolska, Irina. "Symfonizm Witolda Lutosławskiego." *Muzyka* 3 (1992): 37–51.

———. *Conversations with Witold Lutosławski (1987–92).* Translated by Valeri Yerokhin. Stockholm: Melos En Musiktidskrift, 1994.

———. "Niektóre zasady konstruowania melodii w twórczości Witolda Lutosławskiego z lat 1960–80" [Melody and Some Principles of Its Formation in Witold Lutosławski's Creativity in the Years 1960–80). *Muzyka* 1–2 (1995): 59–85.

Nordwall, Ove, ed. *Lutosławski.* Translated by Christopher Gibbs, et al. Stockholm: Wilhelm Hansen, 1968.

Paja-Stach, Jadwiga. "System w muzyce Witolda Lutosławskiego" [System in the Music of Witold Lutosławski]. In *Przemiany techniki dźwiękowej, stylu i estetyki w polskiej muzyce lat 70* [Changes in Sound Technique, Style, and Aesthetics in Polish Music in the 1970s], edited by Leszek Polony, 214–19. Kraków: Academy of Music, 1986.

———. "The Polyphonic Aspect of Lutosławski's Music." *Acta Musicologica* 2–3 (1990): 183–91.

———. "Witold Lutosławski: Dokumentacja" [Witold Lutosławski: Documentation]. *Muzyka* 1–2 (1995), 155–222. Contains: Chronicle of life and work, full list of the composer's works, writings and published interviews, and bibliography (up to 1995).

———. *Lutosławski i jego styl muzyczny* [Lutosławski and His Musical Style]. Kraków: Musica Iagellonica, 1997.

————, ed. *Witold Lutosławski i jego wkład do kultury muzycznej XX wieku* [Witold Lutosławski and His Contribution to the Twentieth-Century Musical Culture]. Kraków: Musica Iagellonica, 2005.

Pastor, Enrique. "*Les espaces du sommeil*, à propos d'un poème de Robert Desnos." *Revue des langues vivantes* 42 (1976).

Petersen, Peter. "Witold Lutosławski: Präludien und Fuge (1972)." *Hamburger Jahrbuch für Musikwissenschaft* 1 (1974): 147–80.

————. "Über die Wirkung Bartóks auf das Schaffen Lutosławskis." *Musik-Konzepte* 22 (1981): 84–117.

————. "Bartók, Lutosławski, Ligeti. Einige Bemerkungen zu ihrer Kompositionstechnik unter dem Aspekt der Tonhöhe." In *Für G. Ligeti*, edited by C. Floros, H. J. Marx and P. Petersen, with M. Stahnke, 289–309. Laaber: Laaber-Verlag, 1991.

————. "Microtones in the Music of Lutosławski." In *Lutosławski Studies*, edited by Zbigniew Skowron, 324–55. Oxford: Oxford University Press, 2001.

Pilarski, Bohdan. "Witold Lutosławski odpowiada na pytania" [Witold Lutosławski Answers Questions]. *Ruch Muzyczny* 7 (1958): 2–5.

————. "Moja muzyka jest grą. Po wykonaniu *Gier weneckich*" [My Music Is a Game. After the Performance of *Jeux vénitiens* during the Fifth Warsaw Autumn]. *Współczesność* 20 (1961): 15.

Pociej, Bohdan. "The Music of Witold Lutosławski." *Polish Perspectives* 7–8 (1972): 24–31.

————. *Lutosławski a wartość muzyki* [Lutosławski and the Value of His Music]. Kraków: Polish Musical Edition, 1976.

Podhajski, Marek. "Formy aleatoryzmu w *Grach weneckich* Witolda Lutosławskiego: próba typizacji" [Aleatoric Forms in *Jeux vénitiens* by Witold Lutosławski: An Essay of Systematization]. In *Z dziejów muzyki polskiej* [From the History of Polish Music], 59–78. Bydgoszcz: Bydgoskie Towarzystwo Naukowe, Filharmonia Pomorska, 1971.

Polony, Leszek, ed. *Witold Lutosławski. Sesja naukowa poświęcona twórczości kompozytora. Kraków 24–25 kwietnia 1980. Wybór materiałów.* [Witold Lutosławski Conference Devoted to the Composer's Work. Kraków April 24–25, 1980. Selected Materials]. Kraków: Academy of Music, 1985. Contains articles by: Danuta Gwizdała, Tadeusz Kaczyński, Maciej Negrey, Bohdan Pociej, Krzysztof Szwajgier, Krystyna Tarnawska-Kaczorowska, and Lutosławski.

Rae, Charles Bodman. "Lutosławski's Golden Year." *Musical Times*, 127 (October 1986), 547–51.

————. "Lutosławski's Late Style?" *The Listener* 121 (January 1989): 36–37.

————. "Lutosławski's Piano Concerto." *The Listener* 122 (July 1989): 36–37.

————. "Lutosławski's Late Violin Works." *Musical Times* 131 (October) 1990: 530–33.

————. "Pitch Organization in the Music of Witold Lutosławski since 1979." PhD diss., University of Leeds, 1992.

————. *The Music of Lutosławski*. London: Faber and Faber, 1994; London: Omnibus Press, rev. ed., 1999.

————. "Witold Lutosławski" (obituary). *The Independent* (London), February 9, 1994.

————. "Danuta Lutosławska" (obituary). *The Independent* (London), April 28, 1994.

————. "Organizacja wysokości dźwięków w muzyce Witolda Lutosławskiego" [Pitch Organization in the Music of Witold Lutosławski]. *Muzyka* 1–2 (1995): 41–58.

————. "Lutosławski's Sound-World: A World of Contrasts." In *Lutosławski Studies*, edited by Zbigniew Skowron, 16–35. Oxford: Oxford University Press, 2001.

Rappoport, Lidia. *Vitold Lutoslavski*. Moscow: Muzyka, 1976.

Rappoport-Gelfand, Lidia. *Musical Life in Poland: The Post-War Years 1945–1977*. New York: Gordon & Breach, 1991.

Reyland, Nicholas. "'Akcja' and Narrativity in the Music of Witold Lutosławski." PhD diss., University of Cardiff, 2005.

Rogers, Harold. "Lutosławski: Poland's Great 'Lone Wolf.'" *Christian Science Monitor*, June 24, 1968: 6.

Rust, Douglas. "A Theory of Form for Lutosławski's Late Symphonic Work." PhD diss., Yale University, 1994.

————. "Conversation with Witold Lutosławski." *Musical Quarterly* 79 (1995): 207–23.

Sadie, Stanley. "Musical 'Games' from Poland." *The Times*, July 24, 1967: 7.

Schmidt, Christian Martin. "Witold Lutosławski: Streichquartett." In *Die Musik der sechziger Jahre. Zwölf Versuche*, 154–62. Mainz: Schott, 1972.

Skowron, Zbigniew. Review of *Conversations with Witold Lutosławski*, 2nd ed., by Tadeusz Kaczyński. *Music & Letters* 78, no. 3 (1997): 462–64.

————. "Spotkania z Witoldem Lutosławskim" [Encounters with Witold Lutosławski]. *Res Facta Nova* 2 (1998): 15–30.

————. "Tradycja, nowoczesność i awangarda jako źródła postawy twórczej Witolda Lutosławskiego" [Tradition, Modernity, and Avant-Garde as Sources of the Creative Attitude of Witold Lutosławski]. In *Witold Lutosławski. Człowiek i dzieło w perspektywie kultury muzycznej XX wieku* [Witold Lutosławski: The Man and His Work in the Perspective of the Musical Culture of the Twentieth Century], edited by Jan Astriab, Maciej Jabłoński, and Jan Stęszewski, 67–75. Poznań: Poznańskie Towarzystwo Przyjaciół Nauk, 1999.

————, ed. *Lutosławski Studies*. Oxford: Oxford University Press, 2001.

————. "Preface" and "Lutosławski's Aesthetics: A Reconstruction of the Composer's Outlook." In *Lutosławski Studies*, edited by Zbigniew Skowron, v–viii and 3–15. Oxford: Oxford University Press, 2001.

————. Review of *The Music of Lutosławski*, by Charles Bodman Rae. *Music & Letters* 82, no. 3 (2001): 483–87.

————. "Improwizacje na zadany temat. Nieznany list Witolda Lutosławskiego do Bo Wallnera" [Improvisations on a Given Theme. An Unknown Witold Lutosławski's Letter to Bo Wallner]. *Ruch Muzyczny* 26 (2003): 29–33.

————. "Witold Lutosławski wobec awangardy i nowatorstwa w muzyce XX wieku" [Witold Lutosławski in Relation to the Avant-Garde and the Novelty in Twentieth-Century Music]. In *Witold Lutosławski i jego wkład do kultury muzycznej XX wieku* [Witold Lutosławski and His Contribution to Twentieth-Century Musical Culture], edited by Jadwiga Paja-Stach, 27–37. Kraków: Musica Iagellonica, 2005.

Stucky, Steven. "The String Quartet of Witold Lutosławski," MFA diss., Cornell University, 1973.

———. "The Music of Witold Lutosławski: A Style-Critical Survey," DMA thesis, Cornell University, 1978.

———. "Lutosławski's Double Concerto." *Musical Times* 122 (August 1981): 529–32.

———. *Lutosławski and His Music.* Cambridge: Cambridge University Press, 1981.

———. "Change and Constancy: The Essential Lutosławski." In *Lutosławski Studies*, edited by Zbigniew Skowron, 149–62. Oxford: Oxford University Press, 2001.

Sznajderski, Tadeusz Krzysztof. "Muzyka a kompozytor" [Music and the Composer]. *Życie Literackie* 13 (1977): 1–6.

Tarnawska-Kaczorowska, Krystyna, ed. *Witold Lutosławski. Materiały sympozjum poświęconego twórczości. Prezentacje, interpretacje, konfrontacje* [Witold Lutosławski. Materials from a Symposium Devoted to His Work. Presentations, Interpretations, Confrontations]. Warsaw: Musicology Section of the Polish Composers' Union, 1985. Contains articles by: Andrzej Chłopecki, Krzysztof Szwajgier, Andrzej Tuchowski, Krystyna Tarnawska-Kaczorowska, Joanna Wnuk-Nazarowa, Bohdan Pociej, and Mieczysław Tomaszewski.

———. "Witold Lutosławski's Third Symphony (1983): A Hermeneutic Interpretation." *Irish Musical Studies* 5 (1996): 375–82.

Thomas, Adrian. "A Deep Resonance: Lutosławski's *Trois poèmes d'Henri Michaux.*" *Soundings* 1 (Autumn 1970): 58–70.

———. "Rhythmic Articulation in the Music of Lutosławski 1956–65," MA thesis, University of Cardiff, 1971.

———. "*Jeux vénitiens*: Lutosławski at the Crossroads." *Contact* 24 (Spring 1982): 4–7.

———. "Your Song Is Mine." *Musical Times* 136 (August 1995): 403–409.

———. "Witold Lutosławski: *Musique funèbre* (1954–58)." In *Settling New Scores: Music Manuscripts from the Paul Sacher Foundation*, edited by Felix Meyer, 256–66. Basel: Paul Sacher Foundation, 1998.

———. "*Jeux vénitiens*: Working Methods at the Start of Lutosławski's Mature Period." In *Lutosławski Studies*, edited by Zbigniew Skowron, 211–43. Oxford: Oxford University Press, 2001.

———. "File 750: Composers, Politics, and the Festival of Polish Music (1951)." *Polish Music Journal* 5/1 (Summer 2002): www.usc.edu/dept/polish_music/PMJ /issue/5.1.02/thomasfile.html (accessed August 1, 2005).

———. *Polish Music since Szymanowski.* Cambridge: Cambridge University Press, 2005.

Trochimczyk, Maja. "*Dans la Nuit*: The Themes of Death and Night in Lutosławski's *Oeuvre.*" In *Lutosławski Studies*, edited by Zbigniew Skowron, 96–124. Oxford: Oxford University Press, 2001.

Tuchowski, Andrzej. "The Integrative Role of Motion Patterns in Lutosławski's Mature Symphonic Works: A Comparison of *Livre pour orchestre* and the Symphony No. 4." In *Lutosławski Studies*, edited by Zbigniew Skowron, 287–304. Oxford: Oxford University Press, 2001.

Varga, Balint Andras. *Lutosławski Profile: Witold Lutosławski in Conversation with Bálint András Varga.* London: Chester Music, 1976.

Whittall, Arnold. Review of *Lutosławski and His Music*, by Steven Stucky. *Music Review* 13 (August–November 1982): 280–82.

————. "Between Polarity and Synthesis: The Modernist Paradigm in Lutosławski's Concertos for Cello and Piano." In *Lutosławski Studies*, edited by Zbigniew Skowron, 244–68. Oxford: Oxford University Press, 2001.

Wilby, Philip. "Lutosławski and a View of Musical Perspective." In *Companion to Contemporary Music Thought*, edited by John Paynter, Tim Howell, Richard Orton, and Peter Seymour, 1127–45. London: Routledge, 1992.

Zieliński, Tadeusz. "Witold Lutosławski's Chain 1." *Polish Music* 1–2 (1985): 17–24.

Name and Title Index

About the Editor

Zbigniew Skowron is a professor at the Institute of Musicology, University of Warsaw. He graduated in Polish philology and musicology from the University of Warsaw, and in music theory at the Academy of Music in Warsaw. In 1987–1988 he studied with Leonard B. Meyer at the University of Pennsylvania on an American Council of Learned Societies fellowship. Among his scholarly interests are aesthetic and historical aspects of twentieth-century music, history of musical aesthetics, the music of Witold Lutosławski, and Chopin's biography and epistolography. He is the author of *Teoria i estetyka awangardy muzycznej* (Theory and Aesthetics of the Musical Avant-Garde) and of the monograph *Nowa muzyka amerykańska* (Modern American Music). He is also the editor of *Lutosławski Studies* and, since 2001, the editor-in-chief of *Przegląd muzykologiczny* (Musicological Review)—a yearbook of the Institute of Musicology, University of Warsaw.